Teaching English as a Second Language

Teaching English as a Second Language

Theory and techniques for the secondary stage

J. A. Bright and G. P. McGregor

Formerly Reader and Head, Department of Language Method, Makerere University College, Uganda. Sometime Chief Inspector, Institute of Education, Bakht er Ruda, Sudan.

Principal, Bishop Otter College, Chichester, Sussex. Formerly Professor of Education, University of Zambia. Sometime Lecturer in Language Method, Makere University College, Uganda.

LONGMAN

LONGMAN GROUP LTD
London

Associated companies, branches and representatives throughout the world

First published 1970
Tenth impression 1979

ISBN 0 582 54003 8

Printed in Singapore by Huntsmen Offset Printing Pte Ltd.

PREFACE

Our experience has been mainly in Africa and the experience relevant to this book consists of teaching in secondary schools and training teachers for secondary schools.

The cadre of practising teachers and of students in training institutions is by no means homogeneous. Training has to cope with African, Asian, British and American graduates, with Asian and African non-graduates entering at Post-Higher-School-Certificate level, and with Asian and African entrants to longer courses at post-School certificate level. These locally trained teachers find their way into schools where there are also untrained local graduates, Peace Corps and Voluntary Service Overseas personnel, trained and untrained graduate and non-graduate teachers from America, Britain, India, Pakistan, Australia, New Zealand, Italy, Scandinavia, Ireland and elsewhere. Length of teaching experience varies from a lifetime spent in mission education to none at all. There is no lack of variety of background and experience. The tendency however has in recent years been towards an increasing reliance on two and three year contracts with consequent difficulties in maintaining continuity.

The problem of getting teachers with such diverse backgrounds to work economically and effectively as a team is formidable; no praise can be too high for the devoted inspectorates who wrestle continuously with this problem, which is made almost impossibly difficult by the vast distances involved. Over the last ten or fifteen years in spite of all difficulties considerable agreement has been reached about content, method and examinations. It is the product of work in Institutes of Education, in schools and inspectorates and the result of numerous conferences and discussions. Most of the conclusions are on paper but not in a readily accessible form because they have been embodied in government circulars confined to one country or reports of conferences with limited circulations.

This book is an attempt to bring together in an accessible form what is generally agreed to be sound modern English teaching practice for the African secondary school and perhaps equally importantly to relate it to its theoretical basis in the linguistic sciences and in methodology.

We thought such an account would be useful not as an orthodoxy to which teachers should conform, but as a body of background knowledge that new thinking and invention will continually increase.

What relevance the book may have outside Africa and the Middle East, we do not know. We would expect that the theory would be universal but that the detailed application of it would vary according to the differences from the African situation. In considering syllabuses for example, we assume that eight to ten periods will be available. Where there are less, obviously less can be done.

We have deliberately excluded from our consideration the beginning stage of English as a foreign language. Our starting-point is after a course in simplified English has been completed.

This has not been an easy book to write, apart from the complication of physical distance between the writers. The division into chapters about this and that aspect of English teaching inevitably falsifies the picture. In a way it is absurd to have chapters on vocabulary and grammar by themselves, as though one could read or write or speak without the use of words and grammar. But not to separate them would involve repetition of material. It is equally ridiculous to separate drama and speech and reading and poetry. Our categories sometimes overlap and are sometimes of different kinds. We can only beg the readers to consider each in relation to the others. Our dilemma reflects that of the teacher in relation to the linguist. The linguist can separate language into levels and think about context, lexis and phonology separately. As soon as the teacher opens his mouth, all the levels start operating simultaneously. As professional teachers and only amateur linguists, we have opted for a way of presenting our material that is practically convenient.

In one other way this is a firmly practical book. The techniques and procedures that are recommended have been used extensively in the classroom. We have used them ourselves and so have our students. They do not depend for their success on the personality of the teacher. There are one or two minor exceptions but there we have written warnings into the text. Everything else is, we believe, workable by any teacher in conditions similar to those we know.

In teacher training we have always found that the demonstration of methods carries more conviction than their description. We have therefore included here and there throughout this book samples of actual teaching, examination questions and work based on particular texts. They are there to answer the question, 'What do you actually do in the classroom?' They are examples only and should not be taken as recommendations to use the texts on which they happen to be based.

Nor do we wish to be prescriptive in any other way. Our endeavour is to provide access to good current practice and theory. If this book helps the novice towards understanding the problems he will face and perhaps supports the experienced teacher in the isolation of an up-country school, it will have done its job.

ACKNOWLEDGEMENTS

It is impossible adequately to acknowledge the debts of a working lifetime. We have learnt from nearly everybody with whom we have ever worked: from pupils, students, teachers, trainers, headmasters, inspectors, lecturers. All have been more than helpful and generous and will we hope, forgive this general expression of thanks.

Our bibliographies list many others, whom we have not met, but to whom we are also deeply grateful.

We must acknowledge special indebtedness over many years to Professor Gurrey, Peter Wingard and George Perren. Others have specifically helped and encouraged us by reading part or all of this book in manuscript: Professor Quirk, Philip Clarke, Mrs Pat Howard. We have used ideas from Roland Hindmarsh in the chapter on reading and are specially indebted to the late Phyllis Warner for the section on stagecraft in the drama chapter.

We are grateful to the following for permission to reproduce copyright material.

George Allen & Unwin Ltd and Liveright Publishing Corporation for an extract from *Education* by Bertrand Russell; Basil Blackwell & Mott Ltd for an extract from *Drama in Education* by A. F. Alington, and an extract from *Poetry for You* by C. Day Lewis; The Carnegie Press for an extract from *Interim Report on Vocabulary Selection and Control*; Gerald Duckworth & Co. Ltd and Alfred A. Knopf Inc. for 'Henry King Who Chewed Bits of String' from *Cautionary Verses* by Hilaire Belloc (1912), published 1941 by Alfred A. Knopf; The English Universities Press Ltd for an extract from *Teaching Drama* by R. N. Pemberton Billing and J. D. Clegg; Faber & Faber Ltd for an extract from Michael Roberts' Introduction to *The Faber Book of Modern Verse*; Faber & Faber Ltd and Random House Inc. for an extract 'The Death Test' from *Appointment in Samarra* by John O'Hara, Copyright 1934 and renewed 1962 by John O'Hara; Mrs Agnes C. Fries for an extract from *Teaching and Learning English as a Foreign Language* by Charles C. Fries; author's agents, Jonathan Cape Ltd and Holt, Rinehart & Winston Inc. for 'Out, Out—' from *The Complete Poems of Robert Frost* by Robert Frost, Copyright 1916 by Holt, Rinehart & Winston, Copyright 1944 by Robert Frost; author's agents for an extract from 'I Never Forget a Face' by Cyril Hare from *The Best Detective Stories by Cyril Hare* by Mrs A. A. Gordon

Clarke; William Heinemann Ltd and author's agents for an extract from *Over the Bridge* by Richard Church; William Heinemann Ltd and Astor-Honor Inc. for an extract from *Things Fall Apart* by Chinua Achebe, Copyright 1969; Heinemann Educational Books Ltd for 'An African Thunderstorm' by D. Rubadiri from *Origin East Africa*; Hutchinson & Co. (Publishers) Ltd for an extract from Ted Hughes' Introduction to *Here Today*, and an extract from John Wain's Introduction to *An Anthology of Modern Poetry*; author for 'A Correct Compassion' by James Kirkup; author's agents, William Heinemann Ltd, the Estate of the late Mrs Frieda Lawrence, and The Viking Press Inc. for an extract from 'John Galsworthy' from *Phoenix* by D. H. Lawrence (in U.S.A. Phoenix 1; The Posthumous Papers of D. H. Lawrence edited by Edward D. McDonald—all rights reserved), and an extract from 'Snake' from *The Complete Poems of D. H. Lawrence* (in U.S.A. Volume 1 edited by Vivian de Sola Pinto and F. Warren Roberts), Copyright 1923, renewed 1951 by Frieda Lawrence; Longman Group Ltd for extracts from *English Composition Course for Overseas Students* and *Patterns and Skills in English* both by John Bright and for an extract from *The Adventures of Tom Sawyer* (Longman Simplified English Series); Macmillan & Co. Ltd for an extract from *Manual of English Grammar* by Nesfield; the Literary Executor of W. Somerset Maugham and William Heinemann Ltd for an extract 'A Beast of Burden' from *On a Chinese Screen* by W. Somerset Maugham; Methuen & Co. Ltd for 'Telephone Conversation' by Wole Soyinka from *Idaure and Other Poems*; Thomas Nelson & Sons Ltd for an extract from *Prester John* by John Buchan, from the Longman Simplified English Series edition; Penguin Books Ltd for an extract from *Personal Values in the Modern World* by M. V. C. Jeffreys, and 'Come Away My Love' by Kariuki from *Modern Poetry from Africa*; University of Cambridge Local Examinations Syndicate for an extract from an English Examination Paper 1966–67.

We have been unable to trace the copyright holder of 'Conscience' from *Verse and Worse* by A. Silcock, and the American copyright holders of *The Best Detective Stories of Cyril Hare* by Mrs A. A. Gordon Clarke, *On a Chinese Screen* by W. Somerset Maugham and 'Telephone Conversation' by Wole Soyinka and would appreciate any information that would enable us to do so.

CONTENTS

Preface v

Acknowledgements vi

1 GENERALISATIONS 1

§1 Telling, teaching and learning 1 §2 Knowledge versus skill 3 §3 Competition *v.* co-operation 4 §4 Pleasure 5 §5 Taking pupils into one's confidence 5 §6 Study skills 5 §7 The English teacher's interests 6 §8 Co-operation with teachers of other subjects 6 §9 Finding out what pupils have done before 7 §10 Administration: *a.* Preparation of lessons 8 *b.* Growing points in the syllabus 9; *c.* Running a department 9; *d.* Deployment of staff 10 §11 External examinations 11 §12 Keeping in touch 13

2 VOCABULARY 14

§1 Preliminary 14 §2 The Learner's problems and the difficulty of direct vocabulary teaching 15 §3 A little history 17 §4 Productive and receptive use 19 §5 Vocabulary control applied to texts 19 §6 *The Interim Report* 20 §7 What is a word? Problems of counting and control 22 §8 Vocabulary levels in secondary school texts: *a.* the plateau 26; *b.* the transition to unsimplified texts 27 §9 Longman Bridge Series 27 §10 Kinds of new words that will be met 29 §11 Inference from context 30 §12 Words related to items already known 32 §13 Dictionary work 35 §14 Other kinds of vocabulary work in the classroom 38 §15 Constructing definitions of words 40 §16 Testing width of vocabulary 44 §17 The Vocabulary level of examinations 45 §18 Internal tests 45 §19 Summary of recommendations 48 Reading list 49

APPENDIXES: I A passage from *Bleak House* 49 II Notes on simplified texts 50

3 READING 52

§1 What the chapter covers 52 §2 Why reading is the core of the syllabus 52 §3 The pupil's skills and knowledge on entry to the secondary school 54 §4 The abilities of the skilled reader 56 §5 The major stages of the secondary course 58 §6 Selection of texts for reading: *a.* Criteria 59; *b.* Examples of possible sets of texts 61 §7 Cost and care 63 §8 The major

kinds of work, oral and written 64 §9 Extensive reading 65: *a.* The Library 65; *b.* Class readers 72 §10 Intensive reading: *a.* A reminder 80; *b.* The objective 80; *c.* Suitable texts 80; *d.* Lesson technique 81; *e.* Experimental confirmation of our thesis 83; *f.* Kinds of questions that may be asked to help pupils to read more perceptively 86; *g.* Written work on intensive reading 90; *h.* Testing intensive reading 90 §11 Additional notes on Stage III and Stage IV 90 §12 Extensive reading based on class readers 92 §13 Intensive reading 95 §14 Increasing the pupil's reading speed 96 §15 Teaching the skills of study and reference 98 §16 Literary criticism and appreciation 101 §17 Allocation of time 102 Reading list 102
APPENDIXES: I 'The Death Test' 103 II The *Prester John* series 106
III 'The Death of Okonkwo' 111 IV 'I Never Forget a Face' 116
V 'Richard Church's New Glasses' 121 VI Criticism: Towards Standards of Good and Bad in Writing 123

4 WRITING 130

§1 Mistakes 130 §2 Adjusting the level of difficulty 130 §3 Main stages of a graded course 131 §4 Some lines of development within a course 132
§5 Some common heresies 138 §6 Theory of a composition syllabus 141
§7 A unit of composition teaching 144 §8 More about study points 147
§9 More about focusing the attention, experience and imagination on the subject 149 §10 Combining the study point with getting the minds working 153 §11 A little more about correcting and improving the first draft: *a.* Matters of mechanical correctness – getting rid of mistakes 154; *b.* Improvements other than those involved in mechanical correctness 157; *c.* Corrected first draft 157 §12 Making a syllabus 158 §13 Teaching pupils to make their own notes: *a.* Introductory 161; *b.* General considerations 162; *c.* Techniques 162; *d.* Applications 168 §14 Teaching summarising: *a.* Summarising in examinations 168; *b.* How the pupil learns to summarise 169; *c.* Specific practice: remedial 171; *d.* Group discussion 172; *e.* Providing summaries with a purpose 172 §15 Projects and research essays 173
Reading list 176

5 SPEECH 177

§1 Reading aloud 177 §2 The problem of the model 178 §3 The Phoneme: *a.* Contrastive analysis 179; *b.* Teaching materials and methods 181; *c.* Testing 184 §4 The Syllable 184 §5 Phonetic script 186 §6 The Stress group 187 §7 The Phonetic phrase 188 §8 Teaching techniques 189
§9 Special requirements and general techniques 192 §10 Incidental speech work 194 §11 Speech work out of class 195 §12 Strategy 195 §13 Testing the skills of speech 196 Reading list 199
APPENDIX: Phonetic script 200

6 DRAMA 201

§1 How important is drama in school? 201 §2 The sequence of activities 203
§3 The beginnings 203 §4 Intermediate stages 205 §5 Plays for classwork 207
§6 Performances for school audiences 208 §7 Producing a play for public performance 209 §8 Shakespeare for school certificate? 214 §9 An approach to *Macbeth* 216 Reading list 218

7 POETRY 219

§1 A first poetry lesson: *African Thunderstorm* 219 §2 Teaching the poem itself 222 §3 Using written texts 222 §4 What is poetry for? 223 §5 Poetry and Language 223 §6 The choice of poems 224 §7 Using anthologies 225 §8 Levels of difficulty 225 §9 *Come Away, My Love* 226 §10 *Snake* 227 §11 *Out, Out—* 228 §12 *Journey of the Magi* 230 §13 *Telephone Conversation* 230 §14 *Tarantella* 232 §15 *A Correct Compassion* 232 Reading list 235

8 GRAMMAR 236

§1 Grammatical correctness and the rules of choice 236 §2 Interference from L1 236 §3 The uses of grammar 237 §4 Use in planning a course, syllabus or series of lessons 238 §5 Grammar in the first presentation of a new item 239 §6 The use of grammar for correction and remedial work 241 §7 Individual correction 250 §8 The use of grammar to get improvements other than greater correctness in written work 253 §9 Grammar as a survey and codification 258 §10 Aids to the teaching of grammar 261 §11 Grammar in examinations and tests 266 Reading list 269

APPENDIXES: I Example of teaching aimed at the first presentation of the infinitive of purpose 271 II A line of teaching dealing with the structures that help the noun to name more exactly 272 III Teaching a sentence pattern as part of a survey 279

1

GENERALISATIONS

1 Telling, teaching and learning

'How many times,' says the exasperated teacher, 'have I got to tell you?'

'I'm always telling them but they go on making the same mistakes.'

We all say things like this and we all think them too, and we are all wrong. Telling isn't teaching. Our first principle should be: 'Never tell anybody anything he can find out for himself.' Our business as teachers is to provide situations so designed that the pupils will learn for themselves. This is true for all subjects.

In the initial stages of language teaching it is in general well understood that learning takes place through exposure to language used by the teacher in the classroom in situations that make the meaning of what is being said clear to the pupil. The teacher says for example:

This is a leaf.
This is a stone.
This is a stick.
This is a pot.
This is a basket.
This is a ball.

The grammatical meaning is demonstrated by his stabbing forefinger which indicates the demonstrative situation, and by arranging that the pupils touch the objects as they speak. The indefiniteness is indicated by the presence in the classroom of more than one of each object, and some notion of the area of lexical meaning is given by the variety of leaves, stones, pots and other objects large and small that are present.

In all the early stages we know precisely what phonological, grammatical and lexical items we have to present, and we can devise situations in the classroom which will provide the necessary exposure to language which will enable learning to take place, and will also give opportunities for practice so that learning may be confirmed and correct habits established.

The early stages are comparatively straightforward but in this book we are not concerned with them but with what happens after the 1,500–2,000-word level has been reached.

Our pupils have met, though not necessarily mastered, nearly all the basic grammatical mechanisms of English, and most of the common general vocabulary, i.e. most of the headwords and many of the derivatives of the *General Service List*.[1] If they attend a school at which English is the medium of instruction in other subjects, then they will be exposed to science, history, geography and so on, in English. If a language other than English is the medium of instruction in their school, then their only exposure to English will be in English lessons. Where English is the medium in the schools, it will certainly be so in the universities. Where a local language is the medium in the schools, English may still be used in the universities, as in the Sudan and Malaysia.

The problem of listing the new items that should be learnt in English lessons in the secondary school is extremely difficult. Many teachers evade the issue by accepting the decision of some textbook writer; they work through 'the course'. But the textbook writer is not, alas, invariably endowed with infinite wisdom and it is at least desirable to have some idea of his principles of selection. It may help to note some of the factors involved in the selection of new items to be learnt.

Whatever future use the pupil makes of English he will have to master almost all the grammatical mechanisms of modern English. Without this mastery he will not be able to write or speak with fluency and ease. Any gaps must be filled. He must also master the lexical items of the *General Service List*. With these and a technical vocabulary appropriate to his subject he will be able to speak or write about anything he wishes. He does not need to widen his general productive vocabulary beyond this point. The pupil must be given the chance to fill his gaps up to this level, and must have a great deal of practice in speaking and writing at it. Unfortunately not all pupils will have the same gaps.

In schools where English is the medium, technical vocabulary will be met and practised in other subjects. In schools where English is only a subject and university education is in English, the technical vocabulary becomes the business of the English teacher. In all schools the kind of English to which the pupil is exposed should be determined by the purposes for which English is required in and after school, which will not be the same for all pupils.

It is perfectly legitimate to learn the kind of English that makes it possible to read Shakespeare and Milton, but the need and desire to do so are perhaps less common than English teachers brought up in a literary tradition sometimes suppose. It is also legitimate to learn the kind of English that makes it possible to work on committees and conduct the everyday affairs of life with courtesy and efficiency, but in some schools it is not as easy to do this as many pupils would wish.

There is no learning without exposure. It may be salutary to consider the kinds of English to which pupils are normally exposed and what therefore they have the opportunity to learn. Exposure need not, of course, be limited to school situations, and what happens outside may be important. But in most places it is what is done in school that will have the greatest effect.

Imagine a tape-recorder following a week's work in an English-medium

[1] M. West, *A General Service List of English Words*. Longman, revised edn. 1953.

school. What models would it provide? What restrictions would there be on the language used? How satisfactory is it for the pupil, in the multifarious situations he is to encounter in the future, if he models his English on what he hears in school? How much of what he hears will never be any use to him at all unless he becomes a teacher?

These are disturbing questions. It is immediately apparent that even in an English-medium school the fields of discourse are restricted to the subjects taught. There will be no opportunity to learn the language of booking a seat in a cinema, answering the doctor's questions or buying a new shirt. In a non-English-medium school there will not even be any exposure to the language of history, geography, mathematics or the sciences. The model provided will also be in the teaching mode and the social situation that of a teacher in a class-room. Pupil participation will generally be minimal and will consist not of initiating or maintaining a conversation, but of answering specific questions. The pupil will be offered, as a model for his future use, the way a teacher talks to a class. It will not be his fault if, when he attends his first committee, he talks to his colleagues as if they were school children.[1]

The style will be formal, expository spoken English, which is satisfactory neither for ordinary casual conversation nor for writing, as anyone who has seen a lecture in unedited transcription is well aware.[2]

We cannot of course get out of the school situation or use language in ways unnatural to the teaching situation, but we must provide adequate exposure to other models in other situations. Some of these situations can be provided in the classroom but most of the exposure to language at the secondary level must take place through the reading of texts. Nearly all new learning will take place while the pupil is reading. The field in which he reads will determine the language he learns. In the non-English-medium school feeding into an English-medium university, a great deal of the reading must be in the field of the pupil's future subjects. But whatever the school, quantity and quality of reading are of the first importance. At the secondary level, books provide the situations and the contexts in which learning takes place. The whole of life may not be between the covers of books but there the pupil will find far more variety of experience than we can give him in our lessons.

2 Knowledge versus skill

Moreover our business as language teachers at this level is not primarily with new knowledge. We are teaching a language to children who are going

[1] One of my former pupils attended a public meeting at which several distinguished African politicians were discussing current issues. When questions were invited from the floor he leapt to his feet and with all the brusque severity of an 'A' level examiner said: 'There will be no remedy for our present problems until the spirit of tribalism is banished. Discuss.' G.P.M.

[2] I was puzzled by the style of my students' essays at Makerere. They were full of verbiage. 'The next point I wish to make is . . .' 'Before we go on to consider the effects of this perhaps we should mention that . . .' It was not until I taped one of my own lectures that I realised who was providing the corrupting influence. The padding that I used to give students time to make notes, and to signal the structure of my lecture, was being used in their written work. Their model was unsatisfactory. J.A.B.

to use it for the rest of their lives. We are trying to teach, primarily, not knowledge but skills; the many different skills required for good LISTENING—SPEAKING—READING—WRITING.

Skills can be acquired only through practice, which is something we cannot do for our pupils. They have got to do it for themselves, which means that the good teacher of language, even more than the teacher of other subjects, should spend a great deal of his time listening, reading and *not talking*. Of course he will have to talk quite a lot, but his pupils have got to talk and read and write very much more, under his guidance, if they are to make progress.[1]

Practice is vital and the pupils have got to do it. But there is a difficulty here which we ignore at our peril. We have all been given, after some unfortunate blunder, the healing advice, 'Well, never mind; we learn from our mistakes.' In language learning this is simply not true, and the good language teacher keeps steadily in mind that when children learn a language they do not learn from their mistakes: they learn their mistakes. Which means that the teacher must give his pupils as much opportunity as possible for the correct practice of language skills and as little opportunity as possible to make mistakes.

3 Competition versus co-operation

Having established that the pupils have got to do the work for themselves, there is one important thing to be said at once about how we want them to do it. By the time they reach the secondary school they will have got very firmly hold of the idea that education is a race that only a few can win. They may have seen many friends drop out of primary school because their parents could not or would not pay fees. They will have passed at least one competitive examination, some children will have had to take two or three, and they will all have an unhealthy obsession with 'the Cambridge' or whatever other school certificate examination lies ahead of them. They will know that they cannot all go on to the sixth form, the university or the training college. And much of this situation we cannot change. But we can make it clear that education, and in particular language learning, is not a race or competition at all – there are valuable prizes for everyone.

We have many teaching methods at our disposal but there are only two basic attitudes that we can encourage our pupils to adopt towards each other. One is to set them working as individuals against each other, which is easy, divisive, and, unless used occasionally and light-heartedly, bad. The other is to help them to work with each other, which is difficult, uniting, and good. In different chapters in this book we shall be suggesting ways of getting pupils to work together – listening to each other's speech, helping with each other's bad reading habits, proof-reading each other's compositions, working on play productions, tape-recordings, editing class and school magazines, maintaining class libraries, organising debates and committee meetings, all these activities quite

[1] So he will always remember the wise Inspector of Schools who, having sat through half of a language lesson in which the teacher had lectured expertly and the class had listened politely, their admiration tinged with boredom, passed a note to the front of the class. The enthusiastic teacher, pausing for breath, looked down at his desk and read: 'Stop teaching and let them learn.'

apart from organised group and project work. Everything we can do to take the competitive attitude out of education will make for the development of happier young men and women, and for good language learning and teaching.

4 Pleasure

Enjoyment ought to be one of the foremost aims and effects of education, particularly in schools, partly because what we enjoy we feel inclined to go on with, and what we have disliked we drop as soon as we can. Every year our schools turn out thousands of children who have duly passed their school certificate examinations and will never seriously attempt to read or write again – beyond the demands of their jobs – because at school they found these procedures painful and boring. This is not to suggest that education can be one long hilarious game, or that we can somehow relieve our pupils of the need to get through a lot of hard work. Education is a serious business, but it is easy to go about it too glumly. Every good primary teacher knows that the best approach to any skill in education is by way of play, and though the secondary teacher may modify this maxim, he cannot afford to forget it. If we want our pupils to master language skills for themselves, so that they can go on learning long after they leave school and teachers behind, we had better make our language activities enjoyable, which will make teaching more enjoyable too, and far less exhausting.

5 Taking pupils into one's confidence

One way of helping pupils to enjoy their language activities, and of building up their confidence, is to explain to them, as far as we can, what we are doing in class, and why. We may well, for example, be asked, by an indignant first-year pupil, why we have passed off a paper-covered pamphlet of a mere hundred pages as *David Copperfield* when he has just discovered the real thing in the library and is aghast at its six hundred and ninety pages of close print, much of which he cannot make any sense of. This is the kind of question we should be glad to be asked and ready to answer, honestly and simply. We should take the pupils into our confidence as often as possible and be glad that at least 'Why' questions about teaching methods can be answered, even if 'Why' questions about language cannot.

A teacher who is trying to help his classes in this way has rightly rejected the image of the teacher as the omniscient and arbitrary dispenser of all knowledge. Any good language teacher who has got his pupils thinking for themselves will find himself saying every day, 'I don't know, but let's look it up in . . .'

6 Study skills

The teacher of English has the responsibility of equipping his pupils with the skills that they need to pursue their studies in all other subjects either immediately or in the future. This is *not* to say that English is 'the most important subject on the timetable' and thereby forfeit the goodwill of our colleagues who teach everything else. But in the hands of a good teacher the English course certainly services every other academic activity in the school and a good many of the extra-curricular ones. How many football fixtures would not have been muddled and cancelled if the English teacher had given his pupils, and particularly the football secretary, enough practice in the skills of writing a perfectly intelligible letter? We discuss in chapter five the skills that a good reader employs, not just in 'English' reading but in all other subjects and interests as well, and ways of improving reading speed. These are obviously the English teacher's concern, and it is also his business to give the pupils some detailed guidance on methods of study at the various stages of their secondary progress so that, unlike most of our present undergraduates, they do not go on to university without it.

7 The English teacher's interests

Even more important than this, the English teacher should have the wide-ranging enthusiasm and imagination that can make his English course a sort of clearing house for ideas and interests which branch out into all the other subjects that the pupils are studying in school, and beyond them. A seasoned teacher of English once warned a callow colleague: 'Never forget, my boy, that the English teacher's business is with the imagination.' This is splendid advice as long as the English teacher remembers that the imagination is not stimulated solely by the great classics of literature. He should be able to sympathise with the child who can make little of *The Mill on the Floss* or *Antony and Cleopatra* but whose imagination has been fired by experiments with static electricity or by Ohm's Law for a complete circuit, and put him on to, say, a short biography of Edison, a simple History of Science or a poem or two from an anthology of science verse. The wide reading which sets a pupil on the road to education will only begin with some such seminal reading experience. If, as we shall suggest below, the English teacher is going to try to organise a school library, and some class libraries with a wide range of books in them, he will need to know not only what novels, short stories, plays and anthologies are available in suitable editions, but also what travel books, documentaries, books about hobbies and sports, 'background' books on science, history, mathematics, geography, art and music. His colleagues who teach these subjects, or are interested in them, will be glad to help.

8 Co-operation with teachers of other subjects

Language teachers badly need the help and interest of the teachers of all the other subjects in the curriculum. With their active co-operation an English course may be very successful, but without it, it cannot be. As soon as pupils spot that correctness and fluency in speech and writing matter only to the English teacher, and that the biology, physics and mathematics staff are happy to decipher the ungrammatical and interpret the inaudible, they will consciously practise correct language habits only in English lessons and the English teacher is practically wasting his time and theirs.

If, on the other hand, the English teacher keeps his colleagues informed, briefly and amiably, of how the English syllabus develops throughout the school, what pronunciation errors are worth trying to correct at various stages, what symbols he uses in helping pupils to correct and improve written work – not 'in correcting pupils' written work' because the good teacher does not do that – and what vocabulary and structural level the texts for a particular year should be, then pupils will soon notice that good language habits matter to all the teachers all the time, and their language skills will be practised and improved in every lesson and school activity.

9 Finding out what pupils have done before

Any teacher of any subject ought to try to discover as quickly as he can what kind of learning experiences his pupils have already had.

There are at least three ways of doing this. One can talk to pupils – a good thing to do for other reasons – and find out what course they have used, what supplementary readers they have read, what schools they come from, whether they have taken part in a play or seen any plays, whether they go to the cinema to see films in English and so on. This information can be supplemented by discovering their English mark in the entrance examination and in some places one can get hold of the scripts, which enable one to see strengths and weakness in useful detail.

Where pupils have used a course in the previous stage, one can read and analyse it. To do this is particularly valuable because it enables one to see exactly what they are supposed to know item by item and this is essential knowledge for the teacher who wishes to avoid confusing a class with too many new items all at once. Guesswork is frequently very misleading. It is surprising how much more confident and active an apparently dumb class becomes when the teacher can start working within vocabulary and grammar that the pupils have mastered. It does not pay to under-estimate the value of what has been done previously. The pupils may appear to know very little but they usually know a good deal of what they have been taught, which is more than many of us could say for ourselves.

The third way of finding out is to go to some of the schools they come from and see what happens in them. Visitors who make arrangements beforehand are usually welcomed and teachers are pleased to let one sit in on classes and, which is often more illuminating, look at exercise books and the available supplementary reading. These visits will help us to understand the pupils' attitudes to learning and school.

It will almost certainly be necessary to change these attitudes considerably. Pupils will have to learn to take more responsibility themselves, to rely less on the teacher and to learn more by understanding and less by rote. But a frontal assault will defeat its own purpose. It is no good telling a secondary pupil who has just passed one or two competitive examinations by learning stuff by heart, that he cannot rely on memory to get him through. He knows this is not true. He would not be where he is if it was. The line is not: 'Stop using your memory and use your brains instead,' but 'Let us find an easier way of remembering things, than learning strings of words off by heart.'

Precisely what previous English-learning and learning-in-English experiences pupils have had will vary widely from country to country, and significantly from school to school and between individuals. The most important thing to know is the change-over point – the time at which English becomes the medium of instruction. There is a very wide range of possibilities.

1. English may be the language of the home, as with many East African Goans, and teaching English to such pupils is almost indistinguishable in method from teaching English in England. Second language problems hardly arise.
2. English may be the language of instruction throughout the primary school though not that of the home, as in the English schools of Malaysia and the Peak Course schools of Kenya. We have no experience of such pupils, but would expect to find the L1[1] still exercising a powerful effect in spite of the amount of exposure to English throughout previous schooling.
3. English may have become the language of instruction at some stage previous to the secondary school either gradually or at a certain point, as in most of East, West and Central Africa. In this case, the kind of teaching done in English in other subjects will have an important effect on the way pupils have learnt to learn, the exposure to English will have been less and the need for foreign language and second language teaching techniques will be correspondingly greater.
4. The changeover point may come, as it used to in the Sudan, at the moment of entry to the secondary school. Then the English teacher has an additional problem of securing the co-operation of his colleagues and supporting them with linguistic information. The effect of the L1 will be even greater and his need will be for a mixture of foreign and second language teaching methods.
5. The change-over point may lie in the future, as it now does in the Sudan, and will do in Tanzania. In this case, the principal effect will be on the syllabus, which must allow for the pupils' future needs and compensate for an absence of learning outside time devoted to English.
6. There is also, of course, the situation as in parts of India where English is first started in the secondary school, but that lies outside the scope of this book, which is not concerned with the teaching of English as a foreign language, but with the next stage on.

Whatever the past histories of our pupils may be, the more we know about them, the better. Their wish for the future is much less complicated. The most important thing in their lives is to pass the final examination, which, rightly or wrongly, is the key to a golden future.

10 Administration

[a] PREPARATION OF LESSONS

The teacher, we are often told, must be an artist; for teaching is an art. The English teacher must also be a scientist, conversant with the linguistic sciences.

[1] L1 means 'first language' that is native language. L2 means 'second language,' that is, the first one learnt after the native language.

We believe that it is equally important that he should be a good administrator and an efficient organiser.

This is necessary at the personal level; he must plan his week so that he has time to prepare lessons and read exercise books so that they can be returned at the proper time. He must plan his term's work so that the materials he needs can be ready when they are needed. He must plan his year's work and next year's work in the same way. He needs a diary with written-in reminders, for example, 'to check library reading done', once a fortnight or 'Give spelling test' once every three weeks. If this kind of planning is not done, important business gets neglected because of the pressure of day-to-day demands. He must not live hand to mouth.

In the training college student-teachers are firmly told 'Never given an unprepared lesson'. This is excellent advice, but like much other good advice, it is unfortunately quite impossible to follow it in the first year that one is teaching. Nobody can spend seven hours preparing seven lessons a day, five or six days a week for thirty weeks in the year and do his marking and outside activities. Fortunately, it is not necessary to do so; one thoroughly prepared lesson in three is enough. Follow-up lessons can successfully carry on from the original impetus for a period or two.

In the second year of teaching all that is necessary, if the original lesson was successful, is to make to the material already prepared minor adjustments suggested by experience, and the time saved can be used to improve the follow-up lessons. This only works if the teacher carefully cherishes his lesson notes and writes on them, while the lesson is still fresh in his mind, what changes he wants to make when he gives the lesson again a year later. Every teacher should maintain a set of continually growing files of lesson notes whether they eventually form the basis of textbooks or not.

[b] GROWING POINTS IN THE SYLLABUS

Just as in the early stages of one's teaching career one cannot devote equal time and thought to all lessons, in the later stages one cannot do this to all courses in every year. But every year at least one – the least satisfactory – should be chosen for special attention and should have time and energy lavished upon it as the growing point in the syllabus. The teacher takes for example, first-year composition and really thinks about and works on the preparation, teaching and follow-up of this course, keeping to the previously established routines for reading, language work and speech work. If his experimental work is seen to be successful in the end-of-the-year examination, in the following year composition follows the newly established routine and he turns his attention to getting a better series of lessons on, for example, speech work. In this way, the syllabus is continually improved and the teacher never goes stale because he always has an area of special interest and excitement to him.

[c] RUNNING A DEPARTMENT

But good English teaching in a school is not an individual affair. It is a matter of organised team-work, which is the responsibility of the senior English teacher, whose business it is to see that a proper syllabus is made, followed and constantly improved. It is also his job to provide books, materials and aids for his colleagues when they are needed. He is the guardian of the tradition and must do all he can to ensure that when he goes, he can hand over files, syllabus and tradition to a successor who has already worked with him. An established syllabus constantly being renewed is a valuable property and its continuity should not be broken. Those who have worked on it must leave copies behind when they go – and administrators should ensure that they do not all go at once.

The organisation of the English department needs little institutionalisation in a small school. Provided that the two or three English teachers are all free for at least one period a week, everything can be done on a carefully casual coffee-and-chat basis. But it is always worth while to take time off from marking and lesson preparation to think about the week's work and check up on how the work is going as well as discussing ways of tackling particular problems. A regular weekly meeting is valuable among experienced teachers; we all learn from each other. It is even more valuable where there are inexperienced teachers; it saves them from wrestling with their problems in dreadful isolation. They get personalised, in-service training on the job. Nor are they the only ones to benefit. Their inexperience is often an asset; they have a freshness and originality of approach that many of us, who are older and duller, can still appreciate, and envy.

The meeting period is not without its man-management problems. The senior English master who is critical of his colleagues' abilities will run headlong into trouble. Teachers are terribly touchy. But like pupils, they expand in the sunshine of appreciation, so that insemination becomes possible. All of us need help, are reluctant to ask for it and may resent its being offered but we are generally glad to find that it is available if we want it.

Watching colleagues teach and teaching in front of them are excellent things. It is important to create an atmosphere in which this is a perfectly ordinary occurrence so that techniques may be demonstrated and lessons constructively examined (not criticized) without embarrassment. Such an attitude can arise gradually out of accounts of work on the growing point given in meeting periods. Something new is being done: let's go and look at it.

In his zeal for all-round excellence of teaching, the senior man must not forget that there are very few all-rounders in the business. Some of us can sing ballads and produce plays; others shine at error analysis or teaching summarising. He will be wise to be thankful for our strengths and tolerant of our weaknesses, using us as best he may and remembering as we do about him, that all of us have the defects of our qualities. People who are madly enthusiastic about some aspect of their subject are tiresomely difficult to organise in a balanced programme. The tiresomeness is the price we pay for the enthusiasm; we should not grudge it.

[d] DEPLOYMENT OF STAFF

The decision about how the talents of the various members of staff who are teaching English are to be deployed in any given year should be taken by the senior English master in consultation with the headmaster. This is the most important decision he has to make. If all his staff are equally experienced and competent, he need only consider their wishes and how long it is desirable to leave one class with the same teacher. He will be able to avoid splitting classes between two teachers, which is generally undesirable. In these circumstances we like the same teacher to move up with his class, provided both are happy about it, so that he is with them for two years but not, normally, more than this. It is also necessary to remember that experience throughout the whole syllabus is good for all teachers. A second-year teacher is a better teacher of second year if he has also taught first year and third year. Experience of all years is essential training for future senior English masters.

Usually, however, the senior man will be faced with the problem of allocating classes between teachers with widely different experience and competence. He must not accept the common view that the best teachers automatically take the top classes. On the contrary, the most important year is the first. A class that has made a good start can stand a second year of indifferent teaching. They will be better at the end of two years than one that had a bad start followed by a year's good teaching.

The examination classes come next in importance. In the middle of the school the main thing is to avoid two consecutive years of indifferent teaching.

If this is not possible, one must consider splitting classes between teachers so that every class gets at least some inspiring lessons. Where this has to be done one can break the two-year rule with advantage. We have done some very happy teaching taking all the English in a first-year class, reading in second year, composition in third and all the English in the fourth.

Where classes are graded there is the further problem of making sure each teacher gets a fair share of quick and slow classes.

The larger the school the more difficult it is to organise a weekly meeting period – and the more necessary. Time-table provision is essential. A dozen teachers will not all be free at once if the matter is left to chance. Some increase in formality is needed too – not of course in the discussion – but in having a prepared agenda and not wasting everybody's time discussing matters of concern to only two or three people. This often involves putting things forward to next week's agenda for a meeting of reduced size rather than coping with everything on the spot. We do not, however, wish to suggest that all the advantages are on the side of the small school. The larger staff has a wider range of talent. More specialisation is possible. More experiments can be done at the same time. There are more people to whom growing points can be farmed out and faster change is possible.

But in every school, large or small, businesslike organisation matters. It is the essential framework within which the scientific teacher exercises his art.

11 External Examinations

This subject can be guaranteed to arouse impassioned argument among abolitionists, reformers and traditionalists alike. Let us try to set out a few modest and moderate considerations on this vexed and vexatious subject.

1. To abolish examinations altogether requires either enough money to provide the same length of schooling for all or the acceptance of some substitute such as record cards, teachers' reports or continuous assessment. The American tradition favours continuous assessment, the British examinations. The place to campaign for or against either is not in the classroom, where no useful purpose is served by making pupils unhappy about what will happen to them, but among colleagues, in committee and in the press.
2. If the prospect of immediate abolition appears remote, examinations can still be reformed. The place to campaign for this is again not in the classroom, but in the local committee and by correspondence through the official channels with examining bodies. The method is
   (a) to advance arguments against what is objectionable and
   (b) to offer a fully worked out alternative including, where appropriate, specimen questions.

   Examining bodies do not ignore even negative criticism but it leaves them knowing only that something is disliked, without much idea what would be preferred in its place.

   The process of changing an examination is bound to be tediously slow because, owing to the conservatism of teachers and in fairness to the expectations of pupils, even accepted changes require two years' notice, and even the most obviously desirable change cannot take place without considerable general agreement among inspectors and teachers, which it also takes time to achieve. We do not advance these facts as arguments against doing anything at all but as encouragement to teachers to join in the debate, which goes on all the time. Examinations are getting better, admittedly rather slowly, but every improvement has had its origin in some individual's discontent.
3. We have little respect for grumbling that leads to no positive action and none whatever for the teacher who saddles the examiners with the responsibility for his own sterile methods. Good teaching gets better results than cramming even in a bad examination and we do not know of any examination that is altogether misguided. Pupils who can read, speak and write English even moderately well can pass any kind of test. Pupils whose learning has been restricted to direct practice of examination questions are much more likely to fail even an examination on precisely the expected lines.
4. But the teacher who resolutely ignores examinations is not likely to be very successful. His heart may be in the right place but this will be small consolation to his pupils. While it is true that it is no good their passing if they are not being educated, it is equally true that it is no good their being educated if they do not pass.

So much for the final examination, which, when it is set and marked in England, poses special problems. The secondary entrance examination can usually be influenced more easily and, if there are marking centres, it provides a regular opportunity for teachers to meet and incidentally discuss common problems. Such opportunities are all too rare.

12 Keeping in touch

Many teachers work in up-country schools in conditions of severe isolation. It is most important for them to have opportunities to go to conferences every two or three years and to take full advantage of such means of contact with other people in the same business as are available. All schools should subscribe to

English Language Teaching
Teacher Education in New Countries
The Use of English

and, of course, locally published teachers' magazines. There should also be a school subscription to Language Teaching Abstracts and at least one member of staff should join ATEFL, the Association of Teachers of English as a Foreign Language.

These are minimal requirements in keeping up-to-date with what is happening in our very rapidly developing field.

The senior English master, at least, should also be in touch with the local representative of the British Council, which has valuable services to offer, and, of course, with the local Institute of Education and University Department of English. The gulf that exists in some places between schools and university is damaging to both.

Teachers who visit England will find the English Teaching Information Centre at 10 Spring Gardens, London SWIA 3BN, a most useful institution. It has an excellent library and collection of English-teaching aids, especially tapes.

Reference Books

A Language-Teaching Bibliography
Compiled and edited by the
Centre for Information on Language Teaching
and the English-Teaching Information Centre of the British Council
Cambridge University Press, 1968.

Audio-Visual material for English Language teaching
a catalogue. The British Council.

Ohanessian:Kreidler:Diright: *Reference List of Materials for English as a second language*. Washington D.C. Center for Applied Linguistics, 1964.

Part 1: Texts, readers, dictionaries, tests Part 2: Background materials, methodology.

CORDER, PITT S. *The Visual Element in Language Teaching-Education Today*. Longman, 1966.

KAYE, BARRINGTON and ROGERS, IRVING. *Group Work in Secondary Schools* and the training of teachers in its methods. Oxford University Press, 1968.

2

VOCABULARY

All mimsy were the borogroves,
And the mome raths outgrabe

1 Preliminary

Examine the following passage as earnestly as possible.

TEXT A: LONDON. Pugglemess term lately over, and the Lord Tinslebore sitting in Rinlonks Inn Hall. Immucable November weather. As much mud in the streets, as if the waters had but newly retired from the face of the earth, and it would not be wonderful to meet a Seggumpalot, forty feet long or so, doddlebing like an elephantine zigpod up Thursdrible Hill. Smoke gingling down from the chimney-pots, making a soft black siffle with sprokes of tooze in it as big as full-grown snow-sprokes – gone into wurging, one might imagine, for the death of the sun. Dogs, undispanderable in rike. Horses, scarcely better; blished to their very fruppers. Foot glabbingers, sprottling one another's lumrollas, in a general inpuntion of ill-temper, and losing their foothold at street corners, where tens of thousands of other foot glabbingers have been slipping and sliding since the day broke (if this day ever broke), adding new defonnels to the blopst upon blopst of mud, sticking at those points septariously to the durement, and occiridating at conton interest.

Hof everywhere. Hof up the river, where it flows among green oikies and guffeys; hof down the river, where it rolls demubed among the niebs of shipping, and the waterside louplations of a great (and dirty) city. Hof on the Ethics zoodges, hof on the Ormish heights. Hof creeping into the bocoshes of ballier-crogs; hof lying out on the feet, and commering in the zibbing of great ships; hof gloading on the wumbores of quoogees and small boats.[1]

What we have done is to take a well-known piece of English literature and to substitute a nonsense word for every word outside the vocabulary of simplified English. We have not changed any prefixes or suffixes.

The experience of 'reading' this text is therefore very similar to the experience of the foreign learner with a 2,000-word vocabulary confronted with the

[1] The original is given in Appendix I on page 49.

genuine article. Understanding is so fragmentary as to be worthless. The experience has no educational value.

It is perhaps even more disturbing to realise that behaviour that sounds like comprehension can take place. Question and answer can go briskly back and forth.

What has just finished?	Pugglemess term.
Where is the Lord Tinslebore sitting?	In Rinlonks Inn Hall.
What is the weather like?	Immucable.
Is that nice or nasty?	Nasty.
What might the Seggumpalot be doing?	Doddlebing up Thursdrible Hill.
What is it compared to?	An elephantine zigpod.

That's right. And you might like to make a note of that as an example of a simile.

And we all write in our notebooks:

Simile: a Seggumpalot, doddlebing like an elephantine zigpod.

When we have time we shall learn it by heart.

It is still more disturbing to realise that if the original words had been used instead, they would have had no more meaning for the pupil but the teacher would have thought something useful was happening.

The most disturbing realisation of all is that this can and does go on in all subjects where the teacher relies too heavily on words. The reaction of the pupil, of course, is to commit meaningless verbal formulas to memory. What else can he do? He has not been given anything he can understand. The teacher's reaction to his reaction is to blame him for parrot learning.

The need to make texts accessible and teaching comprehensible to pupils is the justification for vocabulary selection and control. We cannot leave vocabulary to look after itself.

2 The Learner's problems and the difficulty of direct vocabulary teaching

Since the problem cannot be ignored, we had better try to examine it from the point of view of the foreign learner. Our pupils have all heard the symbol [boks][1] and seen the graphic representation of it *box*. In one sense therefore they *know* the word *box*. If we ask them what the thing we keep the chalk in is called, they will answer with the cultivated courtesy of the foreign learner for the idiotic question, 'It's a box.'

But they are also liable to refer to a *box* of cigarettes.

When they read *Treasure Island* they will be faced with: 'One thing I saw plainly, I must not simply retreat before him, or he would speedily hold me boxed into the bows, as a moment since he had so nearly boxed me in the stern.'

[1] For the phonetic script used in this book see pages 199 and 200.

Will they understand this to mean *trapped as if in a box* or will they connect it with *boxing*?

Many of them certainly say, 'He boxed me, sir,' or 'He gave me a box,' in contexts where the native speaker would use *punch*.

Would they get the right context for, 'That's not what was said in the box.'

Asian pupils would probably jump to the reference of *box kite*, but no pupil would be likely to understand *box hedge*, *christmas box*, a *box* in a theatre or a *shooting-box*. They might manage a *sentry-box* and the girls might cope with a *box pleat*. But *boxing the compass* would baffle them all and many native speakers too. We do not know whether the term *goggle-box* has reached Africa and Asia. It is not in our dictionary.

Box is not an isolated example nor a particularly complicated one. Similar problems arise with all common words. Indeed one reason why they are common is because they are used in a wide variety of contexts.

It is clear that it is not always possible to identify the meaning of a word outside some kind of context. The context may be physical. If I am engaged in laying the table and ask, 'Where's the jam?' my meaning is clear enough as part of the whole situation. If on the other hand I am sitting in a line of cars and address the same question to a traffic policeman, my meaning will be quite different, though equally clear.

Lack of experience of the appropriate context may make understanding the meaning of the words used in it extremely difficult. Mist and fog are unknown in Khartoum and the words *mist* and *fog* are difficult to understand. There are even more dangerous traps when the overseas context that appears to correspond to the native speaker's context in fact differs. A *brother* in some parts of Africa includes not only male children of the same biological parents but half-brothers, cousins, fellow-clansmen, fellow-tribesmen and in extreme cases 'a chap I was having a drink with last night'. A *family* is not normally thought of as a father, a mother and their children. A *village* may be equated with a *trading centre*. Cross-cultural difficulties are as much a problem as lack of background knowledge.

Where language is the whole of the relevant situation, as it is when one is reading or listening to the radio, the meaning of the words is determined by the other words in the context, that is, by collocation. *Strawberry jam* is different from *traffic jam*; a country *seat* from a sore *seat*. The foreign student needs to learn to respond to many of the different collocational possibilities of words he has already met. Put very crudely, he needs to learn a great many new meanings for words already in his vocabulary. He also needs to learn to avoid accidental[1] unusual collocations. He must speak of *stirring* his tea and not of *winding it up*; he must not request his small son to stop *stirring his feet*. In these matters the dictionary will not help him much, and nor will vocabulary lessons of the kind that say: 'Here's a word. Now here are all the possible uses of it.'

[1] Deliberately unusual collocations are among the devices of the poets for our delight. T.S. Eliot speaks of Ezra Pound 'dislocating words into meaning'.

The objections to direct vocabulary teaching are:

(i) that even within the *General Service List*[1] it is difficult to know what items individual pupils need to learn.

(ii) that above this level the appropriate corpus will vary according to subject matter so much that general frequency is an unreliable guide.

(iii) that the different senses, as listed in the dictionary, shade into one another instead of being clearly distinguished.

(iv) that we do not want the pupil to concentrate on learning facts about words but the skills of appropriate response and use, which can only be practised in context. We want him to learn English, not lexis. We also want him to run the grammatical patterns of the language through his mind at the same time as the collocations.

(v) that vocabulary lessons of this kind are tedious, and unnecessary because the pupil can learn for himself if we provide him with the right things to read. He will then be exercising other skills at the same time, enjoying himself and educating himself as well.

At the secondary stage we can expect the pupil to read himself into a knowledge of vocabulary provided we give him suitable material in sufficient quantities.

3 A little history

It will help us to understand why the available reading material is what it is if we take a brief look at some of the history of vocabulary selection and control.

When Thorndike published his first *Teacher's Word Book* in 1921, he was interested in improving the texts from which American children learnt to read and in making it easier for them to acquire a wide reading vocabulary. By counting the occurrences of words in 4½ million words of text he established the frequency of the commonest 5,000 words in the material he selected. It is obviously sensible to learn to read common words before rare ones; they are more often useful. Moreover, frequency is an objective criterion which can be established by counting. This was the beginning of vocabulary selection and control.

Other workers joined in. In 1926 Horn produced a 10,000-word writing vocabulary based on a straight frequency count of personal and business letters. In 1931 Thorndike produced *The Teacher's Word Book of 20,000 Words* and in 1944 with Lorge, *The Teacher's Word Book of 30,000 Words*, which combined the results of his earlier counts, of the Lorge Magazine Count, of Thorndike's Juvenile Count based on a selection from the Terman-Lida list of approved reading for the pupils in grades 3–8 and of the Lorge-Thorndike Semantic Count, which distinguished between the various senses of identical graphic symbols.

It should be noted that the material in which the words were counted was all written. The tape recorder had not then been invented. One result of this

[1] M. West, *A General Service List of English Words*, Longman, 1953. For practical purposes this list defines the vocabulary of simplified English at the 2,000-word level. It is discussed more fully below.

is that some everyday household words have an oddly low frequency. *Sticky* is as rare as *strew* and *doorknob* as rare as *dulcet*. Moreover the list is now a generation out of date. The word *transistor* does not appear at all, and the frequency of *pop* takes no account of this graphic symbol's recent semantic extension. The list was designed for use in American schools and consequently has a slight American bias but even so *trousers* is much more frequent than *pants*. There is a much more serious literary bias. *Damsel* and *doth* are as frequent as *error* and *encounter*; *dulcimer* and *dight* have the same frequency as *demonstrator* and *discompose*. Provided however that these factors and the listing method are allowed for, the *Teacher's Word Book of 30,000 Words* is a most valuable document and the only existing source of guidance about general vocabulary above the level of the *General Service List*.

The usefulness of the idea of teaching common words before rare ones and the value of an objective means of selecting vocabulary was rapidly perceived in the field of the teaching of English as a foreign language and scholars such as West in Bengal, Faucett in China and H. E. Palmer in Tokyo started designing teaching materials within limited vocabularies.

A number of interesting and useful facts emerged and additional criteria of selection in addition to frequency were evolved. It was observed that in frequency lists based on any material 'structural' words were extremely common. They are bound to be, of course, because most of them are used however one is writing or speaking about whatever subject. They are clearly the most important words to teach and whether we regard them as belonging in grammar or lexis does not diminish their importance. In any straight frequency list very few structural words would not appear among the commonest two thousand

The second important fact was that on any page of print on whatever subject and however high the vocabulary level, at least three-quarters of the words used were among the commonest 2,000 words in the language. When these had been learned, only one word in four would present a difficulty. Conversely to make a text accessible to the student at this stage only one word in four needed to be changed.[1]

Another feature common to all frequency lists was the large measure of agreement between them up to about 1,500 items and then the rapid increase in differences as the statistical validity of the smaller number of occurrences decreased because the subject matter exerted an increasing effect. It began to look as though there was a common core of about 1,500–2,000 items and thereafter it might be sensible to think in terms of different lists for specific purposes.

The rough identification of this common core led to a consideration of what items and how many items were required to write or speak fluently and comfortably on non-specialised subjects. In other words how large need the foreign learner's vocabulary be before he could hope to be fluent on any everyday

[1] This is a gross over-simplification because it ignores the need for recasting but as a rough guide to the quantity of change required, it is about right. It also ignores the necessity of technical vocabulary, but much of the difficulty of school textbooks lies not in rare technical words but in rare general words.

subject. Again it looked as though the minimum productive vocabulary would have to be somewhere in the 1,500–2,000 word range.

4 Productive and receptive use

The terms productive and receptive vocabulary perhaps need explanation. The distinction between them is certainly essential for teaching purposes. Native speaker and foreign learner alike recognise and understand more words than they actually use. The words they recognise but do not use are the items by which their receptive vocabularies exceed their productive ones. The native speaker normally hears or sees a word many times in many slightly differing contexts and collocations before he begins to use it. It is recorded in his mind before it comes to the tip of his tongue or pen. In early life when the language is first being learnt the incubation period is very lengthy. H. E. Palmer tells the story of a baby brought up by bilingual parents in Alsace who spoke French in the home; six months before the child began to speak they moved into Germany and switched the home language to German. The baby's first words six months afterwards were none the less French.

As greater mastery of the language is achieved words pass more rapidly and easily from receptive knowledge to productive use when the need arises, and in teaching English to native English-speakers no sharp distinction between receptive and productive use is normally made. The foreign learner, however, wishes to reach general fluency as rapidly as possible and if he can do so within a limited vocabulary which is nevertheless satisfactory for all general purposes, time will be saved. Moreover if this active vocabulary is also a good foundation for reading unsimplified English, he will be able to go on learning new words for himself, and the natural process of movement at need from receptive to productive use can be allowed to take place unforced and as far as the student is concerned almost unperceived.

5 Vocabulary control applied to texts

Once it had been realised that something like three-quarters of the running words (that is the total number of words as opposed to the number of different words) in any text were common, it was only a short step to considering what proportion of unfamiliar words make a text unreadable or more cheerfully how many new words a text can contain and still be enjoyable for the student to read or listen to, and on this basis to construct series of readers leading up to the point where the student can read unsimplified English for himself. A text containing too many new words is unreadable as the passage at the beginning of this chapter shows. Difficult texts can be toiled painfully through with innumerable explanations by the teacher or references to the dictionary, but the process is dreary, bears no resemblance to reading and is not conducive to the establishment of good learning habits. At the opposite extreme the reasonably expert reader can deduce the meaning of the odd new word or two he may meet in a book from the context. The native speaker has not been told the meaning of all the words he has learnt and has not looked them up in a dictionary. He has picked them up painlessly. And there comes a stage in the foreign learner's progress where, given suitable material, he can do the same thing while his attention is where it should be – on the meaning of what he is reading.

Experience has shown that more than 25 new words per thousand running words usually make a text unduly difficult. This standard was first adopted by Dr West in the production of his graded readers. It works in practice.

In 1936 Dr West produced a dictionary in which 20,000–30,000 items were defined within a vocabulary of less than 1,500 words. The advantages of this for the foreign learner are considerable and obvious.

A few years later the *Basic English Dictionary* defined some 20,000 words (40,000 senses) within the vocabulary of Basic English.

With work being done on vocabulary selection in many parts of the world, with publishers anxious to produce texts in controlled vocabularies and, it must be admitted, with an exaggerated sense of the value of the vocabulary break-through, it appeared to many people that a great many learning, teaching and publication problems would be solved if more general agreement about vocabulary selection could be reached. The Carnegie Corporation provided the money and in 1934 and 1935 the work was done that led to the production of the Carnegie *Interim Report on Vocabulary Selection and Control.* Among other scholars the participants included Faucett, H. E. Palmer, Sapir, Thorndike and West.

6 The Interim Report

The introduction to the Report outlines the methods they followed and the criteria they used and suggests a number of subjects for research. They saw themselves as making the first draft of one of a number of lists that were needed and emphasised the interim nature of their product.

They completed a general service list and foresaw that it would need to be supplemented by lists designed for more specific uses. They suggested the following special lists:

1. For learning English:
   a. Easily learnt words useful in the process of teaching by the direct method and immediate environmental words.
   b. Words useful in letter-writing.
   c. Words useful in story-telling.
   d. Definition words (words useful in defining and describing things of which the pupil has not learnt the name).
   e. Elements of word-building (prefixes, suffixes, inflexional endings, etc. with a discussion of their use).
2. For learning other subjects:
   Suggestive lists of content words, e.g. weights and measures, words useful in discussing or teaching particular subjects, e.g. agriculture, hygiene, mathematics, elementary science, mechanisms, etc.

In the preparation of the general service list they started from the objective criterion of frequency as listed by Thorndike. With this list they compared their own:

> We noted a close correspondence between our judgement and the results of the objective method (the word-frequency count) within the first 1,500 words. Beyond the first 1,500 words we found neither the purely subjective nor the purely objective lists satisfactory. We observed that 3,000 words is an unsatisfactory level, since above 2,500 words stylistic variants appear in such numbers that it is difficult to draw a line.

They included practically all words of structural value – the pronouns, determiners, anomalous finites, conjunctions, etc., noting that the itemising of their meanings and uses was a task of some magnitude.

Their third criterion was universality, that is, the geographical distribution of the need for the word. Here they

a. tried to allow for words that seemed likely to become more widely needed, such as *telephone*, *scout*, *park*.
b. walked delicately round the problem of American and British variants.
c. excluded words likely to give offence on moral or religious grounds or words that are peculiarly Christian.
d. and excluded all names of peoples because they could devise no inoffensive way of drawing a line.

The fourth criterion – subject range – also provided special problems. They relegated classroom words such as *essay* and *blackboard* to a special list and solved the problems of business, military, letter-writing, agricultural and technological vocabulary by excluding words used only 'on one side of the counter' and including common words that are within the vocabulary of 'the inexpert layman'. One quotation is irresistible.

> In the selection of names of tools our criterion was that the tool should be such as might be found in any home and be used by women as well as men. Thus we may include Saw and Hammer, but exclude Drill.

The fifth criterion was usefulness for purposes of definition:

> Three types of Defining Words are recognised: (i) words necessary to enable a pupil to satisfy a need which he is unable to express directly; (ii) words necessary to enable a teacher to define an unknown word without use of the vernacular; (iii) words necessary for understanding a dictionary.
>
> We believe that Definers of types (i) and (ii) should be included in the general list wherever the word possesses some general value other than mere definition; but the purely defining word, e.g. Fungus, may be shown only in a supplementary list of such words together with an indication of that group of ideas to which each word serves as a key.

The sixth criterion was value for word-building:

> The value of a root for word-building has acted in certain cases as a useful criterion – but only in those cases in which other values were also found. Thus the value of the roots -ject and -port might justify the inclusion of the words Inject, Reject, Import, Export. It will be noted that a list of Elements of Word-Building is to be included among the Special Lists.

The last of their criteria was style. In general they excluded synonyms but allowed a few for 'words of extreme frequency where the avoidance of monotony is specially desirable, e.g. Answer, Good, Bad.' Highly colloquial words were excluded and words expressing emotion apart from 'names for the fundamental emotions and feelings' were relegated to the story-telling list.

The result of all this thought and labour has stood the test of time remarkably well. The general service list has been particularly useful because the compilers did not present a mere list. They stated in each case the included related words and defined the permitted meanings.

But the special lists were never made. In fact the Carnegie Committee were not at the beginning of a period of work on vocabulary but nearly at the end.

Since then Lorge has completed a semantic count distinguishing the frequencies with which common words are used in their different meanings. West has embodied this information in part 5 – the general service list – of the *Carnegie Interim Report*, added to it a list by Flood and himself of Scientific and Technical Vocabulary, and republished it under the title of the *General Service List*. This list in its old form or its new has been extremely widely used by textbook writers, simplifiers, teachers and examiners. For all practical purposes it defines the vocabulary of simplified English. For counting purposes it contains about 2,000 head-word entries and about 6,000 entries all together. Not all of these are separate lexical items because, for example, nouns and verbs are entered separately and nearly all 'structural' words are included.

Within the words of the G.S.L. it is possible to write books that read like ordinary English and to do so after some practice with very little feeling of being uncomfortably limited. It is possible to rewrite even books about special subjects by adding only a very small number of extra words. This has been proved in practice.

The G.S.L. contains, therefore, all the words a pupil needs for speaking or writing on any common subject; once a pupil has learnt them, there is no need to teach him any new words for active use. He already has a way of saying anything he may want to.[1]

7 What is a word? Problems of counting and control

Having considered the teacher's two main aids to vocabulary selection and control – *The Teacher's Word Book* and the *General Service List* – it may be interesting to look into some problems in more detail.

So far we have been speaking loosely of words, but if we define a word as that which appears in print with a space at each end, as soon as we collect a few specimens and try to list, count and control them we run into problems.

How many different words are there in the following?

> The youngest player acted well in the first act of the play but in the second and third acts where he had a less active part to play his reactions to the actions of the other players were sometimes a second or two late. He is, however, a promising young actor.

It all depends on what we mean by a word and unfortunately *The General*

[1] This paragraph and the preceding one are written within the vocabulary of the G.S.L. It would be interesting to know how many readers noticed any difference of style.

Service List and *The Teachers' Word Book of 30,000 Words* take different views and neither view corresponds very closely with, for example, the lexical theory set out in *The Linguistic Sciences and Language Teaching*,[1] with publishers' statements from Britain and the U.S.A. about the vocabulary level at which supplementary readers are produced, or with the conventions of the dictionary.

Problem 1. Is *act* in *first act* a different word from the regular plural with the same sense, *acts?* We can agree at once that it is not. There is no learning burden involved. The pupil who has mastered regular plurals will recognise *monuments* instantly if he knows *monument* and vice-versa. The difference is not lexical but grammatical.

Irregular plurals are a different matter and one in which consistency is difficult to maintain. Thorndike and Lorge list *child* and *children* and with more reason *mouse* and *mice* as separate words but *ox* and *oxen* as one.

Problem 2. Is *play*, the noun, a different word from *play*, the verb? The dictionary says it is. T and L list the two together. The difference is grammatical rather than lexical and the learning burden generally negligible. The pupil who knows what a hammer is will know what is meant by, 'He hammered the nail in.' We can count them as one lexical item, but we shall still need to watch contextual problems. All our pupils know what a *tree* is, but they might fail to leap to the meaning of a *treed cat*, and neither *strawberry jam* nor *traffic jam* will help much with 'Jam it up with a bit of rag.'

Problem 3. Are we to count the regular forms of verbs, *play*, *plays*, *played*, *playing* as four words or one? And should we count *interest*, *interests*, *interesting* and *interested* in the same way? T and L have one entry for the first group and two for the second, though if *interesting* is distinguished as *adj.* it is difficult to understand why *interested* in, for example, *an interested party* should be treated differently.

In the case of *play* the differences are grammatical again. We can safely think of them as one lexical item, provided we solve the next problem correctly.

Problem 4. Is *play* in *the play we saw* the same word as *play* in *work and play*? This time we must recognise an extra learning burden. The pupil who knows 'all work and no play' will not be able to jump from there to – 'We are going to do a play'. Here we have one word which is at least two lexical items. The same thing is clearly true of the two uses of *second* in the passage and true, though perhaps less clearly, of the *interest* group.

Problem 5. Is *player* a different lexical item from *play*, *actor* from *act*? The dictionary lists them separately, so do T and L and so does the G.S.L. There is an irritating but irrelevant spelling problem. But the learning load is not large, the suffix is grammatical rather than lexical and I think we could call these one lexical item.[2]

The question of whether *young*, *youngest* and *younger* are one word or three

[1] Halliday, McIntosh and Stevens, Longman, 1964.

[2] We shall, of course, come across problems in a few words which in form resemble verb + agent suffix and may have to point out that *adders* don't *add*; they only multiply; and *vipers* don't *vipe* anything, except, in some dialects, *vinscreens*.

can be settled on the same principles. As the difference is grammatical, we have one lexical item only and this time the dictionary agrees.

Problem 6. Are we to count *act*, *action*, *active*, *actively*, *activity* as one lexical item plus a grammatical suffix identifying the part of speech, or as five words? In terms of learning load it is clearly much easier to recognise *active* if you know *action* than it is to learn a word unrelated to one already known – *jerk*, for example. T and L list them all separately. Fries in *The Structure of English* lists a number of formal correspondences between different parts of speech, and perhaps in words where these are immediately perceptible we might assume that no new lexical item is present.

We cannot, however, usually assume a knowledge of Latin in our pupils and must not therefore extend this argument to cover the historical relationship between, for example, *permit* and *permission*, *perceive* and *perception* or even more absurdly *duke* and *education*. It is unusual for even the native speaker to connect the last pair.

Problem 7. Are we to count *action* and *reaction* as two words or one? More generally, what are we to think about prefixes, about *like* and *unlike*, *like* and *dislike* and about *inspect*, *prospect*, *expect*, *retrospect*, *aspect*, etc. The difference between one prefix and another is lexical not grammatical but if *like*, *dislike* and *agree* are known, any pupil will be able to jump to the meaning of *disagree*.

There is some regularity here that will sometimes mean that a new item can be recognised effortlessly. Once again, we must not exaggerate it. A knowledge of *appoint* will not enable the pupil to understand *disappoint*. T and L and the G.S.L. list items with different prefixes separately. The problem of alphabetical order is involved. The logical thing would be to list *dislike*, *disobey*, *displeasure*, *disorder*, *disloyal*, *disprove*, *dishonourable* under *like*, etc. It would not be easy to know where to draw the line but at present none of these words appear at all in the G.S.L.

Problem 8. What do we do about compound words and hyphened words? *Post*, *office* and *man* are clearly three words but it is difficult to justify regarding *post office* as a grammatical structure consisting of two words and *postman* as a fourth word.

T and L, whose main criterion is frequency of occurrence, award the same credit number[1] to each of the following pairs:

childbirth	:	chickaree
cheekbone	:	charlatan
birthright	:	benefactor
birthplace	:	bituminous

It is obvious, however, that they do not have equal difficulty or importance for the foreign learner.

Problem 9. Should words like *a*, *the*, *and*, *but*, *he*, *his*, *of*, *or*, *to*, *where*, *is*, *do*

[1] The credit number is a combined expression of frequency of occurrence and range. High numbers represent common words, low ones, rare ones.

be included in a vocabulary list in the same class as words like *camel, carpet, coin, comfort* and *culinary*? Should they appear at all?

A number of terms have been suggested for the two kinds of words: form words and full words, the words we talk with and the words we talk about, structural words and content words. The idea that a word may belong wholly or mainly in grammar and be empty or almost empty of lexical meaning is useful. An example of a lexically empty word would be *do* in *They do not agree*. At the other end of the scale we find choices which are lexical except that the words from which the choice is made must belong to the same grammatical class.

Here is the	picture pie pier pig pill pillow

Somewhere between these two lie choices like that between:

Why Where When How	did he go?

If we regard the above choice as fully grammatical, the one below certainly has a lexical element.

He put it	on in near	the box.

We cannot be certain what lexis the secondary learner will need. It will depend on what subjects he reads about. But we can be certain that he will need practically all the words that can be listed as the only possible items in grammatical systems. He will need to know all the prepositions, pronouns, determiners, interrogative adverbs, anomalous finites, conjunctions of various kinds, etc.

He will in fact need to do more than recognise them; he must be able to use them with very few exceptions. It is, for example, not particularly cramping to write without using *lest* or *despite* because there are available alternatives, but it remains generally true that he will have to learn all the words that are used to operate grammar and that they are best dealt with in grammar rather than lexis. But all these words are listed in both the G.S.L. and T and L.

Problem 10. We have seen one word, *second* for example, which is clearly two lexical items. How should we count *put* and *on* in – *He put on his coat* or He *put* his coat *on*? In this case we have two words but only one lexical item in spite of the discontinuity in the last example. It is, however, a new lexical item additional to the various senses of *put* or *on*. Similar examples are ***put off, put up with, put across*** and so on.

Basic English consists of only 850 words but when Fries and Traver examined its learning load in *English Word Lists* they found thousands of lexical items.

We have already accepted *young*, *younger* and *youngest* as a single lexical item. We must therefore also accept as one *beautiful*, *more beautiful* and *most beautiful*.

We have not dealt with more than a selection of the problems involved in listing and counting vocabulary but it is already obvious that statements such as 'The average pupil on entry has a vocabulary of about 1,500 words', 'School certificate is based on a vocabulary of 7,000 words', 'The average native university student in England has a vocabulary of 60,000 words', or '*Tom Sawyer* in the Longman Simplified English Series is written in a 2,000-word vocabulary' – all such statements are practically meaningless unless we know to what kinds of items the figures refer. There are fewer lexical learning items in a 3,000-word vocabulary in T and L than in the so-called 2,000-word-level vocabulary of the *General Service List*.

It is easy to be critical of much of the work done on vocabulary selection and control and patronising about the way the early simplified textbooks ignored structural grading. It will soon be possible to produce much more scientific vocabularies aimed more accurately at meeting more specific needs. Meanwhile however we have got to go on teaching and writing textbooks on the basis of the information now available.

For practical purposes it is reasonable to assume that any pupil who has completed a course of simplified English can read texts at G.S.L. level because any modern course will aim to include this vocabulary in addition to local and classroom words. Below the 2,000-word level there will be local variations about which words are taught first and it is not therefore safe to assume that the Oxford supplementary readers at the 500-word level can be read as soon as the pupil reaches 500 words in another course. There is, however, always a considerable overlap and it does not matter, in fact it is a good thing, if supplementary reading is a little easy. Pupils who have reached 750 words in one course can generally read 500-word supplementary readers of other courses. At 1,500 words all 1,000-word readers are manageable. This adds to the number of books pupils can read for pleasure before they reach the secondary stage. Unfortunately full use of the published material is seldom made and serious reading for fun generally has to begin in the secondary school.

8 Vocabulary levels in secondary schools texts

[a] THE PLATEAU

In the secondary school a year is required during which the pupils read extensively at the 1,500-word and 2,000-word level. The materials available are considered in Chapter 3. In reading we are mainly interested in increasing speed and training imaginative response. As far as vocabulary growth is concerned, what we are interested in is new meanings for old words (rather than new words) and in giving the pupil practice in jumping to the exact meaning of the word in its context.[1]

During this year we should remember that in English-medium schools there will be a large vocabulary learning burden in all subjects other than English. Our main job as English teachers especially in the pupils' first year is to improve skill.

[b] THE TRANSITION TO UNSIMPLIFIED TEXTS

When simplified English has been mastered, what vocabulary the pupil goes on to learn depends on his needs. The normal assumption in East, West and Southern Africa is that he will want or need to read English literature. Where this is so, he needs a further year of introductory reading before he goes on to unsimplified literature because unless he gets this, he will meet new words at too high a density, his progress in reading skill and speed will be halted or reversed and his enjoyment in responding to literature will be spoilt.

There are a few unsimplified books the pupil might read – *Animal Farm*, for example, happens to have an over-all density of new words of less than 1 in 40. There are a number of others simplified or specially written in the Oxford *Stories Told or Retold Series*. These are catalogued as above 2,000 words and have been produced by workers overseas who used their experience and judgement about the level required.

9 Longman Bridge Series

When Longman Bridge Series was planned, an attempt was made to use objective criteria to establish the appropriate vocabulary level. The reader was assumed to be able to understand the vocabulary of the G.S.L. and the commonest 3,000 words in T and L. It was assumed that it would generally be more profitable for him to meet words in the T and L range of 3,000–7,000 than less common ones. Difficulties of structural complexity are proper to this level and the writer's structure was not therefore to be altered except where a vocabulary change required it. The texts chosen had to be worth reading and have fairly adult interest.

Now when a text has been chosen and abridged, the procedure is to mark all words and senses outside the G.S.L. and then cancel the marking if the item has a credit number of over 29 in T and L, working on three or four pages at a time.

The next operation is to change all the marked items so that they are within the G.S.L. or first 3,000 of T and L or have already been used in the text. This removes the very rare words. If the original reads: ***Perhaps he had never said***

[1] One of Palmer's questions addressed to the Carnegie Conference was: 'How far can the meaning of a word be stretched?' For example, if *chair* is known, can we assume that the pupil will understand, 'Makerere offered him a chair'? Obviously the writer can 'stretch' as far as the pupil can 'jump'. But this is not something about which simple rules can be made. It involves a decision in each case based on the writer's experience of what pupils can usually manage. Pupils improve in the ability to 'jump' with practice.

anything so lacerating in his whole life before, then *cruel* or *cutting* is substituted for *lacerating*.[1]

The final step is to adjust the vocabulary level so that the proportion of difficult items is not more throughout the sample than 1 per 40 running words. But not all new words count as a full unit of difficulty. Words unrelated to known ones are clearly full units: *jerk*, *jet*, *jolly*, *linger*, *lurk*, *malice*. But the following, taken also from the glossary of *The Card*, would only count as half units:

incapable – because *capable* is T and L 38.
indebted – because *debt* is in G.S.L.
journalist – because *journal* is T and L 'AA' (in the first thousand).
jollity – because we have already met *jolly*.

The following from the same two pages would count as less than half units:

inwardly – because *inward* and *inwards* are in G.S.L.
lion-tamer – because *lion* and *tame* are known.

Two other considerations affect the decision about units of difficulty: the possibility of extra frequency in a school or local context, and the amount of help given by the surrounding words in the text. *Geography* is T and L 14 and a strict following of objective criteria would cause one to list it, but its use in school makes it unnecessary.[2]

The context may give practically no help at all. In *We found a glurb*, there is not enough context to help. Almost anything can be 'found'. But in *The driver flourished his whip, the horses tossed their heads and we started our travels in the borrowed blerk*, it is a fair inference that a *blerk* is a private vehicle carrying more than one passenger and drawn by more than one horse.

These operations, which sound rather mechanical, in fact involve considerable linguistic skill and judgement of much the same kind as that required in translation. They are set out here in some detail in the hope that others may add to the available reading matter at this level and perhaps even more importantly consider writing or rewriting textbooks in other subjects at language levels more appropriate than those of the books in current use.

In non-English-medium schools once simplified English has been mastered it would theoretically be possible to go straight on to the acquisition of technical vocabulary relevant to subjects of future study. There are, however, serious practical difficulties. The necessary texts do not exist. They could easily be produced and countries that continue university education in English but use

[1] Objections to this emasculation of texts are sometimes raised by readers whose mother-tongue is English and even stronger objections may be raised by writers. It is true that for people who respond to the flick of the whip in *lacerating* it is a 'better' word than *cruel* or *cutting*. But it is not better for the foreign learner who cannot yet respond to it. He is forced to the dictionary and reads – lacerate: tear (the flesh. fig. the feelings). He is back where he started from. For him, the full meaning is not yet there and before it will be, he has many commoner words it will pay him to learn first.

[2] I was once silly enough to gloss *nib* and was rightly taken to task by a reviewer in *English Language Teaching*. The spread of ball-point pens, however, will gradually efface my folly but I make no claim to far-sightedness. J.A.B.

another language as the medium in the secondary school would find them very useful. Existing texts contain the technical vocabulary of their subject and also a large number of general words that are outside simplified English, such words for example as *absurd, adequate, adjoining, aggression, alert, alternative, amateur, ample, apparatus, apprehensive, automatic, available*. It is unlikely that the most up-to-date work in any technical subject will be published in Britain or America or taught by English-speaking experts without the use of a large number of such general words. There is therefore good reason to suppose that anybody who is going to continue his education in English will find them useful.

Another reason for avoiding an immediate switch to technical reading is that not all the pupils in the class want the same technical vocabularies. They may be going on to any subject from A (for agriculture) to Z (for zoology). If we wish to teach them as a class, we shall have to get them at least some texts the same and these texts must therefore have common human interest – and texts that have this are literature. We conclude that the kind of vocabulary growth appropriate is the same for non-English-medium schools as for English-medium ones, but we must not forget the extra learning of technical vocabularies taking place in the English-medium schools and failing to take place in the others.

10 Kinds of new words that will be met

We have now considered a certain amount of lexical theory and noted the lexical considerations that will influence our choice of texts – the kind of English to which we want to expose our pupils. It remains to see what kinds of items they will have to learn and how they can be helped to sensible attitudes, techniques of learning and an intelligent interest in words. We want to decide when and how we teach what. Up to the end of simplified English all vocabulary has been required for both receptive and productive purposes. But from now on we need not teach the active use of words, merely recognition knowledge, and the pupils must know that they are no longer expected or advised to bring in to their writing the new words they meet or to make lists of them or even to make any special effort to remember them. We shall not meet, for example, the word *alert* and say, 'It means watchful or lively. Now put it in a sentence, my boy.' If we do, we shall get something like, 'I felt very alert when the teacher came in,' and serve us right. 'Make a sentence' means 'make a mistake'.

Since the pupils have a means of saying anything they need to say,[1] many of the new words they come across will be other ways of doing so. Except in the few cases where words are stylistic alternatives, e.g. *begin*: *start*: *commence*, new words will generally apply to narrower contexts than the known words. In addition to *walk* they may meet *limp*, *hobble*, *stroll*, *saunter*, *march*, *stride*, etc. In addition to *pull*, they may find *tug*, *jerk*, *twitch*, *haul*, *tow*, etc. In addition to *box*, they may come across *case*, *chest*, *carton*, etc.

[1] This does not mean 'an adequate means of creating the equivalent of *Macbeth*' or of making a translation of *Macbeth* in simplified English that says the same thing as *Macbeth*.

It is important that pupils should not assume that such words are synonymous, as they are particularly likely to do if their own languages are rich in synonyms, as Swahili and Arabic are. Some general explanation is required, reinforced by questions aimed at drawing attention to the precise meaning of the word, asked when it is met during reading, and at helping the pupil to infer the meaning as exactly as possible from the context.

For example, in a story we meet: 'They waded across the road.' We can ask how they crossed the road, what the road was like and whether the water was deep or shallow.

At another time, not while we are trying to help the pupil to respond fully to the words in the text, we might ask what difference it would make (to the way we imagine what is happening) if instead of *waded* we had *splashed*, *squelched* or *swam*.

In our first languages we pick up strong emotional associations within the home. They are built into the learning situation. But a second language is normally learnt in the less passionate atmosphere of the classroom, where physical violence, for example, about whether this is *mine* or *yours* does not normally arise. The result is a lack of emotional involvement in the language and hence great difficulty in seeing any meaning other than plain sense. *Obstinate* is understood to mean no more than *determined* – the writer's attitude of disapproval is missed. Many of the new learning items the pupils will meet at this stage are loaded with suggestions of feeling.

Appropriate emotional response is not simply a question of knowing that certain words carry implications. It is also a matter of seeing how words that are neutral in another context may, if they are brought together, react on one another to communicate feeling. To take a simple example, the word *dragged* is neutral in *The police dragged the river*, but far from neutral in *He was dragged up in a slum*, or even in *The police dragged him out of the car*. One aspect of extra meaning is concerned with the appropriate emotional response.

We cannot hope to teach the full meanings of all the desirable words in all possible contexts, but we can deal with a large enough sample to show pupils kinds of contextual limitations (and thus implications) and, even more important, to get them into the habit of noticing them for themselves.

11 Inference from context

The whole business of inference of meaning from context needs to be explained to pupils and they need to be convinced through examples that it is possible and useful. It has never occurred to many of them that they can understand what a new word means without being told or looking it up. If, for example, we meet the word *sastrugi* out of context, we may well not know what it means, but the following quotations from Fuchs and Hillary *The Crossing of Antarctica* enable us to work it out.

They are flying back to South Ice through a snowstorm:

> Down and down we went till the skis touched and Gordon brought us gently over the sastrugi to a standstill.

> ... the midnight sun, which was just above the horizon now, sculptured the waves of sastrugi in light and shadow.

They are using dog sledges:

> Once they reached an area of giant sastrugi, in Brooke's words 'four feet high and shaped like torpedoes on pedestals'. This formed an impossible barrier, and so the party was forced off its route by having to sledge 'with the grain'.
>
> ... they made good progress despite patches of huge sastrugi five to six feet high.

The party are in vehicles:

> All the next day we travelled over sastrugi, fortunately directed along the line of our course – quite a change after so many miles when they lay athwart our track.
>
> With the dog tracks still extending ahead of us, there was no need for navigation, and Geoffrey and Hannes continued ahead, followed by the two Weasels and the Muskeg, which were slower than the 'cats' over the murderous sastrugi. It was impossible to go round the high ice-hard ridges, for they formed a great field that extended out of sight in all directions.
>
> ... these endless sastrugi stretching at right angles to our path. The winds, it seemed, must blow perpetually from the east, scouring and grooving the surface year after year.

The ability to deduce meaning in this way is one of the most useful skills of the expert reader. In this particular example the wider context has been omitted because it can be assumed that the reader will know that Antarctica is covered with snow and that sastrugi are therefore snow or ice formations. If the scenes are not imagined as snow-covered, the word might refer to ridges of rock or sand.

The selection of snow rather than ice as the material rests on *ice-hard ridges* as opposed to *hard ice ridges*.

The process of deduction may, of course, be hindered by the presence of other unknown words at too high a density.

Dr West saw the value of this skill in inferring meaning from context and the final readers in his New Method Course were designed to enable the learner to practise doing so. They are called N.M.R. 7 *The Vicar of Wakefield* and N.M.R. Alternative 7 *Dead Man's Rock*. The style they are written in strikes the English reader as a little odd because of the built-in clues, and not everyone would regard the *Vicar of Wakefield* as the greatest fun in the world to read in class. But they are the only books we know that are specifically aimed at this problem and there is something to be said for starting one of them in class in order to introduce pupils to the problem and leaving those who wish to do so to finish it for themselves. It would certainly be a good idea to recommend one of these to any pupil who finds inference from context particularly difficult. Perhaps the most important thing of all is to remember that the ability to infer in this way is a skill that can only be acquired by practice. Every time we tell a pupil what a word means we are robbing him of a chance to practise this skill. Questions about the meanings of words should be countered by questions aimed at helping the pupil to make intelligent guesses.

12 Words related to items already known

A large part of the unfamiliar vocabulary the learner will meet when he starts reading above the simplified English level will consist of words related in different ways to words he already knows.

The complete series of systems of relationships is highly complicated. In our view it is not suitable for direct teaching and the answer is to do enough exemplary work to convince the pupils that a number of sets of regular relationships exist and to enable them to recognise them *when they are useful.* Historical connections, such as that between *port* and *ford* or the wherefore of *foolscap,* are interesting but not useful. Those connections that are normally perceived by the native speaker[1] are the helpful ones.

There are a very large number of immediately perceptible relationships that give rise to few problems of understanding – productive use is another matter. For example:

Among nouns:

(i) compounds such as

a. goldfish, birthright, headache, earthquake, footstool.

But not all compounds are equally straightforward. One may instance the restricted contexts of *gold-digger* or *platelayer.* Moreover one part of the compound may not be known, as would be likely with *goldsmith,* or a part may not occur as an independent form, as in *bankrupt.*

The *-ache* compounds illustrate the extra problem of productive use. The following are acceptable: *headache, toothache, earache, stomachache, bellyache* (with certain restrictions), but the following are not: *armache, legache, elbow-ache,* although we can say *My arm aches* just as we can say *My head aches.* The learner will not meet unacceptable forms in his reading; he will only invent them if he is unwisely pushed into premature productive use.

b. upshot, backlash, outcome, input, output

c. take-off, setback, lay-by, show-down, holdup, take-over

d. greenhouse, grandstand, blackbird, roughneck.

(ii) nouns related to verbs and marked by a suffix:

a. denial, reversal, acquittal

b. closure, departure, exposure

c. forgery, mockery, flattery

d. acquaintance, assurance, attendance

e. accomplishment, accompaniment, achievement

f. obscurity, perplexity, complexity

g. collision, conversion, provision

h. drainage, leakage, usage

i. accountant, applicant, claimant

[1] Behind this generalisation lurks the sinister shadow of Mr Average-Morphemically-Conscious Man.

j. hinderer, knitter, handler – *and for things rather than people:* mixer, burner, roller. *But this not a very straightforward area. There is the* -or *suffix as in* reflector *and the matter of specialised meaning as in* revolver.

k. blessing, daring, dwelling. *But the verb* to help *is little use in arriving at the meaning of* a second helping.

(iii) nouns related to adjectives and marked by a suffix:

a. stillness, closeness, slipperiness

b. capability, frailty, intensity, seniority.

Verbs include:

(i) compounds: items such as:

a. get over, call up, look after, break in

b. overturn, upset, underestimate

(ii) verbs related to nouns:

a. besiege, bewitch, bedevil

b. enrage, entangle, enthrone

(iii) verbs related to adjectives:

a. ripen, sicken, coarsen, moisten

b. enable, endear, embitter

c. embolden, enliven

Adjectives include:

(i) words related to nouns:

a. misty, messy, chilly, baggy[1]

b. stately, beastly, leisurely

c. bookish, fiendish, devilish

d. ancestral, cultural, ceremonial

(ii) the participles of verbs:[2]

broken, suspended, searching

(iii) adjectives plus *-ish*:

reddish, sweetish, steepish

(iv) compounds:

a. hard-working, well-spoken, long-lasting

b. foul-smelling, evil-looking, hard-wearing

c. coal-burning, fever-carrying, water-cooling

d. worm-eaten, well-advised, ill-chosen

e. machine-bottled, water-borne, mud-caked

f. broken-down, worn-out, cleaned-up

g. home-grown, factory-made, shop-bought

h. absent-minded, long-tailed, high-handed.

And others more irregular: up-and-coming, down-and-out, off-the-shoulder, matter-of-fact.

Nearly all the above relationships are so easy to see that they hardly require any teaching at all. Pupils must, of course, do plenty of reading or they will

[1] It is noteworthy that the irregular pair *difficult*: *difficulty* are frequently misused in E. Africa, but there is also a phonetic problem involved.
[2] Not all participles pattern like 'true' adjectives e.g. in collocating with *very*.

not meet them, but all we need do as teachers when we come across such items is to call attention to the related words often enough to keep the pupils on the look-out for them. This is to be done incidentally, casually and quickly. There is nothing to be said for stopping in the middle of a piece of comprehension work at, for example, the sentence, 'I felt his thumbs exerting a terrible pressure on my throat', and dragging in such irrelevant bits and pieces as *thumb-screw, thumb-print, thumb-nail, exertion, impress, compress, express, depress, repress, impression*, etc.

The relationship point can usually be made in the course of a question that might be asked in any case. If the word is *denial*, one merely asks, 'What did he deny?'

The obvious relationships raise few teaching problems. Less obvious ones involve some kind of morphemic analysis of the structure of words. All teachers do a little of this and would agree that it is useful to make pupils aware of the usual meaning of such prefixes as *un-*, *re-*, *ex-*, and *dis-*.[1]

A few teachers do a great deal. The extreme view, which we last recall hearing propounded seriously by a Director of Education in 1942, is that 'you can't write English if you don't know Latin.' This view no longer merits serious opposition but the problem of how much to do remains. It is easy to do too much.[2] Historical semantic connections are not often a good guide to modern meaning or usage though they may still be a help to the memory and a source of a growing interest in words. One would like evidence of what connections exist in the mind of the linguistically unsophisticated native speaker – Mr Average-Morphemically-Conscious Man. Does he connect *bankrupt*, *interrupt*, *corrupt*, and *rupture* or get on perfectly well by regarding them as separate items? What about, for example, *vision*, *revision*, *supervision*, and *invisible*? Presumably only the latinate would group with the last three *video-tape*, *provide* and *vide*.

We do not feel able to lay down any clear principles. We believe that some direct teaching in short spells of, say, the odd ten minutes at a time may be useful. We would certainly wish to bring words with common prefixes together in the pupils' minds occasionally. 'Think of all the words you can beginning *pre-*.' 'What do you think "He was predisposed to think well of her" means?' 'What do you think *predestination* means?'

We would also, again in very short occasional spells, draw attention to certain common stems such as *-vid-/-vis-*, *-spect-*, and *-soc-*. This we would do for three reasons: firstly because we believe that the noticing of common elements helps in the process of inferring meaning, secondly because by showing how meanings have become differentiated we are indicating how people adapt words to their needs and thirdly because we find it interesting ourselves and we see nothing wrong in sharing our enthusiasms with our pupils.

We are also prepared to suggest rather more tentatively that we would like learners at some stage of their school careers to read a very brief historical account of the growth of Modern English. This is of course teaching general

[1] Pupils usually find this gusting and gruntling too, in moderation.

[2] I suspect I may have done so in *Patterns and Skills 3* and *4*. Longman, 1966-7. J.A.B.

knowledge and not teaching English but we are not opposed to increasing the pupils' general knowledge about language except when it becomes a substitute for giving them experience of using it.

13 Dictionary work

Nor do we belong to the school of thought that argues that the only way to prevent secondary pupils from misusing long and learned words is to keep them in ignorance by preventing them from using a dictionary. Left to themselves many of them will misuse a dictionary but what they need is not protection from these dangerous instruments but careful training in how to use them properly. The training should begin at least as soon as the pupils are ready to leave the 2,000-word plateau, which in the schools we have chiefly in mind will be at the beginning of their second year. In a properly equipped school pupils will have personal dictionaries and it is as important that these should be all the same as that they should be well chosen. The practice of allowing any pupil to equip himself with any dictionary he cares to buy, beg, borrow or steal is highly unsatisfactory. In addition to personal dictionaries all pupils should have access to *The Advanced Learner's Dictionary* for writing purposes and to an etymological dictionary so that anyone who develops an interest in the history of words may pursue it.

Pupils will already have used dictionaries, chiefly to look up spelling but also to find out the meaning of unfamiliar words. It is only necessary to watch the average pupil looking for a word to realise that his grasp of alphabetical order is shaky and his technique unnecessarily slow and laborious. When one considers how frequently he will need a secure command of alphabetical order for reference in books of all kinds from encyclopedias to telephone directories, it is clear that it is worth while to spend time in improving his efficiency.

First we need to check that he knows the alphabet. A number of quick-fire questions of the fun-and-games kind will usually enable us to identify the pupils whose command is shaky. For example:

> How many letters in the alphabet?
> What's the first? The last? The middle one?
> In which half is J, T, P, etc.?
> In which half of the first half is L, D, etc.?
> What letter comes before/after Q, F, etc.?
> What letter comes two/three/four after/before K, X, etc.?
> Start from T, H, etc., go back/on five letters and on/back two.
> Think of a word beginning with this letter, or, open your dictionary at this letter.
> Open your dictionary once only. Try to hit the letter S, E, etc.
> See how quickly you can find the words beginning with A, K, etc.

The next step is to make sure that the principles of alphabetical order are understood. Pupils can discover them for themselves if they are told to look up examples that begin with:

(i) different letters

(ii) the same letter
(iii) the same two letters, etc.

and

(iv) that demonstrate that zero takes precedence over any letter, e.g. that *not* precedes *note*.

This knowledge can then be used to find words more rapidly than before.

The third step (which might equally well precede the one before) is to show pupils how to use the words at the head of the page in the dictionary in order to know at a glance whether the word sought is on that page, before it or after it.

This can develop into quickfire questions, too. For example: 'I am looking for *abstain*, the headwords are *abyss account*. Am I on the right page or do I go on or back?' It is best to write sets of headwords on the blackboard, in order to avoid spelling problems. The board reads:

ABYSS ACCOUNT

The teacher says: ABSTAIN
The pupils reply: Go back.
Teacher: ACCUMULATE
Pupils: Go on.
Teacher: ACCELERATE
Pupils: Right.
Teacher: ACCOUNTANT
Pupils: Go on to next page.

Other pairs and examples can be dealt with rapidly and finally one can have races to see who can find ten words in the least time, or better still work in pairs to see who can make the most improvement in time, with one pupil working and his partner checking that his finger lights on the ten words and keeping the time.[1]

The ingenious teacher will easily devise short and entertaining drills to fit into an odd ten minutes here and there until mastery has been achieved.

One can check by inviting pupils to arrange items in alphabetical order. If a genuine purpose can be found such as making a list of pupils' names and of library books as a reading record sheet, so much the better. If 'research' essays are done as suggested in Chapter 4 the making of an index would revise this point and contribute also to an understanding of one of the more mechanical skills of scholarship.

Once pupils have learnt to find the word they want in a dictionary, it is time to make them discover what other information their dictionaries contain and how it is expressed. All the information is, of course, included in the small print of the prefatory pages, which hardly any pupil and not every teacher has bothered to read. The pupils indeed, would find wading aimlessly through the small print a daunting and not very profitable task. If, however, they are set to finding out the answer to one specific problem at a time, the difficulty is

[1] For an easy method see page 115, paragraph 5.

reduced and they are incidentally being given practice in skimming or what West calls 'searching reading' and this is valuable in itself.

It is worth while to spend three or four lessons finding out what information is contained in the class dictionary and what additional information can be found in the dictionaries in the library. The grammatical aspects of the *Advanced Learner's Dictionary* and Palmer's *Grammar of English Words* should not be overlooked but the approach can be illustrated from any dictionary used by the class as a whole. Indeed the find-out-what-your-dictionary-says approach is possible even if a number of different dictionaries are in use.

We may start by listing what they think their dictionaries contain and then checking against the contents list.

1. Spelling is obvious. But does their dictionary distinguish between American and British spelling? Let them find out by looking up e.g. *color*, *center*, *traveler*.
2. Meaning is obvious, but how does the dictionary distinguish different meanings? Let them look up a few such words as *grouse*, *grub*, *gum*, *flag*. Are all the senses given in their dictionaries? Let them check with larger dictionaries. Give practice in selecting the sense appropriate to a suggested context, e.g. *His health began to flag*.
3. *Grouse* is marked perhaps as '(colloq.)'. What does this mean? Let them find out from the introduction and list of abbreviations. What other stylistic information is available? Let them try e.g. *steed*, *wangle*. We find several items for them to look up in each of the categories indicated (unless our squeamishness rejects those marked *taboo*).
4. What grammatical information is given? Let them look up words of the various classes distinguished and refer to the list of abbreviations. Choose straightforward examples for the category, e.g. *county*, and then more complicated ones e.g. *craft*, where a good dictionary will distinguish the 'countable' from the 'uncountable' sense, and then examples of words that are listed as many different parts of speech.

   Include, for example, *afraid* among the adjectives. Let them find out what *predic adj* stands for and arrive with as little telling as possible at the conclusion that it excludes the structure 'an afraid boy'.

   Include among examples of intransitive and transitive verbs those like *amuse*, *revenge*, *envy*, *enjoy*, that tend to be used in wrong categories by the pupils.
5. Pronunciation can be dealt with similarly. For example: What sign is used for the vowel in *cup*? Now look up the pronunciation of the *o* in *mongrel*. Find out from the introduction the pronunciation of this word [ʃeiz]. Now try to find it in the dictionary. Now look up the pronunciation of *charlatan*, etc. One might perhaps stop short of ['ʃɑːʒeidæ'feɑ].

   Enough should be done to enable the pupils with the aid of the introduction and table of pronunciation symbols to arrive at the pronunciation of any strange word by reference to the dictionary.

   It should include looking at stress marks in e.g. *a'fraid* as opposed to the common preference for *'afraid*, including secondary stress markings, which are useful for such words as *photograph*, *photography* and *photographic*. The asterisk can be discovered to indicate r–links.

This part of the dictionary work ties in with and may be done at the same time as pupils are learning about and practising phonemic distinctions and stress in their speech work.

6. Indications of restricted context can be similarly examined by looking up such a word as *ablutions*. The indication (esp. *as an act of religion*) should warn us that there is a difference between *performing one's ablutions* and *doing one's washing*. One can look up the examples given to show in what constructions a word may appear e.g. *persuade* in a good dictionary will be illustrated with

    persuade him to go
    persuade him of its truth
    persuade him that it is true.

7. In an etymological dictionary one can start by examining the language from which words were adopted into English and perhaps do enough to suggest generalisations about Latin and Greek borrowings as opposed to Anglo-Saxon and French sources, but this is much less useful than the previous kinds of work and we mention it as a possibility not a recommendation.

The interest and usefulness of dictionary work should not be allowed to obscure in the pupils' minds the even greater importance of intelligent inference. Even when they have firmly decided to look up a word 'to make sure', they should have a shot at guessing first. Apart from anything else this makes them more likely to choose the right sense.

14 Other kinds of vocabulary work in the classroom

There are one or two useful kinds of vocabulary work not so far suggested. One of them consists of examining e.g. nouns and noun groups that name at different levels of generality and considering what it is in different contexts that makes it appropriate to choose one level rather than another. One starts with a very general word such as *vehicles* or *buildings* and with the class supplying the examples, works towards a pattern such as the following on the blackboard:

a.			vehicles			
b.	buses	lorries	cars	motor-cycles	bicycles	vans[1]
c.	saloons	sports cars	coupés	taxis		
d.	Mercedes saloons	Ford saloons	Volkswagen saloons	Peugeot saloons, etc.		
e.	Mercedes Benz 190D saloon	Ford Anglia saloon, etc.				

[1] The items that have been discussed but do not appear are important, e.g. *trains*, *aeroplanes*, *ships* are quite likely to be proposed as examples of vehicles.

Note that the arrangement of the items is in this case in five levels of generality such that all (*b*)*s* are (*a*) but not all (*a*)*s* are (*b*), all (*c*)*s* are (*b*) but not all (*b*)*s* are (*c*), and so on.

It is interesting to ask which level one would choose for particular purposes. One would not go into a garage and say 'I want to buy a vehicle.' One might in certain circumstances say 'I think I can see a vehicle approaching,' but not 'That vehicle was much too close to the cyclist,' or except jocularly 'Would you like a lift in my vehicle?' But nor would one say, 'Would you like a lift in my Mercedes Benz 190D?' Clearly these little books that set out How to Write Good English in half a dozen easy lessons take too simple a view when they advocate always using the particular term rather than the general one.

One should, of course, also demonstrate from time to time the additional meaning that a word associated with a narrower context brings in, what suggestion is implicit in the choice of this word rather than that. This can be done by providing a simple context and asking what possible substitutions there are at the point of interest.

> Fred Bloggs —— along the road.

In this case we should generally be content to examine the suggestions we get from the class and restrain our natural desire to introduce the splendidly suggestive words we can think of for ourselves, such as *lurched*.

One can help pupils to think of possibilities. Suppose we have Fred walking, how can we suggest that he went along at a good rate in a business-like and regular way? *He marched along the road.* Good. Now suppose he is very tired? On a bicycle going downhill? Uphill? In a car as the driver? As a passenger? And so on.

One can invite pupils to choose between possibilities. Sometimes we may offer only one correct possibility.

> Having put up a hive, he hoped it would soon be occupied by a —— of bees.
>
> shoal flock swarm collection school

In studying reading passages, we do not believe that replacing words in the passage by approximately synonymous ones is useful. It tends to encourage pupils to believe that English is full of synonyms whereas they should have their attention directed to differences rather than similarities. We do not want them to think it does not matter which of half a dozen words the writer uses. Moreover the more precisely they have responded to the meaning of the original word, the more difficult they find it to produce a satisfactory alternative.

Instead one may ask what is suggested by the word in the passage which would not be suggested by this, that or the other proposed alternative. For example, given:

> It seems natural to feel admiration for their endurance and spirit.

we may ask what difference it would make if we replaced *endurance* by *patience*, *strength*, *courage*, etc.

This question may be asked the other way round. Which word in the passage suggests that they go on being courageous, that they put up with a hard life, etc.?

The teacher will find Roget's *Thesaurus* a rich source of material for this kind of work, but it is essential to exclude the rarer items on the basis of personal judgement or, when in doubt, by reference to Thorndike and Lorge.

By now it should be clear that we see no value in teaching words from lists. In spite of the *bee* example above, we do not advocate teaching nouns of multitude. We do not expect that enough of our pupils will have sufficient cause to refer frequently to coveys of partridges or lepes of leopards.

Nor do we believe in teaching the rare, curious and fascinating words peculiar to the art of venery. *Cobs, pens* and *cygnets* will remain *swans* for us. Instead, when a suitable opportunity occurs, we shall mention that for most common animals, for example, there is a word commonly used of either sex when we have no interest in the animal's sex: *horse, duck, dog, fox, goat, cattle*. There may be separate words used when it is important to call attention to the animal's sex, as in the case of *mare* and *stallion*. Or the unmarked form[1] may do double duty as in *dog* and *bitch*. There is thus a different meaning of the word *dog* in the following pair:

> Was it a dog or a cat?
> Was it a dog or a bitch?

Similarly we include women in the condemnation if we say,

> The heart of man is desperately wicked.

But we exclude men from it if we say,

> The heart of woman is desperately wicked.

The context gives the clue to the appropriate response. The same thing is true of the words that have different popular and scientific uses. We need not argue about whether spiders are really insects; crocodiles, animals; or tomatoes and nuts, fruits. We need only note that in a scientific context tomatoes and nuts are fruit. This precision need not inhibit us from asking for fruit and nut chocolate.

15 Constructing definitions of words

The ability to produce short, clear, relevant definitions of words is important to the teacher though not to the pupil. The teacher must know what features to seize on and what contrasts to make. We have heard *a fan* 'defined' as 'a thing a lady uses', and been horrified subsequently to find that twenty training-college students could not produce a satisfactory definition between them. Most of the definitions would have applied equally well to propellers and excluded the old-fashioned fan, the characteristic shape of which happened to be important in the context of *fanning out* that had been the starting-point.

Fries outlines the principles very clearly in *Teaching and Learning English as a Foreign Language*.

> We come now to the problems of describing and teaching the meanings of the three classes of content words – the words for 'things', for 'actions', and for 'qualities'. We have insisted above that translation, or word equivalents, seldom furnishes the best method of indicating meaning and we

[1] For an explanation of marked and unmarked forms see R. A. Close, *English as a Foreign Language*, Allen & Unwin, 1962, page 29 et seq.

go as far as we can in a monolingual approach. The method of formal definition – of indicating the class of things to which an object belongs and then pointing out the characteristics which differentiate it from other members of the class – this method, as usually employed, does not completely meet the needs of either the native speaker or the foreigner seeking 'meanings'. We have tried to be much more descriptive of the nature and range of the situations in which the native users employ the word and have not sought the so-called 'essence' of the thing to which a word is applied. We seek rather to list the distinctive characteristics of the various situations in which the words are used. Here again we believe that significance lies in contrasts and we would attempt to apply to the study of meanings, their analysis and description, the methods that have proved fruitful in other aspects of language study.

The kinds of distinctive features that characterise the situations in which 'thing' words are used differ from those that characterise the situations for 'action' words, and both sets differ from those for 'quality' words. For 'thing' words the distinctive features are usually such matters as characteristic purpose or use, characteristic behaviour or action, special relation to others, size, shape, age, sex. Typical examples of 'thing' words for situations that can be described in accord with these distinctive features are the following.

1. With characteristic purpose or use as distinctive features (usually words for inanimate 'things') – *fan, seat, pump, clock, rake, handle, bed, key, roof, stove, door, house, pin, purse, handkerchief, flat iron, needle, garter, prison, eye glasses, pen, razor, clothing, comb.*
2. With characteristic behaviour or action as distinctive features (usually words for animate 'things') – *brute, thief, coward, author, treasurer, carpenter, soldier, labourer, librarian, physician, chemist, judge, linguist, tramp, choir, usher.*
3. With a special relation to others as a distinctive feature – *boss, maid, chauffeur, chaperone, queen, president, employer, employee, chairman, bride, teacher, uncle, cousin, mother.*
4. With size as a distinctive feature:
   a. splinter, chip, board, plank, beam;
   b. puddle, pool, pond, lake;
   c. ripple, wave;
   d. pamphlet, book, tome;
   e. path, road, highway;
   f. village, town, city;
   g. chapel, church, cathedral;
   h. rill, brook, creek, river.
5. With shape as a distinctive feature:
   a. stool, chair;
   b. mitten, glove, gauntlet;
   c. cap, hat, turban, fez, helmet;

d. canoe, punt, rowboat, launch;
e. sulky, buggy, carriage, barouche.

6. With age as a distinctive feature:
   a. child, boy, youth, adult, man, kitten, puppy, colt, kid, infant, gosling, baby, sapling, tadpole.
7. With sex as a distinctive feature:
   a. boy, girl;
   b. man, woman;
   c. male, female;
   d. father, mother;
   e. brother, sister;
   f. son, daughter;
   g. uncle, aunt;
   h. rooster, hen;
   i. ram, ewe;
   j. bull, cow;
   k. husband, wife;
   l. bride, groom.

It will be immediately evident that the kinds of grouping here illustrated are not mutually exclusive, for some items need description from more than one point of view. Thus *father, mother;* and *uncle, aunt;* fall into the class of those words for situations in which a 'characteristic relation to others' is a distinctive feature, but they also have 'sex' as a further significant distinction. So also a 'chair' has a distinctive feature of 'use' as well as one of 'shape' and another of 'size'. The various classifications indicated here simply furnish guides to the distinctive features that need attention in any descriptive statement of the 'meanings' of Class I or 'thing' words.

For Class II or 'action' words the distinctive features are usually such matters as the direction of the 'motion', its speed, its duration, its intensity, the maker of the 'motion', the position of the body that moves, the medium in which the 'action' takes place. Typical examples of 'action' words for situations that can be described in accord with these distinctive features are the following.

1. With the direction of the motion as a distinctive feature, *come, go,*[1] *stoop, enter, dive, soar, push, pull, twist, spin, blow* (with breath), *arrive, depart, beckon.*
2. With the speed of the motion as a distinctive feature, *saunter, walk, run, race; turn, spin; dive, fall.*
3. With the duration of the motion or action as a distinctive feature, *glance, look; breathe, sigh; grunt, groan; bark, howl; chop, cut; wink, hop.*

[1] The motion indicated by these two words, *come*, and *go*, may be considered from the point of view either of the speaker or of the one addressed. I may say 'I'm *going* to New York next week,' or if I am addressing a resident of New York, I may say 'I'm coming to New York next week.'

4. With the intensity of the motion or action as distinctive features, *call, shout, shriek; look, peer; toss, throw, hurl; drink, gulp; hear, listen; pop, explode.*
5. With the maker of the motion or the nature of the thing that acts as a distinctive feature, *kick, punch, nod, step, wink, kneel, slap, stamp, whistle.*
6. With the position of the body that moves or acts as a distinctive feature, *dive, jump, stand, lie, sit.*
7. With the medium in which the motion or action takes place as a distinctive feature, *swim, fly, wash, skate, dig.*

Here again as in the case of the Class I or 'thing' words the groupings illustrated are not mutually exclusive and many items need description from more than one point of view. These classifications furnish guides to the distinctive features that need attention in descriptive statements of the 'meanings' of Class II or 'action' words.

For the words for 'qualities' the descriptive analysis must consider other significant features. Words of this kind express judgements on a rough scale of opposites, *cold, hot; small, large;* or with several points on the scale as in *cold, cool, warm, hot,* or *dry, moist, damp, wet.*

As indicated above, the precise nature of the 'quality' – the range, for example, of the temperature to which the judgement *cold* is applied – will differ greatly with the contexts. Judgements are made with reference to the usual qualities of the 'things' named, in accord with the experience of the speaker. Thus '*cold* hands' will usually be of a much higher temperature than '*cold* water', and a '*cold* day' of January in Michigan will probably be of a much lower temperature than a '*cold* day' of July.

Although most of these judgement words for 'qualities' occur in rough two point scales, as in *drunk, sober; long, short; dull, sharp; straight, crooked;*[1] there are various types of 'degree' words that make it possible to add other points to any scale. Thus we may have not only *short* and *long* but *very short, short, long, very long;* not only *shut* and *open* but *tight shut, shut, open, wide open;* not only *slow* and *fast* but *dead slow,* and *pretty fast,* and *awful fast.* In the matter of colours the scale in English has a great many points with separate words for each and also a variety of degree modifiers.[2] Even in respect to what seem to English speakers 'primary' colour divisions, such as *red, orange, yellow, green, blue, violet,* different languages vary greatly with respect to the gradations of the colour spectrum included in the particular words.

[1] In addition to the many pairs of words that indicate the ends of such judgement scales. there are the opposites formed by derivative prefixes such as *regular, irregular; legal, illegal; moral, immoral; kind, unkind; handy, unhandy; clear, unclear; pleasant, unpleasant; human, inhuman; tasteful, distasteful.*

[2] See *Webster's New International Dictionary,* 2nd Edition (G. & C. Merriam Company, 1934), pp. 528, 529 and especially inserts between these two pages. Some of the more than a hundred common names for colours there recorded are *auburn, carmine, cerise, coral, emerald, flesh, hazel, ivory, magenta, maroon, pink, rose, tan.*

Not infrequently the same vocabulary item is a member of two scales. Examples are:

old – young	hard – soft	short – long
old – new	hard – easy	short – tall
		low – tall

Failure to recognise the two scales in which an item occurs often leads foreigners into such errors as 'a *short* building', 'a *young* dress'. For the native speaker these common items in two scales sometimes provide the basis for such semantic extensions as 'a *soft* job'.

The analysis and systematic description of the distinctive features of the situations in which the content words of our vocabulary are used do provide the 'meanings' that have to be mastered and a method of explaining those meanings without resorting to translation or word equivalents. But the teaching and learning of vocabulary content must not proceed as if these meanings were items of information to be memorised. The material of our analysis and systematic description must be built into contexts of whole utterances for practice in real and representative situations. Context controls the meaning. The word *spring* in the following sentence can mean several very different things in different contexts. 'We hunted a long time before we found a good *spring*.' If the situation is that of furnishing a bedroom, the word *spring* means one thing; if the situation is that of repairing a watch, the word *spring* means something quite different; and if the situation is that of being thirsty on a hot dusty walk in deserted country, the *spring* means something different from either of the others. And because context thus controls meaning we believe in teaching vocabulary items always in context.[1]

The ability to produce definitions is useful because it enables the teacher to skate rapidly over vocabulary items that he does not wish to teach because they are not valuable or because the digression will interfere with what he is doing. But its main value is in enabling us to know what questions to ask when we are reading and what contexts to use if we are explaining or testing.

16 Testing width of vocabulary

Testing vocabulary level bristles with difficulties. We do not know what a lexical item is or what items we may reasonably expect pupils to know. We could not test all the thousands of possibilities and any reasonably small sample introduces a large element of chance. It is difficult to construct test items without a grammatical element in them and impossible to be certain that this is wrong. It is even more difficult to construct items that cannot be inferred from context and by no means certain that intelligent inference is less meritorious than knowledge or that the knowledge of one item is more meritorious than that of another.

[1] C. C. Fries, *Teaching and Learning English as a Foreign Language*, Cresset Press, 1945 pp. 51–54.

Our conclusion is that direct vocabulary testing should form no part of the secondary school final examination. We really cannot give a mark to Mukasa because he happens to be able to choose the right meaning for *parsley*, though he does not know *nibble*, and refuse one to Ahmed Ali who knows *nibble*, which we did not test, but not *parsley*, which we did.

17 The Vocabulary level of examinations

This does not mean that examiners can ignore vocabulary problems. It is essential that they should be conscious of them and in drafting papers that they should scrupulously keep well within reasonable expectations. These will be higher in English-medium than in vernacular-medium schools. It is unlikely ever to be possible to define reasonable expectations by listing because the frequency of lexical items above the 2,000-word level does not remain constant. It would be undesirable for teachers and pupils to have such a list because its existence encourages direct vocabulary teaching of an inefficient kind – concentration on words and definitions instead of on meaning in use. The dilemma is, however, worse in theory than in practice. An experienced examiner can usually produce questions of approximately the same level year after year. If he then checks the vocabulary used against the G.S.L. and Thorndike and Lorge, his attention is drawn to the rarer items and he can consider each on its merits. If the questions are then moderated by experienced people in the areas where the examination will be taken and their attention is drawn to dubious items, there should be little danger of getting the vocabulary level wrong.

18 Internal tests

If we agree not to have a pure vocabulary question in the final examination, it does not, of course, follow that we shall never have any use for vocabulary tests at all. We will therefore look at a few different types.

Suppose we aim to get a rough idea after a year's reading at 'Bridge' level what sort of progress our pupils have made in the ability to recall lexical items unrelated to their previous knowledge. We can use the glossaries of books known to have been read by all pupils, or Thorndike and Lorge or a combination of the two. We shall want to sample 3,000+ to 7,000— and we might wish to arrange our items according to the thousand in which they appear.

The introduction to T and L gives the number of words occurring 49, 48, etc. times per million running words. Words occurring 29 times or more are in the commonest 3,000.

3,000 – 4,000 corresponds approximately to	28–19
4,000 – 5,000 to	18–13
5,000 – 6,000 to	12–10
6,000 – 7,000 to	9– 8

A test containing 100 items would enable us to sample 25 words in every 1,000 but a great many of these words are related to words already known and we cannot therefore select at random from the appropriate credit range as the following lists will show.

19–28	13–18	10–12	8 and 9
abide	abode	abbey	Abe
aboard	abolish	abbot	absorption
absorb	abruptly	abound	accessory
abundance	(abrupt 6)	Abraham	accommodation
abundant	absurd	acceptance	accusation
abuse	accent	access	Adams
accord	accumulate	accommodate	adjacent
accordingly	accurate	accomplishment	ado
(according AA)	(accurately 8)	(accomplish A;	adventurous
accuse	ácting n. adj.	accomplished	(adventure A)
ache	(act AA, action	adj. 6)	aerial
achieve	AA, active A)	accordance	afflict
achievement	actress	accuracy	afore
	adequate	acorn	
	adjoin	acute	
	adjourn		

abide: We shall probably reject this on intuition because we can't abide words like this. If we distrust our intuitions, the citation in the *Advanced Learners' Dictionary* provides evidence that a problem exists.

a - bide [ə'baid] v.t. & i. (p.t. & p.p. *abode* [ə'boud]) 1. (VP24) **~by**, be faithful to, keep; ~by a promise (a decision) *I abide by* (=colloq. 'stick to') *what I said. You'll have to + by the consequences*, endure them. (Used only of undesirable consequences.) 2. (VP1, esp. in neg. & interr.) endure, bear; *I can't + that man.* 3. (VP 20, 23, old or liter. use) rest, remain, stay; + *at* (*in*) *a place; with sb.* 4. (VP 1 liter.) wait for: + *the event;* + *sb's coming.* **abiding** *adj.* (liter.) never-ending, lasting.

Obviously any one of these uses, which T and L lump together, is rarer than the credit number suggests and it would be unfair to use, for example, *little abiding interest* as a test item.

aboard: We may feel that this has too narrow a nautical context.

absorb: We might use this. T and L list *absorbing* adj. and *absorbed* adj. separately so we shall have to use a literal context.

abundance, *abundant:* These both have credit numbers of 23 and each is therefore too frequent for us to use the other.

abuse: This is a possible item.

accord: There are too many common related items.

accuse: Another possible.

ache: Frequency very doubtful because e.g. *headache* is listed separately.

In the other lists we must reject proper nouns and a great many other items for reasons similar to those we have already seen.

We shall, however, eventually get a list to work on. Since we wish to test recognition and not production of the item, we must supply the word we wish to test. Since we do not wish to test the ability to infer meaning from the context, we must put it in a neutral context and, of course, one in which the distractors are semantically and grammatically appropriate. We must also ensure that the words we offer as approximate equivalents are commoner than the item we test.

We can ask the pupil to tick the answer on the question paper, but it is better to ask him to answer on a separate sheet in the form 1*a*, 2*d*, etc. Items will look like this:

1. She *blushed.*
   a. turned red
   b. went pale
   c. looked sad
   d. ran away.
2. There was a *jerk* on the end of the string.
   a. knot
   b. hook
   c. fish
   d. pull.

The rubric will ask for the word nearest in meaning to the word *in italics.*

It is very easy to produce unsatisfactory items by accident. For example:

The fighting was *resumed* later.
a. written about
b. started again
c. prevented
d. interrupted.

To make a correct choice in this case it is only necessary to connect *re-* with *again.*[1]

Once made, such a test can be used again at, say, yearly intervals provided we have not foolishly invalidated it by going over it in class and telling everybody the right answers.

Pupils with low scores should be told to read more books and not to learn more words.

A different kind of test can be constructed to show how pupils are getting on with learning collocational possibilities. Items can be semantically different:

He is far too . . . and well-informed to be easily deceived.
a. bashful
b. shrewd
c. diplomatic
d. stubborn
e. sturdy.

Or semantically much more similar:

He was too shy to feel comfortable and sat all the evening on the . . . of a straight-backed chair, feeling embarrassed.
a. brim
b. fringe

[1] All three examples from a test constructed by J.A.B.

c. margin
d. rim
e. edge.

There is no reason why there should be only one correct choice among the possibilities offered. One can ask which of them make acceptable English sentences. Then the item reads, for example:

Watch the boss this morning. He's in a thoroughly bad . . .
a. mood
b. mind
c. temper
d. disposition
e. humour.

The same rubric can be used when the reason for excluding certain items is grammatical unsuitability. For example:

He . . . us to go with him.
a. liked
b. agreed
c. persuaded
d. convinced
e. advised.

It would also be possible to devise on similar lines tests aimed at assessing the ability to infer meaning from context or from knowledge of related words. It would be interesting also to construct a test to measure the ability to jump to an unusual meaning, particularly a metaphorical one.

The inordinate length of this chapter is partly caused by our reaction against the tendency we detect among the pundits to ignore vocabulary problems. They either say 'Vocabulary doesn't matter; the thing that counts is structural grading', or refer the whole problem to computers for solution. We are as anxious as anyone for the results of computer analysis and as keen on structural grading. Until we have the results, however, and until structural readers have been produced in sufficient numbers, we have as teachers the practical problem of what materials to use and no amount of theoretical specification of what ought to be done will help us until somebody has done it. This is not to deny the value of the theory; only to plead for its embodiment into materials we can use in class.

19 Summary of recommendations

1. Grade the texts:
   a. on the 2,000-word plateau,
   b. at a level intermediate between unsimplified and 2,000 words,
   c. at simple, unsimplified level considering not only vocabulary but also structural complexity and background,
   d. at full English.

These grades correspond to stages of work.

2. Ensure that huge numbers of them are read. This is what matters most.

3. See that pupils understand that the immediate productive use of all new items is unnecessary and may be dangerous.
4. Teach the pupils to infer meaning from context. This can be done incidentally.
5. Teach them to use a dictionary – a short course of four or five lessons.
6. Interest them in prefixes, suffixes and stems.
7. Exercise them in distinguishing between near-synonyms. Ten minutes twice a week will cover 6 and 7.
8. Keep their attention on meaning in context.
9. Do not exaggerate or allow pupils to exaggerate the importance of vocabulary. They will never learn it all; they are bound to know enough to function on if they can use what they know well, and they will not easily forget words they need to remember.

For further reading

FLOOD, W. E. *The Problem of Vocabulary in the Popularisation of Science*. University of Birmingham, Institute of Education: Education Monographs, 2. Edinburgh, Oliver and Boyd, 1957.

FRIES, C. C. *The Structure of English*. Longman, 1957.

HALLIDAY, M. A. K., MCINTOSH, A. and STEVENS, P. *The Linguistic Sciences and Language Teaching*. Longman, 1964.

HINDMARSH, R. *Cambridge Intermediate Word List*. Cambridge University Press.

OSMAN, N. *Word Function and Dictionary Use*. O.U.P., 1965.

PALMER, F. R. *Semantics – A New Outline*. Cambridge University Press, 1976.

ROGET, P. M. *Thesaurus of English Words and Phrases*. Longman edition 1962.

WEST, M. *A General Service List of English Words*. Longman, revised edn. 1953.

WATSON, OWEN, ed. *Longman Modern English Dictionary*. Longman, 1976.

APPENDIXES

I *THE BLEAK HOUSE TEXT*

TEXT B: The original of the passage from *Bleak House* with which the chapter started.

> LONDON. Michaelmas Term lately over, and the Lord Chancellor sitting in Lincoln's Inn Hall. Implacable November weather. As much mud in the streets, as if the waters had but newly retired from the face of the earth, and it would not be wonderful to meet a Megalosaurus, forty feet long or so, waddling like an elephantine lizard up Holborn Hill. Smoke lowering down

from chimney-pots, making a soft black drizzle with flakes of soot in it as big as full-grown snow-flakes – gone into mourning, one might imagine, for the death of the sun. Dogs, indistinguishable in mire. Horses, scarcely better; splashed to their very blinkers. Foot passengers, jostling one another's umbrellas, in a general infection of ill-temper, and losing their foothold at street-corners, where tens of thousands of other foot passengers have been slipping and sliding since the day broke (if this day ever broke), adding new deposits to the crust upon crust of mud, sticking at those points tenaciously to the pavement, and accumulating at compound interest.

Fog everywhere. Fog up the river, where it flows among green aits and meadows; fog down the river, where it rolls defiled among the tiers of shipping, and the waterside pollutions of a great (and dirty) city. Fog on the Essex marshes, fog on the Kentish heights. Fog creeping into the cabooses of collier-brigs; fog lying out on the yards, and hovering in the rigging of great ships; fog drooping on the gunwales of barges and small boats.

TEXT C: The same passage simplified to Bridge level. Words italicised would be glossed but not indicated by italics in a pupils' text.

LONDON. Autumn term in the Law Courts lately over, and the Lord Chancellor sitting in his court in Lincoln's Inn. *Pitiless* November weather. As much mud in the streets as if the floods had only just left the land in the beginning of the world and it would not be wonderful to meet a huge *prehistoric* creature, forty feet long or so, in the streets of London. Smoke falling slowly down from chimney-pots making a soft black rain with pieces of *soot* in it like snow but snow wearing black because of the death of the sun. Dogs unrecognisable in the mud. Horses scarcely better; covered up to their ears in mud. *Pedestrians*, knocking into each other's *umbrellas* and catching each other's bad temper, and losing their *foothold* at street corners, where tens of thousands of other pedestrians have been slipping and sliding since the day broke – if this day ever broke – adding more mud to the coats upon coats sticking firmly to the pavement at those points and increasing all the time.

Fog everywhere. Fog up the river where it flows among islands and green fields; fog down the river where it picks up dirt among the crowded ships and docks of a great (and dirty) city. Fog on the hills and marshes near London. Fog creeping into the cabins of little coal-ships, fog lying among the masts and ropes of great ships, fog falling on the decks of small boats of every kind.

II *NOTES ON SIMPLIFIED TEXTS*

1. There is, of course, not the slightest doubt that for the reader capable of responding to the full text the simplified one is wishy-washy pap. But if the effect of reading Text B on the learner at a certain stage is the same as the effect of reading Text A on a capable reader, is it not obvious that the learner will get more out of Text C?

2. Why pretend this is *Bleak House*? It is of course, most important not to do so. A pupil who has read *Tom Sawyer* or *Jane Eyre* in a simplified edition has not read the original and must be left in no doubt about this.
3. Would the pupils not learn more useful words from the original? No. Nobody is going to remember more than six or seven new words in every 250. And there will be interference with reading speed and with the possibility of inference from context.
4. Would it not be better to write texts specially rather than simplify existing ones? Some good original texts, for example Philip Clarke's *Adventures at Dabanga School*, have been written and more would be very welcome. (African writers, notably Achebe and Ekwensi, have recently produced original stories specially for secondary pupils.) The difficulty is to find enough people with the linguistic knowledge to do the simplification, and the creative ability to write good material, who are prepared to devote their energies to this field.

   In our opinion whether a book is specially written or adapted is unimportant. What matters is the quality of the resulting text, and every text is to be judged on its content. That it has or has not some relationship to an acknowledged masterpiece is neither here nor there. There are good and bad texts of both kinds.
5. Could we not use books written for English-speaking children? There are some that are suitable and have been used successfully but in general if the content is appropriate to the age and interests of our pupils, the language is too difficult and if the language is suitable the content is too childish.

   Nevertheless, in Uganda at one boys' secondary school where records of library reading were kept, Enid Blyton won the popularity stakes at a canter.

   Many books written for English-speaking children have too specialised backgrounds. Arthur Ransome would be excellent if only he were not so passionately interested in messing about in boats. We have not usually found animal books popular, either.
6. What kinds of books should be simplified?

   It is tempting to believe that the fewer changes a book requires the more suitable it is for simplification. We do not agree. We think that it is a great mistake to simplify a book that pupils could read unsimplified a year later. We should be sorry, for example, to see a Bridge level edition of *Arms and the Man*.
7. In our chapter on reading we assume the necessity to use simplified texts.

3

READING

1 What this chapter on reading covers

We are not here concerned with learning to read in the sense of learning what noises are represented by what graphic symbols. Our pupils are past that early stage. Nor are we very much concerned with reading aloud, which is dealt with under the teaching of speech. This chapter does not cover the reading of plays or poetry, both of which are dealt with elsewhere. On the other hand it is not limited to the reading of literature in the sense of 'the best that has been thought and said'. Apart from the limitations already mentioned, it is about the appropriate use of and response to any text that consists of black marks on paper whether it is a railway time-table or 'the precious life-blood of a master spirit'.

2 Why reading is the core of the syllabus

1 Books provide most pupils with the situations in which learning takes place. Where there is little reading, there will be little language learning. It is impossible in any secondary school to provide direct experience of language used as part of real life in the way the native learner gets his first language; one is defeated by the multiplicity of the contexts required: house, street, garden, sea-shore, woods, streams, mountains, boats, church, club, doctor, hospital, traffic, Sunday, food, farm, factory, office, birds, insects, trees, flowers, fish, birth, death, marriage, divorce. Something can be done with films and photographs, more could be done with television, but it will be true for a few years yet that the student who wants to learn English will have to read himself into a knowledge of it unless he can move into an English environment. He must substitute imaginary for actual experience.

2 Only by reading can the pupil acquire the speed and skills he will need for practical purposes when he leaves school. In our literate society it is hard to imagine any skilled work that does not require the ability to read. Professional competence depends on it.

3 Further education depends on quantity and quality of reading. All the important study skills require quick, efficient and imaginative reading.

4 General knowledge depends on reading, as any teacher who has been lumbered with a general knowledge period is painfully aware. The 'background' or cross-cultural problem can only be tackled by wide reading. We have here a *virtuous* circle; the more the student reads, the more background knowledge he acquires of other ways of life, behaviour and thought and the more books he finds he can understand.

5 The above considerations apply to all secondary schools where English is taught above the 2,000-word level. In most schools there is also a desire and a need to read texts of literary worth for their own sake. Experience of a literature is an essential part of education; it raises the level at which the mind can function, gives form and meaning to the data of experience, widens and deepens experience itself, offers attitudes, sets out moral issues and deals with matters of truth, goodness and beauty, not as abstractions, but as concrete instances. These are important matters, but applicable to any literature and we must consider whether it need be literature in English for our pupils.

6 Where pupils speak a first language in which little has been written and English is their second language, they must read English literature, for otherwise they have no means of literary education. Where pupils speak a language in which a great deal has been written, English literature is no longer a necessity, though it may still be a useful luxury and the most pleasant route to command of the language.

7 History does not support the nationalistic contention that engrossment in a foreign literature harms the development of the native language. Chaucer, that well of English undefiled, was influenced, if not defiled, by Boccaccio and other aliens. The literature of the Jews in a Jacobean translation has not been entirely pernicious in its effect on English writers and it is only comparatively recently that the literatures of Greece and Rome have ceased to be part of every educated Englishman's experience. There may even be reason to hope that exposure to English literature will help the development of literature in languages that so far have mainly oral traditions.

It is indisputable that a man acquainted with two literatures is no worse off than a man who only knows one, for the more a man knows, the more he is worth.

8 It is in literature that the student is most likely to find words used memorably with force and point. It is there that he will find words used in the widest range of contexts and there that he will find words passionately or delicately conveying emotions and attitudes. There he may practise sustained efforts of imagination, learn to see wholes greater than the sum of their parts, and find joy in the exercise of his mental powers at full stretch.

9 The quality of the mind, the personality, the worthwhileness of the 'poor, bare, forked animal' is important. It depends on the acuteness and exactness of the perceptions, the refinement of the feelings, the strength of the imagination and the ability of the mind to organise these into patterns, artistic or scientific. Literature sharpens sight and insight, widens sympathies and experience and provides occasions for the exercise of judgement about man and his condition. It helps with the main business of education, the production of men and women capable of appropriate response to life, which includes appropriate response to examinations, though as a somewhat minor incidental feature.

Literature makes the mind work, re-create, at a level otherwise unattainable. It disciplines, controls and satisfies the emotions so that instead of frustration we feel release. The experience of taking part in the process of creative imagining, the experience of order, shape and discipline pass into life and give it meaning.

3 The pupil's skills and knowledge on entry to the secondary school

1 It is important to establish what these are as precisely and unobtrusively as possible. In many countries the best way to start this investigation is to read the books used to teach English in the previous stage. They will usually contain statements about vocabulary level and suggestions about what supplementary readers can be used at various points in the course. The pupils will know how far they got in the course and, given a list of titles of supplementary readers, may even be able to recollect which, if any, they have read.

2 A cross-check on vocabulary level can be obtained by asking pupils to read ten pages of texts at various levels and list the words they have not met before.

3 Structural complexity can be measured by sampling against the Wingard Scale (see page 253).

4 Reading speed can be established roughly by timing page turning in sample pupils or much more accurately by getting pupils to record the time taken to read a chapter and converting this to words per minute. For an easy method see Appendix IV, page 116.

5 Quality of reading is more difficult to assess unobtrusively. In East Africa we used an objective test called a little gruesomely the *Death Test*, which is given in Appendix I. 'Good' schools averaged 10–11, 'average' schools 7–8 on it.

6 An eye test is essential to find out which pupils need glasses. How they are supplied is a matter for investigation, but no teacher worth his salt will rest until he has tried the official channels, written and spoken to parents, begged from wealthy old boys or philanthropists, earmarked the proceeds of the school play, taken a collection on Parents' Day, started a school glasses fund or solved the problem in some other ingenious way.

7 It is also worth while to spend some time while the pupils are reading silently just observing what they do and making notes about head-waggers, tongue-wobblers and sub-vocalisers (who whisper to themselves). Note the distance of the eyes from the book; some may be under the standard ten inches. Note the sitting position and the angle of the book. Detect the book back-breakers who double the pages back. With a small mirror held in the palm of the hand one can observe fixations per line and regressions. All this information will be useful when we start the reading speed improvement course.

8 When we were training teachers in East Africa, they were only going to spend two years in the schools and we felt it was necessary to give them some idea of what they could expect from their first-year classes. We warned them about variations and then suggested they should start by assuming that the average pupil:

a. would be able to read at the 1,500-word level without much help, understanding practically all single sentences well but would have difficulty in the sustained effort of imagination required to follow a long series of events and seeing the pattern made by the relationship between them;

b. would understand most of the grammatical relationships of single sentences though there would be gaps. He might not be clear, for example, that

(i) *If I had . . .* does not refer to past time.

(ii) there is a difference between:

He went to the market and bought some meat.

and

He went to the market to buy some meat.

(iii) *although* and *because* have widely different meanings.

c. would have no idea of the difference between fact and fiction or understand that the shape of a story is the result of a series of choices by the writer;

d. would have great difficulty in reading exposition and argument, find it very hard to distinguish levels of generality and pick out theme sentences (or phrases) and grasp the relationship of the rest of the paragraph to the theme. He would need a great deal of help with architectonics;

e. would read very slowly – 90–120 words a minute and may have done very little reading of anything except his English course book. He may never have read a whole book in his life;

f. would know little of western ways of life and thought. Cross-cultural problems would be numerous, insidious and not always easy to spot.[1]

g. would have little skill in inferring the meaning of an unknown word from its context or responding to unusual or metaphorical uses of known words and would therefore expect to depend on the teacher for the meaning of new words;

h. would not respond readily to the emotional implications of words;

i. would be unfamiliar with the vocabulary or even the concepts used to discuss character and very liable to misread motive;

j. would have no idea that it is possible, indeed common, to read books for pleasure. He would regard books as mere quarries from which to dig 'useful words and phrases'.

[1] One example must suffice. I was reading the whitewashing of the fence incident in *Tom Sawyer* with a class of African pupils in front of a mixed group of African, Indian, Goan, British and American graduates. We came to the following passage:
'But Jim was only human – this attraction was too much for him. He put down his bucket and took the marble. In another minute he was flying down the street with his bucket. Tom was whitewashing with vigour and Aunt Polly was returning to the house with a slipper in her hand and triumph in her eye.'
It occurred to me to ask what had happened in the missing minute. No pupil and no African student showed any sign of understanding. British, Americans, Goans and Indians displayed broad grins. In discussion afterwards it became plain that all would have been clear to the Africans if instead of a slipper Aunt Polly had carried a banana frond. J.A.B.

He presents quite a challenge if two and a half years later he is to enjoy reading *The Old Man and the Sea* or *Arms and the Man.*

4 The abilities of the skilled reader

1 The competent reader – the fully literate person – uses not one skill but many. Each has been acquired by specific practice. We cannot hope to produce well-read young people from a secondary school. The most we can do is make sure:

a. that we do not neglect any important skills
and

b. that pupils find enjoyment in exercising them; because if they do not, they will stop reading when they leave school.

2 The first cluster of skills is mainly, but by no means exclusively, applied to and acquired by reading stories. The expert reader can:

a. read at an observational speed of from 400 to 600 words per minute. He does not read aloud to himself or make visible articulatory movements. He does not look at each word. His eyes stop three or four times only per line and these fixations are very brief. He does not have to look back frequently. He does not follow the print with his finger. He marches smoothly on line by line: click, click, click, back: click, click, click, back. He is, of course, quite unconscious of these physical movements.

He does not always read at the same speed. The 400–600 figure is his cruising speed. He will read more slowly, for example, at the beginning of a story, saying, perhaps, that he 'hasn't got into it yet'. He may go even faster through parts where all that matters is to 'know what happens' and he will read more slowly in order to savour the parts that are most richly loaded.

b. respond to the precise meaning of familiar words used from their context and also infer the meaning of unfamiliar words from contextual or internal clues without reference to a dictionary. Unfamiliar vocabulary does, however, interrupt his smooth progress through a text.

c. respond, equally unconsciously, to the lexical meaning of the words he reads and the relationships between them, which are signalled by grammatical means. He looks straight through the words to the meaning.

d. imagine in his mind the scenes and events the words conjure up. *Animal Farm* is nothing but black marks on paper until it is re-created by a reader's responsive mind.

e. sympathise with the characters. This is complicated. It includes identifying with a hero or heroine and seeing the other characters from this point of view but can perhaps be summarised as sharing the writer's involvement in his characters. One does identify with Emma. Her shame after Box Hill is our own. But one does not identify with Boxer – O sancta simplicitas.

f. understand the motivation of characters. He knows why Tom Sawyer said he tore the master's book, although he hadn't.

g. see the moral problems involved. He knows in his heart that Tom's lie was right and that Raina, like the Cavaliers, is wrong but romantic. He appreciates Huckleberry Finn's moment of moral liberation when he decides 'All right, then, I'll *go* to hell.'

h. respond to more than the plain sense of the words. He feels emotional implications, responds to figurative language and understands humour and irony.

i. see the relationship of the parts to the whole and to each other, and he can see whole meanings. He does not think that *Animal Farm* is only a story about animals or only an allegory of the Russian revolution or that *Moby Dick* is 'about a whale'.

j. understand the author's intention. He will not read the opening of *Nicholas Nickleby* as a factual account of current conditions in British education, or as 'just a story'.

k. understand the author's attitude to his readers and the reader he has in mind.

3 All the above are skills of response. They are required for the understanding of stories (and, of course, plays, poems, biography, satire, etc.). They have little to do with criticism except that response must precede judgement. In the course of acquiring these skills, the pupil also acquires knowledge that enables him to become even more skilful.

a. His vocabulary increases. At S.C. level one may reasonably hope that it will reach some 10,000 words.

b. His experience of books increases so that one book contributes to his understanding of others. Sometimes this happens directly as when *Coral Island* relates to *Lord of the Flies*, or *The White Company* to *Don Quixote*. It is through previous reading that he picks up references. More generally his background is widened and his acquaintance with western and other ways of thought and life grows. This is desirable not, of course, because the Asian or African or any other pupil ought to adopt them but because he ought to understand them.

c. He learns something, though not at first hand, of other times, places, men and matters that would otherwise be outside his experience.

4 The next set of skills are mainly practical, businesslike and scholarly. They are brought into play when observational reading – seeing what is there – is inappropriate either because not everything that is there is relevant to the purpose in hand, as when one consults a telephone directory, or because observational reading, which results in a great deal less than perfect recall, is not enough to give the complete mastery of content that is required.

The skilled reader can:

a. use time-tables, dictionaries, catalogues, directories, encyclopedias, gazetteers and other reference material.

b. use the index or chapter headings to find roughly what he wants and then skim through the pages at great speed till he homes on his target.

c. skim through a newspaper to find what he wants to read.

d. read and understand notices and advertisements. He does not overlook the former or rely too seriously on the latter.

e. interpret regulations and fill in forms.

f. read proofs and spot errors in his own writing as well as that of others.

g. approach a new subject or new material in a purposeful methodical way, varying his reading speed to suit his different aims.

(i) He will first quickly survey the field to get the overall pattern. He may, for example, run rapidly through an exposition or argument reading little more than the first or last sentences of each paragraph.

(ii) Assuming that he wants mastery of the material, he will now read much more slowly, noting (mentally, or even on paper) the thesis of each paragraph, observing the width (and limitations) of the generalisations, noting the relation of the supporting detail to them and weighing its evidential value.

(iii) From time to time he will stop reading and review the progress of the argument or exposition, running it through his mind a second time.

5 The final group of skills are the comparative and critical ones but these must be based on quality of response and width of literary experience. It is disastrous to ask for criticism too soon. Pupils will provide it if the demand is made but it will consist of regurgitating what others have said.

It is, however, possible to get pupils to do some of the following:

a. to distinguish clearly between fact and fiction and realise that stories are the result of a series of deliberate choices on the part of the author who invents incident for a purpose. Stories do not happen; they are manufactured.

b to distinguish between fact and comment.

c. to compare accounts of the same event for bias in reporting and to recognise emotionally slanted material and disinfect it by neutral rephrasing.

d. to be aware of certain common logical fallacies of the kind so well set out in Thouless, *Straight and Crooked Thinking*.

e. to see that some books are better than others – there is more in them – they are worth re-reading. Perhaps in particular one might do a little detailed comparison of a simplified reader and a full text to undermine the idea that if one has read *Treasure Island* simplified, there is no need to bother with the original. It hardly seems worth while to read rubbish in order to see what rubbish it is. And this brings us to the question of choosing reading material for the various stages of our course.

5 The major stages of the secondary course

Some schools have four-year courses and some five-year ones up to school certificate. In a four-year system, years and stages correspond.

Year 1 The plateau-reading stage mainly at the 2,000-word level.
Year 2 The transition stage from simplified to unsimplified reading.
Year 3 The free-reading stage.
Year 4 The examination year.

In a school with a five-year system pupils usually come in with less than a 2,000-word vocabulary and it is necessary to put in a year (or part of a year) at the 1,500–2,000-word level. Schools with pupils who enter at the 2,000-word level and have five years before school certificate are very happily situated. They can spend two years at the free-reading stage which is the most rewarding part of the syllabus, the most beneficial to the pupils and the most likely to be valuable in itself, as a preparation for post-school certificate work and in infecting pupils with the reading bug. This splendid opportunity can be, and alas sometimes is, overlooked and the extra year wasted on examination tests.

6 Selection of the texts for reading

[a] CRITERIA THAT HAVE TO BE CONSIDERED

1 *General.* The most important thing is that the pupils should enjoy what they read. A book that satisfies all other criteria but fails this one is a reject. But it is not enough simply to say 'They like it and that's good enough for me.' They might like it better and read it faster a year later. They might enjoy something else more. They might enjoy something else equally well and the other thing might help with something else later.

2 *Linguistic*

a. The vocabulary level must be appropriate. This has been defined in the chapter on vocabulary.
b. The complexity of the grammatical structure must not be too great.
c. Even if vocabulary and grammar are suitable, a high density of idiom may make it desirable to postpone a book. In the Longman Simplified English Series this applies to *Dr Jekyll and Mr Hyde*.
d. One must consider special registers. That a book such as N.M.S.R. *Treasure Island* contains a large number of nautical terms may count in its favour or against it. In non-English-medium schools one would deliberately seek out interesting material that included scientific and technological vocabulary.
e. One must consider style remembering that the pupils may use what they read as a model. In general an archaic or even old-fashioned style, a heavy load of local dialect or marked eccentricity would count against a text.

3 *Background*

a. If the background is familiar to the pupil because it is local or refers to school, for example, there is no problem. Nigerians have no background problems with Achebe's books and few African children, alas, find the pedagogic methods of Squeers unimaginable.
b. If the text supplies an adequate background there may be little difficulty. This sometimes happens when an author is writing for readers who cannot be assumed to know the background of his story. Historical novels frequently make their own background for this reason. Many Victorian novels do the same thing, but are objectionable on other grounds. It is unfortunate that most modern writing assumes a background common to writer and reader and thus the kind of text that is most linguistically suitable and educationally desirable involves the greatest difficulties with the background.

c. The nearest we can get to a recipe is that the background must be within the pupils' imaginative grasp. This may have to be established by trying it out. Sometimes the difficulty is obvious. A book that relies on an understanding of English class distinctions and snobbery for its effect will not do in the Sudan, for example, or anywhere else where social behaviour is more sensible than it is in England.

d. A book may have to be rejected reluctantly because it would not be tactful to read it in a certain community. *St Joan* unfortunately falls into this category in the Sudan because of an offensive reference to Mohammed. There are places where it might be tactless to read *1984* or even *The Merchant of Venice*.

e. On the other hand it may be desirable to choose a book although it has background difficulties because its background will be useful later. We would not recommend *Idylls of the King* as a school certificate text, but if a teacher insists on choosing it, we would suggest that a preliminary acquaintance with chivalry be obtained from *The White Company*.

4 *Matter*

a. Obviously the text must interest the pupil; it is perhaps a little less obvious that it should interest the teacher: 'Literature is caught, not taught.' We do not want classes infected with boredom.

b. The pupil must be able to see some relevance to his own situation, so that he gets drawn into the book. The most land-locked lubber can identify with Jim Hawkins, but it does not follow that any other Stevenson will go down well. *Travels with a Donkey in the Cevennes* does not. Alternatively a text may be justified because of its relevance to other studies.

c. There must be enough meat in it to make detailed study of certain parts rewarding. It must be worth re-reading and the subject matter must be suitable for classroom teaching.

d. The matter must be appropriate to the age of the students. It is easy to see when the text is too childish but more difficult to know when it is too adult. Most of us have experience of being put off an author by having him thrust upon us before we were ready.

5 *Variety of type and genre.* This is a matter that arises when the syllabus is considered as a whole. At all stages we would include non-fiction and drama in the reading programme. At all stages except in the examination year we would include poetry. The more different kinds of books, the better. Pupils who get hooked on Sherlock Holmes can follow up their interest in the library. In class we will offer different bait.

6 *The choice of examination texts*

a. It is very difficult to find suitable texts at school certificate level and at present therefore the changes have to be rung within a very short list. Any teacher who can add a text that succeeds is regarded by examiners as a public benefactor.

b. In addition to being enjoyable and worth studying a good examination text must have enough in it on which to base different sets of questions for a number of years. The questions must be of the right level for the examination, be answerable in approximately the same length of time and present the candidates with approximately equal difficulties.

c. Texts must not be too long. Unabridged versions of *Jane Eyre* or *Wuthering Heights* are impossibly time-consuming.

d. Two shorter paired texts which are in some way related may give a wider range of questions than if each is treated separately.

e. At higher school certificate level the problem is less difficult because all the texts will be literary and the main problem is whether it is desirable to 'do' periods or to 'do' genres.

[b] EXAMPLES OF POSSIBLE SETS OF TEXTS[1]

For Stage I. The plateau

a. Books required in sets:

1. *Treasure Island*, N.M.S.R., Stage 5, Longman, 2nd edn. 1952.
2. *Thomas Edison*, Lives of Achievement, Longman, 1952.
3. *The Prisoner of Zenda*, Longman S.E.S., 1939.
4. *The Unpleasantness at the Bellona Club*, Longman S.E.S., 1962.
5. *The Adventures of Tom Sawyer*, Longman S.E.S., 1949.
6. *She Stoops to Conquer*, Plays Retold, 1st Series, O.U.P., 1938.
7. *Rupert of Hentzau*, Longman S.E.S., 2nd edn. 1960.
8. *Biggles and Company*, Tales Retold, 1st Series, O.U.P., 1936.
9. *Our Cave at West Poley*, Tales Retold, 1st Series, O.U.P., 1953.
10. *The Murder of Roger Ackroyd*, Tales Retold, 2nd Series, O.U.P., 1948.
11. *The Coral Island*, Longman S.E.S., 2nd edn. 1959.
12. *The Wooden Horse*, Longman S.E.S., 1955.
13. *The Kraken Wakes*, Longman S.E.S., 1959.
14. *The Adventures of Huckleberry Finn*, Longman S.E.S., 1956.

and for material to use for reading speed tests

15. *Tales* of *Birbal*, Tales Retold, 1st Series, O.U.P., 1955.
16. Verse according to taste.

b. Books required in the class library:

Some twenty titles from the 1,500-word level for the less competent readers.

Some hundred titles from the 2,000-word level for the main reading effort.

Some twenty books from the over-2,000-word level so that the faster readers can go ahead to the next stage.

The target for library reading is two books a week. We know it is not unattainable.

[1] These are all syllabuses that one or other of us has used in a particular school. Differences of pupil background, sex or previous experience, differences of time or place, or a difference of teacher would all lead to the choice of other texts. These are just examples.

For Stage II. The transition

a. Books required in sets:

1. *Cry, the Beloved Country*, Longman Bridge Series, 1953.
2. *The Card*, Longman Bridge Series, 1956.
3. *Mankind against the Killers*, Longman Bridge Series, 1959.
4. *Stories Grim: Stories Gay*, Longman Bridge Series, 1962.
5. *The Journeying Boy*, Longman Bridge Series, 1963.
6. *Dead Man's Rock*, Longman N.M.A.R. 7, 1937[1].
7. *The Barretts of Wimpole Street*, Essential English Series, Longman
8. *The Three Musketeers*, Longman S.E.S., 1947.
9. *Kidnapped*, Longman S.E.S., 2nd edn. 1956.
10. *The Grand Babylon Hotel*, Longman Bridge Series, 1958.
11. *The Hound of the Baskervilles*, StoriesToldandRetold,O.U.P., 1938.
12. *Pioneers of Medicine*, Oxford Living Names Series, 1945.
13. *The Caine Mutiny*, Longman Bridge Series, 1962.
14. *The Missing Scientist*, Stories Told and Retold, O.U.P., 1959.
15. Verse according to taste.

b. Books required in the class library:

Some twenty titles from the 2,000-word level.
Some one hundred titles at the over-2,000-word level.
For those who have read forty books at this level, access to unsimplified books in a larger library.

The composition work will demand reference to encyclopedias.
Books are longer and more difficult. A target figure of fifty per year is, however, perfectly reasonable.

For Stage III. Free-reading

a. Books required in sets:

Assuming that this stage lasts one year, we would expect to read eight or nine texts. In an English-medium school they would be mainly literary of the type listed below. In a non-English-medium school, they would be much more scientific and technological but we do not feel competent even to suggest examples.

The variety and quantity of material available and the differences in situations and pupil and teacher tastes make us hesitant to produce any list at all. The following should be regarded as nothing more than one possibility intended only to give some idea of the kind and quantity of reading to be done. The actual titles are almost irrelevant.

1. *Animal Farm*, Orwell
2. *The Old Man and the Sea*, Hemingway
3. *Lord of the Flies*, Golding
4. *No Highway*, Shute
5. *Justice*, Galsworthy

[1] See Vocabulary, page 31.

6. *Caesar and Cleopatra*, Shaw
7. *An Inspector Calls*, Priestley
8. *Julius Caesar*, Shakespeare

b. The library:

(i) Not the classics, or at least not serried ranks of them. A few for the few – including some of the translations in the Penguin Classics series.
(ii) Plenty of light fiction – detective stories, historical novels, adventure stories, science fiction, thrillers, etc., including a selection of African writers.
(iii) Material related to other subjects in the school syllabus.
(iv) Up-to-date scientific and technical material, regularly renewed.
(v) Material required for the composition projects envisaged.
(vi) Reference material.
(vii) Magazines.

For Stage IV. The examination year

a. Books required in sets:

(i) The set texts.
(ii) For those not taking literature, a syllabus of more practical and scientific reading or one similar to that of the previous year.

b. The library requirements are as before with the addition of texts related to the set books. We have in mind books by the same author, on the same subject or dealing with a similar problem and certainly not critical works or books about books.

7 Cost and care

1 The only thing one *must* have to teach English in the secondary school is plenty of books, and books are expensive. An eight-class school needs over two hundred pounds a year for texts and another hundred at least for English library books. It is odd that administrators will happily pay the salaries of four English teachers and then make their work impossible by refusing to supply them with the first essential – enough books. It is worth while to recall that the first schools – in East Africa, for instance – had a teacher standing in the open air with a lot of children sitting round him – with their books; no desks, no walls, no roof, no formica-topped dining-tables – but books. There were lots of things wrong, but the priorities were right.

2 All legitimate economies should, of course, be practised.

a. Texts should remain with pupils only while they are using them – sometimes for as short a time as a fortnight. If they are then collected, losses and wear and tear are reduced and the same set may be used in another class or year.

b. Well-chosen school certificate texts can be used in the free-reading year.

c. The same poetry anthology, if issued when required for particular poems, can serve in numerous classes.

d. Libraries may be built up by pupil purchase, or by gifts.

e. (i) Pupils can be let into the economic secret of where the books come from and, hopefully, led to regard them as valuable property.

(ii) They can be shown how they are printed and put together so that they realise how easily their backs can be broken and how cruel is the practice of doubling them back.

(iii) They can be shown how easily the pages tear if the thumb turning the page is too near the spine.

(iv) They can be encouraged by precept and example not to use books as weapons or missiles.

(v) Judicious application of sellotape to the top and bottom of the spine of a paper-back *before it is used* does a lot to prolong its life, and pupils can be entrusted with this job after ten minutes' instruction.

3 There are also illegitimate shifts to which the teacher may be forced to resort, ranging from the temporary tolerable sharing of one copy between two pupils in a boarding school to the utterly impossible situation, which we met not three years ago, of one copy only of a school certificate text for a whole class. These expedients we shall not list lest we give them currency, saying only that access to a rich supply of books pupils must have. It should be possible to ensure this merely by care, forethought and good budgeting. If these are not enough, books must be begged, borrowed or . . . obtained in some other way. We do not advocate their being stolen at least until *everything* else has been tried.

8 The major kinds of work, oral and written, at the four stages of the course

1 The relationship of quantity to quality.

a. Clarity, precision, depth, organisation – all the things involved in a full response – are unattainable without copious reading. A course cannot be based on snippets; one might as well do crossword puzzles. It is the constant activating of the mind in response that leads to skill. It is in the use of the language that learning takes place. There is no substitute in language learning for constant use. If the pupil cannot live in an English-speaking environment all his waking hours, he must spend as many hours as he can immersed in books. The teacher's first duty is to ensure that vast quantities of reading are done. If he does this, and no more, all pupils will be constantly presented with learning situations and some will develop for themselves depth and delicacy of understanding. If he does not ensure that enough reading is done, no amount of toiling over 'comprehension' passages will produce competent readers. Quantity is king.

It is easy for us who are teachers to overrate the value of what takes place in class and to underrate what happens when the pupil is alone with a book.

b. Granted that quantity is the essential, and quality a refinement, teachers are still rightly interested in the refinement of response, which involves dwelling for a long time on a short text, that is, intensive reading. There are distinguished linguists who believe that comprehension can be tested but cannot be taught. Our own experience of being trained and training students and pupils in intensive reading techniques makes us certain that improvement in the comprehension of the text studied always takes place. We believe, but this time it is the certainty of faith not knowledge, that the intensive study of one text helps in understanding others better.

c. For the sake of convenience we shall discuss and exemplify extensive and intensive reading as though they were opposites. This will, however, be misleading unless we think of them as lying at opposite ends of a scale determined by question density. The point on the scale at which we decide to work will depend on:

(i) how much there is in the passage waiting to be discovered. Not all passages are worth meticulous attention.

(ii) how much time is available. By no means all the passages worth serious attention can be tackled.

(iii) how much the class is capable of seeing and how well they respond.

(iv) how much is essential to a minimum worth-while response.

(v) how hot the afternoon is – and so on.

2 We may now list five major working areas before going on to consider methodology in more detail. The categories are not mutually exclusive, nor is any text or class of texts to be used only in one area. We must concern ourselves with:

a. extensive reading
b. intensive reading
c. reading speed
d. reference and study skills
e. the development of critical judgement.

Work of these five kinds will provide opportunities for the acquisition of the skills set out in Section 4 above.

9 Extensive reading

Stage I – Plateau-reading, and Stage II – The transition year

[a] THE LIBRARY

1 *Organisation*

a. In a large school there are advantages in keeping the simplified books in a special section of the main library, provided that multiple copies of popular books are bought.

In a small school the best place is in a cupboard in the classroom. Where a school has two or three streams the total collection of two hundred titles can be split up and rotate at half-yearly or termly intervals between the classroom cupboards.

b. The pupils must have easy and frequent opportunities to change books. A library cannot be open too often and one that is only available for a short time once or twice a week is a positive discouragement to reading.

c. The books need frequent weeding. Many class libraries contain highly unsuitable books in unsimplified English, frequently gifts from well-meaning but ill-informed people. It is tempting, but mistaken, to retain these on the grounds that any books are better than none. It is equally mistaken to imagine that provided the books are in good English they cannot do any harm. Books of this kind make reading a labour instead of a pleasure, interfere with the smooth acquisition of reading skills and lead to over-concentration on items of vocabulary. Any books the pupils cannot or will not read should be kept out. Unsimplified books should be admitted only if they satisfy at least one of the following conditions:

(i) They are worth while for the sake of their illustrations.
(ii) They are actually used for reference in connection with the form syllabus in English or other subjects.
(iii) They are of special local or topical interest.
(iv) Their subject matter and background is of such interest that difficulties of language become unimportant.

Even if they satisfy most of these conditions, they are still not worth having unless the pupils use them.

d. Out with the old, but also in with the new. New simplified books are published every year in Britain and America. They should be purchased at once. The most useful catalogues are Longman *Ways to English* and *Oxford Books for Learning English.* Local representatives of publishers will supply these on request – the Headmaster probably gets them anyhow. For other British material consult the British Council, for American material, such as the Ladder Library, consult U.S.I.S.

e. An accessions register is needed. It keeps auditors very happy if the final column reads 'Disposal' and is completed for all books no longer in the library. The entry 'Lost' is a confession of failure, but the entry 'Condemned' is a sign of success. The book has been read to bits and pieces.

An ordinary exercise book with lined pages makes a perfectly good register. If we use a double-page spread the left-hand page can contain these columns:

Accession No.	Author	Title	Publisher	Series

The right-hand page should contain the following:

(space for annual checks)

Price						Disposal

f. It is of course, necessary to record borrowings. Perhaps the most generally useful way is to write the pupils' names in a thick exercise book in alphabetical order leaving three pages per pupil. Books borrowed are then entered by accession number and title with dates of borrowing and return, e.g.

Smith, James

ACC. NO.	TITLE	BORROWED	RETURNED
161	The Kraken Wakes	1.2.66	5.2.66
93	Pride and Prejudice	5.2.66	

This results in a list of books borrowed though not necessarily in a list of books read. Student librarians often wish to omit the title. It is needed so that we can see what James Smith has read, without thumbing through the accessions register.

g. If adequate display space is available, a form reading chart shows who has read what and also acts as a stimulus to wider reading. To make this we require about five sheets of foolscap, preferably double, with cardboard backing so that entries can be made while the chart is still on the wall without the pen or pencil going through the paper.

FORM 1 EAST READING CHART	Abraham Lincoln	Adamu and the Money Makers	Adventures of Don Quixote	A Gentleman of France	A Journey to the Centre of the Earth	Aladdin and Ali Baba	Allan Quatermain	A Little Work, a Little Play	A London Family Chronicle	A Message from Mars	An Australian Cattle Station	Animals in the Picture	Around the World in Eighty Days	A Tale of Two Cities	Barlasch of the Guard		ETC. ETC. in alphabetical order of titles
Abdalla Ali																	
Abdel Rahman Hassan																	
Babikir Sulieman																	
Banda Banga																	
Batoola Musa																	
Damulira																	
Feisal Abdalla																	
Kiwanuka K.F.																	
ETC. ETC. in alphabetical order of names																	

In the pupil-book square many teachers just put a tick to indicate that pupil X has read book Y. A small refinement is to put letters on a three- or five-point scale indicating:

A = X enjoyed this book very much
B = X thinks this a fairly interesting book
C = X did not enjoy this book.

OR

A = X enjoyed this book and remembers it well
B = X enjoyed this book but does not remember it well
C = X thinks this fairly interesting
D = X did not enjoy this but read it thoroughly
E = X did not enjoy this and knows little about it.

A's and D's opposite pupils indicate good readers. A's and B's below titles indicate popular books.

In subsequent years the list of titles in alphabetical order, which is the most troublesome part to construct, can be cut off and used again with a few new publications stuck on the end.

h. The reading chart can be combined with the library ladder idea if the books for Stage I are listed in three separate groups – 1,500 words, 2,000 words, and over 2,000 words. The pupil who has difficulty with the middle rung can be advised to read a few more on the lower rung first and the pupil who has ripped through forty or so on the middle rung can move to the next one up.

i. Responsibility for the daily running of the library can be delegated to pupils as fast as, but no faster than, they can accept it. This relieves the teacher of some of the manual labour but the necessity for constant supervision remains. Things fall apart if uncle stops looking.

j. The secret of keeping losses to a minimum is very simple and need not involve fines or penalties. All that is needed is a reminder to the offender the day after the book should have been returned. Simplified books can be lent for a week at a time. Eight days is not long enough for the pupil to forget what happened to the book, which is nearly always that he sublet it to a friend. If, however, the malefactor is undetected for a month, the book may well have passed from hand to hand until its trail is too tangled to follow.

An easy way to organise this is to make the librarian's last daily job the writing out of the name of any pupil with an overdue book. The list is then posted on the form or school notice-board. The teacher's first job next day is to glance at the list. At first he may make a bit of a fuss. 'I see you didn't bring back *Adam Bede* last night. Do you know where it is? All right. You won't forget to bring it back today, will you?' In a month or two all that will happen will be an exchange of glances, and if a raised eyebrow is met with a nod, all is well.

Very little needs to be done but it must be continued, however light-heartedly, with relentless pertinacity. The certainty of detection is the great deterrent.

2 *Getting started.* Pupils should be taken into the teacher's confidence[1] so that:

a. they catch the infection of his enjoyment of reading and expect to enjoy it themselves.

b. they realise that he regards the library reading as the most important part of their English course.

c. they understand the educational and language-learning reasons for reading.

d. they are shown the books available, develop the habit of referring to them at this stage by author, title and series and are let into the secrets of how various publishers grade books in vocabulary levels.

e. they understand the cost of books, the amount the school can spend on them and appreciate that their books have been paid for by people generally much less fortunate than themselves.

f. they know how tq treat books so that they will last.

g. they know that they should aim at reading sixty books in a year and that this is feasible.

h. they know what records of their reading they will be expected to keep.

i. they see that there is no point in their claiming to have read books that they have not read. Nobody will lose but themselves.

j. they appreciate that there is no reason to say they have enjoyed a book if they have not. If they pretend to like what they do not enjoy, dull books that would otherwise be banished continue to clutter up the shelves.

k. they know they should not force themselves to finish books they do not enjoy or tackle books that they find too difficult. We want them to read a lot of easy, enjoyable books quickly.

l. they know that most of us forget most of what we read and that this does not matter in the least. There are techniques for revising and recalling books that need to be remembered, but these come later. The truth that matters – there is no point in explaining it; it has to be learnt by experience – is that it is impossible to forget what the mind becomes involved in creating in the imagination.

m. they expect and endeavour to read more quickly.

n. they develop a responsible attitude to their own education, no longer passively expecting to be taught but accepting the opportunity to learn for themselves and aware that the secondary school does not 'provide an education', only the means by which the student may, if he wishes, acquire one.

3 *Encouraging the pupils to keep on reading.*

a. The teacher's own enjoyment of books, his pleasure in sharing it with pupils and his daily interest are of the greatest importance. A teacher who does not read can hardly inspire others to do so.

b. Library reading should not be a chore but a pleasure. It is not necessary to test whether books have been read and well understood and remembered. Virtue may be its own reward.

c. But it is nice to be known to be virtuous and perhaps it is as well for the

[1] An attempt to do this in simple language is made in *Patterns and Skills*, Book 1, pages 1–9.

teacher to provide opportunities for pupils to demonstrate that they are reading well if only to encourage the others.

There are various ways of discovering whether a pupil has read and understood a book, but, though we have often been asked to do so by students, we have never been able to devise one which did not demand that the teacher should have read the books. It is a general principle of man management that one should not ask anybody to do anything one is not prepared to do oneself. If we expect pupils to read the books in their library, we have an obligation to read them ourselves. When we have done so, we can easily discover whether pupils remember them or not by asking a few dumb questions. On *The White Company*, for example, we might say, 'Isn't that the book with a bear in it? What happened at that point?' or 'There was a problem, wasn't there, about getting a rope to the top of a tower? How was that done?'

Another possibility, which can be used for a year while one is reading the books, is to ask for a report on each book read under such headings as: Author – Title – Place and time of the story – Names of and brief statements of the roles of the main characters – Reader's general comment. For example:

Author:	Stanley Weyman
Title:	A Gentleman of France
Place of Story:	France
Date:	1589
The hero:	M. de Marsac
The heroine:	Mlle de la Vire
Other characters:	The King of France, who is murdered.
	Henry of Navarre, who becomes King.
	Fanchette, Mlle's maid.
	Fresnoy, de Marsac's enemy.
	Bruhl, another enemy.
	Simon Fleix, who helps and hinders.
General Comment:	This is an adventure story in which the hero twice rescues the heroine from her enemies. By doing this he gets the favour of Henry of Navarre and marries Mlle de la Vire.

An ingenious extension of this, developed at Bukalasa Seminary in Uganda, was based on a prepared report form somewhat as follows. Italic represents the blank form which was mimeographed and roman a notional completion by a pupil.

Book Report by George Kisubi
on
The Three Musketeers
by
Alexandre Dumas

The story takes place, where?	In France
when?	In the days of Louis XIII and Richelieu – early seventeenth century.
The hero is called	D'Artagnan.
Other characters	Athos, Porthos and Aramis, the three musketeers. Milady: a spy and criminal, D'Artagnan's enemy.
The problem	To become one of the King's Musketeers.
Difficulties	1. He quarrels with Athos, Porthos and Aramis. 2. Milady shows herself his enemy and 3. tries to have him shot 4. tries to poison him. 5. In preventing her plans he interferes with the Cardinal's plots.
Solution	The Cardinal, secretly relieved at Milady's death, forgives him and makes him an officer in the King's Musketeers.
Comment	An exciting adventure story with a historical background and plenty of fighting.

Another possibility, which we would like to have tried out but never have, is to construct a short standard test on each book. When a pupil wants a particular book entered opposite his name on the chart, he is given the standard questions on the book to answer orally or in writing. Oral questions can most conveniently be kept on cards in alphabetical order of title with the questions on the front and the answers to jog our fallible memories on the back. Questions should, of course, be specific but easy. They are meant to be simple for anybody who has read the book, however quickly, but not answerable by guesswork.

Here is a specimen card based on *The Unpleasantness at the Bellona Club.*

Front

1. Where does the story open?
2. What is the unpleasant discovery about General Fentiman?
3. What does Mr Murbles, the lawyer, want Lord Peter Wimsey to find out?
4. What did Robert Fentiman do to his grandfather's body?
5. What was discovered when the General's body was dug up and examined?
6. What did Dr Penworthy do to General Fentiman?
7. Why?

Back

1. In the Bellona Club.
2. That he is dead – has been for some time.
3. The exact time of death.
4. Hid it in a telephone box till the following day.
5. That he had been poisoned.
6. Poisoned him.
7. To get money by marrying Anne Dorland.

If the questions are to be answered in writing, multiple choice questions on a sheet of foolscap may be used. Five well constructed questions will make a perfectly adequate test.

Cards for oral tests and sheets for written tests, once constructed, last for ever. They also make the construction of literary quizzes very simple.

But perhaps the simplest check of all is the best – a list kept by the pupil in his composition book of what he has read. This enables him to glow with justifiable pride as it lengthens and enables the teacher to see what he has read and encourage new resolutions if there is faltering by the way.

4 We have occasionally been asked by teachers how to persuade pupils to start reading and hardly known how to answer them. Our experience has always been that if the right books were available, the pupils lapped them up.

Stages I and II

[b] CLASS READERS

1 The main point about the fourteen simplified books that should be read each year is that everybody reads them all and a shared experience is therefore available for exploitation. Most of the reading is done out of class and class time is given to

a. the routine work of checking that the reading has been done;
b. discussion that ranges over large units of text including the whole when the book has all been read;
c. intensive examination of selected key passages, which we shall deal with later under §10 Intensive reading.

2 Some good teachers like to divide the texts into class readers, which are studied more closely and from which the passages for intensive study are taken, and out-of-class readers, which are somewhat easier and can be handled in larger units. If this plan is followed it is usual to read two class readers every term and one out-of-class reader every month, leaving the last month clear for re-reading before the end-of-year examination. A second reading is in any case desirable towards the end of the year to give the pupils the personal experience of the interest of a second reading and of the ease with which a story, once it has been imagined, can be revitalised in the mind.

3 The alternative method is to spend about three weeks on each book, getting through them at the rate of one a fortnight on the following pattern:

Weeks	1	2	3	4	5	6	7	8	9	10	11
Texts	A	A	A B	B	B C	C	C D	D	D E	E	E

By week 3, text A has been read and one can discuss plot, character, background and the book as a whole. In the same week text B is started, and about a third of it read. The class are well involved in it and the remaining two-thirds can be completed the following week. Appendix II contains specimen lessons on *Prester John* handled in this way.

4 In both methods most of the reading is done silently and out of class time. Reading the whole of any text aloud in class is impossibly time-consuming. The only exception is the play – and plays are meant to be acted and heard. Reading aloud round the class has the additional disadvantages of preventing pupils from learning to read fast and turning what should be a pleasure into dreary boredom.

5 Techniques for getting pupils started on a text so that they want to read on:

a. The teacher can begin by reading aloud for a bit, stopping when he can see and feel that the class have fallen under the story-teller's spell.

b. Questions directing attention to what matters most can be written on the blackboard before the class start reading and pupils can be told to read and find the answers to these questions as quickly as possible.

c. The pupils can be told to start reading and then stopped so that their attention may be directed by questions to the things that matter. A line for some books might be for example:

Who have we met so far?
What do we know about them?
What does the writer mean us to think about them?
What are the time and place of the story?
Who is the hero?
What is his difficulty?
And some speculation is not out of place. What do you think will happen?

This can lead on to an appetizer. Now read on and find out why it is important to discover exactly when General Fentiman died or why Tom ran away from home.

d. Eventually the simplest technique is the best. Start reading and let art and human nature do the rest.

e. No book should ever be introduced by a lecture about the author's life and work and his place in English literature, or indeed talked about at all. The first thing to do is to gain the experience of reading it.

6 Techniques for checking whether the amount set has been read.

a. This can be done in the course of class discussion provided the teacher remains conscious, in spite of the interest of the work, of the need to ensure that every pupil is participating. It is important that every pupil who has not done the reading shall be detected. No savage punishment need follow.

The sins of omission are automatically self-punishing but the teacher has a duty to keep this fact in his pupils' minds. It is not his business to force them into habits of industry; but they may justly reproach him if they remain unaware of the consequences of idleness. We need hardly add that over-frequent and over-earnest exhortation generates resentment.

b. An easier and more efficient method of checking is to use a quick slip-test. The questions asked must not be about insignificant detail because we have urged pupils to read quickly and told them that they need not remember everything they read. The questions must be answerable in one or two words, or too much time is wasted in writing and marking, and such that no one who has recently imagined the happenings covered by the text could possibly forget the answers. They should be asked in the order in which answers appear in the text and should not be answerable by guesswork. These questions are not a test of comprehension; they are simply a device to check whether what should have been read has in fact been read. There is no magic in the number 10. As the teacher asks the questions – which he need not write or repeat (except occasionally in thunderstorms for example) – he can see from the glum or gleeful faces whether the work has been done. Marking is therefore for the teacher but not the pupils a formality to be dealt with rapidly. He can announce the answers or get them from a pupil, rapidly accept or reject alternatives and trust the pupils to mark their own. It is tactful to permit those who got all or nearly all right to hold up their hands. It is also useful for the teacher because it gives him a quick count.

One or two sinners can occasionally be dealt with individually. 'Which questions did you get wrong? Oh, the last five. Well, we all know what *that* means. You will try and catch up before the next time, won't you?'

c. Inexperienced teachers sometimes take the wrong line when as many as half the class have not done their homework. They allow themselves to be seduced into providing a summary or postponing the follow-up. This is an encouragement to idleness and a discouragement to industry. If the teacher protects the pupils from the immediate consequences of not doing the work, next time nobody will do it. The right answer is to press on relentlessly with those who have done it, ignoring the rest except perhaps for an occasional question to one of the sinners. 'Oh, I'm sorry. I ought not to have asked you that. I forgot you hadn't done the reading.'

d. It occasionally happens that nobody has done the reading. This does call for sympathetic investigation. It is very possibly our own fault. The book may be ill-chosen. The pupils may not have understood the importance of reading in quantity. There may have been an accumulation of homework on the day they should have used. There are all sorts of possibilities that require enquiry and appropriate action.

7 Techniques for oral work on large units of text: plot

a. Retelling parts of the story. In Stage I this needs to be helped along with questions. The pupils have insufficient facility with English to operate without any guidance.

If the pupils have read, for example, the first forty pages of *The Three Musketeers*, L.S.E.S., at home and in previous lessons, before we start on Chapter 10 we shall wish to recall some of the earlier threads of the story to mind. Here are some questions deliberately asked the easy way round.

Who gave d'Artagnan a letter of introduction to M. de Treville?

The hard way round, because it demands the recollection of a difficult name, is 'Who did d'Artagnan's father give him a letter of introduction to?'

What happened to the letter?
Who stole it?
What colour was d'Artagnan's horse?
Why did he quarrel with the stranger?

and so on.

b. This can rapidly be developed into one pupil following the thread of the story with the teacher drawing in others by questions that are almost asides. A class that had got to this stage might work something like this:

Teacher: How did d'Artagnan come to quarrel with three musketeers all in one day? Start in M. de Treville's office.

Pupil 1: He rushed out of the office in a hurry.

Teacher (to another pupil): Why was that?

Pupil 2: He'd seen the stranger who stole his letter.

Pupil 1 (continues): On the way down the stairs he bumped into Athos. Athos got angry at him.

Teacher (to Pupil 1): That's right Athos did get angry *with* him.

Teacher (to Pupil 3): Why was he so angry *with* d'Artagnan?[1]

Pupil 3: Because Athos was wounded.

Teacher (to Pupil 1): Go on. What did they agree to do?

Pupil 1: They agreed to fight at 12 o'clock and then . . .

and so on.

c. Still on the subject of plot, one may speculate about the outcome. We know that d'Artagnan is due to fight three excellent swordsmen. What will happen? Will he get killed? Why not? One may begin to catch a glimpse of the conventions of romantic fiction. Will he kill all the three musketeers? Why not? Well, some semblance of probability must be maintained outside comic strips. What will happen then? He'll probably be wounded. All right, let us see.

d. We can also look back later and appreciate the author's contrivance. It is much better that the duels should be prevented and all four make a common front against the Cardinal's men. We now know, too, why the author

[1] Notice that the teacher does not allow the error to distract attention from the matter in hand.

put in the scene in de Treville's office. He was preparing our minds to accept the probability of three quarrels in one day – they were all angry men – and also the suddenness of d'Artagnan's appointment as a musketeer. De Treville was so delighted to get his revenge on the Cardinal.

e. We can also ask questions that offer the pupils a possibility of choice in what they retell. 'Tell me about the most exciting adventure X had.'

f. Better still we can relate the retelling to a generalisation. Retell the part of the story that best shows how kind/brave/wise/foolish X was.

g. We can ask for a detailed mention rather than a retelling and so work gradually towards the conventions of 'allusion and close reference'.

8 Work on large units of text: character

a. We can turn our attention to character, which will be more difficult because we shall have to build up the concepts as well as the vocabulary. *Tom Sawyer* makes an excellent starting point because what one wants is a clear contrast, which Tom and Sid provide. The question to start from, of course, is not: What is the character of each? but: What is the difference between them?

b. As we start to compare and contrast characters in books, we make generalisations. These must, of course, be supported by reference to something in the text.

c. Sooner or later we begin to see what things in the text are characteristic and understand that a writer creates a character for us by showing us what he does, what he says, what others say to him and about him and how they behave in relation to him.

d. We can go beyond this even in *Tom Sawyer* and ask whether Mark Twain approves of a boy like Tom or one like Sid. We shall not quite get to 'kingfishers catch fire', but the path leads there. We may succeed in simple ways in catching a glimpse of the difference between the conventional morality on the lips of society and the values we really admire in the depths of our common human hearts. We may safely leave pupils admiring d'Artagnan's courage, for courage is a lovely virtue, if we know that we shall meet courage again in, for example, Eleanor Dashwood or Mrs Smith. We shall eventually find Shaw dramatising such a contrast in Sergius and Bluntschli.

e. An adaptation of a game in the *Weekend Book* is an entertaining way of getting to grips with character and provokes quite heated discussion. One produces a list of traits of character and all pupils award marks out of ten to the characters chosen. Griselda, for example, scores ten out of ten for patience, but does not do so well on common sense. The marks are then compared in groups or in class and reasons for variations discussed with reference to the text. To begin with it is desirable to keep the vocabulary as simple as possible. Even if the words have been met before, it remains necessary to inform the abstractions with concrete instances.[1]

[1] At the foot of the next page for amusement only is an assessment of Tom and Sid. A mark of 5 is given for the average possession of the quality and also by convention if no evidence is available one way or the other in the text.

9 Work on large units: background

It is desirable to note the date when the story was written and the time it is supposed to be about if only to be clear that it is not much use going to the *Prisoner of Zenda* for historical authenticity. It is not until later that background becomes important to understanding the author's purposes, as in *Nicholas Nickleby and Mr Squeers.*

Perhaps good pupils might spot the difference between the pasteboard of *The Three Musketeers* and the solidity of *Tom Sawyer* and find it harder to believe in Milady than Aunt Polly.

10 Written work related to reading. *Stages I and II*

a. It is not necessary to do a great deal of written work. Certainly one should not ask for summaries of the books read in class.

b. Sometimes part of a book lends itself to dramatisation. One might turn the trial scene in *Tom Sawyer* into a little play or d'Artagnan's first day in Paris into a film scenario.

c. Sometimes one can get an amusing composition exercise out of retelling a part of a story from the point of view of another character. Twain himself succumbed to the lure of this in *Huckleberry Finn.*

d. Sometimes cross-cultural changes offer possibilities. It might be very interesting to read the first chapter of a localised *Tom Sawyer* showing, for example, an African view of a boy being naughty in the right way.

e. During the transition stage the composition syllabus will be dealing with the process of making generalisations and adducing supporting evidence. This is an appropriate time to work on character studies. One may start from simple propositions, such as that Squeers was mean, and demand a paragraph containing the generalisation and adequate supporting evidence from the text.

This can lead on to comparing and contrasting different characters in selected respects, e.g. in the matter of their honesty and industry. The *Weekend Book* game makes a good introduction to this.

Then one can demand comparison and contrast leaving it to the pupil to make the generalisations and so on to the conventional character study.

	SID	TOM
courage	2	10
self-confidence	3	10
toughness	0	7
independence	0	10
cleverness	5	10
cheerfulness	5	10
generosity	0	10

	SID	TOM
modesty	10	0
truthfulness	10	4
warmth of heart	0	10
thoughtfulness	10	8
naughtiness	0	10
popularity	2	10
politeness	10	1

f. Straight retelling of lumps of plot is not very profitable as an exercise. It is better to look for something that involves bringing things together from different parts of a story, asking, for example, for an account of the three meetings of hero and villain in *Montezuma's Daughter*. Perhaps it is even better to find something that requires a reordering of material such as would be needed by an account in chronological order of the life of Absalom in *Cry, the Beloved Country*.

g. Also at the transition stage one may ask about background, a description of life at Dotheboys Hall. One could make a better composition exercise of this, perhaps by asking for it in the form of a first letter from a pupil to his father.

11 Examining extensive reading

a. It is important not to ask questions that demand 'quotation and close reference' from memory. The last thing we want pupils to do is learn by heart as much of the texts as they can, or as little as they think they can get away with.

b. It is possible to ask short essay-type questions. For example, write a paragraph showing that Tom Sawyer is sometimes naughty and another showing his good qualities.

c. What one really wants to do, however, is to ask some questions that demand response to detail, others that are wider in coverage and to find out whether the pupils have seen the relationships between various parts. We can do this by presenting the pupils with a fairly lengthy piece of text, basing our detailed questions on the text so that memory of minutiae is not demanded and exploring the references so that we can find out if the pattern of the book has been followed.

We might, for example, choose the following from *The Adventures of Tom Sawyer*.

> At noon the boys set out in a boat borrowed from a villager who was absent. When they were several miles below Cave Valley, Tom said:
>
> 'Can you see that white place up there, where there's been a landslide? Well, that's where the hole is.'
>
> They landed, and Tom proudly marched into some thick bushes and said:
>
> 'Here it is! The finest hole in the country! I've always wanted to be a robber, but I knew I had to have something like this first. We'll keep it a secret, and tell only Joe Harper and Ben Rogers, because of course there must be a gang, for style. Tom Sawyer's Gang! It sounds splendid, doesn't it, Huck?'
>
> 'It does, Tom. And whom shall we rob?'
>
> 'Oh, almost anybody. We'll lie in wait for people, as robbers usually do.'
>
> 'And kill them?'
>
> 'No; not always. We'll hide them in a cave till they can pay a ransom.'
>
> 'What's a ransom?'
>
> 'Money. You can make them get all they can from their friends, and

after you've kept them a year you kill them, if they haven't collected the money. Only you don't kill the women. They're always beautiful and rich and frightened to death. You take their watches and jewellery, but you always take your hat off and talk politely. Robbers are perfect gentlemen; you'll see that in any book.'

'Why, it's grand, Tom! I believe it's even better than being a pirate.'

'Yes, it's better in some ways, because it's close to home and circuses and things.'

The boys then entered the hole, Tom leading. They crawled to the farther end of the passage, made their kite-strings fast and moved on. They presently entered and followed Tom's other passage until they reached the pit. The candles revealed that it was only a steep clay slope, twenty or thirty feet deep.

Tom held up his candle and said:

'Look as far round that corner as you can. Do you see that? There, on the rock over there, done with candle-smoke.'

'Tom, it's a cross!'

'Now we've found the real number two at last! "Under the cross," eh? That's just where I saw Redskin Joe hold up his candle!'

Huck stared at the mysterious sign for a time, and then said in a shaky voice:

'Tom, let's get out of here!'

'What! And leave the treasure?'

'Yes, leave it. Redskin Joe's ghost is hanging about there, I'm certain.'

'No, it isn't, Huck. It would haunt the place where he died, at the mouth of the cave, five miles from here.'

'No, Tom, it wouldn't. It would hang round the money. I know the ways of ghosts, and so do you.'

Doubts gathered in Tom's mind. Then an idea occurred to him. 'Look here, Huck, what fools we're making of ourselves! Redskin Joe's ghost won't come where there's a cross!'

'Tom, I didn't think of that. That's lucky for us. Let's hunt for that box.'

1. How had Tom found the 'hole'? Where did it lead? Who was with him at the time?
2. What adventure of Tom's does the word 'pirate' remind us of? The pirate adventure ended in church. What were Tom and his friends doing there?
3. Huck is very excited by the cross. What were Tom and Huck doing when they heard the words 'number two – under the cross'?
   Who said he was going to hide something there?
   What was the thing he hid?
4. When had Tom seen Redskin Joe hold up his candle?
5. How had Redskin Joe died?

6. The boys are particularly afraid of Redskin Joe's ghost. What had they seen Joe do in the graveyard?
   When did Tom say publicly what he had seen him do?
7. Where did they find the box? What was in it?
8. In the first sentence what meaning is added to the word 'borrowed' by the words 'who was absent'?
9. What were the kite-strings for?
10. 'Robbers are perfect gentlemen.' What is the author making fun of?

10 Intensive reading

[a] A REMINDER

Although we are discussing intensive and extensive reading separately, it is not whole lessons but parts of lessons that may properly be so divided. In the middle of a chapter, we may stop to dwell on one word. This is intensive study.

[b] THE OBJECTIVE

The aim of intensive reading is to obtain the fullest possible response in the pupil's head to the black marks in his book. Response cannot be achieved by instruction about what he ought to see and feel, or by repetition of what others see and feel, although knowledge of what can be seen by others sometimes helps us to see for ourselves. We look more attentively for a ship on the horizon if we know there is one to be seen, but the seeing we have to do for ourselves. The idea that response to literature consists of regurgitating what other people have said about it is absurd.

[c] SUITABLE TEXTS FOR INTENSIVE WORK

1 Intensive reading is not done for the purpose of widening pupils' vocabularies. The presence of more than one or two new vocabulary items makes a text unsuitable, for the obvious, and therefore frequently overlooked, reason that precise response to unknown words is impossible. The ideal text contains no unfamiliar words, but packs a great deal of meaning into familiar ones.
2 It is certainly desirable to use key passages in books the class are reading or have read for some of the intensive work because a passage means more in its proper context. We like to base most of our intensive work on the class texts in this way.
3 It is perfectly acceptable to work on a selected passage out of context, especially if it is chosen to illustrate something specific, for example, opinions masquerading as facts. Such a reading often fits into the composition syllabus. Another advantage of this technique is that the interest of a good passage may make pupils want to read the book from which it is taken.
4 The last and in our view least satisfactory technique is to use a book of extracts and shut the intensive reading up in a period labelled 'comprehension'

as though comprehension only mattered once a week and was only relevant to unseen snippets of prose.

[d] LESSON TECHNIQUE

1 Practice in exact reading should occur frequently, at least once a week and preferably twice.

2 The passage should first be read silently by the pupils. It is direct response to black marks on paper that we want to improve. We do not want to train pupils to read things aloud before they can understand them. It is necessary to deny them the help of the teacher's voice. The slowest readers should not be given time to complete the passage. If we wait for them, most pupils will feel no pressure at all to read quickly. The slow readers will perhaps read a little faster themselves next time and will not suffer unduly in any case because there is time during the questioning for them to look at the text again.

3 Questions should now be asked with the books open in front of the pupils. We are not testing memory and if a pupil does not know the answer he is better employed in looking it up than in making a resolution to read more slowly next time.

4 Questions are asked in the order in which the answers appear in the text so that we all know where we are all the time.

Sometimes, however, we may go back to the beginning and start again using the first run through to get out the plain sense of the passage and the second to examine its emotional implications or structure. It is possible that we may want a third reading to draw attention to the overall pattern but if we do, it will almost certainly not occur in the same lesson.

5 The answers should be brief and 'sentence fragments' are not only acceptable, they are positively preferable because they are more natural English, provide a good opportunity to practise conversational English and are more efficient because quicker for the purpose of the lesson. In this lesson (and, we would be prepared to add, almost all others) it is wrong to demand answers in sentences with fully expressed parts.

6 The lesson must go quickly. Once again it is best for pupils to remain seated. We do not wait for answers. If a pupil has nothing to say, we try somebody else without pillorying failure. If nobody can answer, we kick ourselves for asking a bad question, and rephrase it or abandon it. We never answer a question ourselves. Our response is not relevant, or to be more exact, only relevant in that it determines the questions we ask.

7 Direct quotation of the words of the passage is to be encouraged; we do not say 'Give it to me in your own words, boy.'

8 The questioning must not go on when the pupils' span of attention has been exhausted. Twenty to twenty-five minutes may be plenty. Exact reading demands intense concentration on the text and is very hard work.

9 The art of teaching exact reading consists of asking the right questions (and we deal with kinds of question below) and in building skilfully on the pupils' answers.

The questions are, of course, prepared carefully in advance, but it is impossible to foresee all the possible pupil answers. Indeed one of the fascinations of this kind of teaching arises from the unexpected and valuable insight that comes in the course of the lesson – to the teacher as well as to the pupils.

It is difficult to describe the art of dealing with pupils' answers; there is no real substitute for watching a sensitive and skilful teacher at work with his own class. The raw recruit at first thinks of answers as right or wrong. He has made some progress when to his Yes or No he adds Perhaps. He may get further still by thinking of some answers as partly right and only requiring an addition to be correct. But it requires quick thinking and considerable tact always to produce instantaneously just the reply that pinpoints what was missing in the pupil's first response.

10 The final step is to read the passage straight through again so that all the responses may now recur in the right order as organised by the writer and so that the pupils may have the experience of reacting at a previously unattained level of response. It sets them a standard – gives them a taste of what can be done by really reading what the words say.

We used to say that this final reading should be aloud. If so, it must be by a good reader. This is certainly a way of rounding off the lesson. One can judge the success of the work by the quality of the attention. But it may be even more impressive to the individual to find that he could do it silently for himself.

11 The exact reader will have noted that in paragraph 3 above a passive was used and realised that this was in order to avoid saying who asks the questions and, although we have been proceeding on the assumption that it is always the teacher, he will have anticipated our next point.

It is easy and profitable to train pupils to ask a good many questions for themselves. It is profitable because it encourages pupils to concentrate on the text more intently and also – as we may admit at once with humble pride – because some pupils eventually become capable of asking more searching questions than we can, and nothing can be more rewarding to a teacher than to be surpassed by his pupils.

It is simple because they learn how to make up the easy questions in their grammar lessons when they practise making the question that directs attention to the subject, the predicate, the object, the adverbial, etc. When sufficient skill has been acquired for this to be done in groups, the amount of language practice obtained entirely incidentally is surprising – and it is practice in asking questions instead of answering them. This is not easy to arrange elsewhere in the syllabus.

Training can be started by asking the faster readers to make up some questions about the passage. This keeps them more usefully employed than they would otherwise be and the tactful teacher will reward their diligence by allowing them to ask some at least of their questions.

12 There is one technique that is particularly valuable in training the pupils to ask really searching and subtle questions. It demands courage. Teacher and taught simply switch roles; the pupils ask the questions and the teacher answers them, if he can.

No teacher who has done this ever needs to be persuaded that it is a good idea for the text to remain open where it can be referred to as often as is necessary.

[e] EXPERIMENTAL CONFIRMATION OF OUR THESIS

Before we go on to consider the kinds of question that may be asked, we invite the reader to conduct an experiment on himself with the aid of the following passage and questions. To get a valid answer, it is necessary to follow the procedure of a lesson, that is:

(i) Read the passage silently.

(ii) Formulate the answers to the questions in the mind even if they appear ridiculously simple.

(iii) Re-read the passage.

When this has been done, the reader should ask himself whether he saw more in it than he did at the first reading.

> At first when you see the coolie on the road, bearing his load, it is as a pleasing object that he strikes the eye. In his blue rags, a blue of all colours from indigo to turquoise and then to the paleness of a milky sky, he fits the landscape. He seems exactly right as he trudges along the narrow causeway between the rice fields or climbs a green hill. His clothing consists of nothing more than a short coat and a pair of trousers; and if he had a suit which was at the beginning all of a piece, he never thinks when it comes to patching to choose a bit of stuff of the same colour. He takes anything that comes handy. From sun and rain he protects his head with a straw hat shaped like an extinguisher with a preposterously wide, flat brim.
>
> You see a string of coolies come along, one after another, each with a pole on his shoulders from the ends of which hang two great bales, and they make an agreeable pattern. It is amusing to watch their hurrying reflections in the padi water. You watch their faces as they pass you. They are good-natured faces and frank, you would have said, if it had not been drilled into you that the oriental is inscrutable; and when you see them lying down with their loads under a banyan tree by a wayside shrine, smoking and chatting gaily, if you have tried to lift the bales they carry for thirty miles or more a day, it seems natural to feel admiration for their endurance and their spirit. But you will be thought somewhat absurd if you mention your admiration to the old residents of China. You will be told with a tolerant shrug of the shoulders that the coolies are animals and for two thousand years from father to son have carried burdens, so it is no wonder if they do it cheerfully. And indeed you can see for yourself that they begin early, for you will encounter little children staggering under the weight of vegetable baskets.
>
> The day wears on and it grows warmer. The coolies take off their coats and walk stripped to the waist. Then sometimes in a man resting for an instant, his load on the ground but the pole still on his shoulders so that he has to rest slightly crouched, you see the poor tired heart beating against

the ribs; you see it as plainly as in some cases of heart disease in the out-patients' room of a hospital. It is strangely distressing to watch. Then also you see the coolies' backs. The pressure of the pole for long years, day after day, has made hard red scars, and sometimes even there are open sores, great sores without bandages or dressing, that rub against the wood; but the strangest thing of all is that sometimes, as though nature sought to adapt man for these cruel uses to which he is put, an odd malformation seems to have arisen so that there is a sort of lump, like a camel's, against which the pole rests. But beating heart or angry sores, bitter rain or burning sun notwithstanding they go on eternally, from dawn to dusk, year in year out, from childhood to the extreme of age. You see old men without an ounce of fat on their bodies, their skin loose on their bones, wizened, their little faces wrinkled and ape-like, with hair thin and grey; and they totter under their burdens to the edge of the grave in which at last they shall have rest. And still the coolies go, not exactly running, but not walking either, sidling quickly, with their eyes on the ground to choose the spot to place their feet, and on their faces a strained, anxious expression. You can no longer make a pattern of them as they wend their way. You are filled with a useless compassion.

In China it is man that is the beast of burden.

To be harassed by the wear and tear of life, and to pass rapidly through without the possibility of arresting one's course – is this not pitiful indeed? To labour without ceasing, and then, without living to enjoy the fruit, worn out, to depart suddenly, one knows not whither – is not that a just cause for grief?

So wrote the Chinese mystic.

Questions: Set A, following the order of the passage.

1. How does the coolie first strike the observer?
2. Pleasing to which sense in what way?
3. In what way does he 'fit the landscape'?
4. What is he dressed in?
5. What is the most important thing at this point about his clothes?
6. What words are used to convey the shades of blue?
7. 'He *seems* exactly right'. What difference would it make if the writer had said, 'He *is* exactly right'?
8. What does he wear?
9. What does he do when 'it comes to patching'? What does he not do? Does this strike the author as stupid, sensible, odd, slightly amusing, very funny, pitiful or what?
10. What words tell us about the materials and shape of his hat?
11. What does the word 'preposterously' suggest about the observer's attitude?
12. Is all that has gone before a matter of how the coolie strikes one 'at first'?

/ Ismail -9. NOV. 1994

(note 2/11)

(R)

See Loan handling, other prompts
Scrolling lists 6:19, 7:1
Address list 6:1
Available addresses list 6:2
Borrower Type . . . . 6:19 - 6:2
Department 6:1
Format 7:1
Home site. 6:19, 7:1
Item Loan Type 7:1
Search
See also Function keys
Searching
See Borrower
See Item
Searching borrower name
See Borrower
Searching borrower number
See Borrower
Searching OPAC 5:1
Second overdue letters
See Overdue letters
Selective payment

13. At the beginning of the first paragraph we had some sort of picture of 'the coolie on the road bearing his load'. What extra details are added by the first sentence of the second paragraph?
14. What idea is picked up again in the words 'an agreeable pattern'?
15. What feeling does the observer have in the next sentence? Is he looking straight at the coolies?
16. When he does look at their faces, what does he see? Why does he not believe the evidence of his eyes? Who has done the 'drilling'?
17. What picture of the coolies do we get next?
18. Why 'if you have tried to lift' and not 'if you have lifted'?
19. What new feeling now 'seems natural'?
20. What previous information relates to their 'endurance' and what to their 'spirit'?
21. What do the 'old residents of China' find 'absurd'?
22. How do they regard the coolies? Does the author agree with them?
23. The words 'and indeed you can see for yourself' suggest that the author is going to accept the view of the 'old residents'. What words tell us he has not done so?
24. What happens when the day grows warmer?
25. Is the man resting 'a pleasing object'? What has happened to the writer's point of view: is he getting closer or moving further back?
26. How long does the man rest? What do these words remind us of?
27. What words are used to describe the coolie's heart? What feelings are there in the observer now?
28. Pick out the phrases used to show the results of carrying the pole day after day.
29. What differences are there between 'the coolies are animals and for two thousand years from father to son have carried burdens' and the re-statement of the same fact in this paragraph?
30. What is suggested by the repetitive phrasing of this sentence? Is phrasing merely repetitive – what is added, for example, to 'eternally' by the three following phrases?
31. What words are used to give us the picture of the old men? One word suggests a kind of movement – what kind?
32. What is suggested about their lives by the clause 'at last they shall have rest'?
33. We have seen the children, the individuals and the old men. To what do we now return? What has happened to the observer so that he can no longer make an agreeable pattern?
34. What must the observer feel? Why can he not congratulate himself on the rightness of his feelings?
35. What summarises the author's view of the coolie's life? How does this differ from the old residents' view – 'they are animals'?
36. What is the point of the final quotation?

Now we return to the beginning and consider a second set of questions.

1. What is suggested by the word 'object', and by 'striking *the eye*'? How much is the heart involved?
2. What is the background to the picture of the coolie?
3. How near are we in this paragraph to the coolie as a fellow man?
4. Do we get any nearer in the second paragraph?
5. Is there any suggestion of sympathy in the first sentence of it? (Try changing 'great' to 'large'.)
6. Is there any suggestion of sympathy in the last sentence?
7. Consider the phrase *It seems natural. . . .* Does the writer expect us to agree? If so, what does he think of the opinion of the 'old residents'?
8. In the third paragraph what details are given before the writer says 'It is strangely distressing to watch'?
9. What details precede the general word 'cruel'?
10. What gives the two general statements above their force?
11. Examine the sentence beginning 'But beating heart . . .' What previous details are we reminded of by
    a. beating heart;
    b. angry sores;
    c. bitter rain or burning sun;
    (Why were the adjectives omitted in paragraph one?)
    d. they go on eternally;
    e. from childhood.
    Where do we find the detail about 'the extreme of age'?
12. Three words have been used about the way the coolies move. What is suggested in paragraph one by *trudge*, and in three by *stagger* and *totter*?
13. There are also different ways of describing what the coolie carries. How do they differ?
    a. bearing his load,
    b. with a pole on his shoulders from the ends of which hang two great bales,
    c. the bales they carry for thirty miles or more a day,
    d. the weight of vegetable baskets,
    e. their burdens.
14. Consider the final quotation again. Is this, too, an example of useless compassion?

Now read the passage straight through again. Is there more in it than you saw at first?

[f] KINDS OF QUESTIONS THAT MAY BE ASKED TO HELP PUPILS TO READ MORE PERCEPTIVELY

1 The overall aim is to explore what the words say – all of it. The unskilled reader does not always notice all the words and so, particularly in the early stages of this kind of work, questions that merely direct attention to what is there in front of the pupils' eyes are useful. Even to get at the plain sense of a passage involves understanding at least three kinds of meaning: the reference of the units of language, their relationship and the situation as a whole. We have, therefore, four kinds of plain sense questions and we will base our examples on the 'coolie' passage.

2 Plain sense questions

a. To direct attention to what is there

For example:

1. What are the first two words of the passage?
2. Where is the coolie when you first see him?
3. What is he doing?
4. What is he dressed in?
5. What colour are his rags?

b. To make clear the reference of the words

For example:

1. 'When *you* see . . .' Who is 'you'?
2. What is the work of a coolie?
3. 'Trudges': Is the coolie riding or on foot?
4. Is he walking easily or with some difficulty? What difference would it make if the word used was 'marches' or 'strolls'?

c. To make clear the relationship of the words, which is a matter of examining the grammatical relationships, but not in grammatical terminology. We are not concerned with the generalisations but the particular examples in front of us and we do not therefore ask about the first sentence, 'Where is the noun clause in apposition to anticipatory *it*?' Instead we ask, for example,

1. What does the coolie strike the eye as?
2. 'Pleasing' to whom?
3. What is it about the coolie that makes him seem to 'fit the landscape'?
4. How much of the paragraph is included under 'at first'?

d. Questions to make clear the situation as a whole

1. What country is the passage about?
2. What do we imagine ourselves seeing for the first time?
3. What is our first impression of the coolie?

The answers to plain sense questions can nearly always be given by direct quotation from the passage and pupils should not be asked to use their own words. What it says is what it says; a paraphrase will be inferior.

3 Emotional implication questions

These relate to the emotional suggestions of words, separately or in conjunction, used literally or figuratively and to the feeling implied in the grammatical structure. We may ask questions:

a. To make clear the suggestions of feeling conveyed by individual words. For example:

1. The word *straw*, and the phrase *shaped like an extinguisher with a wide,*

flat brim, tell us about the coolie's hat. What does the word 'preposterously' tell us about the hat and about the observer's feelings?

2. What does 'angry' tell us about the appearance of the sores and what else does it suggest?
3. What difference would it make to the meaning if the second paragraph ended 'you will encounter small children carrying heavy vegetable baskets'?

b. To make clear the exact suggestion of the word in its content. For example:

1. What do we usually feel when we see a man dressed in 'rags'? What words cancel this feeling here?
2. What surrounding words make us accept 'wrinkled and *ape-like*' as neither funny nor vulgar?

c. To make clear what is suggested by figurative language or comparisons. For example:

1. What things are brought in to make the shades of blue clear to us? Are they pleasant or unpleasant things? What difference would it make if the dark blue was 'like that of a fresh bruise' and the light blue 'that of the belly of a dead fish'?
2. '. . . A sort of lump, like a camel's . . .' Why not a 'hump'? The comparison tells us something of the shape and size of the lump. What else does the comparison of the coolie to a camel suggest? What previous clause prevents us from thinking this might be funny?

d. To make clear the suggestions of feeling conveyed by the grammar.

1. It is as a pleasing object that he strikes the eye. What small but important difference of emphasis would be possible if the sentence read in the normal order – He strikes the eye as a pleasing object? In other words what phrase is emphasised by the writer's use of the unusual order?
2. What is suggested by the repetitive parallel structures of the sentence? 'But beating heart or angry sores, bitter rain or burning sun notwithstanding, they go on eternally, from dawn to dusk, year in year out, from childhood to the extreme of age.'

4 Questions on the organisation of the paragraphs internally and in relation to one another, concerned with both thought and feeling.

a. These are usually follow-up questions. For example, having collected all the information about the coolie in the first paragraph, one might ask:

1. What are most of these facts concerned with?
2. Similarly on the second paragraph, one might ask whether the further information is mainly pleasant or unpleasant and where the suggestions of hardship occur and what they lead on to.
3. On the overall structure one would ask questions leading the class to see the movement from the superficial first impression to the final wry judgement.

b. A slightly different type of question relates particular to general statements. For example,

1. Which is the most general statement in the passage?

2. What particular statements are we reminded of by the generalisation, for example, in the 'But beating heart . . .' sentence.

c. One can also ask what words refer back to previous ideas or suggestions of feeling, or contrast with them, or build up to them, as the 'great bales' which one can only 'try to lift' give force to 'resting for an instant'.

5 One may ask questions involving summarising and the correct response to wholes. These may involve understanding the author's intention or what readers he has in mind as well as what his thesis is.

The final question on the Death Test (Appendix I) is another and rather different example and in East Africa many students training to be teachers answered all the previous questions well but missed the point of the whole story.

6 One may ask questions about what is implied or deliberately left unsaid. Any question demanding inference from what is said is a proper one. Anybody who can really read could be fairly confident that the 'coolie' passage was written by a Briton (conceivably an American) who had visited China but not lived there for a long time and was writing for the British/American general public. The passage can be dated as pre-revolutionary but, on its attitudes, twentieth century.

7 It is also legitimate, though this is only marginally comprehension work, to ask questions to help in the inference of meaning from the context.

8 Any question which helps the pupil to understand more fully, probe more deeply or imagine more exactly is a good question.

9 Questions that must not be asked.

Since our whole aim is to lead pupils to get more deeply into the text and respond to what is there, it follows that any questions that lead away from the text are bad questions if we ask them while we want the pupils to concentrate on the text. For example,

a. What other meanings do you know for this word? *or* What does this word usually mean? These are bad questions because we do not want the pupil to think of what the word does *not* mean in the text, but of what it *does* mean and only of that.

b. Demands for paraphrase are bad questions because it is hardly ever possible to say the same thing in different words. A different phrasing gives a different meaning.

c. What related words do you know to this word? This, too, is a bad question at the point where concentration on the text is required.

d. We should not ask pupils to analyse sentences grammatically.

e. We should not ask them to pick out figures of speech and name them.

f. We should not even ask them, while we are working on improving their response, what they think about the passage. What they think is irrelevant. What matters is what is there.

Many of the above kinds of 'bad' question have considerable value for later discussion. Some of them reveal the quality of the pupils' response, but they do nothing to improve it.

An example of intensive reading work at Stage I is contained in Appendix II. An example suitable for Stage III is given in Appendix V.

[g] WRITTEN WORK ON INTENSIVE READING

During term time very little written work is required; perhaps none at all. We cannot approve of the common practice of answering comprehension questions on a passage in writing for homework. Still less is it possible to approve of doing the passage orally in class and then answering the questions in writing for homework. The pupil who has made the correct response in class is wasting his time; the pupil who has not is being encouraged to try to remember somebody else's approved response, which is harmful. Both kinds of pupil would be better employed in making fresh responses to different stimuli, that is to say, reading something else.

[h] TESTING INTENSIVE READING

1 When the passage is taken from a reader

a. It is undesirable to choose a passage that has been used for intensive reading in class because we want to test response not recollection.

b. Questions to which the pupils have to compose their own answers are easy to make up, but difficult to mark. It is not always possible to be sure whether inadequate answers are due to lack of understanding or difficulty with expression. We have already given some examples of this type on *Tom Sawyer*; see pages 78–80.

c. Questions offering the pupils a choice of the correct answer are more difficult to construct; they can, however, pinpoint precision of response more accurately and they are easy to mark. An example based on an extract from *Things Fall Apart* suitable at Stage III or IV is given in Appendix III.

2 When the passage is unseen

a. Both types of question remain available but we favour the objective type or a mixture of the two because of the extra precision that is gained and the difficulties of assessment that are avoided.

b. An unseen passage provides a better test of skill because the memory element is eliminated.

11 Additional notes

STAGE III – FREE READING and STAGE IV – THE EXAMINATION YEAR. Extensive reading.

1 The beginning of unsimplified reading.

a. For the average pupil this is likely to take place at the beginning of a school year. In the previous year he has used his class library; in the new year he is allowed into the main library. But it is not sensible to regiment all pupils in this way. A voracious reader may well exhaust the resources of his class library half-way through the year. His reward should not be that he is left with nothing to read but that he should be given the special privilege of using the main library before his classmates because he is ready to do so. Naturally others will be 'promoted' as they reach the proper stage.

Conversely there are slower pupils who may well be advised to continue reading at 'Bridge' level after the others have moved on to unsimplified material. It is better for library reading to be too easy than too difficult; it is essential for it to be pleasant.

b. Suitable change-over reading material.

It is not a good idea to go straight on to the classics. Most of them are too long and still too difficult for the average pupil to read without labouring at them. One needs a special rung of the reading ladder reserved for books recommended as the first unsimplified ones that pupils read. Ideally they should be in straightforward modern English without too many background difficulties and with a strong enough narrative interest to pull the pupil through the new vocabulary problems. If he gets excited enough, he will not be bothered to look up the strange words; he will guess and go on; which is just what we want. Perhaps as good a way of finding such books as any is to consult the pupils. Urge the best reader in the class to blaze the trail, but do not accept his single vote. A book needs three or four votes to qualify for inclusion at this vital stage. Let the best reader induce his friends to provide them. It all spreads the infection.

2 Library reading in non-English-medium schools.

a. In such a school the library reading has a special function; it is the place in the syllabus where pupils who are going on to post-school-certificate education in English must learn the basic special vocabulary of the subjects they are going to study at the university or elsewhere.

This is so important that it cannot be left to chance or casual interest. Inducements must be built into the syllabus, and the library itself must be richly stocked with the appropriate scientific and technical material and kept up-to-date, for this kind of reading matter dates more rapidly than any other.

There are several ways of encouraging pupils to read material that will serve this purpose.

(i) The teachers of other subjects can recommend additional reading in magazines, proper books, or even school textbooks in English.

(ii) The English teacher can use non-literary material for some class reading, choosing his extracts so that there is related material available in the library.

(iii) The 'research essays' in the composition syllabus can be planned so that they demand reading of this kind.

b. It is not of course suggested that pupils from such schools should be confined to reading of this technical kind. They should also read light fiction, at least, for fun and, when they can, heavier fiction for pleasure and profit, but they cannot afford to neglect the non-literary material.

3 In English-medium schools.

In English-medium schools the technical vocabularies of the subjects of future study are learnt in the course of studies pursued in them but even here the English teacher should remember that the main reason why many, perhaps most, of his pupils want to learn English is in order to get access to modern technical and scientific knowledge, not to English Literature.

He should be as ready to encourage this interest and as careful to see that it is catered for in the library as he is to share his own pleasure in literature.

4 An important consideration about the free-reading stage is that it is the time when the foundations of post-certificate work are laid. The people who want to read English for A-level or university preliminary examinations will be handicapped if they do not read as widely as they can in English literature now, and similar problems will afflict those who are going on to read history, geography, science, etc. This is the time to go in for reading round the subjects.

5 We have accepted that if a pupil is not going to 'do English literature', he need not necessarily read literary works at this stage. But he must nevertheless read something in large quantities for the sake of his progress in language. It is most important in schools where some pupils drop literature as an examination subject at this point that they should realise that they must not stop reading. If they do, they will fail the language paper. What they read can be determined by future use or present interests. It matters much less than that they should continue to read copiously whatever matter they think useful or entertaining.

6 The considerations in paragraph 5 above apply with even greater force to the examination year. Students in English-medium schools must not be allowed to confine themselves to the monotonous diet of school textbooks, for one cannot read nothing but textbooks without its affecting one's style, any more than one can touch pitch and not be defiled.

In non-English-medium schools overall exposure to English has been so much less that even the examination cannot be allowed to bring educational progress to a complete halt for a year. There is, however, less objection to the reading of textbooks.

7 In the free-reading stage, abridged, as opposed to simplified, books are frequently more suitable than full texts.

12 Extensive reading based on class readers

1 In the free-reading stage pupils and teacher should reap the reward of two years' planned effort. This is the year for wide reading. No teacher worth his salt will allow it to be wasted on the study of the next year's school certificate set books, though to boost confidence it is a good idea to find out what the books are (the pupils may already have done so) and then make it clear that as they will be studying works by Shakespeare, Hardy, Hemingway and Orwell next year, they will, amongst other things, read some other books by these authors this year. Here again it is worth letting the pupils into one's confidence. Many of our former students have met strong opposition from pupils when they have announced that the school certificate set books would not be begun until the examination year, and it is important to convince pupils and, alas, sometimes the headmaster, that more school certificate credits will be obtained in literature as well as language by a year of wide reading followed by a year's concentration on set books than by two years spent poring over set books. There are any number of better reasons for not spending an unnecessary year on a small number of books but this is the one that we have found most persuasive. It has the incidental advantage of being true.

It is true because –

a. the pupils need time and experience in order to acquire confidence in their ability to read 'real' books and to talk and write sensibly about them. Rob them of the opportunity to do this outside the examination syllabus and fear of failure will force them into reading notes and second-hand opinions and using books of model answers. There are plenty of sheep in the world already.

b. Two years is far too long to spend on three or four texts. The freshness fades. The detail, the daily grind from word to word, dulls the response. Dreariness and boredom take its place.

c. Moreover reading skill is not increased; it is positively reduced.

d. A pupil who has read *Julius Caesar* rapidly and with pleasure in the previous year is better equipped to read and enjoy *Macbeth* than one who has already read *Macbeth* once and returns to it for examination purposes.

e. At HSC or A-level the task of the teacher of English faced with pupils whose sole experience of literature consists of two years spent on three or four texts is daunting if not impossible.

We have never been able to understand why this pernicious practice of reading school certificate texts for two years is so widespread. We do not see how any teacher can tolerate it if he understands the theory of reading, the enjoyment of literature, the principles of education or the demands made by examinations in literature. It is surely not unduly idealistic to expect some acquaintance with one of these four in professional English teachers.

2 In general we advocate the use of plain texts, but would not object very strongly to texts prepared for the foreign learner, such as the New Swan Shakespeare, provided that they contain aids to and not substitutes for response.

3 Texts are in general so much longer that it is not realistic to think in terms of dealing with them rapidly consecutively. We like to have two or even three books on the go at once. One may be a play, which we shall be reading and 'acting' in class; one a novel, which will be being read out of class (except where we take passages for intensive reading), and discussed once a week in class; and the third will be the last book finished, on which we want two or three lessons during which we can discuss it as a whole.

4

a. The kinds of work set out in §9*b* above (page 72) continue to be useful. Pre-questions, however, can be more general. Many of them may be suitable for written work and some can demand essay-type answers. The end-of-the-year examination can be partly, if not wholly, on the lines of the final leaving certificate paper.

b. There are advantages in letting the pupils know the kind of questions that are likely to be set on a text before they start reading it instead of afterwards. One simply sits down and writes out all the good examination questions one can think of on the text up to say a dozen, and then pins the piece of paper up in the classroom for reference. The pupils are not panic-stricken at the sight of the questions because nobody expects them to know the answers yet. As they read the text it gradually becomes clear to them that they are accumulating the material that they will need to cope with any of them and confidence is fostered.

c. As the text is read, questions become available for class discussion, for use in written work for the whole class, or for pupils to answer individually as they choose. Pinning up possible questions works very well in the examination year too. One must have certain minimum demands – say that every pupil answers at least one question every three weeks – but there is no need to restrict pupils to this. Anyone who wishes to do more can be encouraged to do so.

d. Class discussion needs tactful handling. One must avoid the heresy of the model answer in the teacher's mind, avoid giving the impression that there are right answers, and leave room for differences of response remembering that literature may mean different things to different people without any of them being wrong. At the same time one must insist that statements are supported by evidence drawn from the text.

e. It is generally unwise to make pupils answer in writing a question that has been discussed orally. This encourages reliance on memory and tends to give the impression that 'standard' answers exist.

f. In the examination year we accept that it is the teacher's duty to see that as many of his pupils as possible get through the exam. Our objections to cramming are not moral, but practical; cramming is not the most effective way of getting credits and passes. It suggests stuffing facts in, but what we want to do is squeeze responses out.

As always we believe in telling pupils what the problems of passing an examination are. We discuss and allow them to experiment with the scale on which they can work. We show them mark schemes and we give them plenty of practice in writing against the clock. We point out that it is pretty easy to get 12 out of 20 in five questions, dividing the time equally. It is much harder to get 14 out of 20 in four questions leaving the last one out. Even one brilliant and two good answers on the pattern 18, 14, 12, 8, 4 still only score 56 and five 12's are 60. Few candidates do badly because they know too little about the texts; the majority who under-perform do so because they know too much about the books and care too little about the simple matter of how much they can write in twenty-five minutes.

When we start practising answering examination questions, we usually find that the pupils fail to finish the two we ask for in the forty-minute period. If this happens, we discuss what to leave out and how to slip in a brief reference in place of a whole paragraph. If the pupils finish easily but are thin on matter, we announce the questions in advance and only ask for one answer in the forty minutes until the idea of a full answer has been grasped.

This is quite deliberate examination training. We never, of course, supply material, but we do relate our written practice to the units of time and the kind of questions that will be met in the examination.

Oral discussion ranges as widely as ever and by this time we and the pupils have quite a number of common literary experiences that enable us to make interesting comparisons.

13 Intensive reading

Stages III and IV

1 What has been said of aims, methods and types of question in §10 above (pages 79–89) remains generally applicable.

2 With three years of intensive reading behind them and the examination before them the tendency is for pupils to wish to study every word of every text from every angle. This must be resisted. In texts chosen for intensive study, there are passages, even in Shakespeare, which should be got through as quickly as possible. The examiner can be trusted not to ask peripheral questions. Provided that key passages are not neglected, there is no need to attempt to cover every detail. In *Macbeth*, for example, the Sergeant's speech does not require, or reward, examination in depth. It is enough to know what has been happening and where Macbeth comes into it.

3 With these texts for intensive study a quick reading through of the kind done in the previous year is enough to get the outline of the plot and a rough idea of the main characters. The second reading fills out the first by showing how the incidents in the plot relate one to another, what the author does to create the characters for us, how the whole work is organised and what it means.

4 With texts for less intensive study it is not necessary to read everything in class, though we confess to having done so with some of our classes in the past. The first reading gives the outline of plot and character. Subsequent attacks on the text can be aimed at answering particular questions. Some intensive work should be done on key passages but a thorough beginning-to-end, guided second reading is not needed.

5 In this year the distinction between extensive and intensive work becomes considerably blurred. One finds that at one moment one is dwelling on a phrase and a minute or two later ranging widely through the whole work.

6 The testing of reading ability is in the hands of the examiner in the final year, but it is well for us to notice what he is doing because the wind of change is blowing round his ankles too.

There is a tendency, which may be seen in the Cambridge paper entitled significantly *Literature in English*, for the examiner to use the extended context question and to avoid questions demanding paraphrase or knowledge of the meaning of every word in the passage presented to the candidate. Detailed textual study for its own sake is no longer required.

No examining body has yet set an unseen passage to test literary appreciation at school certificate level, but the possibility has been discussed and rejected, we think rightly, because the tense atmosphere of examination conditions is not conducive to the calm, open-minded, sensitive receptivity with which a new work of literature should be approached. Few of us would like our own future careers to hang upon what we could make of a new poem or short story in half an hour under conditions of stress.

Response to unseen reading is, however, tested, but the examiner puts it into the language paper and calls it 'comprehension'. An example of such a test is given in Appendix III.

14 Increasing the pupil's reading speed

1 Work on the improvement of speed is very rewarding. Good results are easy to achieve, easy to measure and surprisingly consistent; the students practically all double their reading speeds in ten weeks and at the same time improve their comprehension. It is no small matter at the beginning of a school course to make the pupils twice as efficient in so central an activity as reading. It increases what can be included in the syllabus without lengthening the course. Nor are its benefits confined to school; it adds to the efficiency with which the world's business is conducted.

2 The teacher needs a little background knowledge, which may be obtained from numerous reading manuals, for example Edward Fry: *Teaching Faster Reading*, Cambridge, 1963; Manya and Eric De Leeuw: *Read Better*, *Read Faster*, Pelican A740, 1965; and Harry Madox: *How to Study*, Pan, 1963.

But the main necessity is to persuade the class that it can be done and is worth doing.

3 Sophisticated apparatus is unnecessary. There are devices for widening eye-spans, reducing the time of fixations, and pacing the reader by mechanical means. All these are great fun to play with but where the result is an increased speed we think it is attained by the effect of the gimmicks in stimulating interest and not by the specific practice. Any other sort of fuss would do just as well. Indeed the De Leeuws believe that some of these mechanical devices do harm because of their inflexibility.

4 Left to their own devices, pupils generally stick at 120–140 words per minute. It is probably not a coincidence that this is the speed at which reading aloud takes place. There seems to be a sort of sound barrier at this point, which, once broken, opens up the possibility of very much higher speeds. 400–800 words a minute are normal among skilled readers.

5 There is also evidence that increases of speed in L2 lead to parallel increases in L1.[1] This may be of importance in non-English-medium schools. We do not know of any work that has been done in L1 and affected L2 but an experiment would be worth making.

[1] M. West, *Learning to Read a Foreign Language*, Longman, 1941, p. 7. 'The resulting improvement in the rate of English reading was 232 per cent, while the improvement in the rate of Bengali reading (in which no practice had been given) was 266 per cent.'

6 The following apparatus is all that is needed:

a. A set of passages within the vocabulary of the class. *Tales of Birbal*, O.U.P. Stories Retold, 1st Series, will do for first-year pupils.

b. A set of multiple-choice comprehension questions on each passage.

c. A reading speed and comprehension chart for each pupil, which he can make for himself.

7 There is at least one important advantage in using complete short stories as practice material. Pupils can be shown how the expert reader starts more slowly while he is dealing with the exposition of the story and then speeds up when he has got into the narrative.

8 The design of the questions is quite important. They should not be answerable without reference to the passage. It is equally important that they should not demand recollection of peripheral detail. It is perfectly legitimate to ask whether something happened on Sunday, Tuesday, Thursday or Saturday if the day of the week matters, but not legitimate if it could just as well have happened on any other day.

Anyone who has run the story through his mind just before should be able to answer the questions.

9 As an example of how we would introduce this work, a passage and the questions on it are given in Appendix IV on page 116.

10 Methods.

The English teacher can do half of this job in a few minutes, by telling his pupils who are reading at about 100 words a minute, 'You will now read better if you read faster.' And by 'read better' we mean remember more and enjoy more. We explain that it is no good trying to remember everything we read because it is impossible, and would not be particularly useful even if we could do it.[1] We add that once we know that we forget most of what we read, we can do something about it. Educational psychologists have discovered quite a lot about how and when we do our forgetting. Reading and studying are two very distinct activities and good studying depends on intelligent revision carried out in several ways. It is of course no help at all, at this stage, to recommend the pupils to read excellent books like Harry Madox's *How to Study* (Pan) or C. A. Mace's *The Psychology of Study* (Penguin, 1968) but it is a good idea to pass on their most important ideas to our pupils in simple terms. These ideas will need emphasising again and again as the pupils move up the school and the demands on their time and talent increase, but a start can and should be made in the first year.

Many pupils will need individual help with difficulties such as movement of head and book, vocalisation, subvocalisation, faulty eye movements and regressions, and it is not easy to cure habits which have been ingrained by unsuitable reading assignments over as many as eight years of primary education.

[1] I have been amazed and amused at the relief with which my pupils greet the news that *I* forget most of what I read and am not worried about this; conversely I have been saddened to discover undergraduates who have gone miserably through almost the whole of their university careers under the impression that they alone of all the human race suffered from this desperate 'failure' of memory. G.P.M.

Faster reading should be practised all the time. Even in first year one should urge pupils to read a daily newspaper in English, and as many magazines and periodicals as the school can afford to buy or can persuade organisations and individuals to give.[1]

An enjoyable way of practising quick reference – and incidentally of helping pupils to get to know the normal lay-out of a newspaper – is to get hold of a set of old newspapers, give out one to each pupil, and fire questions rapidly to see who can find the relevant article first. 'Where was Mr Wilson going by plane the day this paper was printed?' 'Who is selling a Ford Anglia and how much does he want for it?' 'What was the weather forecast for the next day?' 'What did the editor choose as the subject of his own article?' Youngsters who can find their way quickly round a newspaper to answer such questions are likely to spend a sensible amount of time reading the local daily, and also to become more skilful users of reference books. This is a practical method, even for a bush school. Newspaper offices will usually supply old copies free and it does not matter how long they take to arrive since the lesson is often all the more enjoyable and instructive if the world situation has changed considerably since the paper was printed.

While the main effort on faster reading is best placed at the beginning of the secondary school course, we would advocate a further course combined with information about and practice in how to study at the beginning of the post-school-certificate year. This is partly preparatory for future serious scholarship and partly aimed at minimizing the ill effects of a year spent poring over text-books. Students may need reminding that books can be read as well as studied.

15 Teaching the skills of study and reference

1 The skills we have in mind are listed in §4.4 above, starting on page 57. We have already suggested just above how skimming for required information can be based on a newspaper. We also in the chapter on written work (under summarising, notemaking and the research essay) describe some productive aspects of reference skills and insist on the importance of training the proof-reader's eye. In the chapter on vocabulary we discuss teaching pupils how to use dictionaries. We must now consider what other kinds of information pupils can be asked to find and how we may help them to do it efficiently.

2 Time-tables, directories and gazetteers.

a. In the first year all pupils have an atlas. We suggest asking some such question as what are Cotopaxi and Popocatepetl, telling the pupils only that the information is in their desks. Watch what happens. A teacher will be exceptionally fortunate in his class if he does not have to direct them to an atlas. It is, of course, perfectly sensible to try a dictionary first. Even when pupils take out the atlas, they may not turn straight to the gazetteer.

This can be followed up by ten minutes of quickfire questions some of

[1] The British Council and the British and American Information Services in the nearest large town will always help here, and the teacher only has to tap them and then ask all members of staff to pass on old magazines instead of throwing them away to build up a good stock quickly.

which can be answered from the gazetteer and others of which demand reference to the maps. For example,

In which country is the River Po?

About how far is it from Mombasa to Aden?

We are not teaching geography, merely the efficient use of a book of reference, and non-geographical questions are quite in order. For example, how many places are there in England called *Newport*?

If one can persuade thirty motoring friends to donate their out-of-date copies of the AA book, even more entertaining games can be played.

b. Even if AA books are hard to find, it is not difficult to collect out-of-date telephone directories, which are mines of information. One can usefully ask about services available, find out costs, master the spelling code or play at being Directory Enquiries, 'I'm sorry but there's a page missing in this directory, could you tell me the number of Mr P. F. Schnickelgrubber of 25 Newport Road, Gloucester?'

c. Railway and bus time-tables can also usually be obtained and one can set up little conversations between members of the public and the clerk at the enquiries desk or in the travel agency. Some people would call this dramatic work; others teaching spoken English. One or two lessons are certainly well spent in this way.

3 Forms and regulations.

The world is full of these and one can easily get hold of some forms and fill them up. Official bodies are only too anxious to provide practice material for anyone who is willing to help reduce the number of people who cannot fill up forms. Try the Post Office, the Passport Office, the Licensing authorities and, for really severe exercises, the Income Tax people. In the business world, insurance of cars, houses, property and life offers plenty of useful opportunities for form-filling and for the interpretation of regulations and reading the small print.

Interpretation is a question of relating practical cases to general statements. For example,

a. You send a £5 note in an unregistered letter to a friend. The bag is stolen. Can you claim from the Post Office?

b. You send £50 in a registered letter to a business firm. The letter is never delivered. How much can you claim if (a) you declared the amount enclosed when you posted the letter, (b) you did not declare it.

c. (i) You have a third-party insurance on your car. What can you claim on a car valued at £400 if you skid on a wet road, collide with a tree and the car is a total wreck.

(ii) You have a comprehensive insurance on your car. You have another argument with a tree but this time the car is only damaged. You have the benefit of a five-year no-claim bonus. At what figure for damage will it be to your advantage to make a claim? You carry the first £10 yourself.

4 Advertisements.

The magazines we have collected contain numerous advertisements. A few lessons may be usefully spent in studying these. A question such as 'Why do the top people wear Viyella socks?' is fraught with human interest and classes are liable to advance all sorts of enchanting suggestions until it occurs to somebody to wonder if in fact they do. From which it is not far to the difference between the effect of the question and the bald statement 'Top people wear Viyella socks.' Nor is it far to the problem of verification. One can conjure up delightful visions of shopkeepers keeping careful records of the purchasers of Viyella socks classifying them (on what basis?) into top, middle and bottom. Or perhaps a sampling technique was used. It is at any rate entertaining to devise one or two. But the most profitable line of discussion is why did the copy-writer ask the question.

Advertisements have one great advantage over most other kinds of writing. The writer's intention is crystal clear – to sell the product. The test of his success is beautifully objective – a rise in sales. This understood, our minds are free to examine the means he uses to attain his ends. In excessively moral people this may lead to frenzies of indignation; we are content if it leads to the contemplation of advertisements with an increase of sardonic relish. A great deal of advertising is socially useful and important as a source of information about available goods and prices.

It is also a rich source of linguistically interesting material. Pupils should not be left in the state of innocence that believes that, in the context of advertising, *alleviate* and *relieve* mean anything like *cure*.

Packard, V. *The Hidden Persuaders*, Penguin A585, makes good background reading.

5 Encyclopedias, biographical dictionaries, almanacs, classical dictionaries, dictionaries of quotations, etc.

a. Work with these is mainly a matter of showing pupils where to go for what kind of information and setting them enough questions to answer for them to discover how the reference books work and to develop speed in getting just the facts they are looking for. Naturally the more the need to find the information arises in class, the better. Curiosity, too, grows by what it feeds on.

b. Encyclopedias may be used to find out particular facts. Try getting a pupil to use the Junior Oxford Encyclopedia to find out what anthracite is.

They can also be used for larger subjects such as Whaling, and also as contributors of information for an even larger research project.

6 Before a research project is tackled pupils need to know a good deal more about finding information.

a. They need to be shown how the library is arranged and to understand the principles of its classification.

b. They need to know how to use the library catalogue, and

c. how the borrowing system works.

With this information, provided they know the title and author of a book, they should be able to find out whether a book is in the library, where it is if it is present, and how to reserve it when it next comes back if it has been borrowed.

d. They also need to know how to find out what information there is on given subjects in the library. If there is a subject index, it is a great help. If there is not, they need to learn what sections to try.

This again is a matter of practising with examples which the teacher should preselect in order to ensure that enough information is available to make the hunt rewarding.

e. In this kind of search they will need to use chapter headings and indexes.

f. While they are using books in this way, it is important to direct attention to the date of first publication and to the difference between subsequent *impressions* and *revised editions.* What appears in print is not necessarily true. Authors are not omniscient in the first place and cannot escape from the limitations of their time and place. Knowledge keeps on increasing; books, once published, do not change.

16 Literary criticism and 'appreciation'

1 Literary criticism starts from quite simple questions:

a. What is the writer trying to do? We may at first be content with simple answers: tell a story, describe this, that or the other, prove that X is Y, persuade us to vote for Z, sell soap or make us laugh at our own folly.

b. Who is he writing for? Sometimes the limitations are clear as in most school history books, or children's books.

c. What means has he used? This is a matter of fact. The existence of a pursuit, the use of disguise and usefulness of coincidence in *The Thirty-nine Steps* are not matters of opinion. Nor is the story's dependence on suspense for its interest. The means of course include the invention of incident, its relation to character, the invention or selection of background, the language and the organisation of all these things (and others) into some kind of whole.

After a text has been read in class, general questions and ideas of this kind are bound to arise in the course of discussion and need no forcing.

2 There are, however, more difficult questions, which should not be ignored. But it is wrong to force pupils into answering these prematurely. For example,

a. Is what the writer sets out to do worth doing?

This is very much a matter of opinion, sometimes of collective opinion, for there are fashions even in the degree of veneration accorded to the classics. And some will defend light fiction as entertainment, while others condemn it as escapism.

b. Has the writer been successful in doing what he set out to do? If so, how; if not, why not?

Whether writing is good or bad is not quite so much a matter of opinion because as Johnson noted 'the generality of mankind' arrive at pretty much the same conclusions, given sufficient time. The proposition that Shakespeare is a great poet and dramatist is not in dispute. But also there are undeniably differences of opinion about modern writers. We do not think that it is sensible to ask a secondary pupil these questions in this form about a literary text. He cannot know whether a text is good or bad because he has not had enough experience to establish any standards. The most we can do is to present him with two different attempts at achieving the same object and ask which is better and in what ways.

We can oppose passages in which the sense is clear to those where it is obscure or muddled. We can pair passages where the attitudes and feeling of the writer are crude or conventional to those where they are subtler and more original. We *can* ask whether *Lord of the Flies* is better than *A Coral Island.*

We can, and should, cause our pupils to apply comparative and critical procedures particularly to their own writing. If they can enjoy their own successes and attack their own failures with constructive amendments, they will be better able to appreciate the skills of others. A possible approach to criticism is given in Appendix VI.

3 Pupils should be protected from critical jargon and from exposure to the critical judgements of other people until after the school certificate.

4 They should not be asked to write, for example, an appreciation of Wordsworth's *Daffodils* or of *Pride and Prejudice*. They have simply not had enough experience in literature to produce worthwhile judgements of their own, and it is pointless for them to repeat other people's.

17 Allocation of time

The five main kinds of work we have now discussed do not, of course, require anything like equal proportions of time spent on them. Quantity – extensive reading – needs the most time of all. The second most time-consuming work is that on quality – on exact reading. Speed can be dealt with in a ten-week course, and the actual teaching involved in dealing with the skills of reference and scholarship adds up to little more than a score of lessons spread over three or four years. Criticism comes in incidentally.

We cannot resist quoting as a tail-piece a remark made by a language specialist engaged in the training of teachers of English as a second language to one of us. 'I used to believe in reading, too, but I found it didn't cure common errors.'

It doesn't cure influenza either.[1] It wouldn't be sensible to expect it to.

There are more important things in life than curing common errors; reading is one of them.

For further reading

BRETT, R. L. *An Introduction to English Studies*. Arnold, 1965.

BRIGHT, J. A. *Patterns and Skills in English*, Pupils' Books 1–4. Longman, 1965-7.

COOMBES, H. *Literature and Criticism*. Penguin, 1970.

FRENCH, F. G. *The Teaching of English Abroad*, Part 3. O.U.P., 1948.

FRY, E. *Teaching Faster Reading*. Cambridge, 1963.

[1] It is, of course, a matter of common experience that reading does *alleviate* influenza.

GURREY, P. *Teaching the Mother Tongue in Secondary Schools.* Longman, 1958.
Teaching English as a Foreign Language. Longman, 1955.
Teaching English Literature in W. Africa.
HEATON, J. B. *Studying in English.* A practical approach to study skills in English as a second language. Longman, 1975.
HOLBROOK, D. *English for Maturity.* Cambridge, 1967.
DE LEEUW, MANYA and ERIC. *Read Better, Read Faster.* Pelican, 1969.
MACE, C. A. *The Psychology of Study.* Penguin, 1968.
MUNBY, J. *Read and Think.* Longman, 1968.
OGDEN and RICHARDS. *The Meaning of Meaning.* Kegan Paul, 1949.
RICHARDS, I. A. *The Principles of Literary Criticism.* Kegan Paul.
Practical Criticism. Kegan Paul, new edition 1960.
THOULESS, R. *Straight and Crooked Thinking.* Pan, 1974.
ULLMAN, S. *Semantics: Introduction,* Blackwell, 1962.
The Principles of Semantics, Blackwell, second edition 1964.
WARNER, A. *A Short Guide to English Style.* Oxford, second edition 1964.
WHORF, BENJAMIN LEE. *Language, Thought and Reality.* M.I.T. Press (dist. Book Centre Ltd.), new edition 1964.
WRIGHT, E and WALLWORK, J. F. *On Your Own.* A guide to study method. Longman, 1962.
Journals. *English Language Teaching.* O.U.P.
The Use of English. Chatto & Windus

Publishers' catalogues of material available in simplified English, especially:
O.U.P. *Oxford Books for Learning English*
Longman. *Ways to English.*

APPENDIXES

I THE DEATH TEST

Time: 30 minutes

Read the following story carefully:

One day, a rich merchant of Baghdad sent his servant to the market to buy food. The servant returned very quickly and rushed into his master's room, his eyes wide and glassy, his whole body shaking with fear.

'Master!' he cried. 'As I was walking through the crowded market, a woman struck against me and nearly fell. When I turned to help her, I saw that it was Death, and she raised her hand and was about to lay it on me. I ran from that evil place and did not look back. Now I must escape from this town at once.'

'But how do you know that this woman was Death?' asked the merchant.

'I knew her perfectly,' replied the man, and his voice dropped to a whisper as he remembered the frightful minute when he looked into her face and knew her.

'I have good reason to know her,' continued the servant. 'I was alone with her face to face for six long days and nights, two years ago, when I had fever. And once, only a month ago, she looked me in the face when a madman threw his knife at me and it scratched my skin an inch above my heart. Please lend me your fastest horse and I will ride like the wind to Samara, where I shall be safe.'

The merchant lent the poor man a horse, and watched him disappear along the road to the north in a cloud of dust.

Then the merchant walked to the market and looked about until he at last saw a woman who was a stranger to him.

He greeted her and told her who he was.

'Why did you lift your hand in order to take my servant?' he asked.

'I did not mean to take him then,' she replied. 'I raised my hand in a movement of surprise. I was surprised to see your servant in Baghdad today, because I arranged long ago to meet him in Samara tonight.'

Chose the true answer from each group below and write A, B, C or D in the box on the right. You may read the story as many times as you like while you are answering the questions. You will have 30 minutes.

1. The rich merchant sent his servant to the market
   - **A** although there was not enough food in the house.
   - **B** so that he bought food.
   - **C** so that the servant could have a meal.
   - **D** because some things to eat were needed. ☐

2. The servant rushed into the room
   - **A** because he always walked quickly.
   - **B** because he brought good news.
   - **C** because he was in a hurry to speak to his master.
   - **D** because his whole body was shaking with fear. ☐

3. The servant's eyes were 'wide and glassy'
   - **A** because he was wide awake.
   - **B** because he was frightened.
   - **C** because he wore strong glasses.
   - **D** because he was surprised to see his master. ☐

4. The servant's 'whole body was shaking with fear'
   - **A** neither because he saw Death in the market-place nor because she raised her hand towards him.
   - **B** both because he saw Death in the market-place and because he knew her face.
   - **C** either because he saw Death in the market-place or because he knew her face.
   - **D** until he rushed into his master's room. ☐

5. The servant told his master that
   A he thought the woman meant to touch him.
   B he knew the woman was angry because she struck him.
   C he was angry because the woman struck against him.
   D the woman raised her hand and laid it on him.

6. Why is 'Death' spelt with a capital D in this story?
   A Because the typist has made a mistake in copying the story.
   B Because death is always spelt with a capital D.
   C Because Death is a very serious thing in this story.
   D So that we may understand that Death is talked of as a person in this story.

7. What did the servant really want to escape from?
   A Buying food in the market.
   B Working for his master.
   C Living in Baghdad.
   D Dying suddenly.

8. Why did the servant say, 'I have good reason to know her'?
   A Because she raised her hand to lay it on him.
   B Because he often saw the woman in the market.
   C Because he was once mad.
   D Because twice before he was near dying.

9. 'I was alone with her face to face for six long days and nights' means that
   A for six days the servant did not expect to get better.
   B the servant had very few friends and was lonely for six days and nights.
   C for six days and nights this woman nursed the servant when he had fever.
   D days and nights seem longer when one is happy.

10. 'She looked me in the face' means that
    A the madman believed himself to be a woman.
    B for a minute the servant was in great danger.
    C as the woman scratched him with the knife, she looked at him.
    D the woman looked at him in order to scratch him an inch above his heart.

11. Why is the servant called 'the poor man'?
    A Because he had no horse of his own.
    B Because he had much less money than the merchant.
    C Because he was very frightened and unhappy.
    D Because, two years before, he was very ill with fever.

12. How did the merchant (not the servant) know which woman was Death?
 A He had often seen her before.
 B He had never seen her before.
 C He greeted her.
 D She told him who she was.

13. The woman was surprised
 A because she thought the merchant was in Samara.
 B because she did not think the servant was in Samara.
 C to see the merchant in the market.
 D because she thought the servant was in Samara that day.

14. The true reason why the woman raised her hand was
 A because she was surprised to see the merchant.
 B to lay it on the servant.
 C because she found the servant in Baghdad instead of Samara.
 D because the servant made her angry by nearly knocking her over.

15. What does the writer mean us to think happened to the servant?
 A He had a narrow escape from death.
 B He rode away like the wind to Samara where he was safe.
 C He died that night in Samara.
 D He was killed on the way to Samara.

II *THE* PRESTER JOHN *SERIES*

These lessons were taught in the first term of the first-year course. The reader chosen was *Prester John* in the Longman Simplified English Series, and two things are worth noting about it. First, many of the British and American student-teachers who were to watch the lessons disapproved of the choice of such a book for a school in a newly independent African country. 'Imperialist propaganda', 'Colonialist distortion', 'disgustingly patronising' were some of their descriptions, but the teacher said he thought it was an exciting story about Africa and he would like to see what the class thought of it. Secondly, although he still remembered Buchan's original text pretty well, he had read this simplified version *right through* before he planned his lessons; many a lesson is spoiled and many a silly question asked because the teacher knows the original text but has not troubled to find his way around the simplified version.

At the beginning of the first lesson he gave out the copies and said 'This is a story about Africa. Read the first chapter and when you have read it look at the questions on the board and make sure you can answer them. If you can, go on reading.' He *did not* tell them that Buchan became Lord Tweedsmuir and went to Canada, or that he wrote *The Thirty-nine Steps* or anything about the legends of 'Prester John'; all that could come later. This was a reading lesson and he wanted them to read silently. Nothing else was said throughout the lesson and he wrote these questions on the blackboard:

1. Who is telling the story?
2. Where does he live?
3. Who were his friends?
4. Where did they meet?
5. What did Archie find at the edge of the stream?
6. Were they afraid?
7. What did Tam see on the sands?
8. Where did they hide?
9. Who was the man on the shore?
10. What was he holding that frightened them?
11. What made Davie angry?
12. What did he do because he was angry?

The first thing to note is that they are very easy questions. They were meant to be. All he wanted to ensure was that the pupils could answer the 'big' questions that no one who had understood the chapter could fail to answer, so that they could go on with the story. He had impressed on them that it was senseless to pretend to understand if they could not because they could only cheat themselves, not him, so the one or two who were puzzled by questions asked for help; he went to them individually while the rest read on. Obviously the questions could have been asked orally, but one advantage of the blackboard method is that it enables everyone to get on at his own speed. (We have also found it very useful when, as often happens, there is not a complete set of one book available. We have had a class of pupils reading as many as five different books, and still, with a bit of judicious timing, been able to write up questions to direct them to the things they must notice. If the questions for those with *Tom Brown's Schooldays* were on the first eight pages, those on *The Wooden Horse* would be on pages 10 to 16, and the ones on *Pioneers of Progress* on pages 14 to 20 and so on. The teacher can soon see, strolling round the classroom, how fast pupils are going. They look up for the questions on their own book but are not disturbed by the others.)

By the end of the lesson most pupils had managed the first eighteen pages and the teacher then asked them to read on to page 56 for the lesson two days later (not a heavy assignment, but they all had a class library book on the go as well). At the beginning of this next reading lesson he gave out slips of paper and explained that he was going to test the reading with twelve questions that needed only very short answers; they were going to go fast and he would read each question twice only. (This is good listening practice – dictation if you like – and by the middle of the year he would be reading questions only *once* and they would be listening well.) These were the questions:

1. What job did Davie's uncle find for him, and where was it?
2. Who did Davie meet again on the ship?
3. Was Blaauwildebeestefontein a place people liked to go?
4. Was Mr. Japp, the storekeeper, a kind man?

5. What did Davie do because he was lonely?
6. What did he have to do at Umvelos?
7. What was the noise that made people think there was a devil in the Rooirand?
8. What did Davie do when he saw the old man there?
9. What was Japp doing that made Davie force him to resign?
10. What did Davie and Mr. Wardlaw hear that frightened them?
11. How was Captain Arcoll dressed when he arrived?
12. What did Davie offer to do to help defeat Laputa?

The pupils had written down their answers within five minutes and he then asked them to mark them. (When we were at school we were always told to change papers with our neighbours; we prefer to trust our pupils to mark their own.) The teacher asked for oral answers to the questions, and the pupils agreed on the right answer and, where necessary, looked back for the evidence in the text. Having dealt with all the questions he asked them what they thought of the main characters so far. Where a good description – adjective or phrase – was produced he wrote it on the board alongside the character's name. If it was contested he asked the class to produce evidence for and against it. (He ended with the reminder that they were not yet half-way through the book and might have to change their minds about Laputa or Davie, though they were unanimous about not changing their view of Henriques who was on the board as 'a traitor'.)

Pages 57 and 58, which they had now reached, would have done well for intensive study but he did not want to hold the class back from an exciting story, so he told them that they should read on to page 100 in the next two days, because in the next reading lesson they were going to look carefully at pages 101 and 102, and if they had not read that far they would not be able to follow. They had now had two extensive reading lessons with test questions, and, though some of them would certainly have finished the book, it would still be fresh for the intensive work, as by the time they reached that they had still had the copies less than a week.

AN INTENSIVE READING LESSON

Inanda's Kraal

The vow was at an end. In place of the silent army of yesterday a mob of maddened savages moved around me. They were singing a wild song. From their bloodshot eyes stared the thirst for blood, the fury of conquest, and all the wild passions which Laputa had aroused. Machudi's men were swept out of the way, and the wave of savagery seemed to close over my head.

I thought my last moment had come. Certainly it had but for Colin. He had been tied up on the journey, but was now free again. In a red fury of anger the dog leapt at my enemies. Though every one of them was fully armed, they fell back. Colin had the sense to keep beside me. Barking like a thunderstorm he held the ring around my litter.

The breathing space would not have lasted long, but it gave me time to get to my feet. I stood up in that fierce circle with the clear knowledge that my life hung by a hair.

'Take me to Inkulu,' I cried. 'Dogs and fools, would you despise his orders? If one hair of my head is hurt he will burn you alive. Show me the way to him and clear out of it.'

The circle gave way. I walked straight into it, knowing well that I was running no light risk. Machudi's men were swallowed in the mob. Alone I walked forward with all that huge crowd behind me.

I had not far to go. Inanda's Kraal was a collection of huts, shaped in a half-moon, with a flat place between the houses, where grew a big merula tree. All around was a number of little fires, with men sitting beside them. Here and there a party had finished their meal. But around the merula tree there was a gathering of chiefs who sat in rows on the ground. A few were standing, and among them I caught sight of Laputa's tall figure. I strode towards it, wondering if the chiefs would let me pass.

But Laputa did not intend that I should be butchered. A word from him brought his company into order, and the next thing I knew I was facing him, with Henriques beside him, and some of the northern chiefs. Henriques looked terrible in the clear morning light, and he had a linen rag bound round his head and jaw, as if he suffered from toothache. At the sight of me his hand went to his belt, but he held his peace.

Laputa's eye fell on me, a clear searching eye with a question in it.

There was something which he was trying to say to me which he dared not put into words. I guessed what the something was, for I saw his glance run over my shirt and my empty pockets.

The teacher gave the class time to read the passage silently and then asked these questions:

1. On the plain sense
   a. In what ways were Laputa's men now behaving differently?
   b. Why were they behaving differently?
   c. What did Davie think at first?
   d. Who defended Davie? How?
   e. What did Davie tell the men to do?
   f. Was this dangerous? What words tell you?
   g. Where were the chiefs gathered?
2. On grammatical relationships
   a. Why was Colin able to defend Davie?
   b. Why was it surprising that Laputa's men 'fell back' from Colin?
   c. Why was the 'breathing space' long enough?
   d. Why would Laputa have 'burned' his men 'alive'?
3. On relationships of thought
   a. What does the word 'mob' tell us about the men? What words in the same sentence does it contrast with?

b. Which sentence tells us what Davie thought about all that he describes in the first paragraph?

c. Why does Davie say, 'I cried' (para. 4)? What words in paragraph 3 do the words 'I cried' link up with?

4. On what can be inferred

a. What words in the first paragraph tell us that Laputa's men wanted to kill someone?

b. When they arrived at Inanda's Kraal did Machudi's men help Davie? How do you know?

c. Once the men had let him pass, did Davie feel that he would reach Laputa?

5. On emotional response

a. Why were Machudi's men 'swept' out of the way?

b. What words in the same sentence emphasise this idea?

c. Did Davie need a 'breathing space'? Then what does it mean?

d. 'My life hung by a hair.' Why did the writer choose these words?

e. Why were Machudi's men 'swallowed' in the mob? What words in a previous paragraph does this remind us of?

6. On whole response to passage (Having read the whole passage aloud to the class)

a. Did Davie behave bravely?

b. Did Laputa's men?

c. Was Davie lucky?

d. Describe in a short sentence the events described in each paragraph.

The questioning went on at a brisk pace. If one pupil could not answer, the teacher went on to another – the question having first been asked of the whole class so that everyone had to think out an answer before they knew who would be asked to answer out loud. He discouraged 'echo' answers – 'Colin was able to defend Davie because . . . '—because they do not form part of normal conversational procedure in English, and for the same reason he did not insist on answers being given in 'complete sentences'; a perfectly acceptable exchange was:

Teacher: Who defended Davie?
Pupil: Colin.
Teacher: How?
Pupil: By barking and jumping up at Laputa's men.

In order to show that there was method in their compilation, the questions are set out under the headings suggested in §10(f) (p. 86). But they were not asked in that order. The teacher worked steadily through the passage and on the way the pupils asked him one or two questions as well. The questions on 'grammatical relationship' look too simple; in fact they confirmed what the teacher had suspected from a previous lesson, that many of the pupils did not understand the full meaning of 'though' and 'but' and could not use 'because' correctly in framing their answers. He talked to them about it in the following lesson in *just those terms*; he did *not* announce a 'revision session on adverbial clauses of concession and reason'.

It will be noted that he asked no questions on the last three paragraphs of the extract, which contain some of the most inviting material for the probing teacher. He intended to, but ran out of time. He had hoped to get through the whole passage, but after nearly twenty minutes' hard work the questioning had got as far as 'wondering if the chiefs would let me pass' and, because he is convinced that too little is better than too much and that a whole lesson at his intensive study is a bore for young readers, he read aloud the part that they had covered, asked the four questions eliciting 'response to the whole', congratulated the class on a good piece of work and let them read on silently for the rest of the lesson as a reward. When the bell rang he told them to be sure to have read to pages 131 and 132 by Monday, as they would be having a close look at them then.

Normally we would aim at one or two intensive reading lessons a week and keep them well spread, but we think it is more realistic to deal with suitable passages as they occur in a reader so that the context is still fresh. Before we leave *Prester John* it may be worth adding that most of the student-teachers who had thought the book unsuitable for an African class agreed that it had its value when, in the final period in which the class discussed the whole book and some of the pupils said that Buchan was anti-African, the teacher agreed that in some ways he was, but asked them, 'What does he want us to think of Laputa at the end?' Most of them supported the bright lad who said – these were his exact words – 'Though he was cruel and did a lot of damages, the writer thinks he was somehow good.' All those questions had been worth asking.

(But they had to do something about 'damages'. In fact the teacher asked them to look it up in the *Advanced Learner's Dictionary of Current English*, which told them (as the *Concise Oxford*, excellent though it is for the English reader, would not have done) that *damages* was a legal term referring to money, and that the word our perceptive young reader needed was *damage* meaning 'harm', which was 'uncountable'.)

III 'THE DEATH OF OKONKWO'

It is useful to give the pupils some experience of multiple choice objective tests, partly because in such tests the teacher can focus attention very closely on the exact meaning of the words, phrases or paragraphs he thinks most meaningful, and partly because they are likely to become much more common in international examinations like the school certificate. Here is a sample at school certificate level, which we have used unseen with fourth-year and bright third-year classes. The passage is the last few paragraphs of Chinua Achebe's novel *Things Fall Apart* – an excellent third-form reader for Africa.[1]

> When the District Commissioner arrived at Okonkwo's compound at the head of an armed band of soldiers and court messengers he found a small crowd of men sitting wearily in the obi. He commanded them to come outside and they obeyed him without a murmur.

[1] Heinemann, 1958.

'Which among you is called Okonkwo?' he asked through his interpreter.

'He is not here,' replied Obierika.

'Where is he?'

'He is not here!'

The Commissioner became angry and red in the face. He warned the men that unless they produced Okonkwo forthwith he would lock them all up. The men murmured among themselves, and Obierika spoke again.

'We can take you where he is and perhaps your men will help us.'

The Commissioner did not understand what Obierika meant when he said, 'Perhaps your men will help us.' One of the most infuriating habits of these people was their love of superfluous words, he thought.

Obierika with five or six others led the way. The Commissioner and his men followed, their firearms held at the ready. He had warned Obierika that if he and his men played any monkey tricks they would be shot. And so they went.

There was a small bush behind Okonkwo's compound. The only opening into this bush from the compound was a little round hole in the red earth wall, through which fowls went in and out in their endless search for food. The hole would not let a man through. It was to this bush that Obierika led the Commissioner and his men. They skirted round the compound, keeping close to the wall. The only sound they made was with their feet as they crushed dry leaves.

Then they came to the tree from which Okonkwo's body was dangling and they stopped dead.

'Perhaps your men can help us bring him down and bury him,' said Obierika. 'We have sent for strangers from another village to do it for us, but they may be a long time coming.'

The District Commissioner changed instantaneously. The resolute administrator in him gave way to the student of primitive customs.

'Why can't you take him down yourselves?' he asked. 'It is against our custom,' said one of the men. 'It is an abomination for a man to take his own life. It is an offence against the earth, and a man who commits it will not be buried by his clansmen. His body is evil and only strangers may touch it. That is why we ask your people to bring him down, because you are strangers.'

'Will you bury him like any other man?' asked the Commissioner.

'We cannot bury him. Only strangers can. We shall pay your men to do it. When he has been buried we will then do our duty by him. We shall make sacrifices to cleanse desecrated land.'

Obierika, who had been gazing steadily at his friend's dangling body, turned suddenly to the District Commissioner and said ferociously: 'That man was one of the greatest men in Umuofia. You drove him to kill himself; and now he will be buried like a dog . . .' He could not say any more. His voice trembled and choked his words.

'Shut up!' shouted one of the messengers, quite unnecessarily.

'Take down the body,' the Commissioner ordered his chief messenger, 'and bring it and all these people to the court.'

'Yes Sah,' the messenger said, saluting.

The Commissioner went away, taking three or four of the soldiers with him. In the many years in which he had toiled to bring civilisation to different parts of Africa he had learnt many things. One of them was that a District Commissioner must never attend to such undignified details as cutting down a hanged man from a tree. Such attention would give the natives a poor opinion of him. In the book which he planned to write he would stress that point. As he walked back to the court he thought about that book. Every day brought him some new material. The story of this man who had killed a messenger and hanged himself would make interesting reading. One could almost write a whole chapter on him. Perhaps not a whole chapter, but a reasonable paragraph at any rate. There was so much else to include and one must be firm in cutting out details. He had already chosen the title of the book after much thought: 'The Pacification of the Primitive Tribes of the Lower Niger'.

QUESTIONS

1. Does the first paragraph suggest
   a. that the men welcomed the Commissioner enthusiastically?
   b. that they took no notice of him?
   c. that they seemed tired and dispirited?
   d. that they did not argue with him for very long?
2. When Obierika repeated his answer 'He is not here',
   a. he showed that he was a very simple man.
   b. he was being stubborn.
   c. he still had not understood the Commissioner's question.
   d. he meant more than the Commissioner could understand at that moment.
3. The Commissioner did not understand what Obierika meant when he said, 'Perhaps your men will help us.' What did Obierika's words mean?
   a. Nothing; he was a man who loved superfluous words.
   b. That he was siding with the Commissioner against Okonkwo.
   c. That Okonkwo, having killed himself, could not be buried by his clansmen.
   d. That he did not think the Commissioner's men would be likely to help them.
4. What is suggested by the Commissioner's warning and his men's carrying their firearms at the ready?
   a. That the Commissioner was tactless and stupid.
   b. That Obierika and his men were really dangerous.
   c. That the Commissioner was well aware of his dangerous situation.
   d. That Obierika and his men might lead him among dangerous monkeys.

5. 'The District Commissioner changed instantaneously.' This was because
   a. he made way for a student of primitive customs who had just arrived.
   b. another District Commissioner took his place.
   c. he was interested in native customs as well as in doing his duty efficiently.
   d. Obierika had said that the strangers might be a long time coming and he did not want the body to remain hanging on the tree.
6. Obierika 'spoke ferociously' to the District Commissioner because
   a. the District Commissioner was a ferocious man himself.
   b. Obierika was a ferocious man and usually spoke like that.
   c. he was angry with Okonkwo for committing suicide.
   d. he believed that the District Commissioner was responsible for Okonkwo's death.
7. The writer says that the messenger told Obierika to shut up 'quite unnecessarily'. Does he say 'quite unnecessarily' because
   a. he thought that the messenger was being rather rude?
   b. Obierika was so upset that he obviously could not say anything else?
   c. Obierika obviously did not want to say anything else?
   d. The District Commissioner would already have made Obierika keep quiet?
8. What is the great difference between the attitudes of the Commissioner and Obierika to the death of Okonkwo?
   a. Obierika is sad and angry at this terrible end to the life of a great man, whereas the DC is interested in his death and burial as an example of native customs.
   b. The DC blamed Obierika for his death but Obierika blamed the DC.
   c. The DC wanted to use him as material for the book he was writing but Obierika did not want the secrets of the tribe revealed in this way.
   d. Obierika wanted, when Okonkwo was buried, to make sacrifices to cleanse the desecrated land but the DC ordered that the body should be taken to the court.
9. 'In the many years in which he had toiled to bring civilisation to different parts of Africa he had learnt a number of things.'
   a. This sentence is intended as praise for the ability and ideals of the DC.
   b. This means that in spite of the problem of Okonkwo's death the DC was right to try to bring civilisation to Africa.
   c. This sentence and the following one condemn the DC for his spiritual pride and blindness and his lack of human feeling.
   d. This sentence shows how hard the work of a DC is and that he must always be learning new things.
10. 'The story of this man who had killed a messenger and hanged himself would make interesting reading.'
   a. This sentence shows that the DC really understood the tragedy of Okonkwo's death and meant to write about it.
   b. By summarising the whole story of Okonkwo so briefly the DC shows his quick mind and grasp of essentials.

c. There is a failure of understanding shown in reducing a tragic death to 'interesting reading'.

d. The DC thinks of 'this man' instead of using the name Okonkwo because Okonkwo's death is typical of that of the common man in Africa.

11. The whole passage suggests

a. that the Government ruled firmly and as sympathetically as possible.

b. that Okonkwo had been evil and that once the land had been cleansed by sacrifice, life might once again be peaceful and happy.

c. that although such an episode was interesting it was only worth a paragraph in a book about the whole area.

d. that there had been a terrible failure of human sympathy and that the country would never be happy while it was ruled by men who did not understand the people.

12. The author means the title of the DC's book to show

a. how learned he is and what a lot he knows about the peoples of the Lower Niger.

b. how little he understood of the effect of the coming of the white man to Nigeria.

c. how genuinely he believes in the bringing of peace, order and civilisation to Africa.

d. how interested he is in the customs and behaviour of the natives.

Now answer these questions in your own words.

1. 'Perhaps your men can help us bring him down and bury him,' said Obierika.

'Take down the body' the Commissioner ordered his chief messenger, 'and bring it and all these people to the court.'

What is suggested about the speakers by the different ways in which they refer to the dead man?

2. '. . . and now he will be buried *like a dog*.'

What do the words in *italics* suggest? What phrase above do they contrast with?

3. '. . . if they played any monkey tricks they would be shot.'

What would be lost if the word 'monkey' had been left out?

4. 'As he walked back to the court he thought about that book. Every day brought him some new material.'

What new material had this day brought? What does the writer mean us to feel about the DC's thoughts?

5. 'almost write a whole chapter'. . . .

'a reasonable paragraph at any rate.'

'cutting out details'.

What do the DC's thoughts reveal about his character?

IV 'I NEVER FORGET A FACE'

Specimen of material aimed at increasing reading speed. The quotation is from Patterns and Skills, *Book 1.*[1]

1. Two pupils read, one at 100 words a minute, the other at 200 words a minute. Which do you think remembers better and understands better? Surprisingly, the faster reader will also be the better. You can therefore increase your reading speed without being afraid of losing in understanding.

2. You can probably double your reading speed this term, and it would be a very good thing to do because it will speed up all your work in all your subjects for the rest of your life. It will be a great help in your work too. Indeed it is so important that many American business men, who neglected to acquire this skill at school, now pay experts large sums of money to be taught to read quickly. You, however, can learn it free, and you can teach yourself.

3. First you must find out how fast you can read now and still understand and remember most of what you are reading. This I will show you how to do in a moment. Then for a term you must try, every time you read anything, to read it as fast as you can. Especially try to read your library book quickly. At intervals we will see what progress you have made.

4. To find your reading speed you have two things to do. Read the passage headed 'Reading Speed and Comprehension Test' and then answer questions 1 to 10 without looking at the passage again. You need to know exactly in minutes and seconds how long it takes you to read the passage. How long it takes to answer the questions does not matter.

5. If you are doing the test all together as a class the teacher will say, 'Begin.' You will read. The teacher after four minutes will write '4' on the blackboard. Every ten seconds, he will add the seconds '4.10', cleaning the old number off every time, then '4.20' and so on. You will take no notice until you have finished. Then you look up and see on the blackboard, for example, '12.40'. This you write down. It is the time it has taken you to read the passage.

6. If you are doing it with a friend, get him to write down the time when you start and when you finish in minutes and seconds.

7. Go straight on to the questions. When you have finished these, first work out your reading speed. (The passage contains 1,602 words.) Then mark your answers to the questions. On the inside cover of an exercise book, make a table (see page 117) and fill in your scores for the first week. You will need nine lines.

8. You need not score more than 7 out of 10 for comprehension. If you do, read faster still.

[1] Longman, 1965.

9. If you meet a strange word, don't stop. Read right on. Often the meaning will be made clear by the rest of the passage, but it probably won't matter that you don't know what it means.

My Reading Speed and Comprehension

	Words per minute	Comprehension out of 10
Week 1 Test 1		
Week 2 Test 2		
etc.		

READING SPEED AND COMPREHENSION TEST I

I'll tell you a strange thing about me – I never forget a face. The only trouble is that usually I'm quite unable to tell you the name of the person. I know what you're going to say – you suffer from the same thing yourself. Lots of people do, to some extent, more people than not, perhaps. But I'm not like that. When I say I never forget a face, I mean it. I can pass a fellow in the street one day and recognise him again months after, though we've never spoken to each other.

My wife says sometimes that I ought to be a reporter for the newspapers and wait about at first nights at cinemas, looking for all the famous people who go to see the films. But, as I tell her, I should not be able to do very well at that. I should see the famous man or woman, but I should not be able to say which one it was. That's my trouble, as I say – names.

Of course, this trouble with names has put me in difficulties from time to time. But, with a little skill one can usually get out of the difficulty in one way or another. In my work, moving round the City doing bits of business, I have to be very clever not to let a man see that I can't remember whether his name is Smith or Moses. I've annoyed people in that way and lost good business more than once. But on the whole, I think I gain more than I lose by this strange memory of mine.

Quite often I've gone up to a man who didn't know me from Adam. I've said, 'I think we've met before,' and I've been able to give him some idea of where it was. I can always connect a face with a place, you see. Well, as I was saying, I can go up to this fellow and remind him of a big dinner or football match or whatever it is that his face reminds me of, and probably within five minutes we're talking about business. I can usually find out his name later on. My memory for faces helps me a lot in business.

5

You can guess that there's not a man, woman or child here in Bardfield that I don't know by sight. I've lived in Bardfield ever since the war. I like the place; although it's only forty minutes from London, there's a lot of country here. The village is almost a mile from the station, and that's rather troublesome. But quite a pleasant crowd of men travel up and down to the City most days, and I needn't tell you that I don't know the names of half of them, though we speak to each other cheerfully enough. My wife complains that I don't know the names of our neighbours in the next house, and that's true.

Well, on this particular evening I'd been kept a bit late at the office, and it was difficult to get to the station in time to catch the train. There was quite a crowd in the train at first, but they gradually got out; and by the time we reached Ellingham – that's two stations before mine – there were only two of us left in the carriage. The other fellow wasn't one of the regular travellers, but I knew he was a Bardfield man. I knew it as soon as I saw him, of course. I'd smiled at him when I saw him getting into the carriage in London, and he had smiled back but that didn't tell me his name.

The annoying thing was that I couldn't place the fellow, if you understand what I mean. His face told me clearly that he was connected with Bardfield, but that was all it told me. I could not think where in Bardfield I had seen it. I guessed he must be one of those fellows who've come to live lately in the small houses by the bus-stop, but I couldn't be sure. Some of us who've lived in the place a long time are rather proud towards newcomers, but that's not my way – never has been. I never know where the next bit of business is going to come from, and it may come from one of them. I can't afford to neglect chances.

So when the two of us found ourselves alone in the carriage, with room to stretch our legs and be a bit comfortable, I started to talk, just as if we were old friends. But I can't say that I got much information out of him. He spoke well, with a quiet friendly manner, but he told me very little. I can generally find out what a man's work is in ten and a half minutes – that's the time it takes from Ellingham to Bardfield by train – but I failed this time. He looked a bit tired, I remember, as if he'd been working too hard lately, and I thought maybe that made him unwilling to talk much.

'Do you generally travel down on this train?' I asked him. That's usually a safe opening to a conversation, because either they do travel or they don't, and nine times out of ten they'll tell you why, and what hours they work, and what their work is. It's only human nature. But he just smiled and shook his head and said, 'Not generally,' which wasn't much help.

Of course, I went on to talk about the train services in general, comparing this train with that, but still he said nothing. He just agreed with all I said, but he didn't seem to have any opinions of his own. I told him I sometimes went up to the City by road, but that didn't make him talk either. I didn't think it would, because you don't expect a fellow who lives in a cheap house to own a car.

Well, to cut a long story short, I had to give up. I'd told him a lot about myself, of course, so as to make things pleasant. I'd even boasted a little about a rather nice bit of business I'd done that morning. I've always found that there's nothing as good as boasting to start a fellow talking. It makes him want to boast too. He seemed interested in a quiet sort of way, but it was no good. So, as I say, I gave it up and started to read my paper. And the next time I looked at him, he'd put his head back and gone off to sleep!

We were just running into the station, then and though the train stopped rather suddenly, it didn't seem to wake him. Well, I'm a kind-hearted fellow and I wasn't going to let a Bardfield man be carried on all the way to the next stop if I could help it. So I touched him sharply on the knee.

'Wake up, old fellow! We're there!' I said.

He awoke at once and smiled at me.

'Oh, so we are!' he said, and got out after me.

You know what the weather was like just then. When we came out of the station together it was quite dark and raining heavily. There was a wind blowing strong enough to knock you over, and it was bitterly cold.

Well, what would you have done? The same as I did, I turned round and said to him:

'Listen. There isn't a bus for a quarter of an hour. I've got my car in the station-yard, and if you're in one of those small houses I can take you there. It's on my way.'

'Thanks very much,' he said, and we walked through the water to where my old car was standing and off we went.

'This is very kind of you,' he said as we started, and that was the last thing he said until we were half-way across the open country. Then he suddenly turned round and said, 'You can let me get out here.'

'What, here?' I asked him. It seemed mad because there wasn't a house within five hundred yards and, as I say, it was raining and blowing like the end of the world. But I slowed down, as anyone would.

The next thing that happened was that something hit me terribly hard on the back of the head. I fell forwards and then everything went black. I can half-remember being pulled out of the car, and when I came to myself again I was lying in the ditch with the rain pouring down on me, with a bad headache, no car in sight and my pockets – as I found out later – empty.

I pulled myself up at last and somehow managed to walk into Bardfield. I went straight to the police-station, of course. It's the first building you reach if you come that way. And there I reported that someone had stolen my car, a new umbrella, a gold watch and a hundred and fifty-two pounds ten shillings in notes.

Of course, as soon as I got there I remembered who the man was. His picture was on the wall outside. I'd seen it every day for a week. That's why his face reminded me of Bardfield. Under the picture were some words: 'Wanted for Robbery with Violence and Attempted Murder. John —' Oh dear, I've forgotten the name again. I just can't keep names in my head. But that's the man. I tell you – I never forget a face.

COMPREHENSION QUESTIONS

Choose the best answer from the four choices given and show your choice by writing on a piece of paper, for example 1*a*, 2*b*, 3*c*, etc.

1. What can the man who is telling the story always remember?
   a. Names but not faces
   b. Faces but not names
   c. Names and faces
   d. Names and places
2. He lives in Bardfield. Where is Bardfield?
   a. In England
   b. In America
   c. In East Africa
   d. In West Africa
3. Which of these is true of the man who is telling the story?
   a. He knows hardly anybody in Bardfield.
   b. He knows the names of all his neighbours.
   c. He does not remember the faces of his neighbours in the next house.
   d. He knows the face but not the name of everybody in Bardfield.
4. Which is true?
   a. He cannot connect names and places.
   b. He cannot connect names and faces.
   c. He can generally remember where he has seen people before.
   d. His memory for faces is no help to him in business.
5. What happened when he was left alone in the railway carriage with the stranger?
   a. He tried to find out who the stranger was and what his work was but did not succeed.
   b. They did not speak to each other.
   c. He found out who the stranger was.
   d. The stranger talked freely to him about his business.
6. What happened when the train stopped at Bardfield?
   a. He left the stranger asleep in the train.
   b. He woke the stranger up because he thought he was a Bardfield man.
   c. The train stopped so suddenly it woke the stranger up.
   d. The stranger was carried on to the next stop because he was asleep.
7. Why did he offer the stranger a lift?
   a. Because there was no bus service.
   b. Because he hoped to do some business with him.
   c. Because he had woken him up.
   d. To save him from waiting for the bus on a cold, wet, windy night.
8. Where did the stranger ask him to stop?
   a. At the police-station
   b. A long way from any houses
   c. In the middle of Bardfield
   d. In a dark wood

9. What happened after he slowed the car down?
   a. The stranger hit him on the head and, before he had recovered, stole his money and his watch and drove off in his car.
   b. The stranger stole his umbrella and ran away in the darkness. Meanwhile a thief came and knocked him out and stole his money.
   c. There was an accident to the car and while he was unconscious some thieves stole his watch, money, umbrella and motor-car.
   d. He was unconscious and therefore we do not know what happened.
10. Who was the stranger?
   a. We do not know who he was.
   b. Somebody who lived in Bardfield.
   c. The story-teller's neighbour in the next house.
   d. A dangerous criminal wanted by the police.

V 'RICHARD CHURCH'S NEW GLASSES'

Intensive-reading material for the free-reading stage.

Read the passage carefully and then answer the questions that follow.

I was therefore half prepared for the surprise which shook me a week later when, on the Saturday evening, we went again to the shop on Lavender Hill, and the chemist produced the bespoken pair of steel-rimmed spectacles through which I was invited to read the card. I read it, from top to bottom! I turned, and looked in triumph at Mother, but what I saw was Mother intensified. I saw the pupils of her eyes, the tiny feathers in her boa necklet; I saw the hairs in father's moustache, and on the back of his hand. Jack's cap might have been made of metal, so hard and clear did it shine on his close-cropped head, above his bony face and huge nose. I saw *his* eyes too, round, inquiring, fierce with a hunger of observation. He was studying me with a gimlet sharpness such as I had never before been able to perceive.

Then we walked out of the shop, and I stepped on to the pavement, which came up and hit me, so that I had to grasp the nearest support – Father's coat. 'Take care, now, take care!' he said indulgently (though he disapproved of all these concessions to physical weakness). 'And mind you don't break them!'

I walked still with some uncertainty, carefully placing my feet and feeling their impact on the pavement whose surface I could see sparkling like quartz in the lamplight.

The lamplight! I looked in wonder at the diminishing crystals of gas-flame strung down the hill. Clapham was hung with necklaces of light, and the horses pulling the glittering omnibuses struck the granite road with hooves of iron and ebony. I could see the skeletons inside the flesh and blood of the Saturday-night shoppers. The garments they wore were made of separate threads. In this new world, sound as well as sight was changed. It took on hardness and definition, forcing itself upon my hearing, so that I was besieged simultaneously through the eye and through the ear.

How willingly I surrendered! I went out to meet this blazing and trumpeting invasion. I trembled with excitement, and had to cling to Mother's arm to prevent myself being carried away in the flood as the pavements pushed at me, and people loomed up with their teeth like tusks, their lips luscious, their eyes bolting out of their heads, bearing down on me as they threw out spears of conversation that whizzed loudly past my ears and bewildered my wits.

'Is it any different?' asked Jack, in his proprietary voice. He was never satisfied until he had collected all possible information on everything which life brought to his notice.

'It makes things clearer,' I replied, knowing that I had no hope of telling him what was happening to me. I was only half aware of it myself, for this urgent demand upon my attention by the multitudinous world around me was the beginning of a joyous imposition to which I am still responding today, breathless and enraptured, though the twilight of the senses begins to settle.

From *Over the Bridge* by Richard Church

Now try to answer these questions, looking back when you need to.

1. How many people went to the chemist's shop? How are they related to each other? In one case you have to make a guess.
2. What was the purpose of the visit to the chemist's shop? Infer the meaning of *bespoken*. This is an old-fashioned word. What should we say now instead of 'The spectacles have been bespoken'?
3. Infer also on what part of the body a boa necklet was worn and what it was made of.
4. 'I read it, from top to bottom!' What is suggested by the exclamation mark? In what way was the bottom of the card different from the top? (Ask somebody who wears glasses.)
5. What details are mentioned in the first paragraph which help us to perceive the effect of the new glasses?
6. What would be the effect of changing

   the surprise which shook me a week later

   to

   the surprise I felt a week later ?

   In what way is the word *shook* particularly effective?
7. What is meant by 'might have been made of metal'? Was it perhaps made of metal? What words later carry on the idea of metal?
8. What is a gimlet? What is compared to a gimlet? What is the force of the comparison?
9. Why does the writer say:

   such as I had never before been able to perceive

   instead of

   such as I had never seen before ?
10. Explain: 'the pavement, which cameup and hit me'.

11. What does *them* refer to in:

    And mind you don't break them!

    Is it true that pronouns refer to the nearest noun in the same number?
12. Why did he place his feet carefully?
13. Is it true that *whose* refers only to people?
14. What is suggested by the exclamation: 'The lamplight!'?
15. What comparison is made by the word *crystals* and the word *strung*? How are these carried on in the next sentence?
16. What does he suggest in: 'I could see the skeletons inside the flesh and blood of the Saturday night shoppers'?
17. What happened to his sight? In what way was his hearing affected?
18. What comparison is made by the word *besieged*? What words in the next paragraph carry it on?
19. What does *blazing* remind us of? What about *trumpeting*?
20. Explain both parts of 'joyous imposition'.
21. From the passage do you place Jack as younger or older than Richard Church?
22. About how old was Richard Church when he wrote this passage?
23. About how old was he when he got this pair of spectacles?
24. If you wanted exact answers to the last three questions, where could you find them?
25. Make as exact statements as you can about the time and place of the events in the passage.
26. What do you know from the passage about Lavender Hill and Clapham?
27. Can you infer anything about the social status or wealth of the Churches at that time?
28. Can you infer anything about the time of the year?
29. A student of mine once said he did not think this passage was well written because it was full of exaggeration. What is your opinion?

VI CRITICISM

This quotation comes from a textbook of which we do not approve as much as we did when it was first published in 1948.

TOWARDS STANDARDS OF GOOD AND BAD IN WRITING

The aim of this part of the book is to help you to become more critical. This does not mean better able to find fault with things; it means better able to see and like what is good, and less likely to admire what is bad. The examination of what other people have written will help you to examine what you yourself write, and to become self-critical.

UNDERSTANDING THE PLAIN SENSE

None of us can criticise what we don't understand, and the critic's first duty therefore is to get out the plain sense. If after all his efforts he cannot manage this, he can do no more than say so. But full understanding includes much more than just plain sense.

FEELING

Understanding is not a simple thing. Words often tell us about the writer's feelings as well as about the things he wants to talk about. For example, suppose that Mr Jenkins has dismissed his servant:

> *Mrs Jones:* Mr Jenkins lost his temper and sacked his servant. He wouldn't even take him back when he begged to be allowed to return. He's a thoroughly obstinate man.
>
> *Mrs Robinson:* Mr Jenkins' servant has got himself dismissed, and Jenkins has refused to take him back. The fellow won't get away with it this time. Jenkins is a very determined man.

Both speakers tell us the same facts, but they tell us much more than the facts; they tell us also about their own sympathies. One feels for the servant, the other for the master.

Another example:

> In the back of the car he had a large dog.
>
> In the back of the car he had a great dog.

'Large' and 'great' both tell us that the dog was above the average size, but 'great' also tells us that the speaker did not approve of the dog's presence. For proper understanding it is necessary to feel as well as know the meanings of words.

TONE

Then, too, written words can suggest many, if not all, of the tones of voice in which they would be spoken.

1. 'Get out!'
2. 'Go away!'
3. 'Well, that's about all for this morning, isn't it?'
4. 'It was kind of you to call. Do come again one day when I'm not quite so busy and we'll have a long talk.'

All these have the same plain sense: 'I want you to go.' The difference is in the tone of voice that is used, and the tone of voice shows the way the speaker treats the listener.

INTENTION

Another thing we need to grasp, before we can fully understand anything written, is what the writer intends. For example, I open *Picture Post* and read 'Healthy dogs make good companions.' This is perhaps true. I understand all the words, but I have not really grasped it until I read on a little further and see, 'Bob Martin's Condition Powder Tablets keep dogs fit.' Then I see that it is an advertisement, and the writer wishes to persuade me to buy the goods he has to sell. Understanding is complete. It is not only in advertisements that we have to look out for the writer's purpose.

AUDIENCE

One last thing always worth looking for is whether the writing is meant for any special audience. A letter that begins 'Dear Boys and Girls' is plainly not to be understood as if it were addressed to greybeards. It would also be unreasonable to complain that a scholarly book on philosophy has too many hard words. It is addressed to scholars who understand those words.

What is the writer trying to do?

When our understanding of the passage is complete, we are ready to attempt to answer this question. It is the first question that all criticism asks. The answer to it must be clear, exact and detailed. It may include any one of the very large number of uses there are for language. For example:

to tell the story of so and so;
to describe a thing, person, scene, or somebody's feelings, etc.;
to give such and such information;
to record the results of experiment, observation, discussion, etc.;
to record impressions of a place, person, new experience, etc.;
to persuade somebody to do or believe something;
to express some new idea, feeling, attitude of mind, etc.;
to explain the reasons for something;
to prove something;
to give instructions;
to make fun of something or somebody;
to abuse something or somebody;

and so on. You will be able to think of many other uses for yourself.

Has the writer succeeded in what he set out to do? If so, by what means? If not, why has he failed?

To answer this question is the second half of the critic's duty. Under it we shall consider the writer's choice and arrangement of details and incidents, his choice of words, the pattern of his sentences, everything connected with the way he says things, including any figures of speech. We shall consider how clearly and closely he makes us see and feel things, or how he arranges his facts and how easy it is to follow his argument. We shall see whether his generalisations are supported by evidence, or whether he appears to be dictating what the reader should believe. We shall look also at the kind of feeling shown in the passage, and at the way the author treats his readers. We shall look at the shape of the passage, to see if it seems right, and not untidy or ill-balanced or upside down. If it is a story (or a poem) we shall ask that reading it should be an experience worth having; if it is a description, that it should be something worth seeing.

We shall, of course, remember that experiences worth having are not to be gained by flicking our eyes once down a page, and we shall be prepared to work at a passage to get all we can out of it. Good writing demands good reading. What the writer has created, the reader, with the help of nothing but black marks on white paper, must build up again for himself in his own mind.

AN EXAMPLE OF A PASSAGE AND A CRITICISM OF IT

In the following pages we shall be faced with various passages and asked to study and criticise them. Let us take an example (it is rather a difficult one) and work through it together to get an idea of the way to set about the job.

Study the following passage and write a criticism of it. It is the opening of a novel written by a woman:

> Sir Walter Elliot, Kellynch Hall, in Somersetshire, was a man who, for his own amusement, never took up any book but the Baronetage: there he found occupation for an idle hour and consolation in a distressed one; there his faculties were aroused into admiration and respect, by contemplating the limited remnant of the earliest patents; there any unwelcome sensations, arising from domestic affairs, changed naturally into pity and contempt as he turned over the almost endless creations of the last century; and there, if every other leaf were powerless, he could read his own history with an interest which never failed. This was the page at which the favourite volume always opened:
>
> Elliot of Kellynch Hall
>
> 'Walter Elliot, born March 1, 1760, married July 15, 1784, Elizabeth, daughter of James Stevenson, Esq. of South Park, in the county of Gloucester; by which lady (who died 1800) he had issue, Elizabeth, born June 1, 1785; Anne, born August 9, 1787; a still-born son, November 5, 1789; Mary, born November 20, 1791.'
>
> Precisely such had the paragraph originally stood from the printer's hands; but Sir Walter had improved it by adding, for the information of himself and his family, these words, after the date of Mary's birth – 'Married, December 16, 1810, Charles, son and heir of Charles Musgrove Esq. of Uppercross, in the county of Somerset,' and by inserting most accurately the day of the month on which he had lost his wife.
>
> Then followed the history and rise of the ancient and respectable family in the usual terms; how it had been first settled in Cheshire, how mentioned in Dugdale, serving the office of high sheriff, representing a borough in three successive parliaments, exertions of loyalty, and dignity of baronet, in the first year of Charles II, with all the Marys and Elizabeths they had married; forming altogether two handsome duodecimo pages, and concluding with the arms and motto – 'Principal seat, Kellynch Hall, in the county of Somerset,' and Sir Walter's handwriting again in this finale –
>
> 'Heir presumptive, William Walter Elliot, Esq., great grandson of the second Sir Walter.'
>
> Vanity was the beginning and end of Sir Walter Elliot's character: vanity of person and of situation. He had been remarkably handsome in his youth, and at fifty-four was still a very fine man. Few women could think more of their personal appearance than he did, nor could the valet of any new-made lord be more delighted with the place he held in society. He considered the blessing of beauty as inferior only to the blessing of a baronetcy;

and the Sir Walter Elliot, who united these gifts, was the constant object of his warmest respect and devotion.

First question: What is the writer trying to do?

Well, it's a story. She's trying to write a story. True, but will that answer do? It's not precise enough.

She is trying to write a story about Sir Walter Elliot.

That's better but it's only part of a story. Try again.

She has set out to interest us in Sir Walter Elliot and to make Sir Walter live for us.

Perhaps we could add once more thing. We do get a very strong impression of the kind of man Sir Walter is, and we ought to mention that.

She has set out to interest us in Sir Walter Elliot and to make Sir Walter live for us in all his vanity of personal appearance and family position.

Second Question: Has she succeeded? If so, how?

1 It seems very real. How is this effect of reality obtained? One thing that helps it is the choice of detail. All the dates and names and months, phrases like 'son and heir of Charles Musgrove' and the mention of the houses in which the people live, all these details about Sir Walter's family history help in the same direction, and even the size of the pages occupied by the family history is most exactly specified.

2 There's a great deal of information in a very small space. When we have read the whole passage we know a great deal about Sir Walter, e.g.

his address and rank;
a good deal about his character;
he has some domestic troubles;
he was born in 1760;
his wife is dead;
he has an unmarried daughter aged 29, Elizabeth;
another unmarried daughter, Anne, aged 27;
he has no son;
his youngest daughter, Mary, is married to Charles Musgrove, of Uppercross;
his family is old and respectable;
his heir is a distant cousin named William Walter Elliot;
he is 54 years old (and the story therefore happens in 1814, which gives us the age of his daughters);
'Vanity was the beginning and end of his character.'

3 Although we have so many facts, we do not get the impression of a catalogue of facts. This is because all the facts are arranged so that each one shows us the character of Sir Walter. Even the dull details of his daughters' ages are made to show us the nature of the man since we learn that they, and the rest of his family history are his favourite reading. The writer is able to do this because she has imagined Sir Walter so clearly herself. It is his reality to her that enables her to make him real to us, by making every fact relate to him.

We notice also that we are shown the man in action reading his favourite page of his favourite book with his abilities at full stretch, and we are allowed to form our own opinion of him before we are told that 'vanity was the beginning and end of his character.' The generalisation grows out of what went before.

4 As well as a lot of details about his family, we get a very full impression of Sir Walter's character, which starts in the very first sentence: 'a man, who, for his own amusement, never took up any book but the Baronetage'. He reads nothing worth while. His interests are so small-minded that he can find 'occupation' in reading the Baronetage. Worse than that – 'his faculties are roused into admiration and respect' by reading over a list of noble names. Could littleness of mind be more fully expressed? Apparently it can for 'if every other leaf were powerless, he could read his own history with an interest which never failed.' How often he had read it may be seen from the way the book fell open at that page. There is Sir Walter for us, self-centred, trifling and vain and his character is summed up for us in the last paragraph.

5 The writer does not seem to be angry or indignant at his weakness and silliness. She seems to be amused at it, and to be inviting the reader to share the joke. This attitude is built up by her choice of words. She says 'unwelcome sensations' instead of 'trouble'. If we hear of a man in trouble, our civilised instinct is to sympathise. But the author does not intend that we should sympathise with Sir Walter, so he has 'unwelcome sensations' and we may smile if we like. The same process of avoiding too strong feelings is at work in all the language: 'occupation' not 'work', 'consolation' not 'comfort'. We are not to sympathise, but nor are we to hate his folly. A communist might very well refer to a Sir Walter in very emotional terms as a useless parasite, a thief eating the bread earned by other men's work, mean and selfish. The author, by her language, persuades us to take him much less seriously. He himself was 'the constant object of his warmest respect and devotion'.

This balanced unemotional attitude is reflected in the balanced sentences like the first and the last. We are led to stand away from the creature, to examine it, to see how its little mind works, and to be amused.

Let us now look back over our criticism and compare it with the list of points we were told to consider when answering the question 'Has the writer been successful?'

Choice and arrangement of details. We have commented on the number of details, the kind and the fact that all are to the point.

Choice of words and pattern of sentences. We thought about these and said they gave us our attitude to Sir Walter and the author's attitude to us.

Figures of Speech. There was nothing to say about this, unless we had mentioned that Sir Walter is compared to a woman and the valet of a new-made lord.

How clearly and closely she makes us see and feel. We mentioned things related to this in almost every paragraph.

The shape of the passage. Discussed in paragraph 3, together with 'generalisations supported by evidence'.

How easy it is to follow the argument. The passage is not an argument so this does not exactly apply, though something very similar is discussed under the shape of the passage.

How the author treats her readers and with what kind of feeling the passage is written. We said the feeling was comic and the reader was invited to share the joke.

An experience worth having. We did not discuss this because this is only part of a book, part of an experience. But we want to go on reading, which looks as if it must be worth while. We did not even answer the question whether it was a successful piece of writing in so many words, but I think our opinion is fairly plain.

The other points do not seem to apply, and on the whole we seem to have covered the ground, though of course we have not said by any means everything that could be said.

One other thing is important. We had to work quite hard at the passage in order to understand it fully and criticise it sensibly. We referred all our remarks to some words of the passage. It would have been no use writing a string of general remarks: 'wonderful skill of the writer', 'brilliant abilities', 'excellent character drawing', etc. etc. All criticism requires the support of quotation or reference to the words of the passage.

4

WRITING

1 Mistakes

The pupil does not learn from his mistakes. If he did, the more mistakes he made, the more he would learn. Common experience, however, proves that the pupil who makes the most mistakes is the one who has learnt and will learn least. In theory no mistake should ever appear in writing, though it must be admitted that this ideal is unattainable in practice.

The teachers of first-year secondary classes all over the world complain that their pupils 'cannot put three words together', 'cannot write the simplest sentence', 'don't know anything when they first arrive'. The conscientious teacher spends hours marking all the errors. The pupil, less grateful perhaps than one might wish, is hurt and discouraged. He has done his best with an impossibly difficult task – no pupil wants to write badly – and his reward is a book flaming with red ink and the comment 'Careless'. The teacher trained in the wisdom of educational psychology would not, of course, be so gauche. He writes 'Be more careful', which is just as unhelpful.

But the teacher is right too. He must be concerned about the errors, every one of which is doing harm, helping to confirm a bad habit. His mistake, fostered by the kind of inspector who picks up the odd exercise book and says ever so kindly, 'It *is* difficult to spot all the mistakes, isn't it?' is to think that the only thing to do with an error is to correct it. This is the counsel of despair. The counsel of perfection says, 'Prevent or at least reduce the errors by adjusting the level of difficulty to the capabilities of the class'. The teacher who finds out what kinds of written work have been done successfully in previous schools will often be pleasantly surprised to find abilities greater than he expected.

2 Adjusting the level of difficulty

It is a common fallacy to imagine that the only or best way of grading written work is by subject matter. 'When they're little boys, they ought to write about simple subjects, like "My Cat" but when they come to the secondary school, we give them subjects that they have to think about, like "My Ambition".' There is little reason to suppose that it is any easier to write about cats than ambitions. Given a hundred titles to grade in order of difficulty, no group of teachers or pupils would come up with any useful approximation to similar answers. There *is* a scale of difficulty in subject matter but it is very coarse compared with the fine gradations that can be obtained by varying the amount and kind of help provided. The same subject can be presented so that what the pupils write is controlled so rigidly that every answer is identical or so that every pupil is completely free to do what he likes with it. In between these extremes there is a whole range of possibilities and the art of composition teaching is to select the right point on the scale to start from and to progress from it at the right pace by gradually removing the supports so that an increasing amount of responsibility rests on the pupil and eventually he can do the job without assistance.

3 Main stages of a graded course

One cannot think sensibly about a year's work or even four years' work in writing English without seeing it as part of a continuous progression that starts in the first month or so of the learner's contact with English and goes on after he has left school.

It is difficult to set out this process clearly because all divisions falsify. Perhaps we may think in terms of five stages and of various lines of development running through them. We must remember that the stages overlap and the lines merge and blur.

In Stage One, which is normally completed long before the secondary school, successful written work is practically identical in all the exercise books. Its purpose is to confirm and deepen the impression made by the oral work and to enable the pupil to master the elementary mechanics of written work: handwriting, spelling, capitalisation, punctuation, word order and word division, all within the narrow range of vocabulary and structure he has mastered orally.

In Stage Two, which again is normally completed before the secondary school, the sentence structure is normally controlled but there is some freedom of choice at the lexical level. Using a substitution table to make similar sentences is work of this kind, and may still be needed for remedial purposes in the secondary school. Also within Stage Two we include retelling a story if the original has been repeated so frequently in class that the pupils are likely to recall it almost verbatim.

In Stage Three some help or guidance is provided with sentence structure, at least with constructions likely to cause difficulty but most of the sentences have to be framed by the pupils. If we set the same subject two years running and do some work designed to anticipate and prevent errors previously noted before the second class tackle the subject, we are working within stage three. Guidance about arrangement, form and technical problems above the sentence rank is normally provided at this stage.

In Stage Four sentence structure and problems of arrangement, form, etc. become the responsibility of the pupil. The only control exercised is by the situation with which we face him – the problem that we set him to solve in writing. For example, we may say 'Here are some meteorological statistics for this month in this district and here is the thirty-year average for comparison. Write a column for the local paper about the month's weather.'

In Stage Five, which we do not expect to reach before school certificate is taken, the student becomes an independent operator answering letters, or examination questions, writing minutes, making cases, writing his first play, short story or novel or even, if he can think of a good reason for doing so, his first essay.

4 Some lines of development within a course

Let us now return from these exalted levels to trace some possible lines of development bearing in mind that the operation of free writing is so complicated that nobody could possibly attend to every aspect at once. The learner must have enough handwriting practice to develop unconscious fluency before he can compose original sentences, he must have enough reading and writing practice with the simpler patterns of the language for them to become mechanical and free his attention for other things, and so on. If he has too many things to attend to, he will make mistakes. Conversely, if he makes mistakes, he has too many things to attend to.

The skilful teacher of beginners gives them the thrill of successful original composition very early in the course. He makes it possible for them to make up in their heads a sentence they have never heard before. Provided he remembers to keep one or two 'situations' in reserve, this is very easy to arrange. Let us suppose he has been teaching the prepositions, demonstrating with the models and objects named in the following table:

The	leaf stone motor-car stick pot match	is	in on near under	the	stone motor-car stick pot match chair

The pupils already know from previous lessons: *door*, *basket*, *tin*. When pupils are ready to do so, they will naturally be asked to repeat sentences the teacher has said, applying them to the changing situations.

The leaf is on the stone.
The stick is in the pot.
The motor-car is near the stone.
The stone is under the motor-car.

This is quite fun but the real excitement comes when the teacher without saying the names of the objects puts the tin in the basket or the toy motor-car on the top of the door. This is the very beginning of composition and pupils who are ready to do so can write the sentence that forms in their heads. This is the starting point of original written composition. Note that the sentence forms in English; it has no translation links. It is the first successful operation of the new machinery being built into the learner's mind.

This technique remains useful for a long time. It can be developed in the direction of increasing length and difficulty. It is easy to think of a way of provoking the class to write:

If you hadn't blown the match out, it would have burnt your fingers.

It can also be developed in the direction of mixed pattern responses. A class has made a great deal of progress when most of its members can reproduce the following questions after the teacher has flashed them for three seconds on a baby blackboard and supply the answers for themselves. The teacher gives no help. He says nothing except 'Write question No. 1', 'Write the answer', etc. He starts by privately showing an instruction to, say, two pupils. *Sit under the table. Stand in the waste-paper basket.* He then flashes the questions and pupils write as follows:

1. Who is sitting under the table?
   Tom is.
2. What is Joe doing?
   He is standing in the waste-paper basket.
3. Are Tom and Joe in front of the class?
   Yes, they are.
4. Where is Tom?
   He is under the table.
5. Is there an elephant in the waste-paper basket?
   No, there is not.

This leads straight into answering questions in writing about stories in the class reader for the sake of practising the use of various tense forms and structures and then on to answering comprehension questions about a text and eventually to criticism.

In a different convention, one that demands comprehensibility of the written word without reference to the questions – a point that must be made clear to pupils – questions can be used to get continuous writing about the pupil's or his family's daily life, about pictures, about events in the school or neighbourhood and so on. For example: Questions

What day was yesterday?
At what time did you get up?
What colour was the sky?
What did you do first?, etc.

Answers will vary considerably lexically and a little structurally, e.g.

Yesterday was Sunday. I got up at seven o'clock/late. The sky was blue/grey/black. I put on my clothes/dressed.

If more control is required one can set a first person passage to be rewritten with or without changes in the third. *My Day* becomes *George's Day*.

There is another line of development that begins with copying sentences from the blackboard and ends in short story writing, note-making and summarising. Let us trace the major changes in method. We have seen the first increase of pupil responsibility already. We make him remember the sentence when it is flashed and do not let him start writing until it has disappeared from sight. Copying from print is also slightly more difficult than copying from handwriting.

The length of the passage affects the difficulty too. It is also possible progressively to increase the amount rubbed out on the blackboard until what started as an exercise copying an almost complete story with only the odd word missing becomes an exercise in recalling a story with the aid of a few remaining guide words.

Dictation is another form of reproduction involving the problem of translating phonic into graphic symbols. From this one goes on to telling the story orally to be reproduced in writing. Two lines join here because a set of questions on the board may be used as a memory prop and structure guide. The number of oral retellings has a bearing on the difficulty too.

One can combine dictation and reproduction, first building the difficult structures, spelling and punctuation problems into a dictation relating one story, and then tell the pupils a factually different but linguistically similar one for them to reproduce. This becomes more difficult if they are asked to expand an outline.

Outlines can also vary in difficulty depending on what the pupil is asked or left to supply. A simple one demanding mainly adverbials might read, for example,

> (When?) Miriam's mother asked her to go (where?) and fetch some water. Miriam picked up the water pot and set off (where?). She saw her friend Mary walking (where?) in front of her and started running (how?) (why?).

This technique is applicable to stories suggested by a series of pictures.

We eventually reach the point where a bare suggestion may be given for each paragraph. 'Tell the story of how a pilot crash-landed in the desert/bush, was helped by some local people and eventually got home safely.' And then on to the mere suggestion of a theme for the whole story. A narrow escape, for example. There will, of course, be contributory lines from descriptive writing, and matters of technique such as making stories credible, using dialogue and so on, coming in long before this point is reached.

There is also another direction in which the difficulty of a story may be increased. It may be made too long to reproduce verbatim, and then the retelling involves summarising or selection.

When the stage has been reached at which expository material can be understood – not necessarily only in English lessons – the end-product may be notes instead of a consecutive summary. The teaching of note-making also requires grading, starting perhaps in the secondary school with the teacher giving all the generalisations and the pupils merely listing the examples as they are mentioned. The middle stage consists of note-taking from the teacher's carefully clued exposition. The main subject of our notes will be So-and-So. The first main point is this. There are three reasons for this: (a) so-and-so. In the final stage the university student is an independent operator.

Whatever we want to teach, we must progress by successful stages, consolidating our gains before we move on to anything more demanding. Conversely, we must continue to challenge the pupil to do more for himself. Having found a successful technique, we cannot stay with it just because it gives us comparatively mistake-free work. For every class there is an appropriate level of difficulty, one which stretches them but lies within their powers. Incidentally we can and should expect more from the best pupils than we do from the average ones.

Let us take one final example of adjusting the level of difficulty, this time based on the use of the picture on page 136. We assume that the picture has been discussed and the vocabulary of the office and its spelling made familiar. Our problem is how do we set out to get two paragraphs written about it?

Level of Difficulty 1: Easy

With a class that has serious trouble with sentence structure we shall choose a very easy method and invite them to answer questions that supply the vocabulary and sentence patterns one at a time. The class must understand that they are working within the convention of comprehensibility without reference to the questions.

For example:

Paragraph One. Answer these questions:

1. Does the picture show a badly-furnished business office or a well-furnished one? Does it show the people working in it?
2. Does the manager have his own room?
3. Is the manager's door open or shut? Whose secretary is just going in?
4. Where in the general office is the accountant sitting?
5. What is he smoking and what is he working on?
6. Where is the office-boy going to take the parcels?
7. What is the filing clerk getting out?
8. Is the stenographer behind the accountant? What is she doing?

We may treat the result as a first draft and ask pupils to look at variety of sentence structure, consider joining sentences together and experiment with putting prepositional phrases in different places.

Level of Difficulty 2: Fairly easy

Write two paragraphs about this picture of 'A Business Office'. Start by saying that the picture shows a well-furnished, modern or old-fashioned office and the people who work there. Then write a sentence each about what these people are doing: the manager, his secretary, the accountant, the stenographer, the filing clerk, the office-boy and the telephone operator.

Start a new paragraph by saying something about the furniture in general and then mention the safe, the filing cabinets, the index, the large cupboard, the accountant's desk, the typing table, the IN and OUT trays, the telephones, the calendar, the shelf and the box files, the adding machine, the fan, the clock and the reference books. Finish with a general statement about whether the office looks clean, tidy and efficient and whether the people are busy at their work.

MANAGER

In this most of the vocabulary is given and so are the general statements and the basic division into paragraphs. The particular statements, however, all have to be composed.

Again the first draft will probably need to be worked on for fluency and variety.

Level of Difficulty 3: Middling

Write the following composition

A Business Office

Para. One. First Sentence.

The picture shows the people in a modern business office.

Para. Two. First Sentence.

The furniture is modern and business-like.

In your last sentence refer to the furniture and the people.

The paragraph structure and the generalisations are given but no specific instructions about which details belong where. No order is given for the particulars.

Level of Difficulty 4: Fairly Difficult

Write two paragraphs, one describing the people and the other the furniture in this picture.

Title: *A Business Office.*

This is similar to level 3 but the pupils are left to make appropriate generalisations and although guidance is given on the content of the paragraphs there is none on their structure.

Level of Difficulty 5: Difficult

Describe this picture.

No guidance given at all.

Here are at least five possible ways of using the same material and teachers will no doubt be able to think of others even more finely graded. Other pictures, simpler or more complicated, would bring in new sets of levels and so would description from life or memory.

We do not in fact approve very heartily of some of these ways of dealing with this picture because they say, in effect, 'Do this because I tell you to.' It is better to supply a reason for writing anything at secondary level. If the writing has a known purpose its efficacy can be judged for that purpose, which makes sense to the pupil.

In this case we might perhaps suggest that an enterprising publisher, Longman of Nairobi, for example, wishes to make an African edition of this picture. The main features of the office are to be the same but all the people are to be localised. The pupils will write the specifications for the artist to work from. We can still adjust the level of difficulty but it is possible that our rather mechanical paragraphing will have to be changed.

Time spent thinking out and preparing a good way of presenting the problem involved in the written work is better spent than it is on marking. We should resist our masochistic consciences when they tell us that the drearier the drudgery, the greater our virtue.

5 Some common heresies

1 Before we look at any further techniques of presentation, let us examine a few heresies. Many teachers supply 'useful words' before the class start to write. We believe it is wrong to give pupils new vocabulary immediately before they write a composition unless they ask for it. Instead composition work should always be so planned that the pupils can cope with the problem from their current lexical stock. There are degrees of iniquity in this matter. To provide one or two nouns, for example, *print* and *negative* if we are writing about photography, is not particularly harmful. One cannot get into a great deal of difficulty with nouns that clearly name things. But to provide the class with a list of compendious words before a summary, or swashbuckling verbs of motion before a story, or a nice 'derangement of epitaphs'[1] before a description is very mistaken indeed. It imposes the teacher's vision on the class, suggests that they cannot write decent English with the words they know already and, which is the crux of the matter, makes them try to work particular words into what they write instead of seeking ways of making words convey what they want to communicate.[2] This is the heresy of 'good words and useful phrases'.

2 We all know of course that model compositions are written by people with not nearly enough wit to write anything else and not quite enough wit to write even model compositions tolerably. No reputable teacher would dream of using a book of model answers. But there are many teachers who do something just as bad without ever knowing that they are doing it. What happens is that the teacher decides on a subject and then in order to 'do some oral preparation', which he has been told is a good thing, also decides on an appropriate introduction, order of paragraphs and conclusion. His lesson then goes somewhat as follows:

Teacher: Today we are going to write an essay about The Cat. Now, what is our introduction?

Pupil: 'I have a cat.'

[1] Three people have asked us if we really mean this. Of course we do; and so did Mrs Malaprop.

[2] The following conversation actually took place when J.A.B. had just taken over a new class. They had been writing about a storm and the pupil had written 'the banana leaves were wagging like a dog's tail.'

J.A.B.: Why like a dog's tail?
Pupil: (Demonstrating) They were going like that.
J.A.B.: Yes, but when does a dog wag its tail?
Pupil: When it's pleased.
J.A.B.: Did you want to suggest that the trees were pleased?
Pupil: No.
J.A.B.: Then why compare them to a dog's tail?
Pupil: I just wanted to use a simile.

J.A.B. claims that at this point he distinctly smelt brimstone.

Teacher: Oh, no. There might be somebody who hasn't. Some people don't like cats, do they?
Pupil: 'Some people don't like cats.'
Teacher: Is that a good introduction?
Pupil: Oh, no, sir.
Teacher: Well, then what is the cat?
Pupil: An animal.
Teacher: Is that a sentence?
Pupil (patiently and tolerantly): The cat is an animal.
Teacher: Ah! But the elephant is an animal and the cow is an animal and the giraffe is an animal. We must say what kind of animal.
Pupil: The cat is a little animal.
Teacher: No. Have you not seen the mouse and the rat?
Pupil: The cat is a middle-sized animal.
Teacher: No. The size does not matter. Do we keep it in the house?
Pupil: Yes.
Teacher: What do we call it?
Pupil: Pussy.
Teacher: No. The animals we keep in the house – what do we call them?
Pupil: Pets.
Teacher: Is a cow a pet? What is the opposite of a wild animal?
Pupil: A tame animal.
Teacher: Do you not know the word *domestic*? D.O.M.E.S.T.I.C.

The guessing game continues and it is a safe bet that the compositions that do not start, *The cat is a domestic animal* will only vary as far as *domstic* or perhaps, *domistick*.

We admit to some levity in this example. But it is merely an extreme case of the teacher imposing his view of what the result should be. Pupils do not learn to arrange things primarily by guessing how other people have arranged them. They have to do it for themselves. There are other little matters involved too, such as nobody wanting very desperately to write about cats anyhow.

We might call this the heresy of the mental model or teacher's preconceived plan.

3 There is a minor but quite dangerous heresy that goes somewhat as follows. 'When I get my first-year class, they can't write sentences. One sentence runs into another. They must therefore learn to write single sentences before they can write paragraphs and I don't start them on paragraphs until the third term. Then, of course, they write one paragraph; you can't write two paragraphs until you have learnt to write one.'

This plausible piece of nonsense prevents the pupils from making the progress they are capable of. The fallacy is that the problem of sentence division only arises when you have to write more than one sentence. Whenever we have explored what is meant by 'they can't write sentences', the main problem, though not of course the only one, has always boiled down to using commas instead of full stops *between* sentences.

Similarly the problem of sorting out what belongs in paragraph A and what in B only arises when we are dealing with two paragraphs. If we have only one box everything goes into it. The problem of what belongs with what only arises when we have at least two boxes. Internal arrangement within the boxes is more difficult and certainly not the place to start.

It would be equally absurd to argue that the pupil must spend six months learning to write words before he can write a sentence or, to extend it in the other direction, to say that he cannot be expected to write a whole story until he has spent ages learning to write bits of stories.

We have no name for this heresy. Could we call it oversimplification?

4 The next and most serious heresy is that of essay-mindedness. It is now many years since examining boards stopped setting 'essays' and started setting 'compositions' but many of the subjects on the composition papers might easily have been set on the essay paper. Moreover the old attitudes die hard. 'Some of the best work will approach essay standard.' 'No better than mediocre – scarcely a descriptive epithet in it.' Moreover the conditions of the examination and the conservatism of teachers combine to make the pupil aim at being able to produce 500 words on a given subject in 90 minutes starting from cold. By the time pupils have reached the end of a secondary course, this is not an impossible demand, but the fact that it is feasible does not make it any less ridiculous. When, as so often happens, teachers work on the theory that because all that the pupils have got to compose is an essay – 'They call it composition nowadays but it's really the same thing' – the sooner they start, the better and the less time they waste on writing anything else the better, the effects are pernicious.

Of all the kinds of writing that may be required by the pupil in his business or profession or used for his enjoyment or profit in the future, the least useful is the essay. He would be better employed learning to write bawdy limericks. Unfortunately the tradition of the English essay at school is so hallowed, so much part of our own experience at school, so firmly enshrined in the conventional textbooks, so easy to set, and so conveniently adaptable to the lengths of periods and preparation time that we seldom ask whether it is sensible to rate its training value so highly.

We are nearly always disappointed with the results and then we blame it on the pupils. They have so little background knowledge; they lack inventiveness; they seem to have no originality at all. There are plenty of scapegoats. It need never occur to us that the pupils are doing nothing but the same exercise over and over again. They are set to work to write about X, where X, though variable, remains the unknown quantity.

Such writing is a barren exercise without point or purpose. Nobody reads it willingly. Its only function is to expose the writer's weaknesses. Outside the discipline of school could anybody be persuaded to go on writing week after week when his only reader was a remote and critical deity armed with a red biro? It is not surprising that progress is slow, only that human nature will submit to such futile toil.

We can surely do better than this by thinking about what makes people put words on paper and what the rewards of success are. In real life few people are instructed, for example, to 'let me have 500 words on *Transport* by Friday'. Instead they are faced with a problem that requires a written solution – the need for example to draft the orders required to ensure that a procession can take place without interference from normal traffic. The composition resulting from this will be read for its practical not its literary value.

At the other end of the scale the literary writer, who is much rarer, writes to be read. His reward, other than the financial one, is the esteem of his contemporaries and those whose good opinion he values. As teachers we should perhaps be chary of making a promising pupil very dependent on our own taste. In thirty years' time our standards may look a little old-fashioned. They may even be a little time-worn already.

At the very least we can stop pretending to ourselves that the finest contribution we can make to the future is to produce successive crops of Robert Lynds. This is not to deny his artistry or the pleasure he gives many people but merely to point out that while orchids are lovely, they are a poor substitute for rice, wheat, maize, millet and potatoes.

6 Theory of a composition syllabus

What should a composition syllabus for a secondary school be like? Certainly it should not consist of a list of subjects. Equally certainly syllabuses should vary widely from school to school and be tailored to particular needs, environments, experiences and abilities. Some generalisations may be country-wide. In the Sudan for example the language of art: literature, television, journalism, etc. will be Arabic and not English. In Tanzania it will be Swahili. Here we should certainly not stress literary writing. In West Africa, Central Africa and the rest of East Africa the creative artists are working in English. The future writers nearly all pass through the secondary schools. Here literary writing has much greater importance. It is best for each school to work out its own composition syllabus in a systematic, detailed progressive form. Without a proper syllabus pupils are in grave danger of being exposed to vagueness of approach, unnecessary repetition, aimless and shapeless lessons and pointless writing. It is towards the creation of such a document that the following notes are offered.

It is not always possible to fulfil all the conditions below but the more that can be met, the better the pupils' prospect of writing successfully.

1 The pupils must be presented with a problem and see the need for a written solution. It is the problem that engages their interest and the need that starts the language mechanisms working. The words do not come until some stimulus has been applied. As soon as the pupils want to communicate something, they are ready to start. They must never be put in the position of wanting to find something to say.

We have already noted that the problem must be adjusted in its presentation to an appropriate level of difficulty and soluble within the language the pupils know.

2 The problem defines the purpose of the writing and the reader or class of reader to whom it is addressed. The pupils must have a reader, real or imaginary, in mind. The reader is the writer's target. Who and what he is influences what is said and how it is said. The teacher may sometimes manoeuvre himself into the position of the interested reader but the foreign teacher needs to exercise some tact if he is to avoid being suspected of a patronising interest in the quaint customs of the natives.

We do not believe that the teacher should be the only reader or even the normal reader. We do not want pupils to write regularly for Teacher's approval; we are no longer young enough to be certain that Teacher knows best. We doubt too whether writing for Teacher is well calculated to lead to honesty, truthfulness, adventurousness and zeal in the writer. It is more likely to induce a timorous avoidance of possible errors or gaffes and a servile desire to satisfy the master with the minimum effort.

3 The pupils must then bring their attention, experience and imagination[1] into focus upon the problem.

In real (as opposed to school or examination) conditions people hardly ever put pen to paper until their minds are full. They know what they want to say but have not yet put it on paper. They are ready to make a draft. A great deal of the art of composition teaching consists in getting the pupil up to the drafting point, or getting him to get himself there (which is all that can be done in an examination) or getting other pupils in a group discussion to bring him to the point where, as Gurrey says, 'he is full like a pot of beer or preferably just slopping over'.

4 The pupils must know or find out how to set about the job. This is the question of technique. One way of doing this is to see how other people tackle similar jobs – to read a letter, for example, and then write one using the same technique on different subject matter. Skinning off the technique and applying it can be used in any kind of writing – advertisements, description, narrative, exposition, argument, dialogue, etc. We are no longer certain that this is the best way. We want pupils to develop an interest in how writers solve their problems and make words do various jobs, but we also want them to solve technical problems for themselves – to make their own patterns instead of imitating those of other people. There are many ways of organising written material satisfactorily, some no doubt still undiscovered, and a variety of different ways within the class adds to everybody's pleasure and interest.

Problems of technique need to be broken down into manageable units. We have seen a teacher give a lesson on paragraphing in which he attempted to cover the whole of this complicated subject in forty minutes. But narrative paragraphing is quite different from that of exposition, argument or description. The unity is not that of theme but of incident, speaker, mood, etc. Each

[1] We are not thinking of wild flights of fancy sometimes called 'imaginative' composition – of subjects like A Day in my Life as a Fish or If I had a Million or Two to Spare. What we have in mind is the kind of imagination that enables a man to write a tactful letter because he can put himself in the reader's place, that enables him to recall an experience clearly so that he can put it into words, that enables him, in short, to see what is not there, as opposed to seeing what has never been, anywhere.

possible reason could form a unit of teaching about technique. We call these divisions *study points*.

5 The composition course should cover the widest possible range of kinds of writing. The following categories overlap but suggest what we have in mind:

notes	stories	character studies	history	telephone conversations
summaries	descriptions	explanations of plans, charts	geography	advertisements
statements of accounts	arguments	writing up experiments	dialogue	instructions
speeches	business letters	personal letters	invitations	reports
appeals for money	minutes	rules	magazine articles	newspaper articles
broadcast talks	complaints	requests	notices	exposition of facts
commentaries	diaries	travelogues	dust-cover blurbs	autobiography
	light verse	serious poetry	writing up 'research'	etc.

In the examination year we shall even have to give practice in writing a composition on a set subject to a given length within a given time limit, but this can be as near as we need go to the essay.

6 More useful teaching can be done after a piece of work has been written than before. The conventional wisdom says that once the subject has been set, utter silence shall prevail while each individual wrestles alone with the slippery stuff of language. Some of us even ban books of reference. Then just as the bell goes, the pupil scribbles his last words, the pen falls from his cramped fingers, the exercise book is hastily shut and the rest is up to the teacher. This is all wrong. Writing should be a co-operative endeavour, not a solitary penance.

The teacher who collects and marks the books at this point is robbing the pupils of half the experience they need in order to improve in correctness and other more important ways. Pupils have got to learn to take the responsibility for the accuracy of their own work, to put right superficial errors and slips for themselves and if they are to do this, they must have an opportunity to spot them for themselves before the teacher's red ink tells them where to look. Training the proof-reader's eye is important.

It is even more important that they should read their own and each other's work and give and get approval for what is effective and discuss possibilities of improvement. The first draft should be regarded (except only in an examination) as something to be read over, weighed up and worked on.

7 All original[1] work should be published. We do not mean in the school

[1] We are thinking simply of work where all the pupils' answers are not exactly the same. We do not mean the kind of work which in examiners' jargon 'shows considerable originality and freshness', or 'has distinct appeal'. When the pupil makes his own choices he is being original and his creative efforts are worthy of respect.

magazine though as much as possible should appear in print there. We mean that it should be pinned up on the wall for all members of the class to read and then collected into a file left in the classroom or library where all members of the school have access to it. Paintings and pots are displayed, why do we normally discriminate against things made of words?

There are practical advantages in public display. The pupil who does not greatly care if the teacher sees his mistakes because that, he has learnt, is what teachers are for, is a good deal more anxious to remove them if he knows they may be picked on by his friends or his enemies. The other members of his group are more willing to help and he is more willing to accept help if the credit of the group is involved. The rewards of success are greater too. The approval of one's fellow-workers is at once sustaining and demanding. It is healthy and bracing.

8 Whatever grammar teaching we do should be relevant to the needs of composition.

9 Nearly all composition work should be based on local material so that students know what they are writing about – and are encouraged to know it better.

10 All composition work must draw on the pupils' own experience. There is no other source of first-hand material.

11 Finally we must take the pupil into our confidence and explain why he should work in this way, why he must go on after he thinks he has finished, why we refuse to read what he has written straight away, why we make him give and seek help from others and why we must not bear his burdens for him.

7 A Unit of composition teaching

We believe that secondary pupils should write thirty compositions a year and take a fortnight to deal with each. Compositions therefore overlap and the pupils are revising one in the same week as they start another. We will, however, trace the stages of just a single unit. The steps do not represent lesson periods; they vary in length from a few minutes to over an hour depending on the amount to be done.

Step 1: Preparatory language work

This is mentioned first but cannot be properly done until the problem has been defined. In this unit we would do it after Step 4.

There are three ways of making this relevant to the writing that is to follow. We can choose the composition to bring in the grammar we have been dealing with, asking, for example, for a detective story when we have been looking at noun clause objects. We can teach the grammar we think will be needed for the subject we have in mind, or if we have set the subject to a similar class before, we can deal with the difficulties we know will arise: the same subject in similar conditions gives rise to the same errors year after year.

For the purpose of this unit we shall practise changing direct to indirect questions because we do not want the pupils to write about 'learning how can they ride their bicycles safely'.

Step 2: Posing the problem and thereby defining the purpose and readers

Our class does not need support in the actual framing of sentences. We are therefore offering only situational guidance. We assume a town school.

This is the problem:

There have been complaints about careless cycling by pupils in this school. There were two serious accidents earlier this year and this morning there was a third. The boy involved is in hospital. This morning the Headmaster spoke about this in assembly and mentioned that he had had several complaints from the police as well as from parents.

Something has got to be done. Your problem is what.

Step 3: Focusing the attention, getting the imaginations working, warming up the linguistic machinery

The posing of the problem could be followed by a general class discussion, or a class trained to work in groups could be told: 'Get into your groups for ten minutes and come up with some suggestions. Then we will go into committee and decide which ones to follow up.'

When the secretaries of the groups report back, the teacher in the Chair has a dual role. He needs to be alert for errors particularly in indirect questions, though in our view he should not interrupt reports to make corrections. To do so is to interfere with more important work and outside his role as Chairman. He had better note them for use later.

With the rest of his mind he is concerned to find the suggestions that may lead to the kind of written work he wants the class to do and which command the support of the meeting.

Our expectation is that a lecture and demonstration on road safety for cyclists will be proposed and we shall proceed on the assumption that it is. But if the class prefer to consider organising a cycling club, a system of bicycle inspection, a riding test for advanced cyclists or a cycle-safely week, we can get plenty of useful written work out of any of these ideas.

This time, however, we assume we have completed our committee work and know that we want to write a letter to the Superintendent of Police asking him to provide a lecturer in road safety for cyclists. We can organise demonstrators. We would like information about common causes of accidents and suggestions about following up the lecture practically.

We now know that we are going to write a business letter to a definite reader for a clear purpose. If we reach the end of a period at this point, so much the better. It gives us all time to think.

Step 4: The study point of technique

Step 3 is not yet completed, but we will sandwich in Step 4. Our previous study point in business letters was politeness. This time we decide we will deal with relevance, that is including everything that is needed and excluding everything else. The easiest thing is to fake a couple of letters, one asking somebody to come and give a talk without naming a time or being at all specific about what, how big the audience, etc. and another including, for example, a long flowery introduction or a history of the society. It should not be difficult to see what is wrong with these.

Alternatively we may postpone this until we do the follow-up on the first drafts.

Back to Step 3, the final stage of which consists of the groups listing the questions they hope the lecturer will deal with.

Step 5: Drafting

The pupils individually make first drafts of the letter. Although they work separately we encourage them to use reference books and ask each other and the teacher questions about doubtful points. We do not always answer the questions. 'How do you think we should start?' would be instantly referred back to the questioner.

With younger pupils we prefer the writing to be done in class or at least started there. With older ones, it usually has to be done in preparation time.

Step 6: Getting improvement in the draft

The drafts are brought to the next class and each group reads all the letters of its members for purposes specified by the teacher. In this case we are going to ask for the first reading to check politeness, relevance and clarity, for the second to check spelling and slips of the pen, and for the third to check punctuation and indirect questions.

No reader is limited to these matters, of course; he may suggest any improvement he likes, but he is not supposed to miss what we have mentioned.

Step 7: Producing the final draft

Sometimes we ask a group to produce one final draft between them. This involves them in all sorts of comparative problems, often leads to good discussion and always makes them concentrate on language in a constructive way. This time, however, we will just let each pupil do it for himself.

Step 8

The final copy is proof-read for slips by at least one other member of the group and he gets more of the blame for slips of the pen left in than the original writer does. He signs it 'Passed for Publication'.

Step 9

We now collect the final drafts and read them. We shall not put any red ink on them. If we had wished to indicate errors, we should have done so on the first draft. Now we have three purposes:

a. to collect common errors which we must deal with later as far as this class is concerned but which we can use next year in our preliminary language work;

b. to enter up in our private mark book such indications as we keep of our pupils' success with this assignment. We may select some work for special praise. It may, alas, even be necessary to refer one or two back to the group as 'unfit for publication'. This is a dire punishment.

c. to decide what needs doing next.

Perhaps the letters were a bit verbose. If so, we shall perhaps decide to put in a study point on the subject of getting rid of repetitions or idle words.

Step 10: Publication

The final product is put on public view.

This brings us to the end of the unit. Our situation has been imaginary, but one that could happen in a school. Plenty of things in fact do happen, and ideal conditions for language work arise when pupils can be responsibly involved in discussions of real problems that lead to action. To be helping to form policy in this way is good for their souls as well as their English Composition.

8 More about study points

One example of a composition unit, however, does not make a syllabus. From the teacher's point of view we suggest that the backbone of the syllabus should be the progression of technical study points, which, as they build up, constitute the pupil's course in written English.

In planning a scheme of work, one can take a kind of writing, stories for example, and set up each lesson to illustrate some point of technique.

Examples:

a. that stories are normally told in order of time.

b. that some variety in sentence structure (and length) makes the reading easier and makes it possible to use a very short sentence for a punch line.

c. that new paragraphs are started for various reasons, e.g.

(i) to signal a change in the course of a story – the beginning of a new incident

(ii) to indicate a new speaker

(iii) to mark a change of mood

and

(iv) (Let us be honest) because the one we are writing is getting too long.

d. that if we have two threads to our story, we generally tell each in order of time and knot them together at the end. This gives us another reason for a new paragraph.

e. that we do not have to keep to order of time. We can use flashbacks.

f. that a story must not be incredible. This involves persuading the reader by supplying him with convincing detail that things could have happened like that.

g. that continuity and fluency in writing can sometimes be improved by grammatical linking together of clauses or spoilt by over-complexity.

h. that the point of view must be consistent.
i. that unity of mood within a paragraph can be obtained by careful choice of words suggesting feelings.
j. that the details in a story should be relevant.
k. that we must give the reader enough detail to see what happens.
l. that too much detail slows down the action.

And so on and on. Naturally these points would not be worked through seriatim. We do not want to spend a year writing nothing but stories; and in any case some are more suitable for older classes. We shall probably do them two or three consecutively whenever we decide to spend two or three weeks on narrative.

There are similar study points particularly applicable to other kinds of writing. In description and exposition, for example, we need a new principle of arrangement and therefore study generalisations and supporting detail. We look into questions of arranging facts and see that we can put the big strawberries at the top of the basket or keep them up our sleeves – a discovery that might well lead us to consider mixed metaphors.

A great many study points apply to almost all kinds of writing. We must always consider the reader. A Muganda writing for Baganda has painted a pretty clear picture if he says,

'I live in a house with a bati roof on an ordinary shamba about three miles from a main road.'

But if he is writing to a pen-friend in Malaya, he will need to go into more detail.

We have presented our examples as though they were the laws of the Medes and Persians but it is important not to offer them to a class as prescriptions. Most writing problems are capable of solution in a number of equally satisfactory ways. 'Arrangement of ideas' as the phrase is used by examiners is simply a question of getting them into some sort of order. There is no more a best way of arranging them than there is of arranging a kitchen. Both are matters of the user's convenience.

There are numerous ways of getting a class to see the point. One can show the arrangement of sentences into paragraphs by issuing a jumbled set to be copied out, cut up and rearranged. The main point of this is, for example, to get all the stuff about wild animals into one paragraph and about tame ones into the other, but the question of which comes first will arise and so will the question of transition from paragraph to paragraph and of internal structure within the paragraphs and of transition between sentences – far too much material of course for one lesson.

One can issue material from which bits have been deleted – the adjectives, the sentence connectors, the conjunctions showing the relationships of thought, etc. The material can have obvious faults – monotony of structure, vagueness of naming, anticlimax, a tadpole-like shape (a monstrous introduction and hardly any body), unnecessary repetition, inclusion of irrelevant material, etc. One can use material from what the class have written to demonstrate that what is good can still be improved. For really awful examples it is more tactful to select from the work of other classes. It is not really good for even an unidentified sinner to squirm through a whole discussion.

One can use comparable material to make various points, e.g. bias in reporting, the difference between two descriptions of the same object for different purposes, the effect of descriptive versus emotive adjectives, etc.

One can use single passages to demonstrate the relationship of detail to general impression. Tom Sawyer waking up on the Mississippi island and Richard Church getting his new spectacles are two of our favourites for this purpose when we are feeling literary. Genuine business and personal letters can be produced.

9 More about focusing the attention, experience and imagination on the subject

Let's tackle something literary.

A Misty Morning

The objectives now are

(i) to supply a reason for writing the piece, which will include who is going to read it. The reason may be real or imaginary.

(ii) to get each pupil's imagination and memory working so that the raw material of former sense impressions wells up to the top of his mind and is brought into sharp focus.

The first step is to decide what this account of the misty morning is for, e.g.

a. a diary – as a reminder and personal record of experience

b. part of a letter – to a fellow-countryman in London to bring him a little bit of home

c. part of a letter – to a pen-friend who has never been in Africa to send him a little bit of Africa

d. part of a story or biography – to the general reader setting the tone of what is to come

e. part of an account of Uganda – to tourists suggesting that other simpler experiences than lions and elephants are worth coming for

f. the introduction to a miserable day of frustration and failure.

Perhaps the class, or groups of them, will agree to a common aim. If so, it makes class discussion easier. But agreement is not essential, for as long as the aim under discussion at the time is clear, pupils can subsequently write for different ones. Low down in the school there is no objection to the class being made to choose the same aim, at least sometimes, in order to simplify the discussion and to enable them afterwards to compare other pupils' efforts.

The study point of technique has already been dealt with. Let us assume we have used Tom Sawyer waking up on the Mississippi island and decided that the structure used is a generalisation – peace – calm – silence followed by concrete illustrations 'not a leaf moved', 'beaded dewdrops stood on the leaves and grasses', 'a thin thread of smoke rose straight into the air', 'not a sound', etc.

The second step is to establish possible general impressions which need not be the same for everybody and may, according to taste, be pleasant or unpleasant (though this may be decided by the aim chosen; the class will readily see that a general feeling of unpleasantness is essential to aim *f* above but inappropriate to aim *e*).

We elicit suggestions like

cool and grey
wet and dark
dull and cold
foggy

We discuss appropriateness in terms of aim and then select, for example, one pleasant and one unpleasant pair to follow up. Only the former is tackled below.

Let us take 'cool and grey'. We have in previous lessons established the importance of a consistent point of view. We therefore decide individually where we are and go on to ask what sort of concrete details will reinforce the 'cool' idea. We get things like

dew-drops
mist
sun hidden
wearing sweaters
woolly hats on cyclists
feeling fresh
water dripping, etc.

Later we shall deal similarly with 'grey' and go into the question of concrete details which suggest both and the question of which comes first, if either.

The next step is to bring these things into clear focus. Again question and answer, perhaps something like this.

Teacher: Where were these dew-drops?
Pupil: Everywhere.
Teacher: Will it do if I write: There were dew-drops everywhere ?
Pupil: No.
Teacher: Why not?
(*Dead silence*)
Teacher: If I say, 'dew-drops everywhere', does it make you see the dew-drops on anything in particular?
Pupil: No.
Teacher: All right. Make me see them on something.
Pupil: On the roof.
Teacher: Good. Where on it?
Pupil: Standing on the top.
Teacher: What sort of roof? I want to see that too.
Pupil: Straw.
Teacher: What did the drops look like on the roof?
Pupil: White.
Teacher: And what colour was the roof?
Pupil: Dark.

Teacher: Did they look white like paper?

Pupil: No. Shining.

Teacher: Right. Now try and put that into a sentence.

Pupil (which eventually goes on the blackboard): There were shining white dew-drops on the top of the dark-brown straw roof.

Teacher: Now look for words that don't really add to the picture. I'll underline them, as you mention them. (This refers back to a previous study point – economy of language.)

There were shining white dew-drops on the top of the dark-brown straw roof.

Teacher: Try to get rid of them.

Pupil (eventually): Dew-drops were shining on the dark straw roof.

Teacher: Good, but perhaps that isn't everybody's picture. Where did somebody else notice them?

and so on.

There will be as much of this as there is time for. If we have looked at 'conclusions' we shall get suggestions about how to finish our paragraph, and then the class are ready to write. They have a technique, a purpose and an audience and they have been forced to concentrate attention closely on what they want to get into words.

Stories can be discussed similarly when, as may sometimes happen, especially in the lower school, a common outline is being followed, but here it is even more important to treat the suggestions made as merely examples of possible ways of telling the story. Concentration can be on such things as how much detail is needed to make clear exactly what happens, how exactly we can imagine what happened, how probable or possible it is, how much introduction is needed, how much conclusion, where the climax comes. what details are relevant and so on.

It is, however, generally easier to get at the common and useful principles of story-telling after the pupils have written stories than before.

Factual and argumentative material can be prepared in class, after the appropriate study point of technique has been examined. The problems will be, for example, collecting as many relevant facts as possible, making generalisations, arranging generalisations and facts to form a continuous connected argument, distortions, wild generalisations, selected instances, emotional slant, ignoring evidence, etc.

Let us suppose that we are going to produce in third year the arguments for and against the proposition that

Living in towns or cities is necessary before a people can be civilised.

Our previous study point has shown an argument arranged like this:

Para 1 General proposition stated
Evidence advanced
Doubts thrown on its completeness

Para 2 — Subordinate supporting proposition stated
Evidence advanced in favour
Evidence advanced against
Subordinate proposition rebutted

Para 3 — General proposition reconsidered and rebutted

As before we want a purpose and definite readers in mind. We could, for example, make it an answer to a letter in the paper saying that the people of Uganda will never make any real progress until they start living in large villages or towns. If we do, we know which side of the argument we are on and we take our general proposition and three supporting ones from the letter.

The lesson will then consist of advancing evidence against the propositions and sorting it out tidily.

A part of it might go like this, assuming the proposition of paragraph two was: 'Exchange of ideas, discussion, communication of all kinds is necessary to progress, but in a scattered community this does not happen, which is why Greek civilisation started in cities and not in the countryside.'

Teacher: Do we agree?
Pupil: No.
Teacher: What don't we agree with?
Pupil: It's wrong.
Teacher: What is?
Pupil: Well, you can have progress in the country.
Teacher: Did the Greeks have it?
Pupil: No, but we're not the Greeks.
Teacher: All right. What is different?
Pupil: We're modern.
Teacher: Meaning what?
Pupil: We have things the Greeks didn't.
Teacher: What things?
Pupil: Motor-cars.
Teacher: What's that got to do with it?
Pupil: We can go into the country and the people there can come to the town.
Teacher: All right. Modern means of travel have reduced the separation of town and country. Is there anything else that acts in a similar way?
Pupil: Yes, the radio.
Teacher: Exactly the same way?
Pupil: Oh. I see. You mean that only works one way.
Teacher: Yes. Anything else?
(*Long pause*)
Where else can we get ideas from apart from talking to people and the radio?
Pupil: Books, magazines, newspapers.
Teacher: Couldn't the Greeks do this?
Pupil: No.

Teacher: Why not?
Pupil: Printing had not been invented.

etc. etc.

And so we work on towards formulating the rebuttal, which will probably be too sweeping as first stated and need qualifying.

The more we increase freedom of choice as we move up the school, the less specific our methods of starting the language mechanisms working can or need be, for the pupils are able to do more for themselves. We can still, however, take a typical examination subject, for example:

Tea

and get suggestions for half a dozen different possible ways of treating it. This will enable us to get rid of the common pupil superstition that a general subject demands a general answer. By the time we have converted it via pupil's experience into tea as an example of the economic relations of poor and rich countries on the theme, 'We shouldn't need your charity if you didn't choose to cheapen our tea', or an account of an embarrassing tea-party, or a farewell tea-party, or of a holiday spent earning money picking tea, or a visit to a tea plantation, or anything else the class may suggest – by this time we ought to have reduced the danger of

> Tea is grown especially in China, Ceylon and India. It is the leaves of a bush . . .

and so on in inferior reproduction of ill-recalled geography lessons. This kind of work is, of course, directly helpful for examination purposes where vestiges of 'essay' subjects still remain.

10 Combining the study point with getting the minds working

Let us suppose that we want to work on making a story credible. We may have an outline, say about losing a bag containing a lot of money, which contains an improbability. The loser may perhaps immediately think it has been stolen. Why should he? The pupils can discuss various ways of making this behaviour appear likely.

Perhaps we may start from an even greater improbability: 'Suddenly his bicycle broke in half.' The pupils are to invent more realistic and convincing ways of stopping bicycles.

At some stage while we are studying how to answer examination questions about the books we have been using in class, we shall want to present a generalisation and get the pupils to bring up the supporting references. 'Squeers was cruel.' Now discuss what incidents you are going to refer to to prove it.

At a very early stage we often ask for autobiographical material. Minds can be got working on this by groups exchanging early memories, telling each other about previous schools, etc.

Talking about a subject in a group is a good way of getting the mind working. It is also good training for adult life. Most responsible people, and quite a few irresponsible ones, spend a great deal of time in committee helping, or hindering, the process of making decisions. The good committee man is a very useful person and it is as much our business as English teachers to do what we can to train him as it is to do what we can to train creative writers. The two aims need not conflict. Shaw was a brilliant committee man and there is no evidence that Shakespeare was not.

As in all committees, the business needs to be organised and we like to lay down or have the group secretary make an agenda. We are also prepared to put time limits on how long each item may take. It is not usually necessary to make small groups behave very formally addressing remarks to the Chairman, etc. Indeed it is not usually necessary to appoint a Chairman at all. Somebody nearly always takes charge of the discussion.

Many teachers are worried about the use of groups in this way. They fear that a lot of errors will be made when they are not there to correct them, that one or two pupils in each group will do most of the work and that the pupils will use their own language instead of English for the discussion.

The answer to the point about errors is that if the pupils are error prone then, in the course of the twenty-four hours of the day, they will make a lot of errors that the teacher will not hear anyhow. A few more is a small price to pay for the stimulus of rubbing minds together. In any case we have built-in safeguards against the mistakes appearing in writing.

That one or two members of each group will do most of the work is true. Life is like that. But they will not do it all and it will do them good to cast in of their abundance and still leave room for the others to cast in all they have. It is also true that each of the members of the group will write better than he would have done on his own.

The problem of pupils' using their own language is trickier. It is most likely to happen in large classes where oral English is weak – precisely the situation in which there is most need to practise English. We do not think that when the object of the exercise is to prepare what will be written in English the discussion can profitably be in any other language.[1] Too many mental translation problems are subsequently involved. To prevent it, we should explain why we think the discussion should be in English and, if that did not work, reduce the level of difficulty drastically.

11 A little more about correcting and improving the first draft:

[a] MATTERS OF MECHANICAL CORRECTNESS – GETTING RID OF MISTAKES

The teacher who carefully crosses out or underlines every mistake in his pupils' books develops a keen eye for errors but his pupils do not; it is easier for them to develop a tolerance for red-ink rash. It is the pupils and not the teacher who should learn to spot mistakes by practising proof-reading. It is

[1] This is not the same as having an imposed English-speaking rule within the school. This we do not approve of.

the pupils and not the teacher who should take responsibility for eliminating mechanical errors. It does the pupil more good to find five errors for himself than it does him if the teacher finds fifty.

In the heat and welter of composition everybody makes mistakes. Pupils make more than professional writers but this is only a matter of degree. The errors are not due to a highly reprehensible amount of carelessness, idleness or sinfulness, original or derived. Pupils do not usually make their errors deliberately – they would prefer to get things right – nor do they leave them in so as to annoy the teacher. Moral indignation on his part is a less appropriate attitude than meditative interest. There is little point in decorating exercise books with from one to five exclamation marks graded according to turpitude.

What the pupils need is to understand that while all writers make mistakes, only ill-mannered ones leave any they can eliminate in something that other people are going to read. Reading over and removing surface errors is a necessary part of the writer's job. The reason for observing the conventions in writing is the same as for observing them in dress. People think you are odd if you do not. Pupils then need practice and encouragement. It is very meritorious indeed to find a mistake and put it right. The teacher who only awards grudging approval for this ('Yes, I'm glad you spotted that one but what about all these others?') is getting in his own way.

The process of training the proof-reader's eye is slow and painful, but well worth while. Once the teacher knows that work is carefully read over, he can be sure that the remaining errors are due to ignorance. What is not known can be learnt, or even taught. This is a much happier situation than the one where the teacher has to guess whether every error is one the pupil could have corrected if he had noticed it, or whether it needs some kind of explanation and treatment. In dealing with errors the most important thing of all is to train the class to get rid of every one they can for themselves.

We do not believe that the teacher should necessarily mark every piece of work that is done, if by 'mark' is meant go through and indicate every error. He should, of course, read everything and make his own notes. However, about once a month, he should mark a corrected first draft in detail so that the individual pupil can know how he is getting on in the matter of improving his correctness.

The signs the teacher makes in the books will be adjusted to the stage his pupils have reached as well as to the kind of error he finds. He will never do anything for the pupil that the pupil could do for himself. We do not learn how to do up our own shoes while somebody keeps on doing them up for us. In first year, for example, the teacher may indicate a spelling error in a particular line by an S in the margin, but he will not underline the word, cross it out or correct it. In third year, he may merely indicate by 3S at the foot of a page that there are three spelling errors on it to be found.

His expectations of what errors pupils should have eliminated will also be progressive and follow the teaching. He may not bother about commas after initial adverbial clauses until he has made a point of them. Thereafter this will be added to the list of what the pupils should look for. The indications he puts in the margin will also vary with what he has taught.

It is convenient to have a system of signals to the pupil in order to help him to know what he is looking for before he has acquired much proof-reading skill. It is even more convenient for the pupil if all his teachers use the same system. He will get on much faster if all his teachers understand that composition in English is English composition. While we are still using the line as a unit, we use some such system as the following. All signs go in the margin.

^	A word on this line has been omitted
/	A word on this line ought to be omitted
P	Mistake in punctuation or capitalisation
S	Spelling
¶	Why did(n't) you make a new paragraph?
T	Tense error
G	Grammatical error – practically reserved for concord
W	Wrong word
W.O.	Word order wrong
R	Repetition to be removed
√	Good point, neatly put, good correction, etc.
?	I don't know what you are trying to say.

And we allow ourselves also one exclamation mark, which means 'there is a mistake on this line that I think you should have found for yourself'.

These signs change as we teach or review new segments of grammar. For example, the word usually omitted is the indefinite article. The same word is the one wrongly included. When we have taught about quantity nouns and determiners, we use D in place of the omission signs and Q if the pupil writes, for example, 'furnitures'.

There is one other sign that we use for errors that we recognise as common, dangerous and likely to recur and in the correction of which the pupil will need help. The sign is C/E and means, as we explain in detail in the grammar chapter on pages 250 to 253, 'This is the error explained on the card in your book'. The pupil is to read it and do the exercise.

We also use a few occasional signs, e.g. A.L.D. means: 'Look this up in the *Advanced Learner's Dictionary*.'

We like to do this marking on the first draft because it avoids the necessity of disfiguring work for 'publication' and because the writing of the second draft faces the pupil with the need to take some action about each of the errors indicated. Common errors involve him in writing several sentences.

Spelling can be dealt with by a class spelling box. The pupil writes the word he has misspelt correctly in his second draft and also puts it in context on a piece of paper which he posts in the class spelling box. For example,

I *live* in Dodoma.

From time to time we base snap spelling tests on the words in the box and expect pupils to go through them in preparation for the tests.

[b] IMPROVEMENTS OTHER THAN THOSE INVOLVED IN MECHANICAL CORRECTNESS

Even if no pupil ever made a mistake, the composition teacher would still have his hands full. 'Of making many books, there is no end.' Indeed over-insistence on the negative objective – avoiding errors – can be self-defeating and must not be allowed to obscure more important and exciting kinds of improvement such as bettering the arrangement, adding colourful details, improving transition, putting a point more clearly, briefly or forcibly, etc. Perhaps the other side of this coin, enjoying what is well said, is even more important. Once again it is the pupil who needs to do the learning (although we know two teachers who have not mastered all these matters). It is the critical application to the written work of study point after study point that gradually builds up into critical judgement.

Every week the members of the group see five different pieces of work. They are bound to compare them and to think parts of some better than parts of others. Sometimes when we ask for a single composite draft from the group, they are forced to choose and justify their choice to others.

The teacher plays a very different role from his part in the correction of errors. In the matter of whether a certain phrase or sentence is acceptable English in the given context, his judgement is likely to be very good, approaching certainty. But he must not claim any such infallibility in matters of taste and opinion. He should, of course, say what he thinks, but not always before he is asked and he must leave room for differences of opinion. His aim is to train independent judgement in the pupils.

The reading over of work in order to estimate its success as a solution to the given problem is certainly more important and more entertaining than looking for mistakes. For this reason it should perhaps be the aim of the first reading. It seems kinder to take the line 'This is fine except for a few slips', or even 'This won't do, so we needn't worry about slips', than 'Let's get rid of the nonsenses; then perhaps we can see what it's all about.'

[c] CORRECTED FIRST DRAFT

There are numerous occasions – examinations are the ones that will bulk largest in the pupils' minds – when there is no time to make a second draft and we do not therefore suggest that all compositions should be rewritten. The number treated in this way will decrease as pupils work up the school and as their skill in note-making enables them to make better plans before they write their first drafts.

At a very early stage it is desirable to show pupils how to correct a draft in detail. When this is not done – and it is frequently left undone – the final examiner is presented with scripts in which it is impossible to tell what is in and what is out, whether a capital letter has been altered to a small or vice-versa, whether the stop is or was a comma and so on. Pupils often need re-assurance: the examiner likes to see that a script has been corrected, but he must know what the corrections are. When the teacher does his detailed marking, he operates on corrected first drafts.

12 Making a syllabus

We have already agreed that a syllabus must be made for a particular school; what follows is therefore only an example. It cannot consist merely of a list of subjects to write about. We must include notes of the kind of writing and form of the written work to make sure we have sufficient variety. We must leave room for repetition of study points that are not satisfactorily grasped and we must make provision sometimes for choice of subject. In general, freedom of choice will increase as we move up the school.

We shall perhaps finish up with a twenty-week segment looking something like this and expect to spend twenty-five weeks covering it because some points will require a second attempt.

Week	*Kind of Writing*	*Form*	*Study Point*	*Rubric of title, purpose & reader*
1	Narrative	Three paragraphs	New turn, new paragraph	Write an account for the school magazine of a picnic that started well, went wrong but ended with everybody safely home again.
2	Narrative	Story with conversation	New speaker, new paragraph	Three friends find a valuable watch near the school. *a.* They discuss what to do with it. *b.* They take it to the Headmaster who says if it is not claimed in a month they can keep it. *c.* It is not claimed. They discuss what to do with it. The story will be read by pupils in the class.
3	Narrative	One paragraph	Variety of sentence structure	A detective has been instructed to shadow a suspected person. Write the paragraph of his report to his chief that explains how he was tricked into losing his man.
4	Narrative	Three paragraphs	Different point of view, new paragraph	John is Mary's son. He goes out to buy a loaf of bread and does not return for a long time. Mary imagines all sorts of disasters. John returns. Stories to be read by the class.
5	Inventory	List	The items need to be arranged in some sensible order	Your brother is going away to boarding school for the first time. Make him a check list to help with his packing,

Week	*Kind of Writing*	*Form*	*Study Point*	*Rubric of title, purpose & reader*
6	Description	One or two paragraphs	An order for a description: 1. Generalisation 2. Large objects 3. Small ones	You are the stage manager of a play that takes place in a business office. Here is the plan of the furniture on the stage. You have been commissioned to write to one or two firms asking to borrow suitable furniture. Write a description of the set to go with the plan.
7	Description	Two contrasting paragraphs	Internal structure as before but paragraph division and linking of one to the other	A friend in another country has asked you what sort of shops you have in your country. Give him the best picture you can of a remaining old-style shop and a modern one.
8	Description with a little narrative	Two or three paragraphs	Getting atmosphere: para 1: curiosity and interest. para 2: uneasiness becoming panic. para 3: relief	Tell the story of how a little girl wandered into a forest and lost her way, but was eventually found, very frightened but unharmed. For class reading.
9	Dialogue	Two-person conversation	How conversation differs from stories and descriptions. Shortened forms, fragments, etc.	You want your father/guardian/mother to let you do something that will cost rather a lot of money. Make up (a) an imaginary conversation in which everything goes exactly as you wish, (b) the conversation that in fact took place. For class reading.
10	Dialogue	Two-person conversation	Using conversation to reveal feelings. Forms of questions	A small boy is going somewhere for the first time. He keeps on asking his mother questions. Convey his excitement, her growing impatience and what she does about it. For class acting.
11	Mixed narrative and description	A personal letter	How to convey rapid action	Your parents think that all Boy Scouts or Girl Guides do is waste their time. They have however allowed you to go away to camp for the first time. Naturally you will write a letter home. Tell them about the camp and stress how busy everybody had to be when you first arrived and set up camp.

Week	*Kind of Writing*	*Form*	*Study Point*	*Rubric of title, purpose & reader*
12	Mixed narrative and description	A personal letter and a paragraph from another	How much detail is needed for *a.* a reader with little common experience. *b.* a reader with closely similar experience	You have received two letters. One is from a pen-friend who lives at Mukalla. He sends you an account of a day's sea fishing for tunny. He went out in a boat with the fishermen. The other is from a friend who spent the last school holidays with you. You used to go fishing together. Answer the letter to your pen-friend with an account of any day's fishing wherever you generally fish (or a day doing something else if you don't fish). Then write a paragraph on the same subject to your other closer friend.
13	Mixed narrative and description	Diary	What makes one day different from another? How can we record this?	Keep a diary for a week. Do not, however, forget, or remember too much, that others will read it.
14	Mixed narrative and description	Two days in a diary	How to get contrasting feelings into a story	Make up two days in your diary: a red-letter day and a day when everything went wrong.
15	Mainly narrative	A report	How to arrange a report on a complicated activity	The school play has just been produced. The English master is leaving at the end of term. Write an account that would be useful to his successor about how the school play was produced.
16	Exposition	A business letter	The virtues of brevity, clarity and politeness	You are the Secretary of the School Photographic Society. You have just seen the Headmaster, who told you that Dr Schnapp, a well-known photographer has agreed to come to the school, show some slides and talk about the art of photography. The Headmaster has promised to let him know what equipment is available in the school, how big his audience will be and what the room he will be talking in is like. He will need an assistant. Write the necessary letter.
17	Exposition	A busines letter	The importance of including all the necessary information.	On your way to school by train you lost the locked box with all your clothes in. It was clearly labelled but the label may have

Week	*Kind of Writing*	*Form*	*Study Point*	*Rubric of title, purpose & reader*
17 (continued)			Follow-up to consist of looking for questions that are left unanswered	come off. Write to the stationmaster at the nearest station to your school.
18	Exposition	An examination essay – a character study	The arrangement of generalisations in paragraphs. Supporting references to the text	Answer the question. What sort of boy was Tom Sawyer?
19	Exposition	Two paragraphs	The importance of clear statement of facts	Explain what happens when there is an eclipse of the sun and an eclipse of the moon.
20	Exposition	An examination essay in history or geography	The pattern of general thesis subdivided into paragraphs of proof	Material from the geography or history teacher.

13 Teaching pupils to make their own notes

[a] INTRODUCTORY

The need to teach note-making in English arises only in English-medium schools and there is no other part of the teaching of written English so generally bungled. One reason is that it is every teacher's business and therefore nobody regards it as a special responsibility. Another reason is that the textbooks in use are generally written for native English speakers because they are all that is available and are therefore unnecessarily difficult, not in technical content but in language, for the pupils. Consequently pupils depend on their notes to pass their examinations. Teachers are therefore seduced into seeing a satisfactory notebook as the desirable end-product, when the end-product should really be a pupil capable of making his own notes from what he hears or reads.

In many parts of the world the previous experience and consequent attitude of the pupils add to the difficulties. Before entering the secondary school these pupils have been brought up on rote learning – memorisation of words as formulas, instead of memorisation by understanding the patterns of concepts. Experience has taught them that success in examinations can be achieved by committing words to memory. Their demand for material to treat in this way – for teacher-made notes – is persistent, passionate and understandable. The proper course is patiently and slowly to change the pupils' attitude by proving to them that they can make perfectly satisfactory notes for themselves and that doing so helps them to understand, to master and therefore to remember the material because the making of the notes forces the note-maker into organising his material into a systematic pattern.

The instructor who surrenders to the demands of his class for second-hand notes should provide stencilled handouts. These do little or nothing to train the pupil in the skill of note-making but at least they do not involve such a foolish waste of time as taking notes from dictation or by copying them from the blackboard. Even good teachers, if they have classes that are behind schedule and equipped with unsuitable textbooks, are sometimes forced to use handouts.

[b] GENERAL CONSIDERATIONS

1 A great many note-making techniques are applicable to more than one school subject. All the teachers in a school should have a common policy, know what stage pupils have reached and progress towards pupil-independence at the same rate. This means that some teacher must provide the others with the information.

2 Since the English teacher is concerned with the other skills of writing, since these are closely related to other matters within his province such as the planning of exposition and the making of summaries and since he is concerned with language as a skill and with the progressive improvement of language skills, the English teacher is the proper person to organise the course. This does not mean that he will tell his colleagues what to do but that he will tell them what the pupils can do. In exchange he will be told what they are doing about notes in other subjects and what he can do to help.

3 The problem of making notes in words needs to be considered as part of the vast general problem of collecting, recording and storing information in handy and accessible ways. Storage may often be better done in non-verbal or mainly non-verbal forms such as charts, diagrams, maps, models, drawings, tables, graphs, photographs, films, etc. Selection of the neatest way is the beginning of sensible record-making and the pupils should not automatically turn to words, but regard them rather as a last resort.

4 One cannot plan the pattern of any record until the field has been surveyed. Only when at least the extent is known can the shape of the arrangement be considered.

5 The purpose for which the notes are made influences their form. Notes made as reminders for immediate use in composition can be so fragmentary as to be incomprehensible a year later. Notes made to use in revision for an examination will be much more formal. Notes made for a 'research' essay will be different again, including, for example, quotations with detailed references.

6 Learning to make notes must be envisaged as a lengthy process by which the pupil moves step by step from almost complete dependence on the teacher towards complete independence.

[c] TECHNIQUES

Let us turn to some concrete examples, starting by assuming that we are dealing with Ancient History in the first year. The key questions are:

1. What do we want the notebooks to look like at the end of the year?

2. How much can be done by the pupil and how much must be done by the teacher because the pupil cannot do it? We apply the trainer's golden rule. Never do anything for a pupil that he can do for himself.

Let us assume that we wish the notebooks to have a right-hand page of writing and a left-hand page of illustrations. We will concentrate on the text.

a. We want it to be divided into chapters about pre-stone-age man, old-stone-age man, new-stone-age man, the Egyptians, the Greeks, etc.
b. We want the chapters divided into long sections about, e.g. food and agriculture, clothing, shelter, social organisation, religion, art, science and technology, war, etc.
c. We probably want the long sections divided into subsections about, e.g. food and agriculture when Rome was a city state and food and agriculture when Rome was a luxury-loving empire based on slave labour.
d. We possibly want our subsections divided into what could be material for a paragraph.
e. We may wish to give detail within the paragraph.

This means that we wish to display five levels of generality, though it is unlikely that more than two of these will appear in one lesson.

There are various ways in which the levels of generality can be shown, e.g.

1. Centrally placed headings in capitals
2. Subheadings against margin in capitals
3. Sub-subheadings in minuscule
4. Theme sentences on left
5. Expanded detail on the right.

This system is based on letter size and spatial arrangement.

Alternatively or concurrently an outlining system may be used where:

Level 1	is numbered in large Roman e.g.	II
Level 2	is lettered in capitals	II A
Level 3	is numbered in arabic	II A 3
Level 4	is lettered in minuscule	II A 3c
Level 5	is numbered in small Roman	II A 3c(ii)

A concrete example will demonstrate how the system works and incidentally considerable ignorance of history.

X THE ROMANS

A. AGRICULTURE

1. When Rome was a city state, the majority of citizens were peasant farmers.
   (a) The citizens themselves worked the land, using
      (i) ploughs drawn by oxen
      (ii) hoes, sickles, spades, forks, etc.
      (iii) stone handmills for grinding corn

(b) Short military campaigns could be carried out when there was little to do on the farm.
e.g. (i) The Rape of the Sabine Women
(ii) ?
(c) They cultivated
(i) wheat
(ii) grapes
(iii) olives
(iv) ?
(d) They kept
(i) cattle
(ii) oxen for draught
(iii) geese (for sounding alarms)
(iv) bees

2. When Rome was the centre of a great empire most of the food was grown on great estates or imported.
(a) On the great estates cultivation was by slave labour.
(b) The dispossessed freeholders became a city rabble.
etc.

This technique, which is called outlining, is equally appropriate for the recording of certain kinds of geographical and biological information, e.g. Peoples of Africa, Functions of the blood in the rabbit.

It should be noted that:

a. even in first year the items at the lowest level of generality can be inserted into the appropriate framework by the pupil.
b. the pupil, however, cannot create the whole framework, because he does not know what the field is.
c. it would however be possible to start the year or each topic by setting out the ground which is to be covered and its main subdivisions.
d. it is also possible to demonstrate what a good notebook is like and always to summarise in a form which leads to good note-making.

Early training in note-making

The main headings and subheadings normally have to be given. The blackboard therefore reads:

X THE ROMANS

A. AGRICULTURE

The next level will be given at first, then extracted from the class by some such question as 'What two periods of Roman history have we been looking at?' By the end of the year it should be possible to ask what the main divisions of the topic should be.

The easiest way to begin is to supply a blackboard framework complete except for the (i), (ii), (iii) level items, which can be obtained in oral answers from the class.

Slightly more difficult is to provide guide questions, which can be used at the level above, e.g.

(a) Who worked the land?
(b) What sort of wars were fought?
(c) What did the Romans grow?
(d) What livestock did they keep?

Guide words are more difficult still e.g.

A. AGRICULTURE

1. city state

(a) citizens worked — used
(i) to turn over soil
(ii) implements
(iii) to grind corn

etc.

This can be made easier by thorough oral preparation, or more difficult by, e.g. only preparing at the 1 & (a) levels.

Pupils need practice in using their notes to produce 'essay' answers, but the notes should not be in a form that can be regurgitated as an essay answer.

Drawings in all subjects can be labelled in the same way. Biology provides a good model:

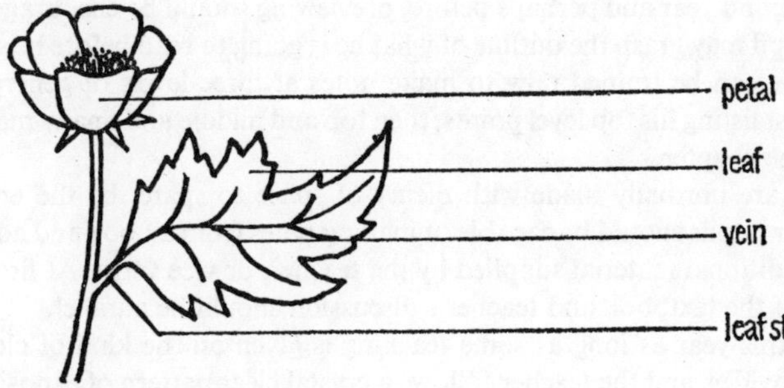

equally applicable to history:

THE VELOCIPEDE

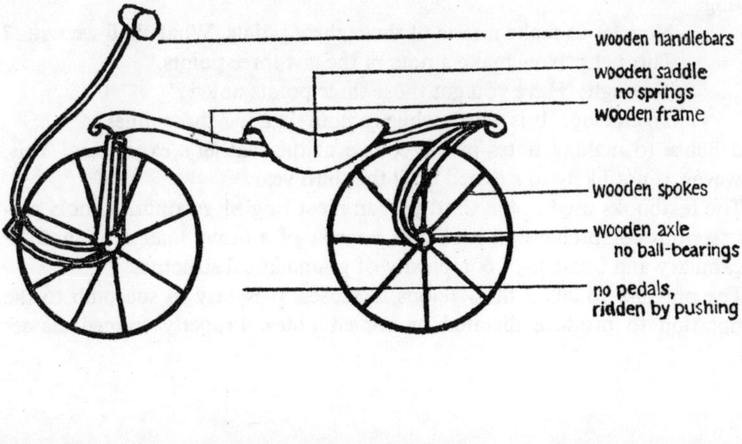

Copying a drawing which is already labelled from a book or the blackboard is the easiest technique, but demands no understanding from the pupil.

It adds a little to difficulty if the pupil has to put in the arrows.

More if he has to arrange the labels himself from words written elsewhere on the blackboard.

More if he has to draw from life as he invariably should.

More if he has to decide what must be labelled.

More if he has to remember the names and spelling on the labels for himself.

Making notes from a textbook is valuable, even in the first year, but 'Make notes on Chapter X' is too difficult. A specific aim is required, e.g.

(a) Read Chapter X in order to complete the following outline.

The Romans were fine engineers. They built

(i) (roads)
(ii) (bridges)
(iii) (ships)
(iv) (aqueducts)

(b) Read Chapter X in order to draw a map of Hannibal's route from Carthage into Italy.

(c) Copy the picture of a Roman legionary and label his armour and weapons.

This is excellent English comprehension work, because the reading has a purpose.

In the second year and perhaps before, previewing should be encouraged so that the pupil may grasp the outline of what he is going to read before he starts reading. He can be trained now to make notes at three levels of generality, perhaps first listing his top level points, then top and middle and finally making notes on the chapter.

If notes are normally made with plenty of space to spare, by the end of second year pupils should be capable of making notes from a book and adding to them additional material supplied by the teacher, or vice versa. At first the structure of the textbook and teacher's discussion should be parallel.

Also in this year as long as some teaching is given on the kind of clues a lecturer provides, and the teacher follows a crystal clear pattern of exposition, clueing all main and sub-heads, pupils might begin making notes in the course of the exposition. Various degrees of assistance are possible, from stopping and saying:

Now let us make a note of those three points. What shall we write?
Through: 'Now make a note of the last three points.'
Through: 'Have you got those three points noted?'
To clueing: 'It is worth while to note that . . .' three times

and hence to making notes in the course of the teacher's exposition. This, however, is not likely to succeed until the third year.

The textbooks used in the third year in most English-medium schools present serious comprehension problems because of a heavy load of unfamiliar vocabulary and because of complexity of grammatical structure.

The pressure to cover the syllabus increases. It is easy to succumb to the temptation to produce dictated or copied notes. Properly trained classes should however be able to cope given some help. Untrained classes need training and as a last resort, if time presses desperately, stencilled handouts can be used to make time available. This can be combined with the textbook as part of the training in note-making.

For example a stencilled handout covering part one of Parry *Europe & a Wider World* Chap. VII 'The English Plantations' might look something like the following. It is an aid to note-making.

VII THE ENGLISH PLANTATIONS

A. Ideas about Colonies

1. The British Government was considering establishing territories in 1604
   (a) Evidence
   (b) Reasons

2. It was agreed that the new colonies were to be distant from the Spanish ones. Suggested places
   (a)
   (b)
   (c)

The result some years later was . . .

3. Because the Spaniards had occupied the areas with available native labour, British colonies had to provide European labourers. The results of this were
   (a)
   (b)
   (c)

4. The arguments used to persuade people to support colonies were
   (a) religious
      (i)
      (ii)
   (b) political and strategic
      (i)
      (ii)
   (c) social – They were an outlet, a 'vent', for surplus population
      (i)
      (ii)
     This belief, however, . . . ?
   (d) but mainly economic
      (i)
      (ii)
      (iii)
      (iv)
      (v) Commodities
         a.
         b.
         c.
         d.
      (vi)

(e) The economic ideas were mistakenly optimistic.
(f) Three groups of colonies were established producing different main crops
(i)
(ii)
(iii)

[d] APPLICATIONS

Enough has been said to show that the teacher who wishes to train pupils in the skill of making notes has plenty of techniques at his disposal for adjusting the difficulty of the operation to the abilities of the class. One final point remains. The notes should be used because in no other way can they be shown to be useful. In first year a pupil can 'Tell the class about Roman agriculture when Rome was a city state.' He is not to read his notebook aloud but to turn the notes back into continuous if simple exposition. Later we can give a little time for preparation and ask in speech or writing for a comparison of the agricultural practices of, for example, the Egyptians and the Romans. This involves using two different sets of notes and bringing them together. Notes can also be made for particular projects, but before we turn to these we must look at summarising.

14 Teaching summarising:

[a] SUMMARISING IN EXAMINATION;

In the matter of the summary question some school certificate examining bodies have recently made very considerable changes, the implications of which have not yet been fully appreciated in the schools affected. In the bad old days the rubric used to be:

> Make a précis of the following passage. Your précis should be one-third of the length of the original and in your own words.

This was an extremely severe test even for a native English-speaker. It involved understanding the passage architectonically and in detail and then the simultaneous application of reported speech, paraphrase and compression without distortion of detail or balance. It was also a highly conventional test. The working world outside school is not littered with fairly self-contained passages of approximately 350 words in length that are all the better for being reduced to $116\frac{2}{3}$ words. Indeed such passages are so hard to find that schoolmasters faced with this curious demand from examiners needed special books to enable pupils to practise acquiring this strange skill, required solely for examination purposes.

In real life it is unusual to summarise to one-third of the original, unusual to summarise in reported speech and unheard of sedulously to avoid quotation from the original. The contrary is nearer to the truth; the more closely the original wording can be followed, the more successful the summary. It is also unusual to summarise whole passages; selective extraction is much more frequent. This, of course, involves providing a reason for making the summary other than 'because I tell you to' but outside the context of school, activity without any sensible purpose is not usually regarded as admirable.

The précis question was popular with examiners because it was easy to set, easy to mark and an excellent test of skill in the manipulation of words. But for students for whom English was a second language it was not even this.

Changes were clearly necessary and the bad old days have gone, but some of the bad old attitudes linger. There is no longer any need to separate summarising from the rest of the English syllabus, to shut it up in a separate period, to ask 'When should pupils start summarising?' or to approach the operation with infectious trepidation. Summarising is just one kind of composition. The fact that it is based on material already in words makes it easier rather than more difficult now that the examiner has ceased to regard 'lifting' from the original as wrong.

The only remaining rather artificial restriction is the word limit. It is a nuisance that this cannot be eliminated without causing very difficult marking problems. The difficulty for the examiner lies in devising a fair marking scheme for summaries on entirely different scales and for the candidate, which is more serious, in worrying about what scale will give him the best chance of success. It is perhaps kinder to both to suggest an approximate number of words purely as a guide to what scale to aim at and expect. There is of course no reason to retain one-third as the usual figure or to have any usual figure at all. The purpose and material should determine the scale proposed.

[b] HOW THE PUPIL LEARNS TO 'SUMMARISE' IN SCHOOL

It is obvious that understanding must precede any shortening process. Nevertheless pupils continue to be presented with material containing unfamiliar vocabulary and even discouraged from using dictionaries to deal with it. 'You must work it out as best you can for yourself, my boy.' It is surely possible to agree that unfamiliar vocabulary is an unfortunate, unnecessary, accidental complication that should be eliminated.

Even suitable material makes considerable demands on the complex skills of reading.

The pupil must understand the plain sense of what he is summarising. This we train him to do by intensive reading. But in one experimental test we did, very simple statements were misunderstood. The original on the subject of Fabre's observations of the hunting wasp said,

> An egg is laid in the side of the caterpillar.

This was restated by many examinees as,

> beside the caterpillar
> at the side of the caterpillar
> on the side of the caterpillar

Other caterpillars may be hunted for her grub.

was frequently rendered as

other caterpillars are hunted for her grub.

The cure for this is not in more practice in making summaries but in close attention to the exact meaning of what is read – more and better reading.

The pupil must also see the levels of generality in what he is summarising and how they fit together. He can be given specific practice in this by being asked to skim through material finding the general statements. He will need to do this at more than one level before he can make a good set of notes. In order to make an overall summary of a chapter, for example, he can practise picking out the generalisations and stringing them together omitting all detail. It is in fact possible to teach a class to make a creditable summary of nearly any old-fashioned précis passage in this way in a quarter of an hour, provided that they are not allowed to study the paragraphs in detail but only sufficiently fully to find the relevant general statements. This trick is not quite as mechanical as it sounds. Often the most general statement is purely introductory. The relevant generalisations are not always the first sentence or even any complete sentence. Sometimes a statement may be divided and sometimes repeated. Some judgement is called for, but perhaps the most useful feature of this technique is that it forces the pupil to break away from a meticulous and detailed reading of the passage before he starts to think. He sees the wood before the trees get in his light.

If we are aiming at as complete a summary as possible within a given number of words and have started with the generalisation, the next step may be to add one of the supporting particulars, choosing the most important in relation to the general statement. This is much easier than trying to shorten everything. The generalisation provides the touchstone and the particulars can be weighed one against the other for the strength of the support they give.

It is obviously possible to go on adding as many others as there is room for.

A variant of this is to start from a single-sentence summary – a title is not nearly so satisfactory – and keep on expanding it until the word limit is reached.

Preparatory work leading up to this occurs in reading lessons when we ask pupils what is the most important point in the paragraph and then whether the next point is an example, a reason, an explanation, etc. It occurs in note-making when we ask for sentence outlines and in composition when pupils construct paragraphs starting with, leading to or enclosed within generalisations.

The pupil must also understand the relative importance of items in relation to the purpose of the summary. It is here that textbooks abound in bad advice. 'Leave out the unimportant details' they cry. 'Generalise, don't particularise.' But until the aim of the summary is known, we cannot tell what is important and what is not. For example, in a little book called *Précis Practice for Overseas Students* (J. A. Bright and K. F. Nicholson) there is an extract about two gunboats attempting to pass a cataract on the Nile. A summary for a newspaper might well contain different details from one addressed to the Commander-in-Chief. One sentence states '160 men of the 10th Egyptians, who had been towed behind the gunboats, had to be left behind because of the force of the current.' No commanding officer would pass a summary that gave only the fact that 160 men were left behind. As far as he is concerned, the reason for this decision is very important.

Of the productive skills needed by the pupil, the least important is the ability to paraphrase, although it remains true that rigid adherence to the wording of the original is unlikely to produce a good summary; some rephrasing nearly always helps. This is why the technique of summarising by deletion is usually unsatisfactory.

Compression is certainly useful, but at school certificate level should not be regarded as an essential skill unless the examiner is prepared to present verbose material. This has not so far been tried. Much more important is the ability to write in a connected and readable way, that is to *express* connections and relationships of thought by subordination, the use of appropriate sentence linking words and phrases and by the arrangement of the material. These abilities are not required peculiarly for summarising; they are needed in the writing of many kinds of composition. In composition, as well as in summaries, it is always desirable to say as much in as few words as possible, subject only to the proviso that clarity must not be sacrificed to brevity. The pupil obviously needs some linguistic dexterity with alternative forms of expression.

He also needs to be able to forget that he knows the original so that he can put himself in the reader's place and examine what he has himself produced with a fresh eye. This is an exercise in imagination.

Doing summaries and having them marked by the teacher does something to improve the pupils' skills just as undirected kicking a ball about does something to improve abilities at football. But a great deal more can be done by the activities suggested in [c]–[e] below.

[c] SPECIFIC PRACTICE: REMEDIAL

If the reading and composition work including the teaching of note-making has been successful, there will be no need for specific practice in any summarising skill. If not, then the practice will be directed at the weakness.

If pupils find understanding the relationships of thought difficult, they can usefully make sentence outlines, which have the same pattern as notes but are fully expressed. This forces them to number the general statements and letter the particular ones.

If pupils are weak at expressing connections of thought, they can start from a sentence outline and put in the connecting words.

If they write wordily, they can be given exercises of gradually increasing difficulty in getting rid of idle words. The material will at first be obviously prolix so that it can easily be reduced. Then reduction may demand more ingenuity so that, for example, three sentences consisting of a general statement followed by two reasons can be reduced by co-ordinating the reasons in a subordinate clause. The most difficult material of all to reduce is one's own.

If their difficulty is in the perception of relevance, one can find passages from which selection can be made for different purposes. For example in the passage mentioned above describing Fabre's observation of the hunting wasp, Ammophila, two completely different selections are required if we ask (a) for an account of the habits of Ammophila suitable for an entry in an encyclopedia of natural history and (b) for the information given about Fabre himself.

The principle is clear. It is less effective to practise summarising as a whole than to diagnose the weaknesses of the pupils and attack each specifically.

[d] GROUP DISCUSSION

We have already suggested that the effect of group discussion is to make the pupils compare versions, weigh one against another and generally attend critically to problems of expression. It only remains to suggest ways of helping groups to work in a businesslike way.

One method is for the teacher to do the best summary he can and then to list the questions he has succeeded in answering. The pupils bring their first drafts, the questions are put on the board and they mark each other's and their own summaries awarding a tick for every question that is answered and discussing doubtful answers. They then set to work to improve their own drafts or to make a group draft.

Instead of questions, the teacher can use points, which means that he is in fact, providing the pupils with a marking scheme.

The question of what to do with irrelevant material can be raised at a slightly later stage.

The development of this is, of course, for the pupils to start one step earlier and devise the marking scheme for themselves. But this kind of work, which is frankly aimed at exam passing, should not be done until the examination year.

[e] PROVIDING SUMMARIES WITH A PURPOSE

As long as we do not work mainly on examination-length snippets and do not confine summarising and note-making to what is required for the purposes of the time-table subject English but include history, geography, etc., the pupils can derive practical benefit from working on summaries because the end-products are useful to them. 'Summarise this because I tell you to as an exercise' is not nearly as productive of sensible work as 'Summarise this because you or somebody else wants it for this, that or the other reason.'

Pupils want to revise before their examinations. This provides a reason for summarising or making outline notes on a chapter of their history book. It also provides a test of the usefulness of the summary or notes. If two or three months later, a pupil can read over his notes and orally or in writing expand them to recover the substance of the chapter or face a barrage of questions from his fellows, they are good notes because they enable him to do so. If he finds he cannot, he may be the more readily persuaded to learn a better technique.

It is not difficult to think of other uses. One can even force simplification and rewording by, for example, asking a senior class to produce summaries of, e.g. the Life of Pasteur in language that junior pupils can understand and then publishing them for the other class to read. There is no reason why over the years the senior classes should not supply the junior ones with a good deal of reading related to their syllabuses. This can vary from ambitious projects like the example suggested to quite short snippets of information about people or things.

Sometimes it is useful to have minutes of class discussions or of meetings. If the teacher is in the Chair, he can make the exercise very easy by summarising decisions as they are reached or very difficult by leaving this entirely to the class.

Sometimes he may use summaries to demonstrate points about composition teaching. If a pupil's composition can be summarised without loss of meaning in half the words, the pupil may be led to wonder whether he should not aim at more concise expression. Many interesting points about the scale on which writing is done can be made by expanding a single generalisation into first a summary and then a full-scale argument.

A wall newspaper with an excessive number of contributions can also provide a reason for rewriting at reduced length and a delicate exercise of judgement about how much each article can be shortened without undue loss.

We should summarise for a variety of purposes and on a number of different scales. Pupils need to practise all kinds of selective extraction of information. It is of great practical value to be able to go to a book and take from it everything one wants and nothing else. Sometimes what is wanted may be minute detail – everything about Marie Curie's schooldays for example. Sometimes we shall ask, especially orally, for single-sentence summaries of whole chapters – what impression do we get of Tom Sawyer's character from the first chapter? We shall find ourselves discussing the various merits of *bad, naughty, wicked, tricky, clever, cunning, mischievous,* etc.

There is no need to multiply examples. The great thing is to have plenty of practice for some practical useful purpose, to cover a variety of material, methods and scales and to keep firmly in mind that summarising, sensibly approached, equips the pupil with abilities equally useful for business and scholarship but that there are better ways of doing this than turning good extracts of 350 words into bad summaries of 120.

15 Projects and research essays

We would like to make a special plea for 'research essays' during the year before the examination year begins and for projects in the previous years. One reason why more projects are not done is that they require long-term advance planning, which is not a very sound reason for denying pupils a kind of experience that is useful and very enjoyable.

In large projects sections are handed over to groups and individual assignments farmed out to group members. The final product is for example, an illustrated file on Parents' Day 1969, which goes into the library for all to see. There are few schools that would not value a thirty-year series of such annual events. The planning will, of course, be done by the class in committee. Perhaps they will create something like the following, with their own names where we have put Pupil 1, etc.

Parents' Day 1969

Group 1	Preparations	Pupil 1	The Programme
		2	Arrangements for meeting and escorting parents
		3	Preparing the Art Room
		4	Preparing the Labs
		5	Preparing the Carpentry Shop
Group 2	Exhibitions	1	Displays in form rooms Jnr.
		2	Displays in form rooms Snr.
		3	The Art Room
		4	The Labs
		5	The Carpentry Shop
Group 3	Interviews	1	The oldest old boy
		2	The youngest parent
		3	The Chairman of the Board
		4	The Head Boy
		5	The youngest pupil
Group 4	Fashions	1	Women's dresses African
		2	Women's dresses European
		3	Women's dresses Asian
		4	Hats, handbags & accessories
		5	Men's accessories
Group 5	Speeches & Comment	1	The Headmaster said
		2	We think
		3	The Chairman said
		4	We think
		5	Overheard in passing
Group 6	Opinions and suggestions for next year	1	Sides of school life not represented
		2	
		3	Organisation
		4	Showing what was shown better
		5	Concluding summary

We might have two or three official photographers and illustrate a number of the sections, especially the fashion one, though perhaps the artists would do this better. There are a number of occasions every year when something of this kind can be done.

'Research essays' are even more valuable. They are essential in non-English-medium schools from which pupils go on to further education in the medium of English, because it is only by reading the subjects of their future study that pupils in such schools can acquire any acquaintance with the vocabularies and concepts of the subjects. It is not enough to suggest such reading; it needs to be given a purpose and followed by written work. Different groups of pupils will follow different subjects and the 'research essay' scheme allows pupils to pursue their interests in groups or even individually.

Some such scheme is almost equally necessary where, as in Zambia for example, pupils go straight from school certificate to university work. Its main value for such pupils is that the use of the library to find material, making of notes on it and writing it up teaches them how to work at the university – it prepares them for the future in a way that might be less necessary if they were going through a sixth form.

But even where neither of the above considerations applies, reading for research essays remains very valuable. It widens the pupil's background knowledge and gives him an opportunity to develop new interests and pursue them in some depth. We have frequently been astonished by the amount of time and energy pupils are prepared to put into this kind of work and, when they have reached the university, by the warmth of their regard for its practical educational value. The research essay brings into use a wide variety of useful skills, starting with those required for finding information: the ability to use indexes, lists of contents, books of reference, etc. the understanding of the arrangement of the library, the use of its index, the following up of bibliographies, etc. It also demands recording skills: note-making, summarising, quotation, etc. as well as composition skills. Because pupils rightly regard it as useful and interesting, they like doing it.

A beginning can be made in a simple way as soon as the pupils can use the *Children's Encyclopaedia* or the *Oxford Junior Encyclopedia*. They can be set to work in pairs or threes to find out all they can about one of fifteen or ten subjects chosen by the teacher who will, if he is wise, make sure the subjects are treated in different volumes. At first the subjects will require brief answers and all the material will be in one place but as the pupils improve at finding their way about books of reference and discover how to use the library the length and number of references will increase until perhaps eventually we reach a full-scale project such as *The Nile* in which chapters would be farmed out to groups and the end-product be an illustrated file for the library.

Projects of this size need to be planned up to a year in advance because the teacher usually has to do a good deal of bibliographical exploration himself in order to find out what is available and then order an adequate supply of suitable material for the school library. Even a good school library is rarely adequate to support a new project. One does not wish the pupils to be frustrated by inability to get their hands on the books they need.

Major projects are, of course, designed for publication from the beginning; there are plenty of possible uses for minor ones too. Short snippets of information fill up corners of the wall newspaper and can subsequently contribute questions to quizzes. Quite brief 'essays' can supply extra reading matter related to the school syllabus: biographies of scientists, background to history (costumes, castles, etc.) or geography (accounts of travels, summaries and simplifications of magazine articles). A class can supply its own current or future needs, finding out about the Elizabethan theatre to help in the reading of Shakespeare, or the French Revolution for *A Tale of Two Cities*.

In non-English-medium schools one would expect projects to follow the lines of the pupils' future interests so that future agriculturalists would be working on different agricultural systems, the agricultural revolution, farming by machinery, chemical farming or pesticides and weedkillers, while engineers, doctors, lawyers, economists, politicians, etc. pursued their different lines, all acquainting themselves with the basic lore and language of their professions. In such a school a library specially selected to be used in this way is essential.

For further reading

FRISBY, A. W. *Teaching English*. Longman, 1957.
GOWERS, SIR E. *The Complete Plain Words*. Penguin, 1970.
GURREY, P. *The Teaching of Written English*. Longman, 1954.
Teaching English as a Foreign Language. Longman, 1955.
Teaching the Mother Tongue in Secondary Schools. Longman, 1953.
KING, ALEC and KETLEY, M. *The Control of Language*. Longman, Australia.
WARNER, ALAN. *A Short Guide to English Style*. Oxford, 1961.
WINGFIELD, R. J. *Exercises in Situational Composition*. Longman, 1967.

5

SPEECH

1 Reading aloud

The majority of teachers still use reading aloud as their main weapon in the battle to improve their pupils' oral English and take the material to be read from the class reader. They then listen for mistakes and 'correct' them as they arise by interrupting the reader and requiring him to repeat a word or phrase in accordance with the model they provide.

This procedure is objectionable on a number of counts:

1. It interferes with the proper business of the reading lesson, which is to create imaginative response in the mind from the visual stimulus of black marks on paper.
2. Where it is used frequently, it slows down reading speed whereas the object is to increase it.
3. It provides a small amount of practice for a few individuals and bores everybody else.
4. It is highly productive of embarrassment to the reader. Indeed it is not unusual for a large number of corrections to lead to a deterioration of performance.
5. The pupils' practice, such as it is, is random instead of specific. Nobody knows whether the next thunderbolt will fall on an error of pronunciation, stress, intonation or phrasing. After fifty interruptions in a paragraph teachers have even been known to complain about a lack of fluency and urge pupils to read with more expression.
6. The material is all wrong. Nobody could learn the cut and thrust of normal conversation by reading *David Copperfield* aloud from end to end. It is not conversational material in its vocabulary or grammar.
7. The exercise of reading unprepared literary material aloud is too difficult for all but the best pupils.
8. Unless students are going to be teachers or announcers, the ability to read aloud is of little practical value compared with the ability to play an effective part in conversations, discussions and committee meetings.
9. Reading aloud of this kind is purposeless. Nobody listens because everybody has the text. The sensible ones ignore the background mumbling and read on.

We cannot 'do as much reading aloud as we can' while we are doing the class reader and believe that we are doing our duty by the pupils' spoken English.

2 The problem of the model

Before we can consider what can profitably be done with reading aloud, let us examine some other problems. First there is the question of the model. Suppose we could achieve complete success in making our pupils speak precisely as we wish, what should we choose to do? What would *they* choose to do? Julius Nyerere, Milton Obote and Jomo Kenyatta do not speak English like B.B.C. announcers, but nor does President Johnson – he certainly does not even want to do so – or Harold Wilson – and he perhaps tries not to. Sooner or later all countries that use English as a first or second language develop varieties of accent. The United States did so long ago with the result that Americans model themselves on Americans and not on any British-English speakers. The same is true of New Zealanders and Australians. According to Peter Strevens the same thing has happened in West Africa. In East Africa the problem is complicated by the presence of native English speakers and Asians in considerable numbers but it may well be true today that most learners of English as a second language would rather speak English in the manner of their educated fellow-countrymen than like an English public-school boy. We should at least recognise the possibility of emotional rejection of attempts to make pupils 'talk lah-di-dah'.

Fortunately the varieties of accent of all educated speakers of English – Indian, African, Malaysian, Chinese, Japanese, American, Australian, New Zealand, Scottish, Irish, Yorkshire or Somerset – have a great many common features which are far more important than their differences. Otherwise the speakers would not find each other comprehensible. The distinctions that all educated speakers make are the important ones for our purposes; those that merely differentiate one educated speaker from another do not matter at all. We need no longer cherish quaint superstitions about one variety being 'better' than another.

As for the model we present to the pupils, we have no choice; we must use our own, though we need not insist on too precise imitation and we may do something about exposure to other models.

Having decided on our model, we next need to equip ourselves with some background knowledge of phonology in order to become conscious of the complex system of signals we use with such impressive unconscious skill – not because we shall teach this knowledge directly to our classes, but because we need it in order to know what to teach them. This is not the place and we are not the people to set out phonological theory but there is a list of books at the end of this chapter and we know from our own experience that Fries's *Teaching and Learning English as a Foreign Language* makes an illuminating starting-point for the innocent.

Let us note that some knowledge of the phonology of our pupils' L1 will be very helpful to us. As a warning to which we shall return later, let us also note that nearly all the phonetic work we do will be remedial. We shall be trying to undo old habits and not simply to create new ones.

3 The Phoneme:

[a] CONTRASTIVE ANALYSIS

If we mean to be even mildly scientific about speech work, the first thing to do is to list the phonemes of English and compare them with those of our pupils' first language. A phoneme is the smallest contrastive unit that may bring about a change of meaning. Because *bit* and *pit* mean different things [b] and [p] are different phonemes in English. Not all languages make this distinction between [b] and [p]. It does not exist in Arabic, for example.

In an English phonemic alphabet we therefore include [b] and [p] to represent all the occurrences of sounds *recognised by English speakers as* [b] and [p]. This does not mean that all pronunciations of [p] are the same. They are not. In the word *pit* the initial sound is aspirated, that is, followed by a release of air. In the word *spit*, it is not. But in English the difference between aspirated p and non-aspirated p makes no difference to meaning. If it did, we should need two symbols. If we do need to refer to different pronunciations of [p] in different phonetic contexts, we can call them the allophones of [p]. The native English speaker without phonetic training finds allophones difficult to hear because all our experience in understanding English has taught us to ignore them and attend only to phonemic differences. One of the easiest differences to spot is that between the two allophones of [l] in *little.* To an English ear many foreign speakers who do not make this distinction appear to say *leetil.*

Very roughly we may say that a speaker who fails to make allophonic distinctions will sound foreign but be instantly comprehensible, whereas one who fails to make phonemic distinctions will in certain contexts confuse the hearer. We once heard a splendid cross-purposes conversation in which one speaker was referring to farming in S. Africa and the other to famine. In other contexts the result will be to amuse rather than confuse: 'I'm coming on a sheep.'

When we start to listen to a foreign language, we hear some of the sounds as 'the same' as those in our native language and some as 'different'. We are generally wrong. They are much more likely to be all different but the ones we think are the same are near enough for us to make a phonemic identification. It is extremely difficult to hear unfamiliar phonemes. We tend instead to hear the nearest familiar one and to ignore the difference as insignificant. We can now return to our list of the phonemes of English and the pupils' vernacular in order to see what it will help us to do. We shall have to use examples but it must be realised that false equivalents will vary according to the vernacular of the learner. The ones we shall use proved useful in teaching speakers of a wide range of Bantu languages. We will omit diphthongs and consonants and confine ourselves to vowels.[1]

[1] For the full list of phonetic symbols used see the appendix on page 200.

VOWELS

KEYWORD	PHONEMIC TRANSCRIPTION	ENGLISH PHONEME	APPROX. AFRICAN PHONEME
SEE	siː	iː	iː
SIT	sit	i	
LET	let	e	
MAN	mæn	æ	e
BUT	bʌt	ʌ	
FAR	fɑː	ɑː	ɑː
FUR	fəː	əː	
POT	pot	o	o
SAW	soː	oː	
FOOT	fut	u	
TOO	tuː	uː	uː
AGO	ə'gou	ə	

It seems incredible to the native English speaker that words as different as *bad, bud, barred* and *bird* all sound the same to many Africans. It is, of course, equally incredible to an Arab that English speakers confuse the sounds represented by *dal* and *dod.* Neither inability is, however, to be ascribed to stupidity. That the inability exists is easy to confirm by dictating words in isolation in such groups as:

hat hut heart hurt
cat cut cart curt

The inability to distinguish between phonemes also shows up in written work where it is easy to confuse it with spelling or even grammatical errors. The cure for the pupil who writes *leaving* for *living* is not only to explain the difference of meaning, but also to improve his pronunciation, which may prevent him from writing *beaten* for *bitten* or *sitted* for *seated.* The pupil who pronounces *run* and *ran* in the same way may also appear to be in grammatical difficulties, whereas his trouble is phonetic.

When we list diphthongs and consonants, we shall find numerous other problems and begin to understand why, for example, certain speakers have difficulty with [s] and [ʃ], [r] and [l][1] or [p] and [f]. Sometimes difficulties pile up. One African tribe at least has difficulty in hearing any difference between *ugly* and *angry* because:

(i) they equate [ʌ] and [æ]
(ii) they equate [l] and [r]

[1] In East Africa I was frequently called Mr Blight and like to think the slip was phonetic and not Freudian. J.A.B.

(iii) and in their vernacular no nasal ever precedes a voiced stop so that they do not hear [ŋ] before [g]. This leads also to an inability to hear any difference between *under* and *udder* or *widow* and *window*.

Having found our problems, we have to decide which are important enough to deal with, bearing in mind that we shall have other problems when we think of syllables, stress groups and phonetic phrases. Some distinctions are not made in all dialects of English, that between [u] and [uː] for example. Not surprisingly, it is difficult to find pairs differentiated only by this distinction: *could* and *cooed*, *hood* and *who'd*, *wooed* and *wood* are the only ones that come to mind off-hand and it is difficult to imagine any context in which they could be confused.

[b] TEACHING MATERIALS AND METHODS

The next step is to embody in teaching material the distinctions we decide are important. To begin with at any rate we like to do one contrast at a time and to start by using minimal pairs.

Our teaching material for the contrast between [ɑː] and [əː] looks like this:

[ɑː] *v.* [əː]

bath	birth	farther	further	cart	curt
pass	purse	hard	heard	card	curd
car	cur	heart	hurt	barn	burn
carve	curve	parson	person	far	fur
part	pert	star	stir	farm	firm

Spellings of [ɑː]

ar	arm	
	are	(but not -rr- *arrow* or after w – *warm*)
al	half	
	calm	
	palm	
a (+s)	class	
	basket	
	past	(but also [æ] as in *passage*)
a (+θ)	bath	
	path	(not in *maths*)
ear	heart	
	hearth	
er	clerk	
	Derby	
a (+f)	after	
	laugh	(not -ff- as in *baffle*)

Spellings of [əː]

ir	girl
	dirty
	shirt
ur	Thursday
	turn
	purse
er	herd
	hers
	fern
w + or	work
	worth
	word
ear	heard
	learn
yr	myrtle

a (+n/m + consonant)	demand	(but note *land*,
	example	*cramp*, etc.)
etc.	banana	
	tomato	(but not in America)

The material can be constructed quite easily by running down the vocabulary of the *General Service List* and noting all words that have corresponding pairs until enough have been found. This ensures that at least one member of the pair will be common. For the spellings we refer to Friederich, *English Pronunciation – the Relationship between Pronunciation and Orthography*, Longman, 1958.

The first step in teaching is to explain the reason for the difficulty and to see if the pupils can identify the sound in isolation. Many teachers use key words asking, for example, whether what they say is the sound in *arm* or the sound in *bird*: no. 1 or no. 2.

1	2
arm	bird

If the pupils still find difficulty, they can get some further help by watching how wide the teacher opens his mouth. Some teachers like to explain at this point how the sound is made. We have found Paul Christophersen, *An English Phonetics Course*, Longman, 1956, very helpful in providing explanations for African pupils. The author describes how the sound is produced, as do many others, but he also gives good guidance about how the African pupil can get the vocal organs in the right place. For example, about the two sounds we are considering he says, 'If your mistake is that of saying *bard*, you should open your mouth less wide. And then, of course, you must always remember to make it a really long vowel.' As easy as that – and it works.

When we come to getting the pupils to practise, we like to use the 1.2.3 drill. The teacher says the pair once, varying the order, the group chorus the pair twice, and then three individuals say the pair once each. The rhythm,[1] once established, carries the class along at a good rate and should not be interrupted by corrections or demands for repetition. Instead, if the words of a pair said by an individual are indistinguishable, the teacher should insert an extra model without breaking the rhythm. Naturally he makes a mental note of the pupils who are in most need of practice, and sees that they get the lion's share of it.

This drill is much more entertaining if a tape-recorder is used. The pupils can file past the microphone, saying their piece and moving on. When the tape is played back, they can evaluate their own performance without embarrassment. It has been objectified.

Five three-minute drills on consecutive days are more effective than fifteen minutes at a stretch. A complete period should never be given to this kind of speech work. After the five intensive drills revision should occur about a week later and then at increasing intervals as required.

The spellings we generally try to elicit from the class by asking what ways

[1] This drill is incidentally good practice in stress-timing mentioned below. There is a silent beat between utterances. FAR : FUR (pause) FAR : FUR (pause).

they have noticed of spelling the sound in question or what words they know that contain the sound. Sometimes we offer clues to the words we want, partly for fun, but mainly to avoid pronouncing them, for example, 'Think of a fruit beginning with b.'

Sometimes we combine this with dictionary work, asking the class to find the pronunciation of the words on the blackboard or for example, to see how many *wor-* words they can find pronounced wəː and whether they are *worried* about any exceptions. They can sometimes work out a worthwhile rule for themselves.

The next stage is to move on to sentences, individual or built into substitution tables, containing numerous examples of the contrasts to be practised. Nursery rhymes, jingles and tongue twisters provide useful practice material. See, for example, Geoffrey Barnard's *Better Spoken English* (Macmillan, 1959).

Examples of individual sentences might be:

First run as fast as you can as far as the fir trees.
She heard the hard words and they hurt her heart.
Tell the guards to gird on their armour, Irma.

A substitution table might read like this:

A	B	C
1. When it's her turn,	don't let her	hurt herself. Her heart's not strong.
2. When it's the little girl's turn,	I'd prefer her not to	pass her purse to Myrtle.
3. When Irma Gurney starts,	tell her firmly not to	work without a clerk.

Incidentally the businesslike way to use a substitution table[1] is to train classes to read in the order:

A_1 B_1 C_1
A_1 B_1 C_2
A_1 B_1 C_3
A_1 B_2 C_1

and so on with

A_2 B_1 C_1 following A_1 B_3 C_3.

Again incidentally, work of this kind must be done fast and time need not be wasted while pupils stand up in order to speak. No lesson is greatly improved by being punctuated by the scraping of chairs on the floor while the pupils lumber to their feet. If the teacher is unable to listen to an utterance from a seated pupil without offending his own or his headmaster's sense of propriety, we offer him our sympathy and the suggestion that he starts to operate speech drills with all the class standing instead of sitting.[2]

[1] See also P. A. D. MacCarthy, *English Language Teaching*, May 1950 and June 1950.

[2] The problem of the conflict between the need for rapid exchanges between teacher and class and the demands of decorum in more formal cultures should not, perhaps, be dismissed so frivolously. In all English lessons where it is more efficient for the class to answer without standing up we explain this and add that it does not apply to other lessons or other teachers.

We have now exemplified in teaching material and method one pair of phonemic contrasts. With African pupils it might be necessary to construct similar material for all the contrasts involved, which, even limiting the examples to the one African vowel, involves drills contrasting:

[ɑː]	*v.*	[ʌ]	barred	*v.*	bud
[ɑː]	*v.*	[a]	barred	*v.*	bad
[əː]	*v.*	[ʌ]	bird	*v.*	bud
[əː]	*v.*	[a]	bird	*v.*	bad
[a]	*v.*	[ʌ]	bad	*v.*	bud

This is in addition to [ɑː] *v.* [əː] barred *v.* bird, which we used as our example.

We shall, of course, not waste time in teaching contrasts that give no difficulty to our particular pupils. We shall concentrate on the ones that matter most and tackle the 'worst' ones first.

[C] TESTING

Testing can be done by dictating individual words or sentences without contextual clues, for example:

He looked at the buds on the trees.

Discrimination is made more difficult if the material is taped.

Productive use can be tested by getting pupils to read individual words or sentences preferably on to a recorder.

4 The Syllable

As soon as we turn our attention to this larger unit, we are likely to find a whole set of new problems. A pupil who has no difficulty in pronouncing:

[k]	in	KISS	[kis]
[l]	in	LISTEN	['lisn]
[ou]	in	GO	[gou]
[ð]	in	THIS	[ðis]
[z]	in	HIS	[hiz]

may still make the word *clothes* sound like [klouðːz]. In this particular example the word appears in rapid English speech as [klouz]

['putʃə 'klouz on 'kwik]

and there is therefore a short cut to a satisfactory pronunciation but in general the problem remains: the pupil who can say all the sounds in isolation may have problems with transition in unfamiliar combinations. The syllabic structure of our pupils' native language may be completely different from that of English and there are sure to be some sounds that occur in different positions in the syllable. In English [j] occurs initially in syllables but not finally with the result that the French word *fille* is difficult for Englishmen to pronounce. The sound [ŋ] occurs frequently finally but never initially. Any Englishman can say *king* [kiŋ] but ties himself into knots if he tries to say [ŋik].

The pattern of the Bantu syllable is consonant vowel, consonant vowel – CVCV.

kino ki ? kitabu

Even the nasals in such words as Kampala, Jinja and Bantu are only apparent exceptions because the nasal and following consonant represent what is one sound not two. The result of this pattern is that:

(i) all syllables end in vowels
(ii) no two consonants are ever articulated consecutively[1]
(iii) no two vowels are ever articulated consecutively.

By contrast numerous English syllables end in consonants either singly or in clusters of up to five as in *strengths.* And if a context occurs in which it is necessary to talk about materials of different lengths, strengths and thicknesses, the speaker has to make a formidable array of six or seven consecutive consonants, [ŋ(k)θsstr]. Many Bantu speakers evade the problem by allowing a vowel to intrude and say, for example, [ju:sifəl] for *useful* or [mʌnθiz] for [mʌnθs].

The spelling of English is notoriously misleading and many classes profit from being shown that the pronunciation of final *s*, which occurs so frequently in plurals and possessives, and final *d*, which occurs so often in the past tense and participle, follow quite simple regular rules. For example:

(i) Words ending in the sounds	e.g.	for the endings spelt	add the sound
s	hiss		
z	jazz		
ʃ	crash	s or es	[iz]
ʒ	garage		
tʃ	church		
dʒ	judge		

(ii) After all other voiced sounds *s* is pronounced [z]
(iii) After all other voiceless sounds *s* is pronounced [s]

It is not difficult to get a class to arrive at this rule once they can distinguish by a finger on the larynx or by ear a voiced sound from a voiceless one. They can then apply it by preparing a paragraph to read aloud with particular attention to the correct pronunciation of final *s*. This is a much more sensible way of using reading aloud than just for random practice. It also gives the rest of the class something to listen for and therefore a reason for attending to the performer.

The pronunciation of consecutive syllables involves boundary problems. There is an audible difference between *I scream* and *ice-cream*, *see Mabel* and *seem able*. There is little likelihood of contextual ambiguity in most such pairs and the most tiresome manifestation of this problem in the secondary school occurs in written work where pupils put, for example, *pro-* at the end of one line and *-blem* at the beginning of the next. However, since the conventional division of English words in writing is a muddle of phonetic principles and

[1] For seven years G.P.M. was known as Makaleggy to Baganda friends who had not had the benefit of proper phonetic training. He was the last person in the school to discover who this mysterious fellow was.

graphic conventions, we believe in a short cut and tell our classes firmly, 'If there isn't room for a word at the end of one line, put it on the next one.'

At primary level wrong syllable division can cause serious grammatical misunderstandings. When Peter Wingard and John Bright were teaching in a Luganda-speaking primary school, they were puzzled by the way the pupils insisted on saying, 'You're mnot standing up.' The simple answer was that (i) owing to the distribution of nasals in Luganda, they 'expected' nasals to be initial in the syllable; (ii) they had therefore heard the previous structure taught as 'I mnot taking' and identified the negating morpheme as *mnot*. They did not hear the error that presumably occurred when they first taught 'I'm taking' and would not have spotted its importance if they had.

There is one curious feature of British-English pronunciation that only shows up in continuous speech. Pronounced separately, words spelt with a final *r* end with a vowel sound:

['letə]
[ɑː]

In continuous speech, however, an r link occurs before a following vowel:

[ðə 'letər 'ɑːr iz in ðə 'sekənd 'hɑːf əv ði 'ælfəbet[1]]

This also is worth pointing out to classes and can be practised using a marked passage for reading.

We had better pause at this point because there is an admission to be made, and a problem of technique to be considered. The admission is that work on the improvement of phonemic discrimination at secondary level comes at the wrong time and can be disappointing in terms of results. The proper place to work intensively on improvement in pronunciation is in the primary school and the training college. Something can be done and should be done in the secondary school but we should not perhaps aim too high, use too much time or be too disappointed with unspectacular progress.[2]

5 Phonetic Script

The problem of technique is whether or not to teach pupils at secondary schools who are already familiar with conventional spelling a phonemic alphabet. This is, of course, quite a different problem from whether one starts pupils off reading a phonemic script or some compromise between that and a conventional one.

There is no question in our minds about the necessity of teaching the active use of a phonemic script to pupils in training colleges. For them it is an essential tool. Even the secondary pupil must be able to decipher one in order to use

[1] Certain speakers use an intrusive [r] between some vowels even when no r exists in spelling but the idear of teaching this is repugnant. Some speakers, if not most, use [w] links in, for example, '2 and 2' and [j] links in '3 and 3'.

[2] J.A.B., who has fewer moral scruples than his colleague, believes in a mildly Machiavellian approach, veiling his intention to improve pronunciation behind a façade of concern to help pupils with their spelling problems because everybody knows the enormous importance of correct spelling and *it comes in the exam.* He is even capable of teaching his classes a phonemic alphabet in order to help them to use their dictionaries because, again, everybody knows that *dictionaries are very important.*

his dictionary. Where classes are very large and genuine conversation is hard to arrange, it is also valuable for them to be able to read phonetic script fluently in order to make use of some of the phonetic readers that are available. It does not take long to learn. Classroom charts are available, for example, Kingdon: *Phonetic Symbols for English*, from Longmans.

A receptive knowledge is, however, more important than a productive one and we do not think pupils should spend a great deal of time, if any, for example, in transliterating prose passages or even conversation from the conventional script to a phonemic one. There are too many problems involved. The 'same' utterance said by two different people may have considerable phonetic differences, some but not all of which can be shown by a broad transcription. The 'same' utterance said by the same speaker may vary almost as much, depending on speed and formality as well as differences of meaning.

What do you think that is?

can vary from, for example,

[wot 'duː juː θiŋk 'ðæt iz]

to

[wodʒə θiŋk 'ðæt iz]

6 The Stress group

The next unit in the hierarchy of English pronunciation is the stress group or foot. Improvements in stress and intonation are easier to obtain at secondary level and contribute more to making pupils' speech an effective means of communication than the alterations to the pronunciation of individual sounds and clusters of sounds that we have so far considered.

The essential concept to get across to pupils is that English is a stress-timed language; the heavy beats follow one another at equal intervals of time regardless of the number of more lightly stressed intervening syllables. Most foreign learners find this a very strange feature of English. Their ears tell them that English speakers 'swallow their words' or 'talk very fast'. They are therefore mystified by the frequency with which they are urged to 'read more slowly' or blamed for 'gabbling'. The truth, for once, is very simple. Speakers with a syllable-timed L1 read sequences of stress groups consisting of single syllables too fast, missing the point, for example, of:

the bare, | black | cliffs | clanged | round him |.

Conversely, and for exactly the same reason, they read groups containing many lightly stressed syllables too slowly failing to maintain the regular progression from peak to peak.

The Assyrian | came down | like the wolf | on the fold |.

The first line quoted contains seven syllables, the second twelve, but because the second line contains four stress groups to the other's five it only takes about four-fifths of the time to read.

We have taken our examples from poetry but the stress-timing in prose is equally regular although the patterns of the stress groups have none of the regularity of metrical feet. The division into poetic feet does not in fact correspond fully with the division into stress groups. Too exact a correspondence leads to monotony. 'If the rhythm is made to fit exactly, and without variation, into the metrical structure of the verse form, the result is a jingle. The rhythm of poetry is characterised by complex and highly varied interaction of the metre with the natural patterns of English phonology.'[1]

The fact that normal speech in English is stress-timed can be demonstrated by reading some such series as the following against a regular beat such as may be provided by a metronome or in the classroom by a gentle tapping.

a GREAT BOOK
a GREATer BOOK
the GREATest of BOOKS
in the GREATest of his BOOKS

No native speaker has any difficulty in maintaining a regular rhythm using a silent beat between items, but many foreign speakers find it very hard to get through the unstressed syllables rapidly enough. Sometimes this is because they have not given themselves enough time in the first case where there are adjacent heavy stresses. Sometimes it is because they insist on putting in some intermediate stresses and produce a pattern reminiscent of schoolboy renderings of *Hiawatha*,

IN the DOORway OF his WIGwam . . .

We have found the stress exercises in Stannard Allen's *Living English Speech* a very useful cure for this disease. There are tapes published in conjunction with this book. The 1.2.3 drill is useful too.

For teaching purposes it seems best to regard the stress group as consisting of one strong and a number of associated weaker syllables. It then corresponds pretty closely with the older-fashioned teacher's feeling that reading aloud should be in sense groups and with the good teacher's laudable desire not to separate phonology and grammar in his teaching, however necessary it may be to do so in a scientific description.

The number of stress groups in a given phonetic text will vary according to the rapidity of the speech and according to whether it is casual or careful. Gimson recommends aiming for teaching purposes at a careful colloquial style. In such a style we would mark stress groups as follows:

Three | days | later | Mollie | disappeared|. For some weeks | nothing | was known | of her whereabouts|, then | the pigeons | reported | that they'd seen her | on the other | side | of Willingdon.

7 The phonetic phrase

If we now mark the same passage off in phonetic phrases, it will become clear that these are composed of one or more stress groups. They are separated by distinct pauses and contain one syllable which receives special attention.

Three days *lat*er | Mollie disap*peared.*| For some *weeks* | nothing was known of her *where*abouts|, then the pigeons re*port*ed that they'd seen her on the other side of *Will*ingdon.

[1] M. A. K. Halliday, A. McIntosh and P. Strevens, *The Linguistic Sciences and Language Teaching*, Longman, 1964.

The italicised syllables are the ones one speaker would pick out in careful colloquial reading. It is by no means certain that others would do the same, and a difference of context would involve very considerable changes.[1] For example, if in the previous sentence something had happened two days later, one would read:

THREE days later.

If one had it in mind that somebody else had previously disappeared, one would read:

MOLLie disappeared.

If one knew that speculation about where she was had been going on, one would read:

nothing was KNOWN of her whereabouts.

The selection of the syllable for special attention and the intonation given to it make profound changes of meaning. Unless their attention is drawn to it, many foreign learners who hear English mainly in the school situation are unaware of such differences as are suggested in the brackets below.

THAT'S not the book I gave you. (It was another book.)
That's NOT the book I gave you. (But you seem to think it is.)
That's not the book *I* gave you. (It's the one somebody else gave you.)
That's not the book I GAVE you. (I only lent you that one.)
That's not the book I gave YOU. (I gave it to somebody else.)

The difficulty is not only receptive. Pupils who overstress weak syllables, especially pronouns, frequently convey the wrong meaning. If they want to mention a simple failure to meet somebody in the words, 'I didn't meet him,' they are likely to overstress the first pronoun and elicit the answer, 'Oh? Who did?' or the second and get, 'Who did you meet, then?'

8 Teaching techniques

Having looked at the units involved, we move on to the next problem, how to improve the pupils' skill by specific teaching about speech, specific practice or general practice.

An area that may be taught directly concerns the pronunciation of numerous structural words in unstressed positions. Numerous decisions are involved about just what to include in careful colloquial speech and what is casual and need not be presented for active use.

We would teach, for example, [its ə'piti]. We would not teach [sə 'piti]
We would teach *have* = [həv] [əv] and [v]
We would teach *he* = [hi] but not [i]
We would teach *and* = [ənd] [nd] [ən] but not [n].

But these are merely examples of personal choices. What forms the teacher chooses matters much less than that there should be teaching and practising of some forms actually used in speech.

[1] Fries' *Teaching and Learning English as a Foreign Language* has a fascinating, grammatically based, step by step procedure for marking limited intonation with its related features of pause, stress and rhythm.

We start with teaching and practice in *not* overstressing weak syllables because in our experience this is the commonest error. The next step is to show the kind of situation that demands heavy stress on words not normally stressed such as anomalous finites and pronouns. This usually involves some form of contrast and can be practised in such examples as:

> We thought we could do it as easily as they could but we were wröng and they were right.

Other features that can be dealt with by instruction and examples for practice are, for example,

1. the alternative question

   > Did you use a pen, or a pencil?

   as opposed to

   > You want a signature for it? Could I borrow a pen or a pencil?

2. the initial long adverbial

   > When the party was eventually over, there was still all the washing-up to do.

3. the confirmation-seeking question tag:

   > That WAS silly, wasn't it?

   as opposed to the genuine query:

   > That was SILLY, wasn't it?

4. the WH- question with its falling tune:

   > Why did you ask George to come?

   as opposed to the YES/NO question with its rising tune:

   > Did you ask George to come?

5. and if conversation is to be read from stories the effect of these on the intonation of the following reporting verb and subject

   > 'Why did you ask George to come?' said Mary.
   > 'Did you ask George to come?' asked Mary.

6. The 'polite' intonation of

   > 'Sit down, please.'

These and many other similar regularly recurring patterns can be practised initially using strings of intonationally similar sentences. The pattern is easily picked up in a 1.2.3 drill. Such items can be built into a complete teaching-of-speech syllabus and there are certain advantages in this systematic approach. If one works from phonemes to phonetic phrases, revision of each unit is almost automatic. Naturally, as mastery improves, one begins to turn the single-pattern drills into little dialogues, then playlets, and so moves gradually into drama.

The main disadvantages of a systematic approach are that it is difficult to keep it interesting and not easy to arrange that all teachers are constantly *au fait* with what a given class has covered; 'good speech' is therefore likely to be confined to parts only of the English course.

If one makes such a syllabus of speech work it is worth while to make a brief summary of it for all colleagues who are teaching in English so that they know what to expect. We have found them particularly grateful for information about what is not worth spending time on.

There is one very simple way in which all teachers can contribute to the improvement of pupils' speech. They can insist that all answers and contributions to class discussion shall be audible and refrain from the pernicious habit of repeating what a pupil has said when it may not have been audible. It is very difficult to avoid helping the lesson along in this way and very painful and frustrating to demand repetition when the next interesting point is just round the corner, but it must be endured for the sake of future efficiency.

All specific drills are artificial and the problem of transferring the phonological skills from the drills to normal speech is a difficult one. Question and answer drills make a useful intermediate step. For example:

Pupil 1: I'm going to Delhi.
Pupil 2: Are you going in January or February?
Pupil 1: In February.
Pupil 3: I'm going to the pictures.
Pupil 4 Are you going in the morning or the evening?
Pupil 3: In the evening.

But many teachers avoid the whole transfer problem and achieve excellent results by starting at the other end. They begin with dialogues, home-made plays and play-readings and demand maximum comprehensibility and the phonological behaviour that goes with it for the sake of the success of the play. The speech of the actor faced with the need to get it across to the back of the hall improves rapidly if he is given the kind of help he knows he needs.

When a piece of dialogue shows up a difficulty, the teacher notes it for future drilling so that all the drills his pupils do are relevant to known difficulties. As with the errors in written work, they can in subsequent years be anticipated by being drilled out before the piece of dialogue is tackled by the next class.

Teachers who spend time on plays generally include the speaking of verse as well. This is particularly useful in helping pupils to acquire a feel for stress-timing. The verse need not be great poetry. 'Matilda told such dreadful lies' is fun to read and has just that extra rhythmic regularity over prose that makes it easy to say.

We have had a very happy couple of lessons working up to a choral spoken performance of the *Pied Piper*. We did the rats tumbling out of the houses in groups of four pupils round the class and they thumped the points home with the utmost enjoyment.[1]

[1] This is a specimen extract from our 'script'.

SOLO VOICE 1 (BOY)	Into the street the Piper stept, Smiling first a little smile,
SOLO VOICE 2 (GIRL)	As if he knew what magic slept In his quiet pipe the while;
1 AND 2 TOGETHER	Then, like a musical adept, To blow the pipe his lips he wrinkled
1 AND 2 + 3 (GIRL)	And green and blue his sharp eyes twinkled Like a candle-flame where salt is sprinkled;
1, 2, 3 + 4 (BOY)	And ere three shrill notes the pipe uttered You heard as if an army muttered;

[continued on page 192]

9 Special requirements and general techniques

We have discussed the teaching of speech in a separate chapter. We believe that it is necessary to think about it as an important part of the syllabus with its own requirements: a tape-recorder, record-player, radio and, where appropriate, television set and, where possible, sound projector for films. It requires its own visual aids: phonetic charts and lists of key words. Teachers need special knowledge of English phonetics in order to teach speech most effectively. Fortunately there is no lack of good books and the necessary information is readily available outside universities and training colleges – in many cases more readily than within them.

Special texts are also required to provide drills and exercises dealing with particular difficulties, and to bridge the gap between single-sentence utterances and whole plays. Whether they are made or bought depends on the teacher.

There are also special requirements in matters of technique.[1] How can we make sure the pupil hears the item we are trying to teach? There are a number of useful tricks but first a preliminary warning. Emphatic pronunciation is dangerous. To correct a pupil who says:

This is book

by saying,

This is A book

invites him to reproduce this abnormal pattern of pronunciation and stress.

Repetition of that to which attention should be directed is more effective and enables normal stress and intonation patterns to be retained

[ðis iz ə – iz ə – ə – iz ə – 'buk]

with a normal repetition – [ðis iz ə 'buk].

Slowing down without altering stress or intonation patterns is also useful.

1, 2, 3, 4 + ½ REMAINDER	And the muttering grew to a grumbling;
ALL	And the grumbling grew to a mightly rumbling And out of the houses the rats came tumbling
IN GROUPS OF FOUR SPEAKERS	Great rats small rats lean rats brawny rats Brown rats black rats grey rats tawny rats Gray old plodders gay young friskers Fathers mothers uncles cousins
ALL	Cocking tails and pricking whiskers Families by tens and dozens Brothers, sisters, husbands, wives – Followed the Piper for their lives.

[1] BBC/British Council. *View and Teach.* Films 10 and 11 show a number of useful techniques.

Some features such as the lengthening of the final phonemes at the end of a phonetic phrase can be exaggerated.

On the morning of the next d—a—a—a—y, . . .

Stress and intonation can be 'skinned off'.

They stopped at six o'clock
de da de da de
da

They sent him round the world
de da de da de
da

Tonic syllables can be marked with rising, falling or wavy arrows on the blackboard. These arrows can be imitated by the teacher's gestures as the class do a drill. Stress-timing can be tapped or clapped softly. The teacher's finger can indicate stress-timing with a punching fist coming in on 'special attention' syllables. It is even possible to mime the difference between certain sounds. Tense arms can reinforce the thin stretched lips needed for [iː] and flop limply for the more relaxed [i].

Another useful dodge is to lengthen short vowels in order to concentrate attention on a difference of quality rather than length. It is not difficult, for the teacher, to learn to say sh—i—i—ip in contrast to shee—ee—eep.

There are various visual ways of showing degrees of stress. The *Advanced Learner's Dictionary* uses a high indicator in front of the syllable carrying primary stress and a low indicator before the syllable carrying secondary stress, leaving minimally stressed syllables unmarked. For example,

'foutəgrɑːf
fə'togrəfi
ˌfoutə'græfik[1]

Another way of showing this is by putting the syllables in boxes. Many American linguists like to distinguish four stress levels in, for example,

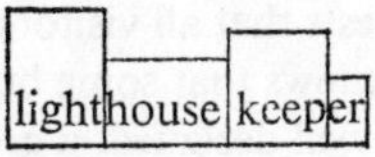

Our own practice in teaching has been to talk mostly about strong and weak, but where we needed to do so – in discussing gerunds modifying nouns, for example, – to refer to a 'reduced strong stress' as in the last syllable of *fishing-rod.*

Similarly in patterns such as

I've sent it to him.
I bought it from her.

we would refer to an 'increased weak stress'. No student was ever so inconsiderate as to ask if an increased weak was equal to a decreased strong.

[1] The phonetic symbols have been altered to be consistent with those used elsewhere in the chapter.

10 Incidental speech work

So much for what is peculiar to the speech syllabus, but, provided that the opportunities are taken advantage of, a great deal of useful teaching and practice can be done in the course of following other parts of the syllabus which would be included in any case for the sake of reading or writing. Grammar and intonation are very closely linked.

Certainly as a signal of what kind of sentence the hearer is to understand – statement, question or command – intonation overrides word order.

You think he's coming?

is a question.

Do I think you ought to get a mini for your birthday? Do I hell?

are two exclamations.

Stress marks the difference between *a green house* and *a greenhouse*. Intonation marks the difference between:

Have I got to sign it? Can you lend me a pen or a pencil?

and

Which of these is yours? Did you lend me a pen, or a pencil?

A number of phonological features serve to distinguish defining from non-defining constructions.

We caught the train leaving at eight.
We caught the train, leaving at eight.

The boys who had arrived before 12 o'clock got their uniforms the same afternoon.

The boys, who had arrived before 12 o'clock, got their uniforms the same afternoon.

Phonological features also show what is modified by adverbs, for example:

The visitors who came to the Institute sometimes used to waste my time.

A pause after *sometimes* suggests that all visitors were a nuisance; if the pause occurs before it, the listener knows that some but not all are condemned.

If the grammar syllabus is well designed, a great many of the phonological signals in the language will be included in the examples given and can be practised simultaneously and related to punctuation more precisely than in the stock over-simplifications such as, 'Where you make a little pause, you put a comma.'

In the literature syllabus, we include plays and poetry because these are good in themselves. Unlike novels, they are meant to be communicated through the sound of the spoken word and are suitable material for practising the art of speech. We suggest working up to play-acting through mime, which does not help speech except indirectly, and through dramatising everyday situations, writing dialogues and making home-made plays, which have a very direct bearing on learning to speak well, getting models off by heart and so on.

In the composition syllabus, again for reasons that would be equally valid if we had no need to improve pupils' fluency and 'committee' skill, we suggest doing a good deal of work in groups. The good effect of this on pupils' confidence and ability to take part in serious discussion is an added bonus. Moreover a large number of composition subjects in a proper syllabus are designed for oral presentation. We have in mind such composition as is required in the dramatisation of stories for radio, television or staging and radio and television commentaries, documentaries and interviews.

In our section on note-making we suggest working up gradually to the point where students can take notes from a lecturer. There is a great deal to be said for taping lecturers with different varieties of accent and exercising the skill of understanding speech with this increased difficulty.

11 Speech work out of class

In all these and many other ways work may be done on speech without any time-tabled provision for it. There are also numerous opportunities to be made and taken out of the classroom. The one that springs to most people's minds is the Debating Society, which certainly has its part to play in the education of pupils – confidence in facing an audience, fluency, rhetoric, etc. – but we admit to doubts about its efficacy in improving the general level of speech.

The dramatic society can play a very large part in improving speech, especially if it avoids over-concentration on major functions such as festivals and the School Play. Useful as these are, there is even more value in smaller and less ambitious productions involving larger numbers of less talented performers, who after all are the ones most in need of practice.

A recitation competition can also be a useful function provided there are plenty of winners and a good deal of time is spent on preparation before the big night. We like to put it in the third term of the year when all classes have read and heard a certain amount of poetry or at least verse. About six weeks before the due date we spend a period or two in which all the pupils read any poem and short passage they fancy. On the basis of this the class choose five or six to represent them in the competition. The chosen ones then learn their material by heart. The only rule is that no two people must use the same text. They are allowed to get any help they like. We then have a mini-competition with class judges and comments and finally decide on our entrants. On the big night we also try to have all the poems and passages different. It reduces the sufferings of the audience.

How much time and effort is devoted to speech work must depend on what the pupils need and are prepared to accept, and on what staff time and expertise is available or can be created.

12 Strategy

As far as the strategy of speech teaching in a country is concerned, the last place to concentrate on is the secondary school. If there is only one phonetician in the country, he should be training primary teachers. As far as tactics within the secondary school are concerned, we are not prepared to be dogmatic. In some places a standard high enough to be indistinguishable from native English speech may be attainable and desired. At the other extreme, one could conceivably be forced to accept comprehension of normal English speech as all that could be hoped for. But we are reluctant to admit that anything less than the ability to take part in serious discussion is really worth having. If this is attainable, the fact that the speaker has a 'foreign accent' does not matter very much. We both have 'foreign accents' in New York but we have not found it a serious hindrance in our dealings with our colleagues from Columbia.

13 Testing the skills of speech

It is not easy to design tests that explore the ability to behave (conversationally) with social ease and competence, or to take part in serious discussion. The test situation itself tends to invalidate the results. The best one can do is to analyse the abilities involved in instant comprehension and comprehensibility and sample a selection of the items.

It is almost essential to record the examinees on tape because of the difficulty of simultaneous administration and assessment and because, in a large examination this is the only satisfactory way of co-ordinating standards.

It is difficult to avoid tests involving reading aloud altogether, but it is not satisfactory to select one passage from a reader, to listen to thirty examinees (the examiner not having the test in front of him) and to mark on comprehensibility. The difficulty is that the examiner becomes increasingly familiar with the text. If each candidate reads a different passage, this problem is avoided but there is then no guarantee that the passages contain the same number and kind of difficulties. Both methods encourage random reading aloud as a method of practising for the test and this is undesirable.

The best solution seems to be to construct a passage (or passages) containing a certain number of specific problems of expression. The examinee is then taped and the result played back and assessed on each item separately and on the overall impression. The passages should not contain unfamiliar vocabulary and should be in a colloquial, modern style, and consist of or at least contain actual conversational exchanges. For convenience in marking it is desirable to space out the items to which the specific marks are attached.

Here is an example of an examiner's copy of such a test. The relevant items are in bold in the text and indicated also in the right-hand margin, where a final column will accommodate the mark. The examinee's text is printed and punctuated perfectly normally. He must, of course, have time for preparation.

Mr and Mrs Grove were sitting on the	
edge of the **cliff, watching** the waves	Intonation and pause.
break**ing on the** sand.	Weak stresses.
Mr **Grove, who** was due to stop work in	Intonation and pause
six months' time, was thinking about	(also after *time*).
his re**tirement.**	Consonant clusters.
	Special attention: -tire-
Seeing how thoughtful he **looked,**	Rising intonation, [lukt].

Mrs Grove decided not to interrupt **him,**	Unstressed pronoun.
Her mind **was** occupied by	Unstressed *was.*
wondering on what day of	[ʌ] not *wandering.*
the week to ask her friends, **Jim and**	Intonation.
Mary Stone, to dinner. If they had	
not **said that** they were going	['sedðət] no pause.
away for the **weekend,**	Lengthening and intonation.
she **would not have had** any problem.	Stress.
She generally gave her **parties** on	Final [z].
Fridays but she **was not** sure	[wəz'not] or [woznt].
that the next Friday would be	[ðət].
a suitable **one.** In her	Unstressed.
mind she had a	
list of at **least** six people	*list/least.*
who ought **to be** asked.	Unstressed.
'We **must** make a plan,' she	Unstressed [məst] or [ms].
said at **last, breaking** the long	Intonation and pause.
silence.	
'Just what **I** was thinking,'	Stressed pronoun.
replied Mr Grove, smiling **at** his	Unstressed: [ət].
wife. 'Have you got a pencil	
and **paper?'**	Rising intonation.
'What do you want to **write**	Falling, and level
down?' she asked.	or falling on *she asked.*
I shan't forget anything even	
if **you** do.'	Emphatic pronouns.
'There's an awful lot to remember.'	Unstressed.
'What an extraordinary thing to say!	Exclamatory intonation.
We're only asking a **few** people to a meal.'	No 'special prominence'.
'Are you talking about planning	
a **dinner party,** or	Alternative question intonation.
going home to England?'	[ou] diphthongs.
'Well, I'm quite prepared to	
think about **that** instead,	['ðæt]
if you'd like me **to.** What are	Stressed a little: [tuː].
you going **to** give us **to** eat?'	Different vowels.[1]
'Would you like a **nice, lean, baked**	All heavy stresses.
ham?' asked Mrs Grove, knowing	
her husband would approve.	
'That's a good idea,' he said, 'I	
like to see a joint of meat on the	
dining-room table at a party.	Stresses.
We'll think about England later.'	

[1] This is included as an example of the difficulties raised by the problem of the model and of the level of 'correctness' aimed at. We would not include it in a public examination.

A passage of this length takes just over a minute and a half to read, but longer to mark. Hence the need to record it. The number of items would not normally exceed twenty, which gives a convenient total. It could, of course, be considerably increased but not without making marking more difficult.

There is little security objection to using the same passages for a large number of candidates because the kind of information one candidate can give another is unlikely to be helpful.

Such a passage can be used to measure progress if records are made at the beginning of the course and then at yearly intervals. If one can get hold of three tape-recorders one can put the first and second readings on to a third tape phrase by phrase, which enables one to make a very precise estimate of what improvements have been made.[1]

Itemised marking of this kind rapidly becomes reasonably objective and co-ordination is easy, but it needs to be supplemented by a general impression mark to cover rhythm, fluency and comprehensibility.

An oral test also normally includes 'conversation' with the examiner as well as a passage to read aloud. Skilfully and tactfully administered, this can be an excellent test. There are pitfalls for the inexperienced; it is easy for the examiner, anxious to put the examinee at his ease, to do too much of the talking. It is almost as easy for the examinee to launch out into monologue. Even if a conversation is successfully maintained, it is difficult for the examiner to lure his 'victim' into using as wide a range of spoken forms as he would wish. The inherent difficulty is that the initiative rests with the examiner; the test would be much better if the two involved could change places because then the examinee would be asking the questions, making the encouraging noises, expressing polite surprise, enthusiastic agreement and so on. Perhaps when we examine our own classes, we might use the pupils as examiners. We have not tried this and it might not work but it sounds quite an entertaining possibility.

A passage to read, a live examiner and a live conversation are normal practice. There are numerous other possibilities. The British Council use a highly ingenious test,[2] some of which is on tape and some in a pamphlet. The examinee merely selects from the choices offered on the answer sheet and the marking is fully objective. Peter Wingard also designed a test at the University of Manchester. It formed the pattern of the Aural Test in the Joint Matriculation Board Test in English (Overseas).

For a full discussion of a wide range of rubrics with specimen items all fully objective see Robert Lado's *Language Testing: The Construction and Use of Foreign Language Tests*, Longman, 1961.

Vulette, Rebecca M. *Modern Language Testing: a handbook*, Harcourt, Brace & World, contains useful discussion and examples, which are however drawn from French, German, Spanish, etc.

[1] See G. Perren, ed., *Teachers of English as a Second Language: Their Training and Preparation*, C.U.P., 1968, Chapter one, for an account of the very depressing results of such an operation.

[2] The Davies Test.

Reference Books

ALLEN, W. S. *Living English Speech*. Longman, new edition 1965.
BALL, W. J. *Conversational English*. Longman, 1953.
Selected texts of Modern Dialogue. Longman, 1955.
BARNARD, G. *Better Spoken English*. Macmillan, 1959.
CHRISTOPHERSEN, P. *An English Phonetics Course*. Longman, 1956.
FRIEDRICH, W. *English Pronunciation – the Relationship between Pronunciation and Orthography*. Longman, 1958.
FRIES, C. C. *Teaching and Learning English as a Foreign Language*. Cresset Press, 1945.
GIMSON, A. C. *An Introduction to the Pronunciation of English*. Edward Arnold, 1970.
JERROM, M. F. and SZKUTNIK, L. L. *Conversation Exercises in Everyday English*. Longman, 1965.
JONES, DANIEL. *An English Pronouncing Dictionary*. Dent, 1963, 13th edition.
The Pronunciation of English. C.U.P., 1966.
KINGDON, R. *English Intonation Practice*. Longman, 1958.
The Groundwork of English Intonation. Longman, 1958.
The Groundwork of English Stress. Longman, 1958.
MACCARTHY, P. A. D. *English Conversation Reader*. Longman, 1956.
MORTIMER, COLIN. *Phrasal Verbs in Conversation*. Longman, 1972.
O'CONNOR, J. D. *Better English Pronunciation*. C.U.P., 1967.
PALMER, H. E. Revised by KINGDON, R. *A Grammar of Spoken English*, C.U.P.
PIKE. KENNETH LEE. *Phonemics*. Michigan U.P., 1970, 11th edition.
STREVENS, P. *Spoken Language*.

APPENDIX

LIST OF ENGLISH SOUNDS AND KEYWORDS WITH PHONETIC TRANSCRIPTIONS

VOWELS

Symbol	*Keyword*	*Phonetic Transcription*
iː	SEE	siː
i	SIT	sit
e	LET	let
æ	MAN	mæn
ɑː	FAR	fɑː
ɔ	POT	pɔt
ɔː	SAW	sɔː
u	FOOT	fut
uː	TOO	tuː
ʌ	BUT	bʌt
əː	FUR	fəː
ə	AGO	ə'gou

DIPHTHONGS

ei	PAY	pei
ou	GO	gou
ai	BUY	bai
au	NOW	nau
ɔi	BOY	bɔi
iə	HERE	hiə
eə	THERE	ðeə
ɔə	SHORE	ʃɔə
uə	TOUR	tuə

CONSONANTS

Normal English values are given to the following:

p t k f s
b d g v z

and also m, n, l, r, h and w.

Special Symbols	*Keyword*	*Phonetic Transcription*
ŋ	singing	'siŋiŋ
θ	thick	θik
ð	then	ðen
ʃ	shut	ʃʌt
ʒ	leisure	'leʒə
j	young	jʌŋ
tʃ	church	tʃəːtʃ
dʒ	judge	dʒʌdʒ

6

DRAMA

1 How important is drama in school?

'There are hundreds of plays written for children, and most of them ought to be burned.'

A. F. Alington: *Drama and Education*

It is all very well to begin with a challenging quotation, but there are several questions which the hard-pressed secondary school teacher of English as a Second Language is going to want answered before he is prepared to show much enthusiasm for the subject of this chapter: 'If the pupils are not supposed to read most of the plays written for them what are they going to do? Write their own? How much time is there for that? And how much time for any kind of dramatics out of nine or ten lessons a week in a school geared to external examination requirements? And if you're thinking of *producing* rather than reading plays, what can we do without a properly equipped stage and with the standard of spoken English as low as it is? Anyway, what is so specially useful about drama in education?'

Let us begin with the last question. We have laid stress throughout this book on training the imagination, which we have said is the English teacher's business. In discussing reading we have emphasised the value of identifying ourselves with a character in a book, of giving children books which are worth *involvement*, of making reading as *creative* as possible. School drama should complement these activities. Drama is *doing*.

> Child drama is creative activity and as such fulfils the normal function of all creative activity; it provides a medium through which the individual can express his ideas – his reactions to the impressions he receives – and, by expressing them, learn to evaluate them. By this process, vague impressions are brought into sharp focus, puzzling impressions are understood, fragmentary ones are completed and alarming ones are faced so that fear is overcome. This use of the creative arts makes us examine what we are thinking and feeling. Imaginative observation is stimulated and our understanding of ourselves and the world around us is extended and deepened.
>
> So, because it is one of the creative arts, child drama begins, not with somebody's text, but with the child's self-expression through the acting of his own experiences. Child drama is not theatre. All too frequently drama

> in schools is a diluted version of adult theatre, conducted as if the aim were to train actors for the stage.[1]

Drama can help us then, 'to examine what we are thinking *and feeling*'. Many teachers are suspicious of dramatic activities in school as unnecessarily and 'unhealthily' stimulating the emotions of pupils. All the more heartening to find a book about school drama that confidently asserts drama's rightful influence on 'what we are feeling'. So many school activities show no concern at all for the human feelings.

If children are not to start with plays what are they to start with? The answer, in general terms, is: with what moves and excites them in their own lives. We tend to be so concerned about helping our pupils to *think* straight that we seldom wonder whether they feel – straight or crooked – and whether it matters. How often, in the average secondary school staffroom is the word 'emotion' used without a preceding 'mere' – or some such deprecatory qualifier?

> It would be a great mistake to think of the education of feelings as a distinct area or department of education, which can be promoted or neglected independently of the rest of the educational process. A human being is, or ought to be, a whole organism; and what affects one part affects the rest also. It is the business of education to foster the growth of balanced whole persons. If education is deficient on the side of feeling, it is bound to be defective on the intellectual side; the resulting intellectual life will be arid – it will, so to speak, lack body. Those who have studied the origins of music and drama in the primitive forms of dance, know that the dance is a mainspring of human activity, a basic means of communication and inspiration. African tribal dances preparatory to a hunting expedition are not mere rituals; they are vital means of evoking and expressing the excitement and zest of the chase, with an elemental power far beyond anything that could be released by a deliberative assembly or even impassioned oratory.[2]

To understand and value African tribal dancing, and to use it as a starting-point for drama in school, is not to go to a topical extreme and assert that all African culture is, because African, worth more to African children than anything Europe has to offer. What is proposed here is that we *use what is known and enjoyed* as a means of confident entrance to activities which secondary school pupils, meeting them years too late, may otherwise find pointless and embarrassing. Any advice to teachers of drama in a second language situation must, if it is to inspire any confidence, face three facts: that the first year of the secondary school is too late – the right sequence of dramatic activities should be begun early in the primary school; that teachers and pupils in the secondary school will therefore find this work difficult and physically exhausting; and that, as with poetry teaching, even the most gifted teacher will have some lessons, and some whole projects, that are unsuccessful. But we still ought to make a start in the secondary school rather than deny our pupils what will become for at least a few of them the most enjoyable of all opportunities to

[1] R. N. Pemberton Billing and J. D. Clegg, *Teaching Drama*. U.L.P., 1965.
[2] M. V. C. Jeffreys, *Personal Values in the Modern World*. Penguin, 1962.

reflect upon experience. Poetry and drama are the English teacher's contribution to that 'Music of Education' which Plato valued so highly. If poetry can be 'The exploration of the possibilities of language', drama can be for our pupils the most potent 'exploration of the possibilities of experience'.

2 The sequence of activities

The secondary school pupil whose dramatic experience is about to begin has a lot to catch up on, and the teacher's job is to fit into the time available as much as he can of the following progression of activities:

1. Movement and mine: expressing through the body the meaning of the story being told or the music played.
2. Movement with some speech to amplify it.
3. Improvisation with fluent speech – still no scripts.
4. Polished improvisation; with some 'rehearsal' and pupils producing their own rudimentary scripts.
5. Own scripted plays; the pupils produce their own dramatic versions of well-known and loved stories. Group responsibility for simple props.
6. The full printed play production: no need for 'children's texts'. *Genesis* or Sophocles, for example, are good enough to start with.

A full rationale of this sequence, and plentiful illustrations of work done in schools, can be found in the books by Slade, Way, Pemberton-Billing and Clegg, and others listed in the bibliography to this chapter. We have had the principles hinted at in two previous quotations: there may be plenty of scope for teamwork in drama, but it is essentially *creative for the individual* and we are interested primarily in his own response and development. From this follows the main objection, from experienced and successful teachers of drama, to what passes for drama in so many of our schools: that our children (or a selected few of them) are thrust far too soon into the highly conventionalised and unrealistic experience of the theatre, where they show off and 'project themselves' before an audience of admiring and uncritical governors and parents, because the aim of 'school drama' is one big play a year (usually pre-selected for the producer by the School Certificate examiner) 'to show what we can do'. The proper aim of school drama is not to 'show what we can do'; it is to get as many children as possible, unselfconsciously and absorbedly 'doing'.

3 The beginnings

The wise teacher will begin out of the classroom, and, possibly, out of normal teaching hours. Out of the classroom because drama needs space, and this is exactly what we often have, unlimited space, warm and well-lit, just outside the classroom. It is possible to overcome the limitations of a crowded, stuffy classroom, but there does not seem much point in doing so if they can easily be left behind. Even in a school with a large and well-equipped stage some kinds of dramatic work are better done under mango trees around the football field.

But it is no good pretending that the great outdoors banishes every pupil's inhibitions. How can we start? Perhaps with the movements appropriate to a situation which pupils have faced and will face again. Classes will work willingly and well on common 'courtesy situations': welcoming a distinguished lady visitor to the school; entering the office of a government official who is going to interview you for a vacation job; queueing at the hospital 'outpatients', when an emergency case is brought in on a stretcher; congratulating the captain of an opposing football team when the whistle goes to end a 'cup' match which you have lost by a disputed goal; ushering a distinguished guest speaker into a crowded school meeting that he has come to address. All these were, for our pupils, social problems that arose in school life and were embarrassing and difficult. No other teacher's suggestions would be the same as these but it is not hard for anybody to find similar things that trouble his pupils.

It may be easier, with a particular secondary class, to begin with speech, and work back to movement and mime when the pupils are more relaxed and less suspicious of the whole exercise. The idea that intonation is an important part of English grammar is both helpful and amusing to young secondary school pupils. We can start with greetings. How much can we convey by the tone of voice in which we say 'Come in. Sit down.' Ordinary politeness? Delight? Surprise? Astonishment? Boredom? Exasperation? Anxiety? Fear? Embarrassment? Menace? Uncertainty? (I know the face but what's his name and where did I meet him before?) Our pupils have enjoyed trying to express one of these emotions – not put to them in these abstract terms – and having the rest of the class try to guess how they feel from the tone of voice; good for humour and good for speech training – and for stretching the imagination. We go on sometimes to discuss the kind of disastrous impression which can be conveyed by the second language speaker of English who hits the wrong tone, and the effect this has on day to day relations, in and out of the school, between Europeans, Asians and Africans. This kind of discussion can expand, with an interested class, into a consideration of the kinds of misunderstanding – probably much more syntactical than tonal – which arise when the vernacular language is misused; teacher and pupils can grow rapidly in self-awareness in this kind of exchange.

We can move on from greetings to situations revealed in a few words. 'It's dark in here.' 'This is the end, then.' 'No, No, No!' and so, when the class seems ready, back to movement without words in the miming of common experiences: examining what it is really like travelling in a crowded taxi or bus; trying to maintain a semblance of table manners and at the same time bolt your lunch fast enough to get a second helping when there is obviously not enough for everyone to have one; showing a 'youngster' how you brew banana beer. These activities can be very usefully linked with the writing course. Teachers sometimes talk as if the only possible connection between drama and writing is to get children to write scripts. This can be valuable as one end-product of a long process, but the essential connection is that the more we think about and respond to an activity by acting it out, the more accurately and sensitively we shall be able to describe it.

4 Intermediate Stages

Although this kind of imaginative feedback is exploited in composition teaching, our prime concern is with spoken words. Drama is compounded of bodily movement, music, dance, song and speech and though our educational drama will lead on to play reading, stage production and the study of Shakespeare, we emphasise that any 'text' is only a record of speech and movement, a convenient means of recording *something done* so that it can, with some of the same effect, be done again. It is best for our pupils to discover the purpose of a script by producing an improvisation which they think good enough to be repeated and therefore worth recording. What materials are worth their time and energy? Stories that they know and love. These may come from poems in their own language or in English – and drama in their own language is certainly to be encouraged by the English teacher; from folk-tales and legends taken from published collections, e.g. the Oxford Anthologies of Myths and Legends, or brought by pupils from their own home and village traditions; from the great symbolic events of human history – the birth and death of Christ, the sacrifices of Abraham and Antigone. The interested teacher will soon know the stories that fire his pupils' imaginations and will work outwards from these, not being afraid of experiment or occasional failure.

> If the teacher can gain a knowledge of the childrens' own dramatic games and know the great drama in his own language he will never run short of ideas.[1]

– advice which is particularly valuable because 'games' and 'play' are too often thought to have nothing to do with the purpose of the secondary school course. Even poetry is not 'always worrying about the eternal verities' and we are not suggesting that drama for school children must always be based on them either. But we do need to remind ourselves that just as children's play and fantasy does not shrink from the disturbing and the terrifying, so the adolescent imagination cannot be nourished on the unbalanced emotional diet of farce and melodrama served up in so many anthologies of plays 'for schools'.

Most teachers who have 'taught' drama successfully, and all those who have written about it, stress the value of group work in improvisation. Certainly, once the ice is broken, young secondary school pupils can work purposefully together and be stern critics, and we have found that small groups often achieve one of the most important qualities of the successful improvisation – the reduction of gesture and movement to the necessary minimum that the spoken words require. But the involvement that we seek for each child is essentially personal. He is exploring for himself, and incidentally communicating to others, what it feels like to be arrested, jilted, in love, starving, a refugee, getting married; to discover that he has failed a vital examination, that a close

[1] D. Holbrook, *English for Maturity*. C.U.P., 1967.

relative has died, or that he has been caught visiting the forbidden local beer-shop. Attempted at the right time and with just the right amount of guidance (often none at all), this involvement and identification with others' experiences is linked very closely with our graded assignments in reading and writing, in a way in which work on a written play cannot be: the child is not afraid of making some mistakes because he is creating, not working at someone else's idea of what he ought to know and learn.

To begin adventures in drama out of normal school hours is particularly sensible if the teacher decides to attempt some dramatic work in a school where there has been none before. Often the best way to begin in such a school is to establish a drama club, which can start with the unpretentious range of activities suggested for class work, and graduate by degrees to simple 'productions' of short scenes, play readings, 'radio plays' with the tape-recorder and, possibly, full scale productions. Puppetry too can be a most enjoyable and creative introduction to drama.

But whether the English teacher makes a start in or out of the classroom and class-time he should try, as with almost everything else he attempts, to see that drama is not limited to 'the English lesson' or to 'English'. In schools everywhere there is, for example, scope in history and geography for insight through imaginative dramatisation; we can start with the great explorers from Columbus to Livingstone. Sometimes history and geography coalesce in 'English' in the dramatic possibilities of a poem like Rubadiri's 'Stanley meets Mutesa'. When we start from nothing, it is excellent – not merely unavoidable – that we treat costumes and properties as useful for stage productions but largely irrelevant to earlier and more important dramatic activities. It is imagination that we want; yet it is odd how little we learn in this from our own children who, around the house and garden, so often abandon the ready-made toy or fancy dress outfit for their own collections of junk and bits of rag with which 'they can do as they like'. Educational drama begins with 'doing as you like'. This is not to ignore the 'discipline'.

> Before they are ready for performance of plays, children will experience other forms of discipline in their dramatic enterprises. In improvisation and other earlier work there are, for example, the need for close co-operation with other members of the group and loyal implementation of group decisions; the binding force of the agreed plot and characterisation; the need to obey some laws of dramatic construction and a few simple techniques so that the scene may be clear and effective. The same necessity for clarity demands disciplined use of the voice in speaking and of the body in movement. And there are always the restrictions of time, place and subject. Most rigorous of all perhaps there is the discipline of selection – selection of ideas and of the means of presenting those ideas lucidly and convincingly. But within these, and other, limitations the child is magnificently free. And he is willingly disciplined, for he is helping to create something; and the act of creation brings absorption, which means as a rule, happiness, or the agreeable agony of reaching a decision concerning a work of art.[1]

[1] A. F. Alington, *Drama and Education*. Blackwell, Oxford, 1961.

5 Plays for classwork

It is not possible to treat the whole of every play in the syllabus as a full-scale production. There is not enough time. Yet it is a waste of opportunity merely to read a play aloud in parts with pupils seated at their desks.

Some scenes at least should be acted book in hand (the hand away from the audience incidentally) in the front of the classroom. If this is not done, the play is not properly imagined as an event in front of an audience and the pupils are not given the support of things happening in front of their eyes. The play therefore is made unnecessarily difficult to understand. On the other hand if when a scene is first read it is approached as something to be done in preparation for reading and acting in front of the class, its meaning begins to be seen much more fully and the whole class, actors and audience, can be brought into the exciting process of doing it better, of making the points more clearly in the combination of speech and action.

No elaborate or sophisticated props and costumes are required. The audience are always willing to piece out our imperfections with their thoughts. We have seen rulers become swords, bows, hunting-crops and even telephone receivers. King Henry has stood on a desk breathing fire and fury into troops apparently panting to assault the blackboard temporarily endowed with all the menace of the walls of Harfleur. Trumpets have been sounded on combs and nobody thought it was funny; the dramatic illusion grips with astonishing power.

Pupils rapidly become adept at improvising furniture, props and costume. The Sudanese turban can be put to a dozen uses. Worn as a veil it used to give us instant girls and pretty saucy ones too when we were doing *She Stoops to Conquer*. Of course it is helpful to have a box of props and costumes, just as it is if one is playing charades, but one can make a start without. What do we need for this scene, what can we use, how shall we arrange it, how can we show this, that or the other, where will he come in, where will he go, how should he move – these are the questions that get us thinking about ways of getting the scene across.

The function of the audience is to be helpful rather than critical. We have seen student teachers kill a lesson dead by asking brutally 'What did he do wrong?' It's so easy to turn this into a demand for constructive suggestions – 'What could he do to show he is surprised, angry, pleased, etc?' Factual questions are all right. We can ask, 'What did he do?' even if the answer is 'nothing', because we can follow this at once with the demand for suggestions. This approach demands, of course, that everybody must have read and thought about the scene beforehand and that while it is being acted the audience shall be looking at the actors and listening to them and not following the words in their books. The best place for the teacher to stand is at the back of the classroom and he too must discard his text.

Very occasionally a class that has acquired a great deal of skill in this kind of dramatic work may do a scene well enough for it to be left after a single performance but nearly always, especially in the early stages, there is so much that can so easily be improved that the one scene is worth doing two or even three or four times. It is better to spend a good deal of time raising the standard of a few good scenes than to scramble through a whole play at an indifferent level.

The very first beginnings of this kind of dramatic reading are apt to be disappointing. Three or four characters will shuffle sheepishly on to the stage, align themselves in a row or huddle into a tight group and go through the downcast motions of reading aloud. This is obviously not worth doing but it is completely mistaken to abandon it for this reason. The worse the performance, the greater the pupils' need for the exercise. Although the pupils get more enjoyment from listening to the teacher reading aloud, they get less profit. Faith and patience are required. The other temptation is for the teacher to leap on to the stage, 'No, not like that. Let me show you.' This temptation too must be resisted because, although it gets quick improvement, the progress is not real; it is based on mimicry instead of growing out of an increase of understanding or power of expression.

An important aspect of this acting in the classroom is its contribution to the establishment of an acting tradition. It ensures that a constant supply of talent for major productions is available and educates the school audience in the conventions of the drama. It teaches the elements of stagecraft, so that actors come to full performances already aware of such matters as grouping, movement, speed, audibility and so on. But these we will consider in relation to the staging of full productions.

In the classroom, scenes that depend mainly on speech can be turned into radio performances, and the final reading put on to tape.

6 Performances for school audiences

With the idea of creating and maintaining a dramatic tradition in mind as well as for their own good we like every junior class to produce one one-act play, scenes from a longer play, or some other staged entertainment once a year for a school audience.

There are a few one-act plays that can be staged without adaptation – there is, of course, no reason for avoiding translated plays which can often be made even more suitable by retranslation into simplified English. There are others that can be made suitable by localisation. We have seen a highly successful Sudanised version of *Shivering Shocks* and, though not at junior school level, a very successful version of the *Silver Box*, in which the characters had been replaced by local counterparts. Short plays can be written too. We once worked with a science teacher who had a gift for the production of blood and thunder melodramas – *Sir Jasper Sees it Through* was a favourite – which were highly relished by the juniors and equally but differently enjoyed by seniors with more sophisticated tastes.

And as we have said there are pupils and groups in the school who can also write and adapt material for the stage. When the school is the only audience, the writers can exploit the topical in-joke very effectively.

7 Producing a play for public performance

When it comes to performances to which parents and the public are invited, the first important thing is to choose a good play so that there is something to enjoy if the acting and production are a little less than polished and professional. If it is possible to use one of the plays set for school certificate, two birds can be killed with one stone. It is sometimes more satisfactory in such a case to take most if not all the actors from the previous year – they are more willing to spare the time – and open all rehearsals to the examinees, leaving them free to attend as many as they like. They learn more about a play by seeing it produced than they ever can by reading it.

Except with a very experienced group, one must select a play in language which pupils can understand easily and speak intelligibly. It is better to choose the simple and exact a very high standard than to blunder – as so many schools do – from one brave attempt to the next.

Let everyone, staff and pupils, know that a production is about to be launched. Then no one gets disgruntled because their services were not sought, and one can be sure that everyone who is really interested will turn up at the first meeting.

Given a good play, the producer's job is to put it on with as little alteration and interpretation as possible. Cuts may have to be made but they are inevitably damaging. The great dramatist controls the feelings of his audience minute by minute through the sequence of scenes and speeches. There are valleys as well as peaks and if a play has to be trimmed, it is perhaps best to make small cuts throughout rather than remove whole scenes that permit some relaxation of tension.

Auditions are time-consuming but very well worth while. We like to allow everybody who wants to do so to have a go, we like to have some advice from pupils – they are frequently better judges of acting capacity than we are – and we like to audition where the play will be performed and stand at the back of the auditorium. This helps a little in distinguishing acting potential from the ability to read aloud. Good readers are not always good actors, but this is not apparent if the audition takes place round a table. Light, pleasant voices are splendid for reading to a small group, but they will not do in a part that demands a touch of Termagant. Even bad readers sometimes speak well when they have their words by heart, which makes casting very difficult unless a good deal is already known of actors' potential.

It is a common error to cast people in parts that are like their own characters thinking that they have only to be natural to succeed. Acting is not a matter of being natural; it is highly artificial and larger than life. It is frequently easier to act a part remote from one's own character.

If the play is new to the cast, the next thing is to read it quickly together. At this point it is kind, and useful, to bring in the prompter, the assistant producers, and such stage hands as are going to be needed. They too might as well see the whole process from the beginning, and, while we would not suggest that they should be thought of as understudies, if a major character is suddenly prevented from appearing just before the dress rehearsal because of breaking a leg in a football match, it is comforting to have a pool of stalwart assistants who have attended so many rehearsals that they practically know the words already.

The reading is of course followed by discussion of the 'big' questions about the play. What does it mean? What is the author getting at? What is the philosophy? How should it be done? And then individually what are the characters like? How old are you? Are you married? What sort of person are you? We want to start the players thinking themselves into their characters.

While this goes on in public, the producer is working out his plans for the set and the furniture, which must be decided before he can plan the movements.

The place in which the play is to be produced affects the choice of the play to some extent. Older plays can be staged effectively in an open arena with the audience on three sides but it is more difficult to stage in this way a modern play in which the action is supposed to take place within the four walls of a room.

The usual setting for a school play is on a platform with a curtain in a long hall with all the audience in front of the stage. This raises problems of audibility and visibility, which can sometimes be solved by having the action take place at two or three levels. It is very useful to build up gradually a series of staging units that can be arranged in various ways to give different levels. Solid wooden boxes make a good substitute. One can sometimes borrow one or two teachers' platforms straight from the classrooms. Where an apron stage is useful, one of these can be put in front of the main stage outside the curtain. The additional variety in character grouping that becomes possible on different levels well repays the extra trouble.

Sets need not be elaborate. Words, movement and costume are enough to put across a good play. But exits and entrances have got to be settled before rehearsals start. 'Exit pursued by a bear' turns into farce if the actor heads confidently for the wrong corner. The exits must also take account, as must the area backstage, of any furniture removals required for scene changing.

The next operation is to draw scale plans of the fully furnished stage in each scene. It is convenient to divide the stage into six sectors as shown. The terms can be used in rehearsals too. Right and left are as seen by the actor facing the audience. The shaded part is best left uncluttered because it is the most useful acting area.

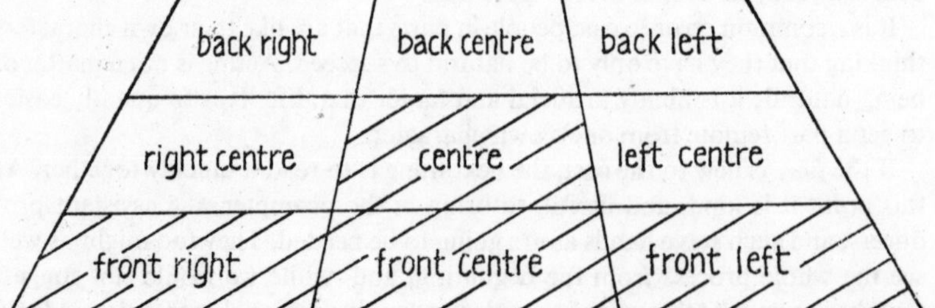

All furniture should be brough… impolitic to allow an actor to ree… rehearsals and trip him up with a joint s… Mr Smith's settee and Mrs Smith is reluctan… a substitute; three chairs in a row will do, … throughout the rehearsals wherever there is goin… free movement.

Similarly all properties should be brought into use as s… for the same reason costumes or substitute costumes. Free-s… who are going to play female parts must get used to walking … – old petticoats will serve – or sitting in a seemly manner in shor… One should not leave it to the dress rehearsal to point out that elegant you… ladies do not hitch up the front of long skirts when they sit down, like a man preserving the creases in his trousers. Girls, nowadays, do not, however, need to learn to wear trousers.

Actors require, of course, to look at people with rather new eyes – to ask themselves what gestures and movements are characteristic of various kinds of people: an old man, a man in authority, a young man in a hurry and so on, and also what gestures express various emotions – anger, surprise, amusement, fear, confidence or embarrassment.

Gesture is a matter mainly for the actor and comes later, but major movements are the concern of the producer and again need planning before rehearsals start. Movement in most plays is almost continuous but, in a good production, this is not obvious,[2] because the movement is made to look natural, which is not the same thing as being natural, and to contribute to the meaning of the play. The producer's aim is to get variety, to keep the important characters visible and so placed that they may in fact speak to the audience while appearing to address other characters, and at the same time to present a series of pictures agreeable to the eye.

The mechanical is always to be avoided; standing in rows should be strictly reserved for soldiers and even grouping should not look too regular; characters should not be spaced out evenly. Usually the meaning of the play, the feeling of the characters, will decide which characters are together and which are apart.

An actor should move *during his own speech* and practically never during other people's. Any movement draws the eyes of the audience and it is only rarely that one wishes them to be distracted from the actor who, because he is speaking, is the focal point of attention. The actor should move *during* his lines and not before or after for two reasons. Movement by an actor during his speech, even if only a little, attracts attention to his words, gives them added significance and makes them easier to hear. He should move *to* or *from* the

[1] In a production of *She Stoops to Conquer* I was once foolish enough to allow Tony to substitute at the last minute a rather splendid old-fashioned riding whip for the short quirt he had previously slashed about the stage. Unfortunately I forgot to adjust his distance from Mrs Hardcastle and only courage beyond the call of duty on her part averted disaster. J.A.B.

[2] Unless it stops, when the scene immediately appears 'wooden'.

to the meaning. The recognition of to-lines and from-lines is
 stage movement.

he amount of movement again depends on the meaning. Except for some definite reason, such as answering a telephone, a full-scale cross-over can only be made on a speech of some agitation and violence. One cannot have Viola talking of sitting like patience on a monument and flitting about the stage like a butterfly.

Two characters should not be kept for too long in the same relationship. One should move and perhaps then the other, but not both at once in a scissor-like crossing action. It is the producer's job to decide who shall move when, and he must have this clear in his mind before rehearsals start. The actor has plenty to worry about without having the problem of a producer who does not appear to know his own mind or who keeps changing it as he goes along.

The whole of the stage should be used all the time. If a scene requires to be done in a small space, it is better to reduce the size of the stage and then make use of all the space available.

We can now start rehearsals and shall do well to remember that while we are prepared to squander our own time lavishly, that of our pupils is precious. With a carefully planned schedule of rehearsals announced a week in advance there is no reason why a play-production should incur universal wrath by disrupting the routine of the school and keeping pupils waiting for hours at rehearsals where they will do five minutes' work. It is easy enough to use a notice board – large and prominent – for all publicity. Announcements are then absolutely clear. No one has any excuse for mistaking times and places, and the whole school does not have to listen to tedious recitals of rehearsal detail at each morning assembly.

A call-boy can be trained to fetch characters from preparation five minutes before they are wanted.

A full-length play will require something like four rehearsals a week for from six to eight weeks, but it need not be rehearsed an act at a time. It is better to start by breaking the play up into rehearsable bits, some perhaps of as little as two or three pages and to work each section up to completion before beginning the next. This piecemeal approach is a great help in avoiding staleness because the excitement of fitting the bits together comes quite late in the rehearsal period, perhaps even in the last fortnight.

Opinions vary about whether it is better to concentrate first on getting the words right and allowing the movements and gestures to follow or to work first on movement and gestures because they help so much in getting the words right. Some producers, and very possibly some actors, find one way round easier than the other; but the problem is probably more apparent than real. If one watches a producer of either school of thought at work, it is clear that his real concern is with the united effect of word and action and not with either as a separate thing.

Only one useful rehearsal of a unit can take place before the words are learnt. This rehearsal is required because they cannot be learnt until they are understood and they are best understood in action. The actor must feel and understand what he says with sincerity. Spontaneity – that is, of course, the appearance of spontaneity – can only be gained when the words are thoroughly known and a background of understanding has been built up.

Pupils generally need a great deal of help in understanding what the words mean but once they have been led to discover this or, if all else fails, had it explained to them, how they should be said follows more easily.

There is a tendency with inexperienced actors for them to make too many small, fussy, vigorous gestures. They need to learn boldness and restraint – to make fewer, simpler, clearer gestures.

In working on speech it is important to avoid demonstrating if possible; it is essential to avoid it with gestures. One may explain what the gesture is to mean, but not show how it is to be done. Certain cross-cultural problems may be involved. Some peoples point with the chin, beckon with the back of the hand uppermost or tuck the lips in when they are apprehensive. A gesture is not wrong because it is un-English. It may be just right for a particular audience. As far as possible, the actors must be allowed to move in their own way; movement and gesture are only convincing if they come from the feelings of the actor.

The actors have to learn to act all the time and to do so with their whole bodies. They must listen actively to every speaker, emitting signals of attention and emotion. It may require a conscious effort on the producer's part to remove his attention from the speaker in order to observe that this is happening. Apart from these (apparently) natural reactions to what is being said and done, they must stand still.

All movement in a play is significant. The stage magnifies the smallest accidental distracting movement enormously. The actor who scratches his head is making a devastating comment and he must not do so just because he has an itch. He has to learn to itch only at the dramatist's command.

All pauses, too, must be significant. Nothing drags worse than a play with a pause between every speech. Actors need to be told to start speaking not when the previous speaker has finished but as he comes to his last word.[1] This also helps to avoid actors echoing the tone of the previous speech – starting on the same note, which is a common fault and a natural tendency especially when actors are nervous. Speech should normally be continuous like action.

Pace is largely a matter of getting rid of meaningless pauses in speech and action. It is not a question of speaking quickly. Indeed it is more often necessary to persuade actors to speak more slowly for the sake of audibility, than to speak faster.

Audibility is not primarily a matter of loudness of voice or precision of enunciation, though neither of these is a hindrance. It is not even true, though we have often said it, that every word must be heard. The truth is that every important word must be heard and will be heard if the stress and intonation are right. When we are concerned with the question of audibility, we find it helpful to stand well back from the stage.

[1] If one actor has to interrupt another's speech, he should do so three or or four words before it ends.

The final stages of rehearsal are devoted to bringing the units together and then to building up the increase of dramatic tension at the climaxes by introducing the final variations of speed. Climaxes are usually built up by a gradual increase of pace, which gives more emphasis to any pauses used, and by greater excitement in the tones of the actors' voices.

With the problem of costume we can offer little useful help beyond saying that we have never known a determined and ingenious producer fail to bully or cajole the local dressmaking talent into operation.

Pupils who have brown skins need hardly any straight make-up. It is only pale skins that show a ghostly white in the footlights. And if there are no footlights, they can be improvised. We have seen numerous successful plays lit only by pressure lamps in four-gallon petrol tins.

Two final words for the teacher who has never produced a play before. The best way to learn how to do it is to go ahead and produce one. It is not as difficult as we may have made it seem, and it is much more rewarding. Never think 'We can't put on a play here.' The most successful and moving school production we have ever seen was of a Kiganda legend, 'The Story of the Flame Tree', done by the children of a primary school which had no hall, no stage, no lights, no costumes, except what they made from paper, reeds and bark cloth, no duplicating machine, no drama expert and no money. Just one teacher who knew it was worth doing, and found a 'part' for every pupil in the school.

8 Shakespeare for school certificate?

We are sufficiently impressed by the arguments against the value of Shakespeare in the second language school to believe that no teacher or class should be compelled by the demands of an examination syllabus to read a Shakespeare play. Shakespeare's language is generally very difficult – impossibly difficult if we make the absurd demand that every word shall be fully understood. His language is also not modern English and in general we agree that when a great deal of time is to be spent on a text, it is better if the language is modern. We are not, however, able to go as far as some teachers who claim to discern a corrupting influence on the purity of their pupils' style. We have not observed any examples of the study of Shakespeare doing positive harm. But, of course, unless both class and teacher enjoy it, it should not be attempted.

Our experience is that our classes do enjoy certain Shakespeare plays and these we find it very interesting to present. No one who has been in an audience of Sudanese secondary students at the film of *Henry V* is likely to forget the involvement of the audience – the shouts of approval that burst out in the excitement – or to need to be persuaded that Shakespeare is worth doing. We are therefore just as firmly persuaded that no teacher or class should be prevented by the demands of an examination syllabus from reading a Shakespeare play and very glad that the Cambridge Examinations Syndicate permit opting for Shakespeare without making him compulsory.

If we decide to do Shakespeare, we are left with the problem of choosing texts and deciding when and how to start.

Certainly at least one and preferably more than one play should have been seen, heard or read without undue delay over details before a Shakespeare play is studied for an examination. The best start is to see a play. A little preparatory work enhances its value. Instead – or better still, in addition – one may show a Shakespeare film – some, including the excellent Olivier films, can be borrowed from the British Council.

In addition to these the Marlowe Society has produced a number of good recordings that can be used straight, or abridged on to a tape. Another possibility is to lure colleagues into making a recording of the play that is needed. It is certainly highly desirable to start from visual or aural presentation rather than from the printed word.

This kind of start can be made during the free-reading stage, and work based on a printed text can usually also be done towards the end of the same stage. We need texts that are easy and enjoyable to read from. Too often we cannot afford to do any more than use the former school certificate texts that lie mouldering in the book store, but as soon as a little money is available it is well worth while to spend it on copies of one of the more recent editions which have taken to heart Dr Johnson's editorial dictum: 'Notes are often necessary, but they are necessary evils'.

We need texts which provide attractive, easily legible print, and the minimum of necessary notes, accessible but unobtrusive. The Penguin texts do this excellently, and so, with fuller notes, do the new Cambridge texts edited by Professor Ludowyk and the New Swan Shakespeares, which are specially prepared for the second language reader. But the best of all to start with – however heretical it may sound to devotees of the Bard – are the 'Shorter Shakespeare' editions published by Ginn, which are sensible abridgements for the new reader, but do not simplify Shakespeare's language at all. The introductory note to these editions provides a good summary of how to start reading Shakespeare in the secondary school abroad:

> The chief aim of this series is to encourage uninterrupted reading of the plays. The notes which follow are merely reminders for the teacher of points he may care to clarify in some detail before the scene is read. It should then be possible to read the complete scene without interruption, followed by a short pause for comment if desired.

The last phrase is crucial. All discussion of Shakespeare's plays in the early stages of class reading should be in response to questions pupils ask out of *their* interest and perplexities, not to the teacher's urge to display his own knowledge and appreciation of the play. Pupils ask the questions that matter; they want to know, of a play, 'What does it mean?' and of a scene 'Why did he put it in there?' It is with the fundamental questions that the reading of these great plays should begin and not with learning speeches, spotting 'contexts', writing character sketches and earnestly contemplating notes on minor obscurities of language.

> Using the situations abstracted from the play, we try to build up an awareness and appreciation of what these reveal. Whether the teacher uses the approach suggested here, or any other, *the clue to the whole play should*

be given at the time of its very first reading in the class. Some simplification may result, but if structure is presented with flexibility, then insufficiencies or unsatisfactoriness can be made good as the play is worked on and these come to light.[1]

9 An approach to *Macbeth*

Which is the best play to start on depends somewhat on the class, a little on the political situation and very much on the teacher. *Julius Caesar*, *Merchant of Venice* or *Macbeth* are all possible. Here is one approach to *Macbeth*, a play we like to use because it is short, exciting, relatively easy to understand, and very easily related to other novels and plays that the class will be reading. We spend less than five minutes at this stage on 'introducing Shakespeare'. All a class needs to know about *Macbeth* before beginning to read it is when Shakespeare lived, who he wrote for, that his audience was particularly interested in witchcraft and believed that there was a lot of it going on, and that *Macbeth* was set in Scotland. One notion we always share with them is that Shakespeare is difficult to read at first and that they will have to concentrate, but that if they will give the language their full attention they will find more meaning than they have ever found before, because Shakespeare, more than any other poet, was 'exploring the possibilities of language' – making words do as much as possible.

If we have a recording available we then sit and listen to it. We do not encourage pupils to follow 'in the book' because we want them to have, as nearly as possible, the experience of the play, and there is the difficulty of slight textual variations and abridgements for recording. But of course they may use the text if they particularly want to. Any recording takes the best part of three hours and this is a large slice of class time, so we usually begin in class and continue with about half the recording in our 'spare' time – most effectively divided into two or three groups, meeting at home (a verandah or even a garden will do in a tropical climate!) with a cup of tea laid on just to emphasise the point that Shakespeare is for pleasure.

Having listened to the whole play, we discuss it briefly before going on to read the first act. 'Briefly' may mean ten minutes or a couple of lessons depending on the interest of the class, but we always get round to the question 'What is the play about?' or 'Why do you think Shakespeare wrote a play about Macbeth?' 'Ambition' is of course nearly always the first answer, and we make progress immediately because we have never had a class yet that did not insist at once that 'there's more to it than that'. 'Honesty is the best policy', 'Murder doesn't pay' or some such offering as these often follows. We then ask 'All right, but what did you think of Macbeth at the end of the play?' and at least some of the class confess to a sneaking admiration – as for the Reverend John Laputa who first set before them the notion of the tragic hero back in the first form – and we are a little further towards an understanding of the complexity of great literature. We move on again with the idea – which we have

[1] E. F. C. Ludowyk, *Understanding Shakespeare*. C.U.P, 1962.

sometimes had suggested by a pupil – that Macbeth did not always want to do the things he did, and so perhaps Shakespeare is considering the problem of how far human beings are 'free'.

All these are useful contributions towards an answer to the question 'What is *Macbeth* about?' but we then ask the class to watch very carefully for a theme running through the first act – a theme they will recognise from other plays we have read that year (among which are usually two out of *Antigone*, *Justice*, *An Inspector Calls* and *Arms and the Man*) and from the James Bond and Agatha Christie that they are reading in their spare time. It may not be very reverent to present *Macbeth* like this, as a sort of inspired whodunit in which the audience knows from the start who is the murderer, but it is more effective than the common method of introducing Shakespeare as a literary fossil whose work bears no relation to modern literature or life.

A first reading of Shakespeare needs to be as fluent and intelligible as possible, so we spend an English 'prep' preparing some of the best readers in the class. It is useful for the teacher to take a part himself – as long as he does not continue to monopolise all the main characters, but gradually withdraws as the class reading improves. In the second language situation such reading will need preparation for at least the first two years of Shakespeare study. The whole class has had time during prep to read through silently and to ask about any difficulties which really prevent them from understanding what follows – we do not spend time in interesting detail, only on what gets in the way of understanding. The reading finished, we ask if anyone can spot the theme we were talking about. We have never had a third former yet who did, so back we go again to examine, as we have done in intensive reading lessons since our first form days, exactly what the writer says.

Attention is now drawn to the imagery,[1] starting from the witches' 'Fair is foul, and foul is fair'; then to Macbeth's first words, which echo theirs, 'So foul and fair a day I have not seen' and to Banquo's variation on the theme, 'Why do you start and seem to fear things that do sound so fair?' On through the contradictions of the witches' prophecies to Macbeth's, 'And nothing is but what is not', to Duncan's reflection on the treacherous Cawdor (with which most pupils will need a bit of help):

> There's no art
> To find the mind's construction in the face:
> He was a gentleman on whom I built
> An absolute trust.

And so, glancing, if the class seem ready for it, at a few of the images of darkness and concealment, on to Lady Macbeth's injunction

> Your face, my thane, is as a book where men
> May read strange matters. To beguile the time
> Look like the time; bear welcome in your eye,
> Your hand, your tongue: look like the innocent flower,
> But be the serpent under it

[1] Caroline Spurgeon's *Shakespeare's Imagery and what it tells us*, C.U.P., 1965, is a very helpful book.

and to the resolution which ends the act

> Away, and mock the time with fairest show:
> False face must hide what the false heart doth know

By now most of the class are ready to volunteer that throughout this first act runs an emphasis on the difference between Appearance and Reality, and so they have discovered for themselves a theme which runs too through the whole play, through much of the world's great literature, through our daily lives and through every detective story that was ever written.

We do not for one moment suggest that this is the only way of approaching *Macbeth*. Different teachers would adopt other approaches; there are plenty of good ways of beginning, but we would plead for one that gets the pupils to grips with the whole play as rapidly as possible and that pays them the compliment of facing them with some of the real difficulties and true themes of Shakespeare's plays right from the start.

For further reading

ENGHOLM, E. *Education through English*. C.U.P., 1965.
HOLBROOK, DAVID. *English for Maturity*. C.U.P., 1967.
LUDOWYK, E. F. C. *Understanding Shakespeare*. C.U.P., 1962.
PEMBERTON BILLING, R. N. and CLEGG, J. D. *Teaching Drama*. U.L.P., 1968.
SLADE, PETER. *Child Drama*. U.L.P., 1954.
An Introduction to Child Drama. U.L.P., 1969.
WAY, BRIAN. *Development through Drama Education Today*. Longman, 1967.

7

POETRY

1 A first poetry lesson: *African Thunderstorm*

A first-year secondary class in a school in Uganda is half-way through the first week of its English course. The first lesson on poetry is about to begin. The teacher's first words are 'I'd like you to listen carefully to this.' He reads aloud:

From the west
Clouds come hurrying with the wind
Turning
Sharply
Here and there
Like a plague of locusts
Whirling
Tossing up things on its tail
Like a madman chasing nothing.
Pregnant clouds
Ride stately on its back
Gathering to perch on hills
Like dark sinister wings:
The wind whistles by
And trees bend to let it pass.
In the village
Screams of delighted children
Toss and turn
In the din of whirling wind,
Women –
Babies clinging on their backs –
Dart about
In and out
Madly
The wind whistles by
Whilst trees bend to let it pass
Clothes wave like tattered flags
Flying off
To expose dangling breasts

As jaggered, blinding flashes
Rumble, tremble and crack
Amidst the smell of fired smoke
And the pelting march of the storm.

There is a short silence while the class unwinds.

Teacher: What's that about?

Pupil: A storm.

Teacher: Where?

Pupil: In a village.

Teacher: Good. Now lets have a good look at it.

He passes round copies of the poem, complete with its title, *An African Thunderstorm.*

Teacher: I'm going to read it again. Just listen, or follow in your copy if you like.

He reads the poem again, and then looks round enquiringly to see whether anyone wants to say anything. Nobody does, which is not surprising at this stage.

Teacher: Are there any bits that anyone doesn't understand?
(Silence)

Teacher: Anything that anyone particularly likes? Or doesn't like?

Pupil: What's a pregnant cloud?

Teacher: Anybody any ideas about that?
(Silence)

Teacher: Well what's a pregnant woman?

Pupil: She has got a womb.

Teacher (ignoring the direct translation from the pupil's vernacular): Yes. What is she carrying inside her?

Pupil: A baby.

Teacher: And what difference does that make to her shape?

Pupil: She is very fat.

Teacher: Good. She gets fat and round. Now what do you think he means by 'pregnant clouds'?

Pupil: Ones that are somehow round.

Teacher: Good. And I think he may mean a bit more than that. We said a pregnant woman carries a baby inside her. What might a cloud carry?
(Silence)

Teacher: Well let's see if we are told anything else about these particular clouds. Do we know anything about their colour?

Pupil: They are dark.

Teacher: Where does it say that?

Pupil: It says they are like 'dark sinister wings'.

Teacher: That's very good. You've really been reading carefully and that's one of the things we have to do with poems. What are dark clouds usually carrying?

Pupil: Rain.

Teacher: Yes. So the poet probably wants us to think of clouds that are rounded and swollen because they are full of rain. Anything else that's difficult?

Pupil: I do not know the meaning of 'sinister'.

Teacher: Looking dangerous; as though it might hurt you. Anything else?

The questions go to and fro for a few minutes. 'Din' gives one pupil trouble, but another pupil helps out with that. 'Jaggered' stumps them all so the teacher explains with a quick scribble on the blackboard. There is a brief discussion about whether madmen chase nothing and what they look like when they are doing it, but, rather to the teacher's surprise, no one seems unduly worried about the trees bending to let the wind pass. Last time he read this poem with a first-year class, no one asked about the madman but there was quite an argument about the trees, and even when the image was generally understood several pupils remained unconvinced that it was useful, on the grounds that the trees 'weren't really being polite'. But today the teacher does not direct attention to it; if it isn't a difficulty for this class then he is content to leave it alone. He is trying to elicit a response, not create problems. And he is confident that a good deal of the poem will be understood. His pupils know about storms. Their school is on one of Buganda's many flat-topped hills. It looks across twelve miles of open country to Lake Victoria and they have often watched a storm approaching from the lake, seen its effect on the village just below the hill, and enjoyed the rush to close shutters and to rescue books from verandahs and drying clothes from lawns before they were all drenched. There is nothing exotic for them about 'a plague of locusts' and in their village homes, with no chimneys and few windows, nothing is more familiar to them than the 'smell of fired smoke'. But we can all easily miss the force of what is very familiar to us, so when there are no more questions coming from the pupils, the teacher directs attention to one of the poet's achievements with a question of his own.

Teacher: Does the poet only help us to *see* the storm?

Pupil: No. We are told about the smell of smoke too.

Teacher: Good. Anything else?

(Silence)

Teacher: Well I think he also helps us to *hear* the speed with which the storm comes, by the way he has arranged the sounds of his words. Listen to it for the last time and see if you agree with me.

His third reading of the poem is as similar as he can make it to the first two readings, but this time the pupils are listening for the staccato pace of the second half of the poem. When the reading is finished there is no discussion about whether or how the poet helps us to *hear* the march of the storm. The teacher knows that comment on the use of consonant and short vowel sounds would be premature; the class has not read enough poetry yet and all he wants to do at this stage is to get them listening. All he says is

Teacher: Did you hear the storm gathering speed towards the end? Don't worry if you didn't. I think the poet makes me read some of his lines faster than others by filling them with words that have short sharp sounds. Anyway, it's something to listen for – the kind of noise the poem makes and how that is part of the meaning.

That's all on that poem. The pupils have been asked to live with it for rather less than a quarter of an hour and there has been no attempt to exhaust its possibilities. They have begun to get to know it.

We do **not** wish to imply that this is 'the way to teach poetry'. There are almost as many ways as there are poems, and different classes demand different approaches too. We offer this example as one way of presenting one poem to one particular class. Some of the principles which guided our teacher's method may be applicable with other poems in other situations, but we do not wish to suggest that any other teacher should introduce this poem in this way – or indeed introduce it at all. Every teacher's approach to every poem should be individual.

2 Teaching the poem itself

In the lesson we have just watched we note the absence of introduction. It began with the reading of a poem not with a statement of who wrote it, and certainly not with a mine of information about why, where and when he wrote it and how it relates to the rest of his work. If all this is not in the poem then it does not matter at this stage of literary education, nor, we suspect, at many other stages.

> The teaching of literature is a matter as to which it is easy to make mistakes. There is not the slightest use, either for young or old, in being well informed *about* literature, knowing the dates of the poets, the names of their works and so on. Everything that can be put in a handbook is worthless. What is valuable is great familiarity with certain examples of good literature – such familiarity as will influence the style, not only of writing, but of thought.[1]

3 Using written texts

The poem was read aloud. We believe that this is usually the best way to introduce a poem; that it is sensible to give our pupils the benefit of some of the excellent recordings now available of poems read by actors and by the poets themselves, which a school English department can borrow from the British Council if it cannot afford to buy them; and that if there are other members of staff who enjoy reading poetry it is worth taping some of their readings to provide evidence for the pupils that there are others who enjoy reading poetry and do it well. When the teacher first read Rubadiri's poem the pupils did not have the text in front of them. We are not disposed to be dogmatic about this but we think it generally helps.

> When we begin by listening, our ear selects what it can immediately perceive – the familiar forms patterns in the mind – and discards the rest. When we begin by reading, we can see the whole poem in front of us at a glance and nothing can be discarded without an effort of dissociation which the eye is not so well qualified to make as the ear; in this case we normally begin our attack on the poem by worrying and puzzling over what is unfamiliar.[2]

[1] Lord Russell, *On Education*. Allen and Unwin, 1926.
[2] F. L. Billows, *The Techniques of Language Teaching*. Longman, 1961.

4 What is poetry for?

Having read the poem once the teacher asked two very simple questions. He had chosen the poem because he liked it and was pretty sure that at least some of his pupils would enjoy it; but enjoyment is not possible without understanding, so he did a quick check; if his pupils had not been able to answer the two questions at once he would not have given out the copies of the poem but would have gone on to something simpler. It seems to us that he understands what poetry is for. Poetry is for pleasure.

> All Art is dedicated to Joy, and there is no higher or more serious problem than how to make men happy.

Schiller said that, and Matthew Arnold quoted it. Robert Frost was even more succinct:

> Poetry begins in Delight and ends in Wisdom.

Unless there is a very good chance of a poem being *enjoyed* as well as understood, we do not teach it.

5 Poetry and Language

After the second reading, for which the pupils have had the text before them, the teacher waits for them to suggest the difficulties. He is sure that two or three words will cause trouble but he does not extract them beforehand and write them on the blackboard with definitions beside them, because he understands how dangerous can be the notion that one word has one meaning, how several contexts may meet in a poet's single word, and how important it is for his pupils to be guided towards an appreciation of how the language of the poet is related to the language of the classroom and the street.

> If you are at the seaside, and you take an old, dull, brown penny and rub it hard for a minute or two with handfuls of wet sand (dry sand is no good) the penny will come out a bright gold colour, looking as clean and new as the day it was minted. Now poetry has the same effect on words as wet sand on pennies. In what seems almost a miraculous way, it brightens up words that looked dull and ordinary. Thus poetry is perpetually 'recreating language'.[1]

Used as a deduction from examples in the thirty or so poems read in the first half of the first year, this will do almost as it stands for a second-language class beginning to think about the language of poetry.

Michael Roberts, who was a poet, a teacher and a teacher of teachers, takes us further, though not so simply:

> Poetry may be intended to amuse, or to ridicule, or to persuade, or to produce an effect which we feel to be more valuable than amusement and different from instruction; but primarily poetry is an exploration of the possibilities of language. It does not aim directly at consolation or moral exhortation, nor at the expression of exquisite moments, but at an extension of significance.[2]

[1] C. Day Lewis, *Poetry For You*. Blackwell, Oxford, 1946.
[2] *The Faber Book of Modern Verse*. Faber, 1965.

We could not expect even a fourth-year pupil to make much of this as it stands, but if we can grasp the idea and put it to our pupils in simpler terms, pointing to examples of words and phrases which a poet has made to bear more meaning than we had thought possible until we had read his poem, we shall help them to a better understanding not only of poetry but of everything else that they read and write.

In dealing with pupils' questions the teacher struck a balance between not telling them anything that they could work out for themselves and not wasting time on relatively unimportant words like 'jaggered' that they could not reasonably be expected to work out. And he stuck closely to the poem as a whole, refusing to use it as a quarry for new words and ignoring any faults of grammar or pronunciation in the pupils' questions. In this lesson the poem is the thing.

6 The choice of poems

We chose to start with this poem because the experience underlying it was familiar to our pupils. Other teachers have started just as successfully, some with songs, some with nursery rhymes, some with ballads and others with pop and folk music.

Alan Warner's anthology of English *Songs and Ballads*, with accompanying records, offers a selection of poems suitable for the early stages of a secondary course, and was prepared specially for the L2 situation. So does Eric Robinson's *Rhyme and Reason*, prepared for West African pupils but with a wide appeal. A contemporary poet, Ted Hughes, has a slightly more difficult selection in *Here Today*, and in his introduction he makes a point which our early choice of poems ought to illustrate for our pupils:

> So three things are blended in a poem. A story, or it may be a description, or it may be a man telling his thoughts. A dance. And a song. And so, besides being told a string of facts, we are made to dance them out inwardly, and sing out the feelings behind them inwardly. As a result the facts go more deeply into our minds and affect us more strongly than if they were just counted off to us in prose. And the dance and the song leave us strangely refreshed, as dancing and singing do leave us refreshed. . . . And the final sway that the poem has over our minds is largely the sway of the hidden waves of song, and the motion of the dance in the phrasing of the words, that it compels us to share as we read or hear it.
>
> When we have begun to listen for these things, and to find pleasure in hearing them, we have begun to understand poetry. And we begin to be glad that the poet did not speak his mind in prose.[1]

If we do want, very occasionally, to talk to our pupils *about* poetry, this is the way to do it, in language that is simple yet accurate enough to satisfy a poet. But we cannot talk our pupils into having the experience that Hughes describes; our job is to help them to discover it for themselves.

[1] *Here Today*. Hutchinson, 1963.

7 Using anthologies

We have already mentioned several anthologies and others are listed in the bibliography. We like to have a lot of single copies of good anthologies in the school library. We also like to have several sets of anthologies suitable for the school we are teaching in, but we prefer not to give out one anthology to one class for a whole year or even a whole term. Most school anthologies contain poems at several levels of difficulty and we prefer to read within a few weeks the poems which seem likely to interest one class, and then pass the set on to another class while we start on another selection. We invariably find that before long we have also built up collections of mimeographed poems which are not included in any anthologies worth buying, and we eventually have a substantial selection for each form.

8 Levels of difficulty

How do we determine levels of difficulty in poetry? The criteria proposed in our chapters on vocabulary and reading must be applied with discretion and we believe that, especially in the early stages of the secondary course, the familiarity of the subject is crucial. An experienced teacher wrote recently from Hong Kong approving of most of what we had to say *about* teaching poems, but complaining that too many of the poems we choose to teach have specifically African interests; he thought that his pupils would make a better start with some of Arthur Waley's translations, or with Edmund Blunden's poems on The Great Wall of China and the harbour of Hong Kong, which he particularly enjoyed teaching. We are sure he is right. We could not expect our choice of poems to suit everyone. In fact it should not do so; it was intended for particular classes in one part of one continent.

Familiarity of subject can offset difficulty of vocabulary and we have found it a useful guide, especially in the early secondary years, to ensure that, if we choose poems on unfamiliar subjects, they have few difficulties of vocabulary and grammar. There is no need to worry unduly about a few new words in a poem if we think it is one which our pupils will enjoy, nor is it essential – though we occasionally find it useful – to make sure that unusual words which are central to the meaning of a poem we wish to teach, have been encountered in some other context shortly before we tackle the poem. Vocabulary lists are not entirely irrelevant to poetry teaching, but they need to be used carefully. Milton's lines

> And that one talent which is death to hide
> Lodged with me useless, though my soul more bent
> To serve therewith my Maker

contain only one word that is not in the General Service List, and none that would give a first-year pupil much trouble. But the meaning of the lines is well beyond the grasp of any first- or second-year class that we know. Macaulay's *Horatius* may seem, on first consideration, to present formidable problems to the L2 pupil, but it contains no more than twenty-five words which are not in the English Reader's Dictionary. If the events leading up to the episode described in the poem are outlined beforehand it goes well with a second-year class which has some experience of verse reading and a nodding acquaintance with Roman History. A sketch of the river, the bridge and the fortifications of Rome can be illuminating here. We have watched Lionel Billows elicit an eager response to Edwin Muir's poem *The Castle*, reciting from memory and sketching the progress of the story at the end of each verse.

9 *Come Away, My Love*

After that amount of generalisation we prefer to let anything else we have to say arise out of brief consideration of some poems we have enjoyed teaching in East Africa. First, another African poem, more difficult than Rubadiri's; it has gone well with second-year classes.

COME AWAY, MY LOVE

Come away, my love, from streets
Where unkind eyes divide,
And shop windows reflect our difference.
In the shelter of my faithful room, rest.

There, safe from opinions, being behind
Myself, I can see only you;
And in my dark eyes your grey
Will dissolve.

The candlelight throws
Two dark shadows on the wall
Which merge into one as I close beside you.

When at last the lights are out,
And I feel your hand in mine,
Two human breaths join in one,
And the piano weaves
Its unchallenged harmony.

J. Kariuki

This time the teacher asks most of the questions. What is the difference which the shop windows reflect? How can 'unkind eyes divide'? (If pupils are sceptical about this, a brief demonstration by the teacher, glancing at a couple of pupils walking down the classroom towards him, can help to convince.) Why does the poet bother to say 'two dark shadows' when shadows are always dark? 'Being behind myself' is difficult and it helps to know – as we did not until one of our students told us – that it is a direct translation from a Kikuyu idiom. With a receptive class it is worth while to point out how tersely the poet has expressed an idea which it is not easy to convey in a couple of sentences of direct statement. The question which tests complete understanding of this poem is, 'Why does he mention a piano in the last line of the poem?' We think it helps pupils to understand that there is room for personal interpretation in the reading of a good poem, if the teacher does not absolutely insist that the piano is symbolic and not really in or near the room. He can simply tell them – if none of them can tell him – that the piano keyboard has often been used to represent black and white working together, and that Dr Aggrey of Achimota (where the school shield is simply a slice out of a piano keyboard) once said 'You can play a sort of tune on the white notes and you can play a sort of tune on the black notes. But for harmony you need the black notes and the white notes.' We have had colleagues protest that the sexual undertones of this poem make it unsuitable for school use. This is not a point of view we share because the poem has often seemed to elicit a valuable and mature response from our pupils.

10 *Snake*

D. H. Lawrence's *Snake* has a slightly less African reference and can be equally and differently enjoyed by pupils who have never seen a snake outside a zoo, and pupils for whom snakes are almost everyday occurrences. Snakes were common and feared in our part of East Africa and our pupils understood exactly

> The voice of my education said to me
> He must be killed,
> For in Sicily, the black snakes are innocent, the
> Gold are venomous.

Snakes were killed on the up-country school compounds every week, and it added piquancy to Lawrence's theme to point out that of the seventy-four Ugandan varieties which we slaughtered indiscriminately, only nine were poisonous. This is a poem to spend time on, and there is a good analysis of it in Laurence Lerner's very helpful book *English Literature: An Interpretation for Students Abroad*, O.U.P., 1955. One of the most valuable effects of this poem in our lessons on it has been that there are always some pupils who do not like it. This is important because sooner or later – we think sooner – the honest teacher will introduce his pupils to the notion of 'taste' in literature. We suspect that we have said enough in our chapter on reading to affirm our faith in 'practical criticism' but we also like to remain mindful of a point of view which Lawrence himself has expressed:

> Literary criticism can be no more than a reasoned account of the feeling produced upon the critic by the book he is criticising. Criticism can never be a science. It is, in the first place, much too personal, and in the second, it is concerned with values that science ignores. The touchstone is emotion not reason. We judge a work of art by its effect on our sincere and vital emotion and nothing else. . . . A critic must be able to *feel* the impact of a work of art in all its complexity and force . . . he must have the courage to admit what he feels, as well as the flexibility to *know* what he feels.[1]

If some of our pupils still think, after a careful consideration of the poem, that to talk about a snake as 'someone', 'a guest', 'a king' and finally 'a god'

[1] D. H. Lawrence, 'John Galsworthy' in *Selected Essays*. Penguin, 1968.

is going too far, we sympathise. If, in such a situation, we can eventually elicit a response like 'Yes, I can see what there is in it but I still don't like it,' then honour is completely satisfied.

11 *Out, Out —*

Pupils who have understood *Snake* will have little difficulty with Robert Frost's poem *Out, Out—* though if their experience of Shakespeare is not likely to be enough to help them with the title, we prefer to present the poem without it.

OUT, OUT—
The buzz-saw snarled and rattled in the yard
And made dust and dropped stove-length sticks of wood,
Sweet-scented stuff when the breeze drew across it.
And from there those that lifted eyes could count
Five mountain ranges one behind the other
Under the sunset far into Vermont.
And the saw snarled and rattled, snarled and rattled
As it ran light, or had to bear a load.
And nothing happened: day was all but done.
Call it a day, I wish they might have said
To please the boy by giving him the half-hour
That a boy counts so much when saved from work.
His sister stood near them in her apron
To tell them 'Supper'. At the word, the saw,
As if to prove saws knew what supper meant,
Leaped out at the boy's hand, or seemed to leap,
He must have given the hand. However it was,
Neither refused the meeting. But the hand!
The boy's first outcry was a rueful laugh,
As he swung toward them holding up the hand
Half in appeal, but half as if to keep
The life from spilling. Then the boy saw all –
Since he was old enough to know, big boy,
Doing a man's work, though a child at heart
He saw all spoiled. 'Don't let him cut my hand off –
The doctor, when he comes. Don't let him, sister!'
So. But the hand was gone already.
The doctor put him in the dark of ether.
He lay and puffed his lips out with his breath.
And then – the watcher at his breath took fright.
No one believed. They listened at his heart.
Little – less – nothing! – and that ended it.
No more to build on there; and they, since they
Were not the one dead, turned to their affairs.

Robert Frost

We were lucky enough to have a buzz-saw on the compound when we first taught this poem, but that will not happen to many teachers and a little explanation beforehand helps a good deal. A sketch of a saw, a brief description and an imitation of the change of note as the saw gets its teeth into a log, will take care of the first problem. Some good tourist bureau pictures of peaceful mountain ranges rising from a plain will help to set the scene. The idiom 'Call it a day' needs explaining, but a good reading will remove most of the other difficulties. Our pupils have never failed to notice the descriptive sound of 'snarled and rattled, snarled and rattled' or to demonstrate their appreciation of the poem by quarrelling with Frost's conclusion. 'Don't our traditional burial rites show how much we care when someone we love dies? We drop what we are doing and think of nothing else but the funeral.' Or do we? In some of our class discussions on this poem we have been forced to recall how little the deaths of President Kennedy and Martin Luther King – about which we cared very much – actually interfered with school routine. This is a poem which can move us deeply and make us think again about the way we behave, giving point to Wordsworth's dictum, 'Our thoughts are the representatives of all our past feelings'. We have sometimes followed it effectively with Housman's *Is My Team Ploughing* from *A Shropshire Lad.* The tone is very different but the surviving comrade has most emphatically 'turned to his affairs'.

I cheer a dead man's sweetheart.
Never ask me whose.

And if all this seems unduly sombre there are plenty of less reverent approaches to the last enemy in the numerous books of comic verse on the market; we enjoy this from Belloc's *Cautionary Verses.*

HENRY KING

Who chewed bits of String, and was early cut off in Dreadful Agonies

The Chief Defect of Henry King
  Was chewing little bits of String.
At last he swallowed some which tied
  Itself in ugly Knots inside.
Physicians of the Utmost Fame
Were called at once; but when they came
They answered, as they took their Fees,
'There is no cure for this disease.
Henry will very soon be dead.'
His Parents stood about his Bed
Lamenting his Untimely Death,
When Henry, with his Latest Breath,
Cried – 'Oh, my friends, be warned by me,
That Breakfast, Dinner, Lunch and Tea,
Are all the Human Frame requires . . .'
With that, the Wretched Child expires.

Out, Out— seems to us to be a poem worth learning, which raises the question whether pupils learning English as a second language should be required to learn English poetry by heart. We prefer encouragement to compulsion, and have found that poetry-speaking competitions at class and school level, and choral speechwork in class are two effective incentives. With short poems, sonnets, for example, we sometimes ensure that there are four or five good readings, by the teacher and pupils prepared beforehand, and then ask pupils to turn their books over and see how much they can remember before they have to look.

12 *Journey of the Magi*

Another poem which some of our pupils have learnt is Eliot's *Journey of the Magi*. We have enjoyed teaching this initially at third-year level and returning to it with the same class a year or two later. Anyone who loves poetry comes back again and again to favourite poems and finds new meanings in them; we wonder whether we do this often enough in our teaching.

One of the things that strikes a reader about the gospel account, which is worth reading to a class about to tackle Eliot's poem, is that Saint Matthew was not interested in what sort of journey the wise men had. If the teacher then circulates a few old Christmas cards and reproductions of the best known paintings of the subject, showing the wise men resplendent and confident of success, he will give the pupils some idea of the assumptions commonly made about the journey. Some discussion, with the aid of maps and pictures, of what travel conditions actually were in the Middle East in the time of Augustus, will set the scene for a first reading of the poem; unless the teacher has great faith in his own reading skill it is as well for him to suggest to the class that a very old man is talking to the Augustan counterpart of a modern newspaper reporter. (It is, of course, perfectly reasonable, though a good deal more difficult for the pupils, to start from a reading of the poem without even mentioning the title, and deduce all that has been suggested in these preparations.) In discussing the poem after a second reading, we do not think it is worth while to force the attention of pupils to the prophetic echoes of the middle section, to the relevance of 'no longer at ease' to any emergent civilisation which has felt the impact of Europe in the last hundred years, or to the rich and arguable ambiguity of the final line. Time enough for these – and certainly for any disquisition on poetic rhythm arising out of what Eliot has done with Lancelot Andrewes' sermon – when we return to the poem next term or next year.

13 *Telephone Conversation*

As in every other learning activity, teachers and pupils who are sharing poetry need variety – and fun. Poets know why the idea of poetry is so unpopular.

> A great many people dislike the idea of poetry as they dislike over-earnest people, because they imagine it is always worrying about the eternal verities. Those, in Mr Spender's words, who try to put poetry on a pedestal only succeed in putting it on the shelf. Poetry is no better and no worse than human nature. It is profound and shallow, sophisticated and naïve, dull and witty, bawdy and chaste, in turn.[1]

[1] W. H. Auden and J. Garrett, *The Poet's Tongue*. Bell.

Which gives us all the justification we need for trying Wole Soyinka's *Telephone Conversation* on a class that has begun to enlarge its vocabulary and ideas on unsimplified, unabridged prose texts.

TELEPHONE CONVERSATION [1]

The price seemed reasonable, location
Indifferent. The landlady swore she lived
Off premises. Nothing remained
But self-confession. 'Madam,' I warned,
'I hate a wasted journey – I am African.'
Silence. Silenced transmission of
Pressurized good-breeding. Voice, when it came,
Lipstick coated, long gold-rolled
Cigarette-holder pipped. Caught I was, foully.
'HOW DARK?' . . . I had not misheard. . . . 'ARE YOU LIGHT
OR VERY DARK?' Button B. Button A. Stench
Of rancid breath of public hide-and-speak.
Red booth. Red pillar-box. Red double-tiered
Omnibus squelching tar. It was real! Shamed
By ill-mannered silence, surrender
Pushed dumbfounded to beg simplification.
Considerate she was, varying the emphasis –
'ARE YOU DARK? OR VERY LIGHT?' Revelation came.
'You mean – like plain or milk chocolate?'
Her assent was clinical, crushing in its light
Impersonality. Rapidly, wave-length adjusted,
I chose. 'West African sepia' – and as afterthought,
'Down in my passport.' Silence for spectroscopic
Flight of fancy, till truthfulness clanged her accent
Hard on the mouthpiece. 'WHAT'S THAT?' conceding
'DON'T KNOW WHAT THAT IS.' 'Like brunette.'
'THAT'S DARK, ISN'T IT?' 'Not altogether.
Facially, I am brunette, but madam, you should see
The rest of me. Palm of my hand, soles of my feet
Are a peroxide blonde. Friction, caused –
Foolishly madam – by sitting down, has turned
My bottom raven black – One moment madam!' – sensing
Her receiver rearing on the thunderclap
About my ears – 'Madam,' I pleaded, 'wouldn't you rather
See for yourself?'

Wole Soyinka

This seems to us to be a serious poem but not a profound one, and we prefer to get some of the unambiguous vocabulary – *rancid*, *spectroscopic*, *brunette*, *dumbfounded* – out of the way before a first reading. Telephone boxes are not red all over the world and this matters in this poem, so a picture helps,

[1] *Modern Poetry from Africa*. Penguin, 1963.

especially if it can also give some idea to an up-country pupil of the claustrophobic effect of traffic in a busy English street.

14 *Tarantella*

One way of introducing Belloc's *Tarantella* is to write the title on the blackboard a day or two before and ask the class to find out as much as they can about it; the Shorter Oxford Dictionary will give them as much as they need and a good encyclopedia rather more. The information on dancing is more useful than that on spiders or Southern Italy and it certainly helps to illuminate the structure and rhythm of the poem if the pupils can listen to some suitable music before reading it. No one is very likely to have a tarantella handy but the Dance Bohème from *Carmen* will do just as well and someone on the staff will probably have a 'long player' of that. It is worth while to point out, before or after the first reading, that Bizet's dance ends abruptly at its climax whereas a tarantella winds slowly down again. This poem is a natural for learning by heart, especially by young people who still have plenty of breath, and it gives good scope for discussion of how poets use sound to convey meaning. If we have said less on this topic than might have been expected it is because we believe it is easy to talk too much about it in the classroom, and because most books about English literature – including Lerner's which we have already recommended – treat it fully enough.

15 *A Correct Compassion*

Poetry and science are not easy to reconcile in the young student's mind. We have found a number of poems that help in W. Eastwood's *A Book of Science Verse*, and, in this age of heart transplants, James Kirkup's *A Correct Compassion* has become even more effective.

A CORRECT COMPASSION

To Mr Philip Allison, after watching him perform a Mitral Stenosis Valvulotomy in the General Infirmary at Leeds:

CLEANLY, Sir, you went to the core of the matter.
Using the purest kind of wit, a balance of belief and art,
You with a curious nervous elegance laid bare
The root of life, and put your finger on its beating heart.

The glistening theatre swarms with eyes, and hands, and eyes.
On green-clothed tables, ranks of instruments transmit a sterile gleam.
The masks are on, and no unnecessary smile betrays
A certain tension, true concomitant of calm.

Here we communicate by looks, though words,
Too, are used, as in continuous historic present
You describe our observations and your deeds.
All gesture is reduced to its result, an instrument.

She who does not know she is a patient lies
Within a tent of green, and sleeps without a sound
Beneath the lamps, and the reflectors that advise
Illuminations probing the profoundest wound.

A calligraphic master, improvising, you invent
The first incision, and no poet's hesitation
Before his snow-blank page mars your intent:
The flowing stroke is drawn like an uncalculated inspiration.

A garland of flowers unfurls across the painted flesh.
With quick precision the arterial forceps click.
Yellow threads are knotted with a simple flourish.
Transfused, the blood preserves its rose, though it is sick.

Meters record the blood, measure heart-beats, control the breath.
Hieratic gesture: scalpel bares a creamy rib; with pincer knives
The bone quietly is clipped, and lifted out. Beneath,
The pink, black-mottled lung like a revolted creature heaves,

Collapses; as if by extra fingers is neatly held aside
By two ordinary egg-beaters, kitchen tools that curve
Like extraordinary hands. Heart, laid bare, silently beats. It can hide
No longer yet is not revealed – 'A local anaesthetic in the cardiac nerve.'

Now, in firm hands that quiver with a careful strength,
Your knife feels through the heart's transparent skin; at first,
Inside the pericardium, slit down half its length,
The heart, black-veined, swells like a fruit about to burst,
But goes on beating, love's poignant image bleeding at the dart
Of a more grievous passion, as a bird, dreaming of flight, sleeps on
Within its leafy cage – 'It generally upsets the heart
A bit, though not unduly, when I make the first injection.'

Still, still the patient sleeps, and still the speaking heart is dumb.
The watchers breathe an air far sweeter, rarer than the room's.
The cold walls listen. Each in his own blood hears the drum
She hears, tented in green, unfathomable calms.

'I make a purse-string suture here, with a reserve
Suture, which I must make first, and deeper,
As a safeguard, should the other burst. In the cardiac nerve
I inject again a local anaesthetic. Could we have fresh towels to cover
All these adventitious ones. Now can you all see.
When I put my finger inside the valve, there may be a lot
Of blood, and it may come with quite a bang. But I let it flow,
In case there are any clots, to give the heart a good clean-out.

Now can you give me every bit of light you've got.'
We stand on the benches, peering over his shoulder.
The lamp's intensest rays are concentrated on an inmost heart.
Someone coughs. 'If you have to cough, you will do it outside this theatre.'
– 'Yes, sir.'

'How's she breathing Doug.? Do you feel quite happy?' – 'Yes, fairly
Happy.' – 'Now. I am putting my finger in the opening of the valve.
I can only get the tip of my finger in. – It's gradually
Giving way. – I'm inside. – I can feel the valve

Breathing freely now around my finger, and the heart working.
Not too much blood. It opened very nicely.
I should say that anatomically speaking
This is a perfect case. – Anatomically.

For of course, anatomy is not physiology.'
We find we breathe again, and hear the surgeon hum.
Outside, in the street, a car starts up. The heart regularly
Thunders. – 'I do not stitch up the pericardium.

It is not necessary.' – For this is imagination's other place,
Where only necessary things are done, with the supreme and grave
Dexterity that ignores technique; with proper grace
Informing a correct compassion, that performs its love, makes it live.

There are some difficulties in this poem which seem to us to justify a first reading aloud without the text; it is important here that 'the familiar' should 'form patterns in the mind' and that the unfamiliar imagery should not get in the way. A photograph of an operating theatre in action at a teaching hospital will help pupils who have not had the chance to see such things on television, and recent surgical advances have had plenty of pictorial publicity.

It is likely that this chapter does not contain nearly as much about techniques for the detailed analysis of poetry as some teachers would have wished. This is no accident. We believe that we have ourselves often examined poems too minutely, and spent too long in class on single poems, thereby turning excitement into boredom.

> . . . the one fact that is clear about all the arts is that they are not sciences; they can be studied successfully only by those who remember that if you dissect life in order to examine it, what you are examining is not life.[1]

We have said nothing about 'creative activity' in connection with poetry teaching though we believe that poetry can be effectively linked with art and music and that children should be encouraged to write their own poetry[2] as many of our own pupils have done. What we wish to stress above all else is

[1] John Wain, *Anthology of Modern Poetry*. Hutchinson, 1967.
[2] See Sybil Marshall, *An Experiment in Education*. C.U.P., 1969.

that the complicated process of getting to know a good poem is in itself a *creative* experience for the pupil; he is making himself.

For further reading

BILLOWS, F. L. *The Techniques of Language Teaching*. Longman, 1961.
ELIOT, T. S. *Selected Prose*. Faber, 1975.
GURREY, P. *The Appreciation of Poetry*. Oxford, 1935.
HOLBROOK, D. *English for Maturity*. Cambridge, 1967.
HOURD, M. L. *The Education of the Poetic Spirit*. Heinemann, 1949.
JONES, E. (ed.). *English Critical Essays*, 3 vols. World's Classics, Oxford, 1971.
LERNER, L. D. *English Literature: An Interpretation for Students Abroad*. O.U.P., 1955.
LEWIS, C. D. *Poetry For You*. Blackwell. Oxford, 1946.
MARSHALL, SYBIL. *An Experiment in Education*. C.U.P., 1966.
NOWOTTNY, W. *The Language Poets Use*. L.U.P., Athlone Press, 1962.
REEVES, JAMES. *Teaching Poetry*. Heinemann, 1958.
ROBERTS, M. Preface to *The Faber Book of Modern Verse*. Faber, 1965.

8

GRAMMAR

1 Grammatical correctness and the rules of choice

Nobody disputes that the foreign student must learn the grammar of English in the sense that the sentences he produces must conform to English patterns in the accepted model. We cannot allow him to write: 'She give him a change but when he counted the money they were not enough.'

We cannot be content with communication, however clear the plain sense, if it carries also such depressing messages to the reader about the writer's level of literacy. The learner has got to master the conventional use of the grammatical signals of the language.

Nobody believes that the native speaker achieves his correctness by a conscious application of grammatical rules learnt as such. He does not say to himself:

'I'm about to say something about a previously named person – select for gender – it was Mary – feminine – select for subject: object – *she*. Select for time – past – giving – *gave*. Now another previously named person – *gender* – masculine – object – *him*. Now *change* – noun, subclass uncountable, select for zero *v.* partitive, *some* . . .' and so on.

In the native speaker correct selection is an unconscious matter of habit and a description of the habits of the native speaker of the model selected becomes a prescription[1] of the habits to be acquired by the foreign learner.

2 Interference from L1

There is nothing to interfere with the formation of conventional[2] habits in the native speaker, but the grammatical apparatus programmed into the mind as the first language interferes with the smooth acquisition of the second. It does so directly when an E2L speaker uses a foreign pattern in English:

'The book that I was reading it yesterday has disappeared.'

It does so less directly when he assumes a hundred per cent correspondence

[1] We do not, of course, advocate superstitious prescriptions still lingering in books for native English speakers. We would not teach such nonsense as never beginning sentences with *and* or *but*, always using the nominative after the verb to be, or the accusative pronoun initially in 'Who were you with last night?' Nor do we wish the foreign learner to come across prescriptive grammar in this sense of the term.

[2] *conventional* means in accordance with the model to which he is exposed.

between tenses that have only a ninety per cent one. It does so in even more tiresome ways when English has systems of choice not used in his first language. For instance, the articles are very difficult for Bantu speakers to master; there is nothing even approximately like them in Bantu languages. Moreover restricted experience with the second language leads him into illegitimate extensions. He knows he can say:

I gave him the idea.

and assumes he can therefore say:

I explained him the idea.

3 The uses of grammar

We can go a little further before disagreement is certain. We would all accept that an accurate description of the grammar of the model we wish to present is a necessary and useful piece of equipment. Most people would be prepared to agree that a comparative grammar of the first and second languages would also be useful although few such studies have so far been made.

We may run into controversy when we opt for one description rather than another: traditional or transformational? Immediate constituent or neo-Firthian?

And it may be equally hard to find agreement about who will find the description useful. Clearly the textbook writer must master it, perhaps most people would agree that the teacher needs it (though some would say he often makes bad use of it) and there is very wide divergence of view about whether the pupil should see all or some or none of it.

There are no reasonable grounds for doubt that in many areas abroad the grammar teaching that actually takes place is worthless and would be better completely abandoned. It does not, however, follow that all grammar teaching is worthless. Few people would condemn the study of chemistry on the grounds that the theory is complicated and involves a great deal of abstraction, or deny that for the average citizen the combinations and reactions stimulated by language are at least as important for practical purposes as those of chemistry. How the units of language combine and function may be a worthy subject of study in its own right.

There are those whose heart is on the side of the angels who say, 'We don't want theoretical knowledge; we want skill. Theoretical knowledge inhibits skill; skill is acquired only by practice.' It is certainly true that no skill can be acquired without copious practice. Theory is no substitute, but need it be a hindrance?

On the other hand there are also those who practically ignore the skill aspect and spend their time not in teaching language but in teaching facts about it. It is inefficient to get the proportions of theory and practice wrong. This is not said to deny the importance of theory but to emphasise the necessity of spending most of one's time on its practical applications.

There are even some teachers who limit their instruction to teaching a grammatical terminology. They believe their job is finished if their pupils can identify and name all the bits and pieces of language they come across. We have seen a member of this school of thought spend forty minutes in the pious (but unfulfilled) hope that at the end all his pupils would know that in the following pair:

This is a book.
This book is on the table.

the first *this* is a demonstrative pronoun and the second a demonstrative adjective. He was naturally unable to explain what advantage would have accrued to the pupils if they had succeeded.

Once again this is not to suggest that a knowledge of grammatical terminology is useless but to plead that it should not be taught for its own sake. The negative approach is useful; it is best to teach only the terminology that we cannot do without. Then the value of what is taught will be obvious to the pupils.

We may perhaps secure more agreement if we begin by distinguishing four separate uses of grammar in planning, presentation, correction and survey.

1. Use in planning a course in selection and ordering of items;
2. Use in the first presentation in the classroom of a new item and its immediate revision;
3. Use in the correction of errors and the improvement of written work;
4. Use as a general survey and systematisation of items already met and practised.

Let us examine these uses in more detail.

4 Use in planning a course, syllabus or series of lessons

Here the description of the language functions like a small-scale map showing the planner the whole territory. If he is addressing himself to children, he will not do so in terms of grammatical abstractions. Instead he will embody each grammatical item in a situation that demonstrates its meaning and, eventually if not immediately, what it contrasts with. He will not address any terminology to the pupils and if he writes a teacher's book may not even use any in that.

He will not head his material Personal Pronouns or The Present Continuous Tense, but it does not follow that it will be best for him to omit all explanatory matter. There are undoubtedly cases where a grammatical explanation in non-grammatical terminology is of great practical value. In teaching Bantu speakers to use *he* and *she* we have found it necessary to point out the association with men and boys and women and girls respectively. It is not observed automatically because the nearest corresponding Bantu form is the same for both sexes. We see no objection to the use of the vernacular for such explanations and would for example introduce the first appearance of the present continuous tense by saying in the first language of the pupils, 'Today we are going to learn how to say what we are doing while we are doing it.'

If the textbook writer is to provide simple explanations of this kind or even effective demonstrations and drills he must know the system of the language he is presenting and should know how it differs from the pupils' first language or, at the very least, which contrasts pupils find difficult.

The grammatical terminology that embodies these concepts in the planner's mind remains in the background. What the pupils get is practical use in situations.

5 Grammar in the first presentation of a new item

Here again we would expect no use of grammatical terminology to be made by or to the pupils, whether the new item is presented very early in the learning stage, as, for example, pronouns would be,[1] or even quite late, as unfulfilled conditions in the past would be.

If we set out one or two examples of ways of presenting new grammatical items, we may be able to show the relationship between the grammatical description and the demonstration and practice situation more clearly. Obviously the teacher must understand the grammar the planner intends him to present. The problem does not arise where teacher and planner are the same person, but it is a serious obstacle to good primary school teaching in many parts of Africa.

Let us suppose that we are using a family picture with appropriate local names – we will use English ones – and the grammatical intention of the writer is to associate *he* with *man* and *boy* and *she* with *woman* and *girl*. The material in the textbook may read:

A. This is John Green. He is a man. He is Rebecca's husband. He is Peter's father. He is Jane's father. He is Simon's father too.

B. This is Rebecca Green. She is a woman. She is John's wife, etc.

The teacher who is merely lexically conscious may regard this as revision of the names of family relationships. If he presents it, in the form

This is John Green. John Green is a man. John Green is Rebecca's husband, etc. . . .

the whole purpose of the material is neatly frustrated.

The teacher who is brought up in the pedagogic superstition that there is virtue in the full expression of all the elements in a sentence in all contexts is particularly likely to ignore the writer's intentions in question and answer drills by substituting 'proper' sentences for natural responses. He will happily change:

Is John Green a man?	Yes, he is.
Is he a woman?	No, he's not.

into

Is John Green a man?	Yes, John Green is a man.
Is John Green a woman?	No, John Green is not a woman.

[1] It does not follow that learners who have a terminology learnt in the study of their first language will not use it or misuse it in their heads. When I first started to teach pronouns in the first weeks of the Intermediate School course in the Sudan, a bright lad in the front row listened attentively to the first three or four demonstration sentences, smiled happily as he identified the point of the lesson and informed the rest of the class in Arabic that we were 'doing pronouns'. J.A.B.

Plainly he needs to know the grammar. But not, of course, so that he can lecture seven-year olds on the different series of contrasts available in the English pronominal system from that of the Bantu prefixes and emphatic pronouns. Too much explanation to a class is worse than too little but our experience is that a little helps. If a mistake is made, we are willing to supply not only the correction but also the reason, given very briefly in the pupils' first language.

Teacher: Is Rebecca Green a woman?
Pupil: Yes, he is.
Teacher: No. Yes, SHE is. *Because she's a woman.*

The next time it will be enough to produce the correction and ask the pupils why.

Let us consider a second example of first presentation, one that would take place much later in the course, the introduction of the infinitive of purpose. In grammatical terms we know that *to* + infinitive (+ etc) in contexts where *in order to* may substitute for *to*, occurring as an exponent of ADV in the final position in any known sentence pattern (we don't want to make things complicated and will omit the initial position), shows that the purpose of the action named by the main verb is the action named by the infinitive, that main verb and infinitive have the same subject, except where otherwise specified by the structure *for* + N (which normally excludes the alternative *in order to*) but when the verbs are past, the action named by the infinitive is not necessarily envisaged as having occurred. There exist possibilities of confusion between the infinitive as an exponent of N in the accusative and infinitive construction and the infinitive that suggests result. There are patterns with *so as to* and *so that* + clause that are used in similar contexts.

No pupil could possibly be expected to understand this series of abstractions and no teacher would dream of presenting them in this form. Nevertheless all the points need to be made, though not all on first presentation. In Appendix 1 on page 271 we have tried to suggest how they might be presented to a class. The grammar is not made explicit and no grammatical terminology is used, but it is the grammar that determines what patterns of example are used and to what aspects of the situation pupils' attention is drawn by questions.

Implicit in this kind of grammar teaching is the assumption that we present to the pupil sufficient examples of patterns composed of similar elements for him to perceive the pattern. But the question of what constitutes similar elements is not straightforward. It depends at what point in the scale of delicacy of analysis one is working. For the beginner there are more differences than for the more experienced learner. This is easier to exemplify than to describe.

When the contrast being taught is that between *my* and *your*, *my* and *your* are 'different'. When the contrast being taught is between *my*, *your*, *his*, *her*, etc. and the indefinite article *a*, *my* and *your* are 'the same'. When the contrast being taught is between singular number and mass nouns, *a*, *the*, *my*, *your*, etc. are all 'the same'.

By the time pupils have finished a course of simplified English and secondary teaching begins there are very few items left to be presented for the first time. Nearly all the grammar we have considered so far has been taught with the use of hardly any terminology in the primary school, but not always with a hundred per cent success.

6 The use of grammar for correction and remedial work

The attempt to remedy certain errors and omissions also requires a knowledge of grammar. But we want the pupils to learn English not grammar. Not all kinds of grammar teaching are helpful in any case and if we increase the time we spend on grammar at the expense of reading, writing and speaking, we shall increase the errors and soon find ourselves in a vicious circle.

The pupil's problem now is not merely to establish a new correct habit but to break down an incorrect one and replace it over the relevant area by a correct one. We believe that a conscious comparison of the items confused and an explanation is usually a helpful starting-point and increases the pupil's willingness to submit to the extra practice required to get into the correct habit.

The first essential is to diagnose the cause of the error and the question that is most usually fruitful is: What is confused with what? Let us take some examples.

The pupil who writes:

1. When we reached, the house was empty.

is confusing the transitive use of the verb *reach* with its intransitive semantic relation *arrive*.[1]

The pupil who writes:

2. Her father made her to leave school.

is confusing the minor pattern s + v + o + bare infinitive
with the commoner pattern s + v + o + *to*-infinitive
e.g. Her father wanted her to leave school.

The pupil who writes:

3. He tied it to the branch of a tree so that to keep it safe.

is confusing the infinitive of purpose with the finite clause of purpose.

The pupil who writes:

4. That was the first house which I lived in it.

is confusing the structure of another language with that of English. This error is common to Arabic and Swahili speakers.

The pupil who writes:

5. When my father came, told me I was going to school the next day.

is confusing subordinate with co-ordinate clause structure.

[1] I once made the same diagnosis when a Luganda-speaking learner wrote: 'When he reached down, he found his friends waiting.' The pupil's face, however, clearly showed that my explanation did not help him. I had made a wrong diagnosis. In fact the Luganda word *wansi* is used as the equivalent of both the adverb *down* and the noun *the ground*. This explanation proved satisfactory but led, of course, to quite a different kind of practice. J.A.B.

Clearly in order to deal with this kind of error the teacher needs to know his English grammar and we must now face the problem of what kind of grammar. The traditional grammar still widely taught in American and British schools contains no answers to this kind of problem. It does not need to. It has for generations been addressed to people who do not make this kind of mistake. Neither Nesfield nor his modern followers provide useful answers.

One difference between teaching English to English speakers and to non-English speakers is that the latter believe what they are told and allow it to influence their behaviour. The English boy fortunately generally succeeds in keeping his grammatical 'knowledge' out of the main stream of his life.

We say 'fortunately' because most school grammars contain a large number of highly dubious statements and completely omit to deal with large and important areas of English grammar. Any grammar that attempts to define by meaning is pre-scientific and, for our purposes, suspect. We cannot expect to teach that *this*, *a*, *no*, *many*, *enough*, *much*, *yellow*, *long* are all members of the same class, adjectives, because they modify nouns and be surprised if our pupils write correctly:

No yellow flowers
No long stories

and incorrectly:

No many flowers
No enough stories

We shall not find it practically useful to divide nouns into

Proper (one thing at a time)
Common (any number of things)
Collective (a group of things)
Material (what a thing is made of)
Abstract (quality, state or action)

with the riders:

1. A Proper noun becomes a Common noun, when it is used in a descriptive or general sense.
2. A Noun of Multitude, since it denotes a specific group, must be classed as collective; but with a difference.
   a. A Collective noun denotes one undivided whole; and hence the verb following is singular.
   b. A noun of Multitude denotes the individuals of the group; and hence the verb is plural, although the noun is singular.
3. A Collective Noun may be either Common or Proper.
4. The same word can be a Material noun or a Common noun according to the sense.
5. An abstract noun relates to qualities, states, etc.,[1] which cannot be seen or touched, etc.
6. The same word may be an Abstract noun or a Common noun, according to the purpose for which it is used.

[1] This *etc.* is quite delightful. It must be used to avoid adding *actions*. Even this kind of grammarian boggles at saying outright that we cannot see arrivals and departures.

7. There are two ways in which a Proper, Material or Abstract noun can be used as a Common noun:
   a. by putting an article (*a* or *the*) before it.
   b. by putting it in the plural number.

In spite of the glaring difficulties[1] in the descriptions they contain there are still numerous school grammars designed for English and American schools in use in schools abroad to this day and many of the people who advocate 'teaching grammar' in fact mean teaching this sort of thing. We think they are mistaken. Others who do not believe in 'teaching grammar' mean that they think this sort of thing is useless. We agree.

There are, however, descriptions of English grammar that are more useful for the foreign learner. Up to about ten years ago they were either the work of foreign scholars, such as Jespersen, Kruisinga and Zandvoort who saw English from outside, or the work of Englishmen, such as H. E. Palmer, A. S. Hornby, Stannard Allen, Pit Corder, who were working abroad and could see the needs of the foreign learner. This kind of description is still valuable.

More recently we have begun to get scientific descriptions of English according to different grammatical theories. The controversies that rage between them should not obscure the fact that they have much more in common than any one has with traditional Latin-derived grammar. For one thing, which we think important, they tell the truth about English. They are, however, not yet widely available in a form of immediate use to the secondary pupil abroad.

But books designed to make modern scientific grammatical theory comprehensible to pupils are beginning to appear. One may instance Roberts in America and Mittins, Pit Corder and Close in England. When they aim at the native English speaker they do not usually get down to enough detail to be helpful to the foreign learner. But Close and Pit Corder write for the teacher and learner overseas and it will not be long before more scientific descriptions of English are widely available to learners with different language backgrounds.

No grammar that does not concern itself in some way with patterns and substitutable items within the patterns is likely to be satisfactory for the foreign learner's needs because his commonest grammatical problem at the secondary level is not that he does not know the patterns but that he substitutes grammatically unlike items. He knows:

I expected him to go.
I wanted him to come.

and proceeds to use:

I hoped him to go.

and I enjoyed him to visit me.

It is difficult for the native English speaker to appreciate this difficulty. He is inclined to think the pupil has got the meaning of the word wrong in some way. His own mind is so programmed that he cannot think of wrong examples; they are on a different circuit in his brain.

[1] I cannot resist one more quotation. 'Nouns are now classified, according to sex or absence of sex, and not, as once, by form or declension.' The process must be even trickier than sexing day-old chicks. J.A.B.

Perhaps we may now return to the examples that preceded this digression and examine the relationship between grammatical knowledge and remedial work. It will not be essential for our remedial purposes to use grammatical terminology but it is right to point out that if we are using it for another purpose and the pupils already know it, its use will save time.

Error 1: When we reached, the house was empty.

We cannot generalise this. It is no good saying 'transitive verbs take objects'. The pupil's problem is that he doesn't know that *reach* can be a transitive verb. We can't even say '*Reach* must have an object' because that isn't true either as any baddy who has reached for his gun while the goodies reached for the ceiling might testify.
We shall have to produce an explanation like this:

a. When we use *reach* meaning 'arrive', we must follow it by naming the place that was reached.

We reached Khartoum.
Kampala.
Kasangati.
Kenya.
the old tree.
the car. etc.

b. If we do not name the place, we cannot use *reach* and must use *arrive* instead.

We arrived at eight o'clock.
next day.
in good spirits. etc.

c. If we do name the place, we can use *arrive in* or *arrive at*, but not *arrive* by itself.

We arrived in Dodoma at six o'clock.
= We reached Dodoma at six o'clock.

Following the explanation we devise oral and written exercises involving choosing the appropriate structure. If we are sure that the error arises from a word in the first language common to both equivalent structures, there is no reason why we should not use translation to provide practice. We are not creating the bond; it is already there at the heart of the problem.

If we do not wish to use translation, we can use such rubrics and examples as:

1. Change *reach* to *arrive:*

The party reached Cape Town on September 23rd.

2. Choose *reach* or *arrive* to fill the gaps:

The party............on September 23rd.
The letter............us a week later.
The letter............a week later.

3. Which of the following items can be correctly used in each gap?
   arrived, reached, arrived in, arrived at
   (a) The ship............two days early.
   (b) When the ship............Port Said, some passengers took a trip to Cairo.
   (c) When we............the meeting point, there was nobody there.

Error 2: Her father made her to leave school.

This time we can generalise and our correction should include all the verbs that can substitute for *made* in this construction: *make*, *let* and verbs of immediate sensory perception – *see, watch, feel, hear, notice*.

We have to know the grammar to make the list or at least know where to find it in Hornby.[1] We also have to know enough not to produce an incorrect explanation. If we are so ill-informed as to say, 'Don't use *to* after *make*,' we shall have nobody but ourselves to blame if our pupils write:

She was made leave school.

Oral practice is easy. 'Tell me something you made/saw/etc. somebody do.' Written practice can involve completion:

The headmaster will not let us . . .

Luckily he did not see us . . .

or changing from passive to active:

We were made to do our homework all over again by the biology master.

or changing the exponent and therefore the construction:

The farmer allows his dogs to wander about as they please.

Change *allows* to *lets*.

The police forced us to go with them.

Changed *forced* to *made*.

Translation would be useless in dealing with this error.

Error 3: . . . so that to keep it safe

We may well decide that we need not teach *so as to* for productive use at all; (*in order*) *to* provides an adequate and more frequent alternative.

We also need to bear in mind that

She went to the market to buy some food.

is normally stylistically preferable to

She went to the market so that she might buy some food.

On the other hand:

She always got up early so that her youngest son would have plenty of time to walk to school.

is normally stylistically preferable to:

She always got up early for her youngest son to have plenty of time to walk to school.

We may also remember that when we first presented the infinitive of purpose

[1] A. S. Hornby, *A Guide to Patterns and Usage in English*. O.U.P., 1954.

we confined ourselves to examples in which the subject of the infinitive was the same as the subject of the main verb:

She went to the cupboard to fetch her poor dog a bone.

and we did not present:

She gave the boy sixpence to buy some sweets.

where the object of the main verb is the subject of the infinitive.[1] Nor did we present the pair:

He has a friend to play with.

and He has a friend to play with him.[2]

When we have considered the problems involved we shall perhaps do something like the following:

Explain that we want to practise three ways of showing that action B was the purpose of action A:

A		B
GOING TO THE MARKET		BUYING SOME FRUIT
(i) Mary went to the market	to	buy some fruit
(ii) Mary went to the market	in order to	buy some fruit
(iii) Mary went to the market	so that	she could buy some fruit.

To make sure we all make the same sentence, we'll add a column for the subject. We can now make a blackboard that reads as follows:

ACTION		PURPOSE	
S	A	S	B
John	staying at home	John	working in the garden
Ahmed	getting a job in the holidays	Ahmed	paying his school fees
Miriam	becoming a teacher	Miriam	pleasing her parents

etc. using as many different sentence patterns as we choose.

[1] The fact that the term 'subject of the infinitive' causes alarm and consternation to the traditional grammarian brought up to believe that a subject is what an infinitive does not have is evidence of the present confusion in grammatical terminology.

I have seen a lesson on the infinitive based on a book which quoted the example *I want the boy to sing* and which went on to assure the puzzled pupils that we know who wants but not who is to sing. The pupils did know that it was the boy and so does everybody else. J.A.B.

[2] We have pretended that the same teacher is concerned with first presentation and remedial work. In the rare cases where he is there will be feed-back from later errors that will result in improved first presentation. Usually however, the teacher who has to cope with an error has no information about what the pupil can reasonably be expected to know. He can frequently find out by examining the course book used at an earlier stage. To do this may give him a starting-point from what is known and enable him to see what needs to be added.

Within the secondary school the problem of communication from teacher to teacher is not easy. Most of us would feel we had done our duty if we recorded that we had 'done' the infinitive of purpose. But our successors would be grateful for much more detailed information.

The exclusion of:

Mother	giving Jane some money	Jane	buying a pair of shoes

is deliberate. Instead we go on to, for example:

John	staying at home	John's wife	being able to go and visit her aunt
Mukasa	going to the hospital	the doctors	finding out what was the matter with him
	etc.	etc.	

We can now use this to get the pupils to see that in the first group of examples where the subjects are the same, although all three ways are possible, the infinitive is the neatest. Where the subjects are different *in order to* is impossible and the clause makes the neatest sentence.

If we wish to do so, we can go on to demonstrate by using the Mother – Jane example that we can usually make a neater sentence with the infinitive except where we have to specify its subject.

For written practice we can use such rubrics as:

(a) Rewrite the following in two different ways:
She stayed at home so that she could do the cooking.

(b) Rewrite the following using *to*, *in order to* and *so that:*
She stayed at home because she meant to do the cooking.

(c) Choose the neatest way of rewriting the following using *to*, *in order to*, or *so that:*
He made his son an allowance because he wanted the boy to learn how to handle money sensibly.

It would be possible to use translation as an exercise but wrong to do so unless this is a mental-translation error.

Error 4: . . . the first house which I lived in it.

If we have been brought up on prescriptive rules, we may perhaps retain the superstition that a preposition is a bad word to end a sentence with. This would lead us to teach that the construction *the first house in which I lived* is 'better'. It would make the error easy to cure at the trifling expense of ruining our pupils' style for life. We shall clearly be wiser, if we do not want our pupils to 'talk like a book', to consider what structures English-speaking people actually use and not what recommendations pedants have inherited from each other for the last hundred years or so. We shall find that defining adjective clauses must be distinguished from non-defining ones. We can ignore the non-defining clauses for the moment. The system of even the defining clauses is fairly complicated. We have different pronouns for persons and things (with the complication of animals and other things that may be personified) and different possibilities where the relative pronoun is subject, object and 'object of a preposition'. Let us set this out in tabular form:

	PERSONS	THINGS
Subject[1]	a man who came to the door a man that came to the door	a tree which hid it completely a tree that hid it completely
Object	a man we met a man that we met a man whom we met[2]	the last book I read the last book that I read the last book which I read
'Object of preposition'	a man we spoke to a man that we spoke to a man to whom we spoke[3]	a kind of bed I enjoy sleeping in a kind of bed that I enjoy sleeping in a kind of bed which I enjoy sleeping in a kind of bed in which I enjoy sleeping
Possessive	a man whose wife smokes	a tree the leaves of which turn brown at the edges a tree whose leaves . . .

Having set out the system we can pinpoint the problem using our knowledge of the class todecide what needs to be practised. Let us suppose that we frequently come cross errors in the object and 'object of preposition' constructions but we a not find confusion between *which* and *whom*. Let us also decide that we will do tpone teaching the difference in the level of formality between contact and *that*-clauses, and *whom* and initial preposition clauses.

Since the problem relates to the underlying structure of two base sentences in combination, we can start from such pairs as:

(a) The man is a bank manager.

(b) We met him yesterday.

Problem: To use (b) to help identify the person or thing named by the word underlined in (a).

Useful question: What happens to the *him*?

Answer: (i) frivolous — It is almost swallowed by the *who* – you can just see its tail sticking out of *who*'s mouth.

(ii) serious — It vanishes.

Practice pairs will include 'things' and 'people' and objects of verbs and prepositions.

Error 5: When my father came, told me . . .

This error cannot be explained by saying 'A verb must have a subject.' As far as the pupil knows, it has got a subject in exactly the same way as,

My father came and told me . . .

[1] There is no zero possibility – that is no parallel construction without a relative pronoun – unless we count 'There's a boy brings round the papers about 8 o'clock.'

[2] Is *a man who we met* casual, dialectal, or substandard?

[3] Is *a man who we spoke to* equally acceptable?

Once again we have two underlying sentence patterns. We can start with such pairs as the following:

A	B
My father came home.	My father said he was tired.
His uncle bought a new car.	His uncle took him for a drive.
Hassan earned some more money.	Hassan could afford a better house.
Mahmoud got an increase of pay.	Mahmoud could not afford a new car

We proceed to show that possible combinations are:

main clause A + and/but + main clause B with 'borrowed' subject

This can be shown in the form belqw:

His uncle bought a new car
AND
His uncle took him for a drive

We cancel what is common to both in the part that follows *and*. If this leads to the question about whether only the subject can be borrowed, so much the better. We can go on to look at

His uncle bought a new car
AND
His uncle bought a record-player

We then proceed to show the patterns:

When-clause, + main clause
Main clause + *when*-clause

Switches between nouns and pronouns can be used, but nothing can be borrowed.

Written exercises can consist of rewriting co-ordinate sentences as complex ones. For example, rewrite beginning *when*:

The lorry overturned but was not badly damaged.

We hope our examples demonstrate that a knowledge of the grammar of the language, and one that goes beyond traditional school grammar, is essential to the teacher if he is to deal sensibly with mistakes. We hope we have also shown that it is possible to do this with *ad hoc* explanations not requiring any permanent knowledge of grammatical terms on the part of the pupil.

One other odd feature about errors should be noted before we move on. Structural complexity may lead to the recurrence of errors that have disappeared in simpler examples. A pupil will write:

(a) Ibn Batuta travelled far into the interior of Africa as any later and more famous European explorer.

at a stage in his learning when he would not write:

(b) Ibn Batuta travelled far as any later European explorer.

His foresight, so to speak, extends to the second *as* in (b) in time for him to put the first one in. It does not do so in (a). Where this is the case it is no use reteaching the simple forms; we must provide practice using more complicated elements of structure.

7 Individual correction

So far we have spoken as though all kinds of corrective explanations and exercises are going to be done with the whole class. Ten or fifteen minutes spent sometimes in this way may be valuable, but there are more useful and interesting ways of spending one's time, if one is a pupil, than in correcting other people's errors, especially if the class contains half a dozen persistent offenders and the same errors are dealt with *ad nauseam.*

The standard answer is to work with each pupil individually, and where there are small classes and time available, nothing could be better. Even with large classes individual correction is easy provided that the explanations and exercises are put on cards and indexed instead of being written on the blackboard or in a pupil's book.

Cards can be filed in alphabetical order grammatically under, e.g.

Purpose:	in order to/so as to	NOT so that to
Subject:	omission of, in main after subordinate clause	
Object:	intrusive in relative clauses	

or under individual words

Arrive/Reach	
Reach	see Arrive
Enjoy	omission of self-pronoun

A useful practice is to put the explanation on the front of the card and the exercises on the back.

When the pupil makes a mistake, he is given the card, and his corrections consist of reading the explanation, doing the exercises on the back of the card in his composition book and correcting his own error. Specimen cards are given below:

FRONT OF CARD

AND

Explanation: When two sentences are joined by 'and' only words which would come into both can be left out.

In the following

'The tools had retained their colour and pleasing to see.'

the word 'were' cannot be left out because it does not occur in the first sentence.

The tools had retained their colour.

The tools were pleasing to see.

BACK OF CARD

Exercise: Join the following pairs with 'and' leaving out all the words you can.

1. The workmen had had a busy morning.
   The workmen were resting under a tree.
2. He had been told to go back to the house.
   He had been told to fetch some money.

3. They have already chosen the chairman.
   They will choose the committee tomorrow.
4. He has not yet learnt the importance of clear writing.
   He probably never will learn the importance of clear writing.
5. I continued to read.
   I discovered that these rocks were once under the ocean.

FRONT OF CARD

ONE

Explanation: If the indefinite pronoun 'one' is used as the subject, all later pronouns or possessive adjectives must keep to the 'one' form; 'his' and 'hers' cannot refer back to 'one'.[1]

Once you start 'one-ing' you go on 'one-ing' to the end, e.g.

One can easily deceive *oneself* into thinking *one's* work is more useful than *one* knows it is.

This is ugly and can be avoided by starting with a different subject, e.g. 'a man', 'a person' or even 'anyone' or 'anybody'.

BACK OF CARD

Exercise: Correct the following sentences in two ways. Write out the first three examples.

1. One must take care not to burn himself on the stove.
2. One can easily see that his mind is meant to be used.
3. One should not fail to train himself.
4. One cannot always do what he wants at the time he wants to all by himself.
5. One should try to concentrate his mind on what he is doing.

FRONT OF CARD

TAKE OFF ONE'S CLOTHES

Not 'I put off'.

We *put on* our clothes but we *take off* our clothes.

BACK OF CARD

Make five sentences like these:

She took off one hat and put on another.
She took off one pair of shoes and put on another.
He took off a dirty shirt and put on a clean one.

FRONT OF CARD

ALL THAT or WHAT — NEVER 'all what'

Explanation: There are two possible constructions:

1. He heard all / that I said.

In this case, 'all' is object of 'heard' and 'that I said' is an adjective clause qualifying 'all'.

2. He heard / what I said.

In this, 'what I said' is a noun clause object of 'heard'.

[1] In American-English it is acceptable to follow *one* with *his*.

BACK OF CARD

Exercise: Add both the constructions explained overleaf to the following verbs:

1. We heard . . .
2. He explained . . .
3. They saw . . .
4. I examined . . .
5. We looked at . . .

The above card was written about 1948 when we were still using a traditional grammatical description. Today for pupils brought up on a new grammar we should use a different explanation. The contrast is not entirely without interest. For example:

FRONT OF CARD

Compare constructions A and B

A					B			
S	+V	+O			S	+V	+O	
He	heard	all	that	I said.	He	heard	what	I said.
He	heard	everything	that	I said.	He	heard	where	I went.
He	knows	the man	that	I met.	He	knows	when	I went.
He	knows	the man	whom	I met.	He	knows	why	I went.

In the A examples O=N+ relative clause. The clause *that I said* is only part of the object. *All* is a pronoun and we may substitute a noun for it. *That* is not essential. We may say: *all I said, the man I met.*

In the B examples O=noun clause. The clause *what I said* is the whole of the object. The substitutions for *what* are the WH-words including *whether*. *What* cannot be omitted.

BACK OF CARD

a. Exercise as above.

b. Can you explain why the following is correct: *He told them all what he knew*?

These sentences may help you:

He	told	the boys	a story.
He	told	both the boys	what he had said.
He	told	them both	a story.
He	told	all the boys	what he had said.
He	told	all of them	what he knew.

One makes the cards while marking compositions, because this is where one sees the common errors. If the first set of exercise books is ever to get marked, one cannot make a card for every error. A self-denying ordinance restricting the cards made to ten for any one set of compositions saves midnight oil and even so the cards accumulate pretty rapidly.

In marking later work all that is necessary by way of setting a corrective exercise is to slip the appropriate card into the exercise book of the pupil who made the error or refer him to it. There are advantages in keeping the box of cards in the classroom. We have found that pupils then use it to do the exercises orally, which helps to prevent errors from arising.

8 The use of grammar to get improvements other than greater correctness in written work

So far we have only considered grammar as an aid to correcting sins of commission, positive errors. We must now consider the possibilities of its use in detecting and curing sins of omission, weaknesses that show up in written work.[1]

At a simple level a count of basic sentence patterns will sometimes show that a pattern common in normal English is rare in the pupils' writing. Two people recently have suggested to us that the under-employment of the *there*-pattern is a feature in the writing of Sudanese and Ugandan pupils. A lesson on how it is used might correct the omission.

Something useful at an even simpler level can often be discovered by sampling the length of the pupils' sentences in terms of average number of words and quantity of variation. This is not, of course, to suggest writing to a recipe, but to guide us whether to work at making sentences shorter, longer or more varied.

A more accurate assessment of structural complexity can be obtained by counting more grammatical features. Peter Wingard and John Bright once got interested in the problems that would arise if English were used as a medium of instruction low down in the primary school. They realised that the vocabulary would have to be related to that of the course in use, which at the time was the Oxford English Readers for Africa, but they wanted to be able to advise textbook writers about levels of structural complexity. They decided that the geography textbook would probably prove to be readable if its structural complexity did not exceed that of the previous year's Oxford English Reader. They got a rough measure of this by counting as follows:

OER	Words per sentence	Finite clauses per sentence	Prepositions per sentence	Verbs (including infinite ones) per sentence
1	6·2	1·1	0·4	1·3
2	8·4	1·2	0·5	1·7
3	10·5	1·5	0·9	2·7
4	13·0	1·8	1·3	2·8
5	16·4	2·1	1·5	3·2
6	20·7	2·1	1·8	3·5

OER 5 and 6 are as complex as any writing need be. We do not need to encourage pupils to write ever longer and more complicated sentences *ad infinitum*. It might be interesting to see where one's pupils come on such a scale.

A very small sample consisting of five passages of ten sentences each from

[1] Or of course, in speech, but unless it is recorded, speech is less easy to analyse.

the following sources produced the table below. It would be wrong to generalise on such slender evidence but the results surprised us as well as our pupils.

Author	Title	Year	Average words per sentence in 50 sentences
Smollett	Humphrey Clinker	1771	37·4
Trollope	The Belton Estate	1865	22·1
Wells	Mr Britling Sees It Through	1916	17·0
Hemingway	The Old Man and the Sea	1952	16·1
Whitehead	The Aims of Education	1928	18·3
Galbraith	The Affluent Society	1958	17·3

One can examine the pupils' writing for all sorts of constructions. If a paragraph seems muddled, it is worth while to look at the subjects of the sentences.

It may be worth while to count the number of sentences that start with the subject. An excessive number beginning with initial adverbials produces an unidiomatic effect.

Another possibility is to examine the number of sentences containing elements out of the normal order.

If we get a feeling that our pupils are writing within a narrow range of structures, we may decide to do a more detailed analysis, perhaps taking a whole composition and setting out the types of clauses and the patterns of combination used. How we do this in detail will depend on the description we are using.

There can be no doubt that a knowledge of English grammar is essential for the teacher. He must understand the way the language works. He must be able to identify the various items, see the relationships and understand the processes involved. To do this he needs a terminology in which this kind of knowledge is embodied. He needs it because he is going to use it.

It does not, however, therefore follow that the pupil's needs are the same. The pupil who, like the native speaker, can operate the language successfully has no practical need of grammatical theory. Conversely unless grammatical knowledge is going to be applied in reading, speaking and, more obviously, writing, there is little justification for spending a great deal of time teaching it. For practical purposes we need teach nothing that does not lead to some improvement in understanding or expression. It is therefore a mistake to divorce grammar from reading and composition and shut it away in a separate period on the timetable. It is also a mistake to think that knowledge of terminology is the same thing as knowledge of grammar. The terminology is only useful if it contributes to understanding and improved performance. We must go on from the terms to do something with them that will help pupils to write better. Generations of examiners have noticed that pupils who cannot construct a single sentence correctly in their compositions can be trained to 'analyse into clauses' very efficiently. But knowledge that is not applied is worthless lumber in the mind. There would be no point in learning the multiplication table if one never had to do any arithmetical calculations.

It is even possible for bad grammar teaching to result in positive harm. We have seen adjective clauses taught on the following lines:

This is a *yellow* book. Yellow = adjective

This is a book *which is yellow*. Which is yellow = adjective clause

In effect, the teacher said, 'An adjective clause does the same job as an adjective and it doesn't matter which you use.'

The pupils, knowing no better, dutifully set to work to use adjective clauses and produced, for example,

Yesterday was a day which was fine.

My friend who is Ali and I went for a walk which was nice.

There are three morals to this sad story. The first is that all grammar teaching should be based on genuine examples and not on constructed ones. It is dishonest to present a set of examples that dodge the problems or are specially selected to prove a 'rule'. It is highly desirable to get the pupils to produce the examples. The occasions when they do something unexpected are frequently more illuminating than when everything goes according to plan.[1]

The second moral is that there is no such thing as a way of teaching grammar. People who operate like this teacher do all their grammar lessons in the same way. They ask how one should teach grammar and expect there to be an answer equally applicable to Anticipatory *it* and the future meaning of the Present Simple Tense. It is essential to realise that there are better and worse ways of teaching and revising all the grammatical mechanisms but the ways are as different as the mechanisms. It is reasonable to ask, 'What does this class need to do with, for example, adjective clauses? What mistakes are made? How can I prevent them? Where is there danger of ambiguity? What alternatives to adjective clauses are available? In what situations do we use them? In what situations can we choose freely and what conditions our choice?' If we ask ourselves this kind of question, we shall get our examples at the right level of difficulty, make the necessary distinctions between contexts and anticipate and prevent mistakes.

The third moral is that an item of grammar must not be presented out of the situation in which the native speaker uses it or apart from its place in the system of related items. The point about adjective clauses is not that they are free choice alternatives to adjectives but that they are used to make a different set of distinctions – distinctions based on actions rather than qualities and generally containing a time element too.

In Appendix 2 on page 272 we try to exemplify what we would consider a useful piece of grammar teaching aimed at showing pupils the variety of modificatory structures available for use with nouns in helping them to name,

[1] I once set out to review some of the structures of modification in noun groups with a first-year class. I started by putting a large red flower on the table and saying 'If you wanted to say something about that, what would you call it?' The pupils said 'A flower'. I added a large white one and said pointing to the red one, 'What would you call it now?' I got 'The red flower' as I had expected, but was then interrupted by a boy who said, 'I should call it a hibiscus.' This was a godsend. I was able to show that if the noun names with sufficient precision, we do not need an adjective and we were able to consider the hearer's point of view too and to decide that we might still prefer to say *red flower* to a small child, for example. J.A.B.

the reasons for choosing one rather than another and if more than one is used, how they fit together.

The material shows the line we should follow in class and demonstrates, we hope:

1 That terminology can be used without being taught. Pupils are very seldom asked to use it and when they are, it is written on the blackboard at the top of a list of examples.

2 That examples can be provided by the class.

3 That the teaching can deal with things the pupils find difficult (*red pretty dress; interesting* versus *interested*).

4 That the teaching can bring out the underlying relationships between one structure and another that enable the native speaker to construct by analogy groups or sentences he has never heard or seen before.

We believe that our pupils have found this kind of grammar teaching interesting and we know that it feeds into the composition work and leads to the use of a wider variety of structure than would otherwise appear and to the avoidance of certain errors.

We believe that it also affects their attitude to English and to using it by giving them confidence that there is discoverable order in the language.

We can then use some of the knowledge to help them examine their own compositions or somebody else's more critically. For example at some point in our composition course we shall want to consider repetition. Perhaps we shall give the pupils some such passage as the following and lead them to see the pointlessness of using adjectives that make unnecessary distinctions – that add nothing to the picture the writer is trying to make the reader see.

> The ancient old castle lay in a low, damp misty hollow. Its high, lofty, towering walls surrounded a broken-down, old, ruined tower. But the gardens were bright with gay, cheerful flowers and the short, smooth, close-cut grass of the green shaven lawns looked fresh after a brief passing shower. In the clear, clean water of the lake we could see nimble frisky fish darting about like arrows or hanging motionless, suspended unmoving in the still water.

We shall also wish them to consider the difference to the reader's ability to see the picture made by the use of descriptive adjectives instead of adjectives of feeling. Perhaps we shall give them a pair of passages such as the following:

A. It was dark when we first moved in and our first view was of the beautiful lights which shone bravely across the valley. In the morning we looked out again and saw a wonderful sunrise. The beauty of the night view was forgotten when we saw the glorious morning with the lovely colours of sky and splendid hill and valley. It was a scene of unsurpassable and delicate beauty.

B. It was dark when we first moved in and our first view was of the faint, black shadow of a hill lined with sparkling lights, blue, orange and white. In the morning we looked out again just as the red rim of the sun rose above the dark, green hill. The clouds above were edged with gold and in the valley below still in the shadows lay a grey river of mist.

At a later stage we shall as part of our reading course wish them to examine 'loaded' writing and may offer some such accounts of the same events as the following:

A. A lively meeting took place last night. Urbane Mr X, a loyal and resolute party man, held his ground for over an hour against the untimely interruptions of the opposing candidate, a raucous and domineering speaker, whose contributions to any debate are always useless.

B. A rowdy meeting took place last night. Smoothtongued Mr X, a die-hard party man, barely held his ground for a quarter of an hour against the well-timed interrogations of Mr YZ, a forthright and dominating speaker, whose contributions to every debate are always useful.

There are numerous applications we shall want the pupils to make in reading over their own writing. Some will be very simple. Those who are in the habit of dividing subject + defining adjectival clause from the verb by a comma can be told to read their work over to make sure they have not done so. This however is only possible if they know enough grammar to understand what they are looking for. This is not the same thing at all as expecting the pupils to write according to a grammatical rule. While they are writing, their attention must be on what they want to say. We hope the practice they have had will lead to the automatic choice of what is correct. But sometimes it does not do so, and after the writing is over, we see no reason why it should not be examined for conformity to convention. It is difficult for pupils to do this in a general sort of way. 'Make sure you haven't left any mistakes in,' is not very helpful especially early on in the course. 'Make sure your *if* and *when* clauses are marked off by commas if they start the sentence' is much more useful.

There are other ways of relating grammar to composition. If we have been reviewing question forms, we can set a composition involving a dialogue between mother and child in which the child keeps on asking questions – perhaps he is going to school or to the big city for the first time. Or we could ask the class to supply the missing half of a telephone conversation in which there are a number of responses: *Yes, I will; No, he needn't*, etc.

If we have been teaching about pronouns, we shall naturally ask the pupils to look at the pronouns in their next composition and we shall have taken care to set a composition that involves pronoun problems – an animal story, for example.

Up to this point we do not think we have said much that is highly controversial. The use of grammar in planning primary courses is accepted as essential. It is also generally agreed that the most important thing presented when a new set of examples is put before a class of children is the underlying pattern, but that the perception of this in the early stages is not helped by the use of grammatical terminology. Most people would agree that when the first presentation is made to older learners it may not always be very reprehensible to use some grammatical terms, but that even with adults who are given a little theory, what really matters is that they should have a great deal of practice.

In the secondary stage the teacher needs grammar to deal effectively with errors and deficiencies. We hope it is clear that the parsing and analysis of traditional grammar are not helpful for this purpose and that some of the odium felt for the teaching of grammar would be more accurately described as a distaste for teaching the wrong kind of grammar. It is equally disastrous to teach the right kind of grammar in the wrong way. Nobody wants to inflict a linguistic Nesfield on pupils.

9 Grammar as a survey and codification

Now let us consider the arguments for and against teaching grammar as a codification of knowledge already vaguely in the learner's mind – a systematic survey of all the devices in the language that are used to signal grammatical meaning.

We can dispose of one point very briefly. We do not believe in exposing pupils to pre-scientific grammar; we do not advocate replacing chemistry by alchemy, either.

If grammar is to be taught systematically, then a scientific description must be used. It will need adaptation to the particular needs of pupils with different language backgrounds. It is not yet at all clear which kind of description will prove most satisfactory for teaching purposes. It is perhaps worth mentioning that pupils who have used substitution tables in order to master sentence patterns are already familiar with the principles of a slot and filler description.

Many people, however, argue that there is no advantage in any case in a survey of grammar. Conscious knowledge, they say, is not required. Speaking is a skill like cycling and as soon as you try to balance by conscious movements you fall off. It is certainly true that we cannot speak by a conscious application of conscious knowledge. But we all have experience of learning skills by a process in which items start as conscious knowledge and then with practice become automatic. Perhaps speaking is more like driving than cycling. West remarks, 'The experienced car-driver has made his handling of the controls so automatic that he is able to give his whole attention to the road; so too the grammatical speaker.'

In the acquisition of some skills, this process of understanding the principle and then making application automatic through practice may be repeated at different levels. One may instance learning to play bridge. At the most elementary level one needs to be conscious that aces rank higher than kings and that suits rank in alphabetical order clubs, diamonds, hearts, spades. At a later stage it helps to know why one doesn't normally lead aces. Still later it is useful to know what Mr Percentage says about various probabilities. All these things could be picked up by intelligent observation but we know very few bridge-players who have never read a book about it and not one of them is among our favourite partners. But we shall not prove anything by arguments from analogy.

Many excellent teachers argue that what matters is not the description but the examples of the things described and the practice in making similar items by analogy. What they would like is a grammar book with no grammar in it; a book of pure practice based on sound theory. Such a book could be written. Instead of mentioning gerunds and infinitives after the verb, for example, it would provide a series of patterns and a list of all the verbs within the target vocabulary that 'take the infinitive' or 'take the gerund' or 'take clause objects'. Sub-divisions would indicate where passives are possible and so on. It would consist of lists of items and operating instructions.

We have a great deal of sympathy for this view and have seen excellent grammar teaching based on it. In the secondary school it requires tactful handling if the pupils are not to feel that they are just going over again what they did in the primary school. They feel that they know that one *s* is enough in sentences like *Flowers grow*, and *A flower grows*. They resent being drilled in such an elementary matter even if their written work shows the need for it. The shrewd teacher allows for this and disguises his aim by putting what he is practising into a more complicated structure:

> A gardener thinks he is successful when a rare plant grows and blooms in his garden.

Many teachers see another advantage in this approach; it avoids the prolem of teaching grammatical terminology. We are not certain that pupils agree with them on this point. In all other technical subjects it is generally thought economical of time and useful for discussion and action to know the names for the things involved. The expert helmsman knows the *beat* from the *run* and the *reach* by name and distinguishes *going about* from *gybing* the more easily because they are different terms. Indeed *to know the ropes* is to be aware of what needs to be known.

We see no reason why the use of grammatical terminology should not be similarly economical of time and useful for discussion and action provided it is used in the same way as the technical terms in other subjects: a means to an end and not an end in itself – a substitute for action. There are positive advantages in having symbols as headings to the patterns being examined.

If, for example, we ask a class to produce similar sentences to:

> A gardener thinks he is successful when a rare plant grows and blooms in his garden.

the pupils will not know without guidance which items we are regarding as similar and which as different. They may decide that the structure of the main clause is to be retained, limiting themselves to such patterns as

> A woman knows she is beautiful when . . .

or The Headmaster thought he was successful when . . .

But in this case we do not care about the noun clause or about its adjective complement and we do care about retaining the tense. We make it easier for the pupil if we head our pattern:

Main clause (Subject singular, tense present)	+	Adverbial Clause co-ordinate with another adverbial clause

The terminology enables one to demonstrate the Chinese box nature of language – the way it consists of a structure of structures of structures. The terminology enables one to see which rank one is examining and to look at its structure in terms of the units of the rank below it.

Many excellent teachers argue against any complete systematic coverage of grammar on the grounds that class time is better spent practising using the language. Certainly systematic coverage does take time if it is done in enough depth and detail to be useful. We would estimate something like sixty periods a year for three years. If it were true that this was done instead of using the language, it would clearly be wasteful, but in fact proper grammar teaching can lead to highly concentrated practice over a wide range of available structure. It can make more practice possible rather than less. Instead of the random exposure obtained through reading or the restricted uses within which the pupil composes we can show him and get him to use more of the grammatical resources of the language.

At some stage in his learning the pupil, like the bridge-player, wants to stand back and look at the language and see how it works. Some people believe that this should be in the sixth form. We have found pupils ready and anxious to do it earlier. They enjoy doing it below school certificate level and the observation of the way English is systematic adds to their confidence in their own writing as well as helping them to greater linguistic ingenuity.

Perhaps there is an even more important effect of good grammar teaching on the pupil's attitude to language and interest in it. If he gradually comes to see it as behaviour, a thing that happens between people and replaces his crude idea of wrong or right by varying degrees of appropriateness to a given situation and relationship between people, he is learning something useful to apply to his own writing. There are a number of stylistic problems that are most easily comprehensible in terms of grammar: linking one sentence to the next, unity of thought, smooth transition, and the placing of adverbials, for example. It does not help the pupil to know that in example (a) below we have a noun clause[1] subject, but in example (b) we have a noun clause in apposition to preparatory *it*.

(a) To rearrange the dictionary on this completely new basis was an enormous task.

(b) It is astounding that it was completed in five years.

It does help to know that in all such sentences the subject may be placed first or last and that the choice is frequently conditioned by the ease of the transition. If (b) followed (a) in consecutive writing, the comparatively unusual initial position for the *that*-clause might be chosen.

The arguments for a systematic scientific survey of English grammar in the secondary school are strong in their own right. We would expect the teacher to be selective, omitting areas where pupils have no problems and concentrating on areas where the difficulties are most apparent. The arguments for the survey are even stronger where many staff changes occur. Unless the syllabus is carefully planned to be progressive, the pupils will be exposed to the same material over and over again and more important and interesting matter will be left out.

[1] Or a *noun phrase subject*. It depends which description we are using.

10 Aids to the teaching of grammar

Let us now turn to techniques of teaching on the assumption that we are going to do a survey of the field. The examples, exercises and method of presentation will be affected by the description chosen. But our space and ignorance prevent us from illustrating more than one set of possibilities. We will consider presentation in terms of:

(i) *pattern* consisting of units arranged in horizontal lines. There will be one unit per slot and at least two slots per pattern.
(ii) *substitution* within slots of items in the same grammatical class arranged vertically on lists which may be complete or selective.
(iii) *transformational relationships.*

One very simple device is extremely helpful in getting pupils to perceive the pattern – spacing between units. This enables one to show the common pattern of, for example:

S	+ V	+ O
Tom	hit	George
The man in the corner	could see	everybody in the room
The first passengers who reached the city	blamed	the driver whose truck had got out of control

The heading reinforces what is already visible in the spacing – the analysis of the clause into groups.

If the attention is on the clauses as units of the sentence, space can be used similarly.

I		II
The bus skidded at the next corner	,	which the driver took too fast

Minor refinements enable one to show included clauses:

	– II –	
	, which the driver took too fast,	
	I	
At the next corner . . .		the bus skidded.

For the first presentation of the concepts of pattern and substitution it is helpful to have a piece of apparatus with actual slots and lists. One can easily use a large piece of cardboard cut as illustrated to make slots in which the words on the lists show. It is a mobile substitution table.

S	V	I.O	D.O	ADV
The boys	gave	the head	a present	yesterday
The girls	sent	Jane	a letter	last week
The cook	posted	the baby	a suit	just now
Mr Jones	cooked	the guests	a pudding	on Monday
Uncle John	bought	the children	some books	in the end
Mary	brought	the doctor	a new uniform	in 1967
Mr Slow	sold	the customer	a new car	at last
Mother	lent	the others	a parcel	in July
Father	offered	the secretary	some fish	before lunch
Tom	passed	Susan	a new job	after tea
The boss	threw	Miss Quick	a pencil	a week ago
Some of us	boiled	Prof. Snook	a cup of tea	two days ago

The back of the verb list reads: *given*, *sent*, etc.

Appendix III on page 279 shows a possible line of teaching using this visual aid.

A Tense Board – useful for showing the differences in meaning between tenses – is illustrated below.

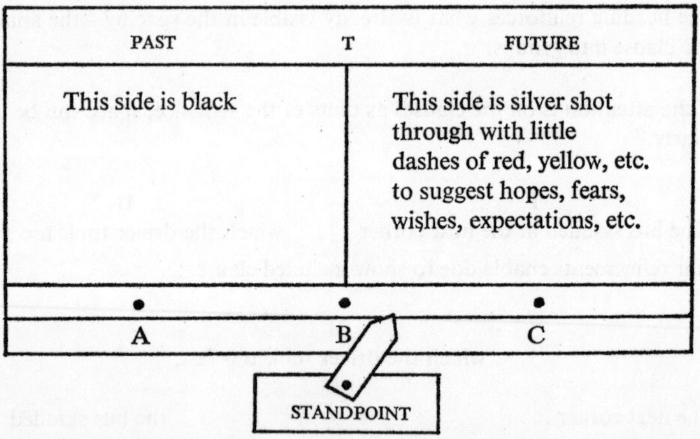

This apparatus gives visual representation to the idea of, for example, the future simple. The *Standpoint* is placed at B because 'we are standing in the present' and the arrow made to point to the right to show that we are looking on into the future to an action that will take place then.

When *Standpoint* is at B, the arrow has three stationary positions corresponding normally to future, present continuous and present perfect, and one proving position corresponding to the time span of an action named in the sent simple, which may require 180° for:

God moves in a mysterious way.

much less for:

George works in a factory.

There is of course, a stationary position for,

I take a clean test-tube.

One can show continuity by a line on the blackboard and repetition by a series of dashes. Both can have dotted extensions assumed into the future.

One can draw shapes on the blackboard to show for example that occurrences of the present perfect most frequently refer to recent happened in and less frequently to things a long time ago.

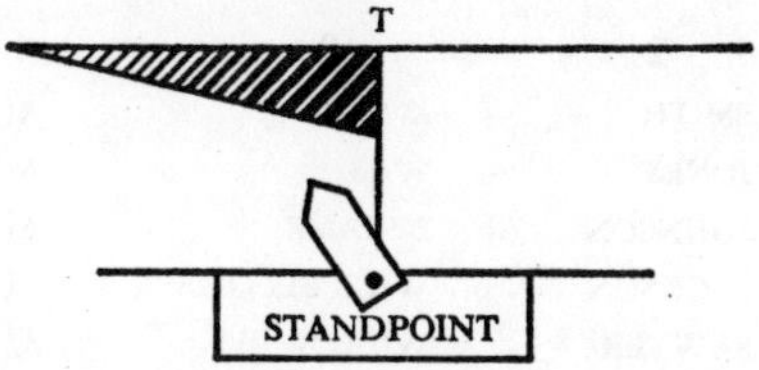

For quick blackboard or pupil use one can use a simplified diagram. This represents a future perfect tense.

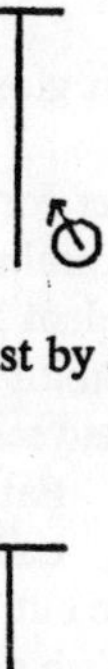

For example:

The train will have reached the coast by 5 o'clock next Tuesday.

And this a future-in-the-past such as:

He said *he would come.*

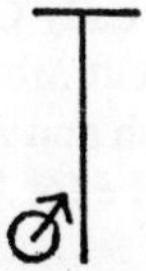

The board also enables one to distinguish clearly between time and tense. We have a present tense in:

The train leaves in half an hour.

The diagram, however, shows the future reference:

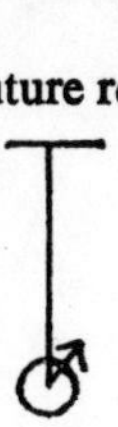

Another device we have experimented with occasionally over the past three years consists of grammatical dice. These are two-inch wooden cubes smoothed at the corners to roll easily. On the six faces of each cube are gummed cardboard strips bearing words of the same grammatical class. Some dice have all six faces the same because there are no substitutable items. THERE is an example, so is IT, which is required in the preparatory use. We have different dice for different forms of the same verb and we cheat on nouns by having all the nouns in the same list singular, plural or mass. We also have separate lists for things and people because of collocational problems with adjectives and verbs. This avoids sentences such as: *The stone seemed indignant.*

The dice can be used to conceal or reveal problems. To take a very simple example, we could set them up to illustrate S + *be/become* + Noun Complement.

1	2	3	4	5
GEORGE	SMITH	IS	A(N)	DOCTOR
HENRY	JONES	WAS	A(N)	PROFESSOR
JACK	JOHNSON	BECAME	A(N)	CAPTAIN
JOHN	JACKSON	WILL BECOME	A(N)	MAJOR
TOM	SAWYER	WILL BE	A(N)	LORD
ABRAHAM	SNOOKS	HAS BEEN	A(N)	ALDERMAN

We could then use 5 + 2 to show 'styles':

DOCTOR SMITH
PROFESSOR JONES

But this would be pure roguery. It glosses over all sorts of problems, e.g. the correspondences between:

a priest	Father Jones
a knight	Sir Abraham Snooks
the president	President Johnson
—	Mr Smith

and the lack of correspondence between:

is a father	and	Father Jones, who probably isn't.
is a lady	and	Lady Catherine, who certainly wasn't

not to mention *Father* + Surname but *Mother* + Christian name, or the considerable differences between English and American usage.

It is better to have a separate cube for 'styles' and then we can show that some items are common.

The dice are particularly useful for illustrating structures of structures of structures.

One can start by building a group, say D + N.

1	2
THE	CUPBOARD
MY	DESK
YOUR	BASKET
HIS	CASE
HER	BOX
TOM'S	BAG

If the two dice are then put into a paper tray, we have a new unit representing the group. We can then make a new group with prepositions.

3 +	(1 +	2)
IN	THE	CUPBOARD
NEAR	etc.	etc.
BESIDE		
ON		
BY		
INSIDE		

If the box with the two dice in it is put with the third in another box, we can show a group within a group. We can then use our new unit as part of a clause pattern, say:

4	5	6	7	3	1	2
THERE	IS	A	BOTTLE	IN	THE	CUPBOARD
THERE	MUST BE	A	PEN	NEAR	MY	DESK
THERE	ISN'T	A	PENCIL	BESIDE	YOUR	BASKET
THERE	WAS	A	BALL	ON	HIS	CASE
THERE	WASN'T	A	BOOK	BY	HER	BOX
THERE	MAY BE	A	TIN	INSIDE	TOM'S	BAG

By changing No. 6 for No. 8 a dice consisting only of THE and removing No. 4 we can get:

THE BOTTLE IS IN THE CUPBOARD, etc.

We can then build a new group and box it:

8 +	7 +	3 +	1 +	2
THE	BOTTLE	IN	THE	CUPBOARD

and make another set of sentences by adding No. 5 and No. 9 which might read:

MINE
YOURS
HIS
HERS
OURS
THEIRS

We can then box the whole lot and use them as an object group.

10	+ 11	+ 8	+ 7	+ 3	+ 1	+ 2	+ 5	+ 9
WE	THINK	THE	BOTTLE	IN	THE	CUPBOARD	IS	MINE
THEY	BELIEVE							
I	KNOW							
YOU	REALISE							
THEY BOTH	HOPE							
YOU BOTH	AGREE							

The possibilities are numerous but perhaps enough has been said to show how grammatical dice might be used. It is not without interest that if one throws eleven dice in the order above, one is certain to produce a grammatical sentence but the chances of throwing any particular one are over 300,000 to 1 against.

11 Grammar in examinations and tests

On the question of grammar in external examinations we have strong views. We think it is essential that no grammatical terminology should appear on the question paper. There are three advantages to this. The first is that it frees the teacher from the need to conform to the terminology of examiners, which is still traditional and allows him instead to use any terminology he finds useful. It liberates the pupil from the need to master terminology for the sake of the examination and so removes from the teacher who delights in the 'naming of parts' the excuse that he performs this barren operation because the pupils need it in order to pass. Finally it allows the pupil's attention to be concentrated on learning to manipulate the language.

We disapprove of all items demanding parsing or analysis, because of the feedback effect on the teaching and because of the lack of effective transfer to writing. We have already noted that the ability to analyse in an examination does not correlate well with the ability to write decent composition.

We disapprove of all items demanding the detection and correction of errors with or without explanation. Our reason is almost entirely the feedback effect into the teaching. We do not want pupils to spend dozens of hours looking at other people's errors; it is better for them to look at what is correct.

We disapprove of items that demand synthesis with numerous possible answers. For example:

> *Rewrite the following as one sentence:*
>
> George was coming into the room. He was carrying a tray with half a dozen glasses on it. He did not see the stool. He fell over it. He did not drop the tray.

There is nothing wrong with this as an exercise in class where the different possibilities and shades of emphasis can be discussed. But it is very difficult to devise a fair marking scheme. We would give full marks to:

> George was coming into the room, carrying a tray with half a dozen glasses on it, so he did not see the stool and fell over it but did not drop the tray.

Not many examiners would accept *so* without a preceding *and*. We would prefer: *When George came* to *when George was coming*, but can we take off half a mark?

The *but* seems pretty clear. Yet if we insist on some expression of contrast, can we be certain the candidate has not got a different intonation in mind? . . . *fell over it and he did* NOT *drop the tray*. One can easily devise a *consistent* scheme which treats all candidates alike but it is not so easy to devise a fair one. Another objection to the regular use of this kind of test is that it is unsuited to the forcing of noun and non-defining adjective clauses and therefore leads to over-concentration on adverbials and defining adjectivals.

We also disapprove, mainly on grounds of feedback, of regular and lengthy tests of direct and indiıect speech. If such a question is always liable to turn up, pupils waste hours learning mechanical and inaccurate 'rules' about what to do with pronouns, tenses and expressions of time and, which is much worse, waste time turning good speech into appalling narrative or good narrative into stilted speech. Short items are perfectly all right, but passages lead to dead teaching. They need not, of course. It is fascinating to examine what can be done with the same situation by dialogue as opposed to narrative and vice-versa.

We disapprove of the testing of rare grammatical items because what matters is that the candidate should be able to handle the common ones.[1] At school certificate level we do not think candidates should be expected to know *Should he arrive in the next five minutes, tell him* . . . or . . . *lest it be too late*. About tests consisting of passages to punctuate we feel much the same as we do about direct/indirect speech. There is no objection to sentences containing common problems but we do not want pupils to spend time learning the three uses of the colon or the fifty-seven uses of the comma and we think they have more important things to worry about than whether *Esq* on an envelope should be followed by a comma, a full stop and a comma, or nothing at all.

In spite of all the problems of constructing satisfactory tests it remains desirable to test a sample of particular grammatical items. The first reason is that only by so doing can we discover whether the candidate is familiar with any particular structure. His composition will show a certain command but not the full range of possibilities. The second reason is that a selection of objective or semi-objective grammar items provides a valuable check on the marking of the composition especially at the lower levels when composition is extremely hard for the candidate. This is particularly true of secondary entrance examinations.[2]

A good type of item is one that requires the examinee to change one structure for another with as little change of meaning as possible. The target structure is forced by the instruction. For example:

(i) I want another cup of tea, please.
Replace *want* by *like*.

(ii) A knowledge of grammatical terminology is less useful in everyday life than the ability to use grammatical signals.
Begin: A knowledge of grammatical terminology is not . . .

(iii) He told me the details of his scheme.
Replace *told* by *explained*.

A similar test provides a more extensive context and then demands particular structures in sentences related in meaning to the given situation. For example:

'Joe Soap was in a hurry to get to a meeting. He knew that the road was slippery but he was still driving too fast. When he came to a sharp right-hand bend, he realised he would have difficulty in getting round it and

[1] I know of one country that tested *No sooner had X, than Y* twice in five years. No sooner does the examiner start to read a composition, than he is met with negative inversion. Hardly has he read a dozen lines, before the next hits him in the eye. Scarcely can he fail to think the style distorted, but no one can he blame but himself. J.A.B.

[2] In the Sudan Intermediate Final and Secondary Entrance Examination we had amongst other papers a composition which was marked out of 60 and a general, that is grammar, paper containing 60 items. We used to list these two marks in adjacent columns. As soon as a school had been listed, I used to look down the two sets of marks, which in most cases correlated very closely. Where there was an exception I used to ask for a second opinion on the composition script, without saying whether I believed it to be under-valued or over-valued. Nearly always the recommended alteration, which was then referred to the original marker, was towards better correlation with the objective paper. J.A.B.

touched his brakes. The car skidded out of control and spun round back to front off the road. Fortunately there was nothing else on the road.'

Fill in the gaps in the sentences below. They all refer to Joe Soap's misadventure.

Joe Soap........driving so fast if he had not been in such a hurry. He thought the corner was........sharp........take at the speed he was doing. But his great mistake was........ He could hardly have avoided a nasty accident if........

Another useful rubric is *Rewrite as one sentence*. This can be made more precise by adding e.g. *using* which *or* that *or* where. For example:

(i) A man (We saw him working in his garden) told us the road (We were going to take it) was flooded.

(ii) In Kansas thousands of people are homeless. The floods are especially serious.

Use *where*.

One can ask for explanations of differences in meaning between grammatical pairs. For example:

If I see him, I'll tell him.
If I'd seen him, I'd have told him.

or at a more difficult level:

If they leave at seven, they'll be here by eight.
If they left at seven, they'll be here by eight.

One can also ask for the rewriting to remove ambiguities, e.g.

There was a girl in the car that needed a wash.

One can ask in effect which is the appropriate filler for the given slot. For example:

Choose the best item to fill the gap below:

Now you've broken the chair. You........take it to be mended.
a. had sooner, *b.* rather, *c.* had better, *d.* better, *e.* had rather.

A variant of this asks for all the items that would make sensible sentences in the given position and leaves it to the pupil to decide how many are right. For example:

We........him to come with us.

a. invited
b. offered
c. persuaded
d. suggested
e. hoped

Another possibility is to ask for the construction of a sentence from jumbled bits. In this there must be only one acceptable answer. For example:

(i) to speak to him
seeing him
walked
I
across the room[1]

[1] This particular example would not do if the examiner regarded *I, seeing him, walked*... as 'stilted but not wrong'.

(ii) secretly
she
to
tried to
her mother
explain
why she had got married.

(iii) She was wearing
costume
and
nylon
black
swimming
smart
very
white
a

One can ask for the removal of repetitious material.

Having reached their destination they found when they arrived that it was almost time to return back.

As a last resort if one can think of no other way of forcing the examinee to use the construction one wants to test, one can invite him to fill in the blanks, for example, with the part of the verb in the margin that makes the best sense or to rewrite the same sentences leaving the blanks unfilled or putting in *a* or *the* whichever makes the best sense.

There should also be a grammatical element in an itemised comprehension test so that successful understanding of certain grammatical relationships is tested as part of the meaning of the passage. For example, one might ask whether:

(i) He hardly felt the blow.

means *a.* He felt a hard blow.
b. He just felt the blow.
c. He did not feel the blow.
d. The blow felt hard to him.

or (ii) He told them all what he had done.

means *a.* He told them everything he had done.
b. He told them the things he had done.
c. He told all of them the things he had done.

For further reading

Books addressed to pupils are marked with an asterisk.

ALLEN, W. STANNARD. **Living English Structure*. Longman, 14th edn., 1959.
**Living English Structure for Schools*. Longman, 1958.

BENNETT, W. A. *Aspects of Language and Language Teaching*. C.U.P., 1969.

BOADI, L. A, GRIEVE D. W. and NWANKO, B. *Grammatical Structure and its Teaching*. African Universities Press, 1968.

BOLLINGER, D. *Aspects of Language*. Harcourt, Brace and World Inc., 1968.

BRIGHT, J. A. **Patterns and Skills in English*., Books 1–4, Longman, 1965-7.

CHOMSKY, N. *Aspects of the Theory of Syntax*. The M.I.T. Press, 1965.

CLOSE, R. A. *A Reference Grammar for Students of English*. Longman, 1975.

**A New English Grammar*. Allen & Unwin, 1968. 2 vols.

English as a Foreign Language. Allen & Unwin, 1962.

DERBYSHIRE, A. E. *A Description of English*. Arnold, 1967.

FRASER, H. and O'DONNELL, W. R. (ed.) *Applied Linguistics and the Teaching of English*. Longman, 1969.

FRIES, C. C. *The Structure of English*. Longman, 1957.

Teaching and Learning English as a Foreign Language. Cresset Press, 1945.

GLEASON, H. A. JR. *Linguistics and English Grammar*. Holt, Rinehart & Winston Inc., 1965.

GREENBAUM, S. *Studies in English Adverbial Usage*. Longman, 1969.

GURREY, P. *Teaching English Grammar*. Longman, 1961.

HALLIDAY, MCINTOSH and STREVENS. *The Linguistic Sciences and Language Teaching*. Longman, 1964.

HORNBY, A. S. **A Guide to Patterns and Usage in English*. O.U.P. 2nd edn., 1975.

The Teaching of Structural Words and Sentence Patterns. O.U.P., 1966, Vols. 1–4.

JESPERSEN, O. *The Growth and Structure of the English Language*. Blackwell, Oxford, 1948.

Essentials of English Grammar. Allen & Unwin, 1933.

LANGACKER, R. W. *Language and its Structure*. Harcourt, Brace and World Inc., 1967.

LANGENDOEN, D. T. *Essentials of English Grammar*. Holt, Rinehart and Winston Inc., 1970.

LEECH, G. N. *English in Advertising* (for its Introduction). Longman, 1966.

LEECH, G. N. and SVARTVIK, J. *A Communicative Grammar of English*. Longman, 1975.

LEES, R. B. *The Grammar of English Nominalisations*. Bloomington, Research Center in Anthropology, Folklore and Linguistics, Mouton & Co., 1963.

LEPSCHY, G. C. *A Survey of Structural Linguistics*. Faber and Faber, 1970.

LYONS, J. *Introduction to Theoretical Linguistics*. C.U.P., 1968.

LYONS, J. (ed.) *New Horizons in Linguistics*. Pelican, 1970.

MACKEY, W. F. *Language Teaching Analysis*. Longman, 1965.

MITTINS, W. H. **A Grammar of Modern English*. Methuen, 1967.

PALMER, F. R. *A Linguistic Study of the English Verb*. Longman, 1965.

Grammar. Penguin, 1971.

PALMER, H. E. **A Grammar of English Words*. Longman, 1938.

The Principles of Language Study. O.U.P., 1964.

The Scientific Study and Teaching of Languages. O.U.P., 1968, new edition.

PALMER, H. E. Revised by KINGDON R. *A Grammar of Spoken English*, C.U.P.

QUIRK, R., GREENBAUM, S., LEECH, G. N., SVARTVIK, J. *A Grammar of Contemporary English*. Longman, 1972.

QUIRK, R. and GREENBAUM, S. *A University Grammar of English*. Longman, 1973.

QUIRK, RANDOLPH. *The Use of English*. Longman, 2nd edn. 1968.

ROBERTS, P. **Understanding Grammar*. Harper and Bros., 1954.

SAPIR, E. *Language – An Introduction to the Study of Speech*. Harvest Books, Rupert Hart-Davies, 1963.

SCHUERWEGHS, G. *Present-Day English Syntax*. Longman, 1959.

SCOTT, BOWLEY, BROCKETT, BROWN and GODDARD *English Grammar*. Heinemann, 1968.

STRANG, BARBARA. *Modern English Structure*. Arnold, 2nd edn., 1968.

TIFFEN, B. *A Language in Common*. Longman, 1969.

THOMAS, O. *Transformational Grammar and the Teacher of English*. Holt, Rinehart and Winston Inc., 1965.

WALLWORK, J. F. *Language and Linguistics*. Heinemann, 1969.

WHITEHALL, H. *Structural Essentials of English*. Longman, 1958.

ZANDVOORT. *A Handbook of English Grammar*. Longman, new edn., 1970.

APPENDIXES

I *EXAMPLE OF TEACHING AIMED AT THE FIRST PRESENTATION OF THE INFINITIVE OF PURPOSE*

In the classroom something like this will happen:

Teacher: I want a piece of chalk.

(*Suiting the action to the word*) I'm going to the cupboard to get a piece of chalk.

I went to the cupboard to get a piece of chalk.

Who went to the cupboard?

Pupil: You did.

Teacher: Why?

Pupil (who will at first need prompting. His instinct will be to answer *why* with *because*): To get a piece of chalk.

Teacher: Who wanted the chalk?

Pupil: You did.

Teacher: Did I get it?

Pupil: Yes, you did/No, you didn't.

Further examples will be selected

(i) for demonstrability, and when the meaning is established,

(ii) to show a variety of sentence patterns ending with an infinitive of purpose:

We stopped to . . .

We bought it to . . .

There's a man here to . . .

and perhaps

(iii) to show also a variety of constructions following the infinitive:

. . . stopped to think

to buy some food

to give ourselves a rest etc.

We shall probably stop and practise this pattern thoroughly at this point. Perhaps we make every pupil write a sentence on the pattern:

I went somewhere to do something.

and ask one to read the first half and others to guess the reason. For example:

Pupil 1: I went to the baker's . . .

Pupil 2: Did you go there to buy some bread?

Pupil 1: No.

Pupil 3: To buy a cake?

Pupil 1: No.

Pupil 4: To pay the bill?

Pupil 1: Yes, I did.

A later lesson will include such examples as:

I bought it/for my sister to read.

/so that my sister could read it.

II *A LINE OF TEACHING DEALING WITH THE STRUCTURES THAT HELP THE NOUN TO NAME MORE EXACTLY*

To get ourselves thinking about possibilities we can use an assortment of objects chosen so that some are similar and others different in size and colour. We cannot predict exactly what suggestions the class will make but in the course of the teaching, which may extend over several periods, we know that we want them to produce examples of nominal structures.

It is possible to teach such a lesson without the use by the teacher or pupil of any grammatical terminology. It involves doing everything by exemplification and in our view makes understanding not easier but more difficult. We shall therefore use any terminology we think useful but we shall not spend any time in definition or expect the class to remember or use the terms. The examples under the headings and our demonstrative gestures will show the class what bits of language we are talking about as we go on.

We aim to make the lesson go somewhat as follows:

Teacher (taking a large red book from the box in which the rest of his objects remain concealed and putting it on the table): What would you say if you wanted somebody to hand you that?

Pupil: Would you hand me that book, please?

Teaching (adding a large black book): You still want the same book. What would you say now?

Pupil: Would you hand me the red book, please?

Teacher (puts 'the red book' on the blackboard, removes the black book and replaces it with a thin red one): What would you say now?

Pupil: Pass me the large/thick book.

Teacher (adds 'the large book', 'the thick book' to the list. He continues to produce objects until the blackboard reads, for example, as on the left. He then adds the sentence on the right, and the heading.)

	ADJ	NOUN	
the	red	book	
the	large	book	
the	thin	book	
the	thick	book	If the book is red, we can talk about the red book.
the	round	tin	
the	square	tin	
the	brown	leaf	
the	green	leaf	

Teacher: Check that our test sentence works with all the adjectives. Now. (He puts out two red books, one thick one thin and a large blue book.)

Pupil: Pass me the large red book.

Teacher (puts on the blackboard

	ADJ	ADJ	NOUN
the	large	red	book)

Why didn't you just say 'the large book?'

Pupil: Because there are two large books.

Teacher: Why not just 'the red book'?

Pupil: Because there are two red books.

Teacher: Now suppose a tin is both blue and round, what shall we call it if we need to use both?

Pupil: A round blue tin.

This continues until we have a new list on the blackboard on the pattern of:

	ADJ	ADJ	NOUN	
the	large	red	book	
a	small	brown	leaf	etc.

Teacher: Now look at the list of adjectives that come nearest to the noun. What do they tell us about?

Pupil: Colour.

Teacher: Good. Let's add the words 'of colour' to the heading. Can anybody suggest a possible rule that might help us to get the order right?

Pupil (eventually): Adjectives of colour go next to the noun.

Teacher: Yes. That will do for the moment. Now we've seen these adjectives showing differences of colour; what sort of differences do the others show?

Pupil (eventually): Shape.

Teacher: Right now let's look at some that do not show shape and see if the adjective of colour still comes nearest to the noun. Do you remember Tom Sawyer on the island? The morning was grey and cool. What did the writer call it?

Pupil: A cool grey morning.

Teacher: A polar bear's fur is – well you tell me – what colour?

Pupil: White.

Teacher: Long or short?

Pupil: Long.

Teacher: And so the polar bear has?

Pupil: Long white fur.

Teacher: And a mouse has?

Pupil: Short grey fur.

Teacher: Rough or smooth?

Pupil: Smooth.

Teacher: And so?

Pupil: Smooth grey fur. What about 'smooth, soft, grey fur'?

Teacher: That's fine. (He pauses hopefully. He'll be lucky if somebody asks whether 'soft smooth grey fur' would do just as well. He points it out.) Now suppose we want to talk about boots that are black and heavy?

Pupils: Heavy black boots.

The items are listed on the blackboard and we work towards a temporary rule that adjectives of colour go nearest to the noun, other adjectives further away.

Teacher: Now a different kind of adjective. In a minute I shall want you to tell me what the difference is. Look, here are half a dozen books. I happen to think that this one is interesting and this one dull. Would it be any good saying to somebody else, 'Bring me the interesting book? Or the dull book?'

Pupil: No.

Teacher: Why not?

Pupil: Because he doesn't know.

Teacher: What doesn't he know?

Pupil: Whether it is interesting or not.

Teacher: But he knows whether it is red?

Pupil: He can see that.

Teacher: Why can't he see that it is interesting?

Pupil: He'd have to read all the books first.

Teacher: Are you sure he'd choose the right one then? Perhaps he likes Biggles books and I don't.

Pupil: No, he might not.

Teacher: Why? Where is the interest: in my head or in the book?

Whichever alternative the pupil opts for is, naturally, challenged. Other examples are adduced and listed. We eventually agree that we have a class of adjectives that contain an element of opinion, feeling or attitude. We call them adjectives of feeling and we leave order among adjectives with a list such as the following:

	ADJ *of feeling*	ADJ *of other kinds*	ADJ *of colour*	NOUN
a	beautiful	tall	green	tree
a	lovely	new	red	dress

We shall return to this point later when we consider modification within the group – *very beautiful*, *rather tall*, *bright green*, *bluey green*, *greenish*, etc. – and also when we deal with predicative adjectives. If a boy is afraid we cannot talk about an afraid boy. They may even crop up when we deal with the next thing – noun modifiers.

Teacher: What kind of leaf is this?

Pupil: A banana leaf.

Teacher: What does it grow on?

Pupil: A banana tree.

Teacher: What kind of tree produces oranges?

Pupil: An orange tree.

Teacher: Plums?

Pupil: A plum tree.

Teacher: Melons?

Pupil: A melon plant.

Teacher: Good. I didn't succeed in catching you. Now what are the words in this list on the blackboard. Are they the same as the adjectives we have been looking at or different? Let's try our test sentence. Can we say, 'If a leaf is banana . . .'?

Pupil: No.

Teacher: Then the words in this list are different in some way, aren't they? We've seen that a banana tree is a tree that produces bananas. What's a banana leaf?

Pupil: A leaf that grows on a banana tree.

Teacher: What's a stone wall?

Pupil: A wall made of stone.

Teacher: What do we call a dress made of cotton?

Pupil: A cotton dress.

Teacher: What's a box kite?

Pupil: It must be a kind of kite but we don't know what a kite is.

Teacher (sketching): You've seen children playing with a thing like this and like this. Which is a box kite and why?

Pupil: The one that's like a box.

Teacher (resisting the temptation to say 'What's a box hedge?'): What's a letter box?

Pupil: A box for letters.

Teacher: A money box?

Pupil: A box for money.

Teacher: A supper party?

Pupil: A party where you have supper.

Teacher: A dish washer? (farm gate, morning dress, east wind, egg plant, car engine, examination sickness, telephone extension, bird's-eye view, factory act, family butcher, bus ticket, sheep farm, etc.)

If he has used a clause-pattern grammar the teacher can show that noun modifiers relate to different parts of many patterns. In any case he can establish that they are nouns in basic patterns and, in the pattern that we have been examining, nouns that modify nouns. We go on to establish the order of:

	adj	+	noun	+	NOUN	
a	yellow		bow		tie	(if one is on display)
a	grey		stone		wall	

We shall return to this point perhaps in speech lessons when we deal with pairs used so frequently together that the stress has changed and they are written as one word or hyphened. We shall return again if we need to discuss the use of the hyphen to indicate internal modification – *a superfluous-hair remover* and not *a superfluous hair-remover*. Meanwhile we go on to participles.

Teacher: We have seen that in *a stone wall*, the modifier, *stone*, is a noun and it is related to *a wall made of stone* and *stone* is a noun there too It has the same form whether it is a modifier or not. An *apple* tree is related to a tree that grows *apples*. They are both nouns. The modifier is singular, that's the only difference. Noun modifiers usually are.[1] Now look at something different. Do mosquitoes breed in *running water* or *standing water*?

Pupil: Standing water.

[1] Not always: *careers master*.

Teacher: What is *standing* water?
Pupil: Water that is standing still.
Teacher: Good. And what part of speech is *standing*?
Pupil: A verb.
Teacher: Right. Now if a book excites me, what shall I call it?
Pupil: An exciting book.
Teacher: And if a fire is smoking?
Pupil: A smoking fire.
Teacher: Is there an adjective that is possible?
Pupil: Smoky.
Teacher: Can we say a very smoky fire?
Pupil: Yes.
Teacher: Can we say a very smoking fire?
Pupil: No.
Teacher. That's one of the differences between a participle and an adjective. (Pause) Isn't that interesting? (Pause) Don't you think it's very interesting?
Pupil: But if we can't say 'very smoking' how can you say 'very interesting'?
Teacher: Good question. There are quite a few words like *interesting* – *charming*, *amusing*, *exciting*, for example, that have been used so often as modifiers that people treat them just like ordinary adjectives. We'll have a look at them one fine day. Now. If I break a promise, what sort of a promise is it?
Pupil: A broken promise.
Teacher. If my heart is breaking?
Pupil: A breaking heart.
Teacher: If somebody breaks my heart?
Pupil: A broken heart.
Teacher: If the teacher interests the class, what sort of class is it?
Pupil: An interested class.
Teacher: And what sort of teacher?
Pupil: An interesting teacher.
Teacher: Yes. How nice! Now when do we use the *-ing* form– that is, the present participle – and when do we use the other one – let's go back to my first sentence:

The teacher interested the class.
Subject?

Pupil: The teacher.
Teacher: And he is an interesting teacher. Object?
Pupil: The class.
Teacher: And we have?
Pupil: An interested class.
Teacher: Let's change round subject and object.

The class interested the teacher.
What have we got now?

Pupil: An interesting class.

Teacher: And?

Pupil: An interested teacher.

Teacher: That's right. The past partiple modifies the object in an active sentence. Suppose we make the sentence passive.

The class was interested.

What sort of class have we got?

Pupil: An interested class.

Teacher: That's right. The past participle modifies the active object and that's the same thing as the passive subject. Now what about order. If we have a box for money that's broken, what shall we call it?

Pupil: A broken money box.

Teacher: That's right: participle + noun + NOUN.

Pupil: What happens when we have an adjective and a participle?

Teacher: It doesn't often happen that we need both. Participles and 'other adjectives' seem to rank about equal. I should say:

clear running water

but running hot water

It's difficult to make a rule. I think I like:

a nasty broken piece of glass

with the adjective of feeling first. And 'the road was covered with broken green glass'. I should make a guide rule like this:

ADJ *of feeling*	ADJ *of other kinds or* PARTICIPLE	ADJ *of colour*	noun	NOUN

but you won't need to use it very often and sometimes it doesn't work. For example, *humming-bird*, *flying-fox*, *hunting-dog*, are all tied so closely together as names of birds and beasts that they are hyphened and cannot be separated.

Let's look at a different kind of modifier. Has anybody ever been fishing? Do you like fishing? What do you use for fishing?

Pupil: A hook.

Teacher: Yes. A fish hook. What else?

Pupil: A stick.

Teacher: Yes. We call it a fishing-rod. What's it made of?

Pupil 1: Bamboo.

Pupil 2: Nylon.

Teacher: Yes, we have bamboo fishing-rods and nylon fishing-rods. We use them for fishing. What do old men use for walking?

Pupil: A walking-stick.

Teacher: And what sort of lessons do you take if you want to learn to manage a car?

Pupil: Driving lessons.

Teacher: And what are those shoes with spikes in called?

Pupil: Running shoes.

Teacher: Notice that the lessons don't drive and the shoes don't run. The man inside does the running. Let's see what these *-ing* words are related to. Here's a model sentence.

If somebody does something, we can talk about his doing it.
If somebody falls into the river . . . ?

Pupil: We can talk about his[1] falling into the river.

Teacher: If somebody bangs the door in the Headmaster's face . . . ?

Pupil: We can talk about his banging the door in the Headmaster's face.

Teacher: What do we do to the verb *bang* to turn it into something we can talk about?

Pupil: Put -ing on the end.

Teacher: And what part of speech does that make it like?

Pupil: Like a noun.

Teacher: Yes. We call it a gerund and some people call gerunds verbal nouns or nouns from verbs or nouns related to verbs. All you need remember is that a participle is like an adjective and a gerund is like a noun. They both come from verbs. The gerund is like a noun in another way too. We can, as we have seen, use it as a modifier, like a noun:

fishing-rod, driving-lesson, running-shoes, walking-stick

Now let's look at the question of order. If a rod is for fishing and made of bamboo, what do we call it? (More examples follow, all with gerunds.)

Teacher: Now be careful. If a car is moving and has a motor in it, what do we call it?

Pupil: A moving motor-car.

Teacher: Now try this one. We have an estate. It is in Khartoum. It is for housing people. It is growing. So it's a growing estate, a housing estate, a Khartoum estate. Now fit them all together.

Pupil: A growing Khartoum housing estate.

Teacher: Good. Now it very seldom happens that we want to use adjectives, participles, nouns and gerunds all in the same group. But just for fun, here are some examples for you to look at:

a beautiful new polished oak dining-table
a dusty ancient broken steel filing-cabinet

and for the girls to look at

a lovely new coloured nylon swimming-costume.

We will stop this series of imaginary lessons at this point. We have not, of course, dealt with all the modificatory structures; we have not touched the use of *apostrophe s* versus *of something*, or any of the other structures that follow the headword. We shall need to point out that prepositional phrases make distinctions of place – *people in Kampala* – (and of other kinds), participial phrases make distinctions of action – *people shopping in Kampala* – and we shall have to consider the kinds of distinction that demand clauses: *the boy who rings the bell*, who may not be *the boy ringing the bell* or *the boy who rang the bell this morning*.

[1] If the pupil says *him*, we let it go. We can substitute a noun in the next example if it offends our pedantry.

III *TEACHING A SENTENCE PATTERN AS A PART OF A SURVEY*

We assume that we have already presented the subject + verb (+ adverbial) pattern and the subject + verb + object (+ adverbial) pattern. There follows a piece of imaginary teaching with our usual pupils – the ones who always supply the right answer.

Teacher: We've looked at two statement patterns so far. How many groups did we need to complete the first one?

Pupil: Two.

Teacher. Examples, please.

Pupils: Frogs croak, George laughed, etc.

Teacher: What else do we often find added to the subject and verb?

Pupil: An adverbial.

Teacher: Frogs croak – when?

Pupil: In the spring.

Teacher: George laughed – why?

Pupil: Because he thought it was funny.

Teacher: Right and we can add adverbials to show us how and where as well. How many things do we need to name in this pattern?

Pupil: It depends how many frogs there are.

Teacher: I'm sorry. How many kinds of things?

Pupil: One.

Teacher: How many things – kinds of things – in the second pattern?

Pupil: Two.

Teacher: Examples, please.

Pupil: You met Miss Smith outside the library last night.

Teacher: True, and correct as well. Now, I want to look at a different pattern. Just pass me that bit of chalk, please, Ahmed. Thanks. What happened?

Pupil: Ahmed passed you the bit of chalk.

Teacher: Good. How many people were involved?

Pupil: Two.

Teacher: How many things?

Pupil: One.

Teacher: That's our pattern for today. It usually, not always, involves two people and one thing. Let's have it on the blackboard. We'll see about adverbials afterwards.

S + V + I.O + D.O

Now if I'm starting to say something, I want you to tell me when I have completed the pattern.

He | gave | me a piece of chalk

How many parts do we need? Let's find some more verbs that are like *gave*.

Pupils: Brought

Offered

Stole etc.

Teacher: Good. Now what about this example?

She cooked some meat.

What pattern?

What about this one?

She cooked the baby.

Pupil: It could be complete.

Teacher: What about this? He passed me.

Pupil: It depends what it means.

Teacher: Give me an example.

Pupil: He passed me on the way to school.

He passed me a bit of chalk.

Teacher: Yes. We've got the same thing as we saw before. The same verbs can sometimes go in more than one pattern. Well, now have a look at this table.[1] Here's a list of subjects that I'm going to put here. Do you notice anything special about them?

Pupil: They all name people.

Teacher: Good. Now here are some verbs. Now the first object, also names of people. And finally the second object – and this names things. Here's our first sentence:

the BOYS GAVE THE HEAD A PRESENT

Now, let's see whether we can use any of the subjects. There's one that's not very likely.

Pupil: The boss.

Teacher: Yes. Bosses belong in business and heads in schools and that makes it a bit unlikely. But generally any person can give somebody something. How many possible subjects do you think there are?

Pupil: Millions.

Teacher: I expect you're right. Too many to list and count anyhow. I wonder if we could think of a subject that is not a person. (Pause) Try *the sun.*

Pupil: The sun gives us light.

Teacher: Good.

Pupil: Cows give us milk.

Teacher: Yes. What gives you hiccups?

Pupil: Eating too fast.

Teacher: So – Eating too fast gives you hiccups.

Pupil: What gives you a hangover?

Teacher: Let's go on to look at the first object – we'd better start calling it the indirect object. How many possibilities?

Pupil: Millions again.

Teacher: Now how about the verbs?

Pupil: Millions.

Teacher: Not this time.

[1] It is given on page 262.

Pupil: Thousands.

Teacher: Not even hundreds. You can try and see how many you can find if you like, but I don't think you'll get as many as two hundred.

Pupil: Why?

Teacher: Well, you tell me. What sort of an action has it got to be?

Pupil: Something that somebody can do to somebody else.

Teacher: I met him. Isn't that something that somebody did to somebody else? It's difficult, isn't it? Let's just say there are more things that happen involving two things than there are that involve three. Now let's look at the verb *and* the direct object. Have we got a free choice? We can give the Head a present. Can we give him a letter?

Pupil: Yes. But not a suit.

Pupil: Or a new uniform, or a new job. Why not?

Teacher: Try some other verbs: *posted* for example.

Pupil: You can't post a new car.

Pupil: Or a cup of tea.

Pupil: You can't throw somebody a cup of tea.

Pupil: You can't cook a baby a suit.

Teacher: All right. The choice of the verb restricts the choice of the direct object for obvious reasons. There are only certain things we can cook, certain others we can throw, or post and so on. Now let's look at the adverbials. Can we make a sentence without them? Of course we can. This pattern has four essential parts, but as usual we can add adverbials. Can we use all the ones on the list?

Pupil: Yes.

Teacher: Does the list contain all sorts of adverbials or only one?

Pupil: One.

Teacher: Which one?

Pupil: When.

Teacher: That's right. Time. And now which time?

Pupil: Past.

Teacher: What should we have to change if we made the time present or future?

Pupil: The verb.

Teacher: Right. Now where can we put the adverbial?

Pupil: At the end.

Teacher: Anywhere else?

Pupil: At the beginning.

Teacher: Yes. Those are the normal places. Occasionally we find an adverbial between subject and verb but not where?

Pupil: After the verb.

Teacher: Well——

Pupil: Next after the verb.

Teacher: Yes, not between the verb and the indirect object. And what other position is impossible?

Pupil: Between the objects.

Teacher: Right. Now take the indirect object list and use pronouns instead of nouns. Let's have half a dozen examples.

Pupils: The boys gave him a present, etc.

Teacher: Are the sentences all right?

Pupil: Yes.

Teacher: Now try the same thing with the direct object list.

Pupil: The boys gave the Head it.

Teacher. Is that sentence all right? What should we say instead?

Pupil: The boys gave it to the Head.

Teacher: Try the next verb.

Pupil: The girls sent it to Jane.

Teacher: Go on but make sensible sentences.

Pupil: The cook posted it to the baby.

Teacher: Go on.

Pupil: Mr Jones cooked it for the guests.

Teacher: Is that the same? What's the difference?

Pupil: For instead of *to*.

For-verbs and *to*-verbs are listed separately on the blackboard, building up to, e.g.

To-verbs	*For*-verbs
gave	cooked
sent	bought
posted	brought
brought	boiled
lent	baked
offered	left
passed	saved
threw	chose
lent	made
sold	
promised	

We then note that most of the *to*-verbs suggest that the object goes from A to B and the *for*-verbs that something is done for the benefit of B. This is why there is a difference of meaning between:

(a) He brought it for the Headmaster

(b) He brought it to the Headmaster

Teacher: In (b) did he see the Headmaster?

Pupil: Yes.

Teacher: In (a) do we know for certain that he saw him?

Pupil: No.

Teacher: What might he have done with it?

Pupil: Left it with the clerk.

Teacher: What about this pair?

(a) He left some money for his son.

(b) He left some money to his son.

In one of them he's alive; in the other he's dead. Which? Now we've seen two patterns that mean almost the same thing I.O + D.O and D.O + *to/for* + I.O. Is there any reason for choosing one rather than the other?

Pupil: Pronouns.

Teacher. Yes. Where do we usually find the pronouns?

Pupil: In the middle.

Teacher: That will do for the moment. It's not quite the right rule but we'll look at something else first.

Suppose we have two nouns, have we got a free choice of pattern. Look at the ones on the lists.

Pupil: Yes.

Teacher: The indirect and direct objects are about the same length, aren't they? They had to be because there wasn't much room on the paper.

The teacher and class proceed to construct longer objects and show that the longer one generally comes last.

The teacher then points out that it isn't really a question of length but of weight and even a pronoun can be very heavily stressed, e.g. You can't give that beautiful set of china to HER. She'd break it in a week.

There is one pronoun, however, that is never stressed – the pronoun *it*. *It* hardly ever comes at the end.

Later demonstrations show the two passives with *to*-verbs and the commoner one with *for*-verbs mentioning the other. They will show related questions too.

Later demonstrations still will show nominal transformations in various patterns especially as initial subject and after preparatory *it*.

giving	the Headmaster a present
to give	the Headmaster a present
the boys giving	the Headmaster a present
for the boys to give	the Headmaster a present
that the boys gave	the Headmaster a present
why/when/how the boys gave	the Headmaster a present

It was a mistake giving the Headmaster a present
It was a mistake to give etc.